THE PRACTICE OF POWER

The Practice of Power

US Relations with China
since 1949

ROSEMARY FOOT

CLARENDON PRESS · OXFORD

Oxford University Press, Great Clarendon Street, Oxford OX2 6DP

Oxford New York
Athens Auckland Bangkok Bogota Bombay
Buenos Aires Calcutta Cape Town Dar es Salaam
Delhi Florence Hong Kong Istanbul Karachi
Kuala Lumpur Madras Madrid Melbourne
Mexico City Nairobi Paris Singapore
Taipei Tokyo Toronto
and associated companies in
Berlin Ibadan

Oxford is a trade mark of Oxford University Press

Published in the United States
by Oxford University Press Inc., New York

© *Rosemary Foot 1995*
First issued as paperback 1997

British Library Cataloguing in Publication Data
Data available

Library of Congress Cataloging in Publication Data
Foot, Rosemary, 1948–
The practice of power: American relations with China since 1949/
Rosemary Foot.
Includes bibliographical references (p.   ) and index.
1. United States—Foreign relations—China. 2. China—Foreign
relations—United States.   I. Title.
E183.8.C5F66   1995   327.7305'09'045—dc20   95–7963

ISBN 0–19–827878–0
ISBN 0–19–829292–9 (Pbk.)

1 3 5 7 9 10 8 6 4 2

Printed in Great Britain
on acid-free paper by
Biddles Ltd, Guildford and King's Lynn

In Memory of
Christopher Thorne

ACKNOWLEDGEMENTS

Of all the stages that it takes to complete a book it is always a great pleasure to reach the point of acknowledging the encouragement and support received from others. So many friends and colleagues have given generously of their time and offered valuable suggestions. My thanks go especially to Warren Cohen, Tim Kennedy, and Nancy B. Tucker, who have each read the entire manuscript, challenged my interpretations at several key points, and tried to rescue me from any inaccuracies. Steven I. Levine, Robert O'Neill, Marc Williams and Ngaire Woods—each with different perspectives and areas of specialism—have also focused on particular chapters and offered helpful advice. An anonymous reader for the press gave warm support for the draft manuscript and combined it with genuinely constructive criticism. The International Relations group at Oxford has provided a stimulating and supportive environment, and various opportunities to give papers on parts of the study. (I, of course, remain responsible for any errors that remain.)

Laura Stone kindly helped facilitate my discussions and interviews in Washington, and Rhoda Smyth and Shao-yun Kan willingly offered to assist with the translation of some material in Chinese. David Shambaugh gave valuable advice in planning my interviews in Beijing, and the British Academy–Economic and Social Research Council Exchanges Scheme with China provided the institutional and funding support that made the trip possible. The Chinese Academy of Social Sciences and its Institute of American Studies were generous as hosts during my stay. I am very grateful to have had the opportunity to discuss the US–Chinese relationship with Chinese colleagues.

The major part of my funding for this research has come from the British Academy, and I remain indebted to that body for its support of my work over many years now. Useful additional sums for later stages have been provided by the Cyril Foster and Related Funds of Oxford University. Such funding has enabled me to visit a large number of presidential libraries, the National Archives in Washington DC, and several research libraries in the

United States, and I would like to record my gratitude to those individuals in such institutions who have assisted me in my quest for source material.

Chen Jian has generously agreed to allow me to quote from his path-breaking paper, 'The Failure of an "Alliance Between Brotherly Comrades": China's Involvement with the Vietnam War, 1964–9', first given at the Nobel Institute, Oslo, April 1993. An earlier version of Chapter 5 appeared in *The Journal of Northeast Asian Studies*, 10, no. 3, 1991. The journal has kindly given permission to reprint parts of that article.

I have dedicated this book to the late Christopher Thorne, whose standards of scholarship have long been a source of inspiration. I greatly miss his warm friendship and wise counsel.

A NOTE ON TRANSLITERATION

In general, the Pinyin system of transliteration has been used for most Chinese names and places, except where they occur in different form in quotations, or where familiar names might be confused if changed.

Rosemary Foot

CONTENTS

1

Introduction: Power and the US–Chinese Relationship

In 1972, Richard Nixon became the first American President to go to Beijing to meet the leaders of a state once overwhelmingly reviled in his home country and still espousing an ideology antithetical to his own. He described those days in China as the week that changed the world.[1] It was hardly that, but it was a striking event and one that sent diverse signals to various audiences. Whether a member of a liberation movement, a capitalist or socialist society, an international institution or a non-governmental organization, perceptual shifts had to be made, policies re-examined, and expectations about the future adjusted.

The main objective of this book is to uncover the range of conditions that led to a change in American relations with China: from hostility to *rapprochement*, and finally in 1979 to the normalization of relations. Additionally, it examines the management of that relationship since normalization. The most parsimonious explanation of the change available to us—a realist one—concentrates on China's deteriorating relationship with the Soviet Union, America's desire to take advantage of that in order to put pressure on Moscow and advance its policy of *détente*, and Washington's aim to recapture some of its standing and leverage in Asia as a result of its decision to withdraw from the war in Vietnam. However, such an explanation, while powerful (and it is central to the later discussion on the Sino-Soviet alliance), leads to a focus on relatively short-term events and obscures broader currents of change that were taking place in the period after 1949. The argument proffered here is that American relations with China were embedded in a wider structure of relationships at the

---

[1] Richard M. Nixon, *The Memoirs of Richard Nixon* (London: Sidgwick & Jackson, 1978), 58. Nixon first made this statement as he was leaving China in 1972.

global and domestic levels; they also embraced areas other than bilateral concerns about the global strategic balance. It is that wider, contextual, structure that is the focus in this study, in an attempt to deepen our understanding of the evolution in American attitude.[2]

As will become obvious to those who read beyond this introduction, the framework of the book is predominantly thematic, focusing on domestic political, diplomatic, economic, and strategic aspects of the relationship. The first three chapters are concerned with US efforts to build and then maintain a consensus behind its China policy, first in the international and then in the domestic environments. The maintenance of that consensus depended largely on US administrations' ability to demonstrate the legitimacy of their approach towards the People's Republic of China (PRC)—to allies and the domestic public alike. As many have argued before, policy that is not consented to, that relies therefore on a degree of coercion, is more costly to enact and more likely to result in non-co-operative behaviour or open defiance, features that will all be depicted here.

The next four chapters deal with the perceptual understanding of the capabilities of the Chinese state in the political, economic, and military fields. The assessment of those capabilities altered over time as a result of changes in China's policies; opportunities to test assessments of previous calculations about Beijing's resources; advances in intelligence gathering operations; the introduction of new China specialists into American administrations; and developments in the scholarly contribution to the understanding of the PRC. As will become clear, the perceived consequences of the rift between China and the Soviet Union, and the failure of the Great Leap Forward were important to the develop-

---

[2] The book, then, is not intended as a detailed policy-making study which, anyway, cannot yet be written for the period after the Johnson presidency. The *Foreign Relations of the United States* series on China does not go beyond 1957 as of writing, and State Department records are thin after that. Military records stop in the early 1960s. Of the presidential libraries, Truman, Eisenhower, and Johnson have important source material; the Kennedy library is somewhat trailing behind in the declassification process. On the Chinese side, some documents have been made available on a selective basis, sometimes for particular political rather than academic purposes, and several memoirs have been published; but in no sense is there open access to archival material. For insight into Chinese sources see Steven M. Goldstein and He Di, 'New Chinese Sources on the History of the Cold War', *Cold War International History Project Bulletin* (Spring 1992).

ment of an argument that, in a weakened political and economic condition, a more flexible US approach towards China would not necessarily serve to empower it in ways that would be detrimental to Washington's interests.

The final chapter examines American relations with China after normalization. In this period, China came to be viewed as less of a challenge, but not quite a full supporter of the prevailing international economic, political, and security orders. Nevertheless, it is suggested that China's economic reform policies have given rise to foreign policy behaviour that frequently has served to legitimize many of the international norms that reflect the interests of developed Western states, and especially those of the United States. In this respect, therefore, the book also represents a contribution to the debate about America's supposed decline relative to other states from the late 1960s to early 1970s.

Each chapter of the book may be read in isolation from the others. However, the chapters can also be understood as parts of a complex whole, linked together by a concentration on the concept of power. Certainly, the theoretical literature on power demonstrates that the concept is a contested one; yet it is suggested here that eclectic use of this rich, conceptual literature is valuable to an understanding of the evolutionary processes in a relationship where aspects of power have seemed central.

The Concept of Power

This study is concerned with the practice of power, but before tackling that in the context of American–Chinese relations, it might be helpful to outline briefly some of the major ways in which the concept of power has been defined and how it has been seen to operate. In recent years, the scholarly writing on power has expanded the concept to take account of its range between the coercive and visible forms and the consensual, less visible aspects. This discussion has taken place not only in the strictly theoretical realm but also in more practical, applied areas, in part because of a preoccupation with the question whether the United States has been in decline as a hegemonic power in the post-Vietnam, post-Bretton Woods era.

In its simplest form (what Lukes has referred to as its 'one-dimensional' form[3]) power has been defined as X's ability to get Y to do something that Y would otherwise not do. Power in this sense is to do with conflict, not co-operation, and with unwilling compliance not consent. In the realm of international relations, the ability to enforce compliance has often been related to the capabilities of states—usually a combination of demographic, economic, political, and military resources—and the ability to bring those resources to bear on a particular issue. Since certain of such resources are measurable, we have a ready if crude means of determining which states are more powerful in the global system and which are less so. In effect, it is often the perceptions of those capabilities rather than their determination in an objective sense that is the more important factor in a relationship.

Although this resource-based approach to power can be made operational to some degree in international relations, nevertheless it raises further questions. For example, the relationship between power resources and the achievement of policy goals needs to be specified; we need a clear identification of the issue that is at stake; and some indication of whether, in the act of bringing pressure to bear, X's own behaviour has also undergone change. There is the question of reciprocity to consider therefore.[4] Above all, there is the matter of preferences to take into account: if we consider power only in terms of altering the behaviour of others, then we have to know what they would have preferred to do.[5]

Once the matter of preferences is raised, then the shaping of those preferences requires exploration. An actor can exercise power prior to the operation of a bargaining relationship, by 'setting the agenda', 'mobilizing the bias of the system', determining which issues are to be considered and which are to be

[3] Steven Lukes, ed., *Power* (New York: New York University Press, 1986), introd. See also Lukes, *Power: A Radical View* (London: Macmillan, 1974). The one-dimensional view of power is most frequently associated with Robert Dahl. See his 'The Concept of Power', *Behavioral Science*, 2 (1957).

[4] For an exploration of the term reciprocity see Robert O. Keohane, 'Reciprocity in International Relations', *International Organization*, 40, no. 1 (Winter 1986).

[5] See on the points raised in this paragraph, Keith Krause, 'Military Statecraft: Power and Influence in Soviet and American Arms Transfer Relationships', *International Studies Quarterly*, 35 (1991); and Joseph S. Nye, Jun., *Bound to Lead: The Changing Nature of American Power* (New York: Basic Books, 1990).

silenced.[6] Consideration of this phenomenon from a Gramscian perspective would lead to the conclusion that those unable to set the agenda might be unaware of their oppression, thereby 'consenting' to the subordination of their values.[7] On other occasions, however, the ability to silence might depend on an acknowledged element of fear and submission in a relationship. Compliance might be engendered by an individual's perception of powerlessness and the lack of alternatives: that is, individuals can be constrained by their 'own fettered imagination'.[8] More positively, issues might be silenced because of the attractiveness of a particular advocate.

Joseph Nye has adopted the term 'cooptive power' to explain this phenomenon of agenda setting, an indirect form of power which might rest 'on the attractiveness of one's culture and ideology or the ability to manipulate the agenda of political choices in a manner that makes actors fail to express some preferences because they seem to be too unrealistic'.[9] Pushed somewhat further, as Nye and other authors do, there is an obvious relationship between some features of co-optive power and legitimate action. Legitimacy is important to the exercise of power because it represents the moral or normative aspect, and affects the costs associated with a power relationship.

David Beetham has argued that power becomes rightful or legitimate when it is acquired and exercised according to 'justifiable rules'.[10] Power can be said to be legitimate if it derives from

[6] For discussion of this definition of power see Peter Bachrach and Morton Baratz, 'The Two Faces of Power', in Roderick Bell, David Edwards, and R. Harrison Wagner, eds., *Political Power: A Reader in Theory and Research* (New York: Free Press, 1969); Nye, *Bound to Lead*; Lukes, *Power: A Radical View*.

[7] For a discussion of Gramscian approaches in international relations see Stephen Gill, ed., *Gramsci, Historical Materialism and International Relations* (Cambridge: Cambridge University Press, 1993).

[8] Jürgen Habermas, *Legitimation Crisis* (London: Heinemann, 1973).

[9] Nye, *Bound to Lead*, 267 n. 11. Kenneth Boulding uses the related concept of 'integrative power' by which he means the power to persuade, not power based on threat or exchange. See Kenneth E. Boulding, *Three Faces of Power* (London: Sage, 1990).

[10] David Beetham, *The Legitimation of Power* (London: Macmillan, 1991). Similarly, Robert Cox, drawing on a Gramscian definition of hegemony, has argued that as well as having material power a legitimate hegemon must be able to universalize its own values and interests to the extent that they correspond with the dominant norms and global institutions that are features of the international system. See Cox, *Production, Power and World Order* (New York: Columbia Univer-

a recognized and valued source of authority and if subordinate actors demonstrate by their actions their consent to the power relationship.[11] Without legitimacy, the powerful have more often to resort to coercion and thus must concentrate their attention on maintaining order, draining energy that might otherwise have been available for the achievement of other goals.

Determining how the beliefs of the subordinate are shaped and reproduced involves consideration of the process of socialization. With respect to international relationships, socialization might be said to have occurred when foreign elites 'internalize the norms and value orientations espoused by the hegemon and accept its normative claims about the nature of the international system'.[12] Such an internalization of norms could come about as a result of a hegemon's repeated ability to dominate events and situations, or more indirectly because of its ability to control the structure of values and meanings in a given social system. However it occurs, it remains a facet of power that is difficult to make operational since it does not generate empirical evidence and requires taking a stand on the subordinate actor's 'objective' interests;[13] nevertheless, it is clearly a feature of power that intuitively is present.

The United States as Hegemon

Discussion of hegemonic world orders in the international relations literature has often involved interpretations of the US role in the global system post-1945. It has been quite widely acknow-

sity Press, 1987), and his 'Social Forces, States and World Orders: Beyond International Relations Theory', *Millennium: Journal of International Studies*, 10 (Summer 1981).

[11] But note here remarks made earlier about the Gramscian concept of hegemony where the subordinate gives 'consent' out of a lack of awareness of oppression.

[12] G. John Ikenberry and Charles A. Kupchan, 'Socialization and Hegemonic Power', *International Organization*, 44, no. 3 (Summer 1990), 285. J. D. Armstrong argues that socialization 'denotes a process whereby an increasing entanglement within an existing structure of relationships brings about an increasing degree of adaptation to the normal behaviour patterns of that structure'. See his *Revolutionary Diplomacy: Chinese Foreign Policy and the United Front Doctrine* (Berkeley: University of California Press, 1977), 12.

[13] Krause, 'Military Statecraft', 326.

ledged that in the immediate post-war era, the United States was the hegemonic power in the state system. It had been the major economic beneficiary of the Second World War, becoming the workshop of the allied effort, a role that gave it a privileged economic position once the war had ended. America's GNP more than doubled over the course of the war, it had come to control some 70 per cent of the world's gold and foreign exchange reserves, and its economy experienced a threefold expansion in manufactured goods and a 60 per cent increase in the extraction of raw materials. It had an unrivalled merchant fleet, the world's most powerful navy, a sophisticated air force, a well-equipped though rapidly demobilizing ground army, and until 1949 a monopoly in nuclear weaponry. Its cultural products were being widely disseminated, it played a major role in global institutions that were being established, and over four-fifths of the world's economy was controlled by capitalist countries, led by the United States. Washington may not always have been able to translate these resources into the policy outcomes that it precisely desired, but the liberal economic and political order that came to be established corresponded reasonably closely with its wishes. Joseph Nye additionally points to the three major power resources of America's major rival: the Soviet Union's vast conventional army; its geographical location; and what he terms its 'soft power' resource of transnational ideology, and the political institutions of communism.[14] Such resources did indeed generate a perception among Western politicians in the early cold war era that there was a balance of power, not American hegemony. Yet, in terms of the range and depth of American resources, the United States has clearly been predominant.

The period of American hegemony has been variously dated as lasting between 1945 and 1967, 1945 and 1973, or is thought not to have ended at all. In addition, there has been debate over the domain of its hegemonic power. Nye has seen that domain as restricted, no more than regional in its geographical scope, and issue specific, consistently being brought to bear only in the

[14] Nye, *Bound to Lead*, 70–1. Nye describes soft power resources as including culture, ideology, and institutions, and also refers to them as intangible power resources that help to establish preferences. He contrasts these to hard, command power resources which tend to be tangible and to include military and economic strength. See Nye, p. 32 and 267 n. 11.

Caribbean and in the early post-war years in the establishment of rules governing finance and trade. John Gaddis, Stephen Gill, Bruce Russett, Susan Strange, and Robert Cox,[15] however, have seen US hegemony as operating over a long period and far more widely than this. Gaddis, for example, has noted that although the Soviet Union came to develop military strength roughly comparable to that of America, it 'did so only as its influence was diminishing in economics, politics, culture, and even the ideological arena of competition Lenin himself had created'. From a political economy perspective, Strange has argued that America's hegemonic power, or what she terms its structural power, has been found in four separate but interrelated structures: the ability to exercise control over other people's security from violence; to control the system of production of goods and services; to determine the structure of finance and credit; and to have influence and control over the generation, acquisition, communication, and storage of knowledge, whether technical, religious or relating to ideas.[16] Similarly, Russett, who sharply distinguishes the decline in America's power base—its relative power—from its power over outcomes—a form of structural power—has argued that the international system has been structurally transformed largely by the United States. Such a transformation of expectations and preferences continues to produce the 'goods'—that is, the norms and rules of behaviour in the security, political and economic fields— that the United States and its major allies find conducive to the maintenance of a compatible international system.[17] Although these authors are generally willing to acknowledge that there has been a decline in America's power base, pointing to such indicators as loss of a reliable coalition in the United Nations, of nuclear superiority, of a conventional military lead, and in GNP per capita, they nevertheless would argue that structural power is

[15] John L. Gaddis, *The United States and the End of the Cold War* (Oxford: Oxford University Press, 1992), 4–9; Stephen Gill, 'American Hegemony: Its Limits and Prospects in the Reagan Era', *Millennium*, 15 (Winter 1986); Bruce Russett, 'The Mysterious Case of Vanishing Hegemony; or is Mark Twain Really Dead?', *International Organization*, 39, no. 2 (Spring 1985); Susan Strange, 'The Persistent Myth of Lost Hegemony', *International Organization*, 41, no. 4 (Fall 1987); Cox, *Production, Power and World Order*.

[16] Gaddis, *The United States and the End of the Cold War*, 5; Strange, 'The Persistent Myth', 565. Clearly, Strange's structural power is close to the idea of co-optive power as used by Joseph Nye.

[17] Russett, 'The Mysterious Case'.

far more significant than relational power because it shapes preferences and therefore outcomes.

Power and the American–Chinese Relationship

These various facets of power pertain to the relationship between the United States and China in a number of respects. In particular, the idea of co-optive or structural power, the relationship between power and legitimate action, the notion of states having hard and soft power resources (or, more exactly, being perceived as having such resources at a particular level), from which certain consequences derive, are helpful to an understanding of the evolution in American relations with China.

Turning first to China, it is undeniable that China's leaders over a long historical period and certainly since 1949 have been preoccupied with power in many of these forms. Each successive regime since the Imperial era has sought to discover and implement a development strategy that would transform China into a powerful and prosperous country, able once again to stand proudly, perhaps even to recapture the aura that surrounded it when it was regarded as a great civilization whose accomplishments surpassed those of the West.

During the post-1949 period, the conceptual framework that China's leaders have brought to bear on the analysis of international affairs has involved a focus on the rise and fall of hegemonic powers, powers that have been willing to use their resources in an attempt to achieve global domination and to constrain the actions of others. China's strategy has been to try to form a united front against such a hegemon in order to contain its ambitions and ensure its decline.[18] This framework has encouraged the Chinese to see their own security concerns as a function of the global strategy of the hegemonic power of the moment. For the 1950s and 1960s, the hegemon was the United States, while in the late 1960s and 1970s Chinese leaders perceived the Soviets to have taken the lead. It has driven a Chinese sense of impermanence in international relationships and of a world in constant

[18] Harry Harding, 'China's Changing Roles in the Contemporary World', in Harding, ed., *China's Foreign Relations in the 1980s* (New Haven: Yale University Press, 1984), 211.

flux. In such circumstances, independence and flexibility are to be maintained, multilateralism and alliances to be avoided.[19]

The Chinese concept of hegemony, therefore, is resource-based, but importantly also includes a willingness on the part of the hegemon to employ those resources to establish control. It is a deep-rooted concept, and remains prevalent still in their world-view. Sensitivity to behavioural hegemony derives from the so-called 'century of humiliation' during which strong powers interfered in China's internal affairs, imposed their will on China, and substituted the unequal treaty system for the former tributary arrangements. This has led to a concern with concepts of sovereignty, territorial integrity, and status in the global system, a strong desire to right past wrongs, and a powerful need to be treated as an equal by the major powers.[20] Chinese leaders have often depicted the revolutionary triumph in 1949 as essentially one of national liberation, and Mao in particular has been described as 'extremely sensitive to whether foreign powers—especially the United States—would grant China true equality'.[21] As the Chairman put it in his oft-quoted statement in October 1949: 'we are all convinced that our work will go down in the history of mankind, demonstrating that the Chinese people, comprising one quarter of humanity, have now stood up'.[22] Premier and Foreign Minister Zhou Enlai during the same year used the same metaphor, accusing previous Chinese leaders of conducting foreign affairs on their knees. Each later advance was hailed as further evidence that the people had indeed stood up: Zhou

[19] David Shambaugh, 'Growing Strong: China's Challenge to Asian Security', *Survival*, 36, no. 2 (Summer 1994), 44–5.

[20] The Chinese attachment to the strong state is reflected in many other parts of the developing world. For one explanation of this see Hedley Bull, who was to write in 1979: 'Among the Third World Countries the idea that we must all now bend our efforts to get "beyond the state" is so alien to recent experience as to be almost unintelligible. Because they do not have states that were strong enough to withstand European or Western aggression, the African, Asian and Oceanic peoples, as they see it, were subject to domination, exploitation and humiliation. It is by gaining control of states that they have been able to take charge of their own destiny.' Quoted in J. D. B. Miller, 'The Third World', in Miller and R. J. Vincent, eds., *Order and Violence* (Oxford: Clarendon Press, 1990), 90.

[21] He Di, 'The Most Respected Enemy: Mao Zedong's Perception of the United States', *China Quarterly*, 137 (Mar. 1994), 154–5.

[22] Mao, 'The Chinese People Have Stood Up', 21 Sept. 1949, *Selected Works*, v (Beijing: Foreign Languages Press, 1977), 16.

Enlai's triumphant remark after the testing of China's atomic device in 1964—'Has not the label "sick man of the East", fastened on us by Westerners, been flung off?'[23]—further testified to the desire to demonstrate that China's past humiliations had been left far behind.

Yet, in the period after 1949, the United States more than any other state in the global system struck at the leaders' sense that China's status had indeed been transformed. From their perspective, US and not Chinese actions diminished the country's security, prevented its territorial unification with Taiwan, and denied it fulfilment of a world role. The United States stationed its troops and most deadly weaponry around China's borders, formed military and economic alliances with its regional enemies, threatened the country with nuclear destruction, and interfered in its internal affairs. Washington also obstructed Beijing's establishment of diplomatic relations with a number of states, imposed a strict trading embargo upon it, and denied it entry into the United Nations—the most important international organization of the post-war era. Communist ideology dictated that the leading imperialist nation was doomed to extinction in the final stage before the transition to socialism, and Mao additionally argued that the United States, though it seemed powerful, was in fact a 'paper tiger' because it lacked popular support; nevertheless, the longevity of imperialism was troubling, and often required a prudent response from China in the short to medium term.

China's method of dealing with its inferior position in the global system drew on hard power as well as soft power resources. To enhance its security, in the 1950s it formed an alliance with the Soviet Union, and used that link to build up its military and economic capabilities, including a nuclear capacity. Mao made constant reference to his belief that only a strong China, one that could produce the goods of an industrialized economy—such as steel—in quantity, or had advanced, nuclear weapons, would be taken seriously by Western nations.[24]

---

[23] This is discussed in Ch. 7, where I deal with China's development of nuclear weapons.

[24] Stuart Schram makes a point which is slightly different but related to this when he states that in 1958 Mao 'measured progress in terms of numbers of machine tools; in February 1959, his criterion was the size of the Chinese working class. The very slogan "Steel as the key link!" which Mao made peculiarly his own

Chinese leaders also made reference to the ideological appeal of the new China compared with the demoralized, unpopular West. They pointed to the shallowness of American power given that its leaders were divorced from the people and had become targets of resistance. Beijing, conversely, could project itself to newly decolonized states or those in the process of decolonization as a potential economic and political model. When its alliance with Moscow began to founder, Beijing adopted self-reliant policies referring proudly to its anti-imperialist credentials against those of a revisionist Soviet Union. In the international community, it claimed status as the one serious contender to the imperialist states and to the exploitative capitalist order. It depicted the developing nations, including itself, as the main agents of revolutionary change, propelling the wheel of world history because of their common experience of oppression. There was, it claimed, a virtue in having been poor and oppressed.

The results in terms of enhanced security and economic advancement were decidedly mixed, however. China's self-reliant economic policies, launched under the slogan 'Great Leap Forward', resulted in a famine of major proportions, and a need to expend precious foreign exchange on purchases of grain from abroad. And when a new and serious military threat was identified, coming from its neighbour to the north, it was the United States that would offer the protection it desired. With that strategic realignment came a steady improvement in security and status, including entry into the United Nations in 1971, and new diplomatic and trading relationships, all of which served to undermine (for a time) Taiwan's place in the global system. As ties developed with the United States, leading to the full establishment of diplomatic relations in 1979, and China at about the same time embarked on a major economic reform programme under the guidance of Deng Xiaoping, Beijing obtained further benefits, including support for its entry into the keystone economic institutions, access to technology and knowledge, and entry into new markets. What it lost was the moral dimension of its policy as its previous principles seemed lightly to be cast aside. Its 'virtuous' quest for autonomous non-capitalist development had been re-

in these radical years encapsulated the view of quantitative economic growth as a central and dynamic factor in revolutionary change.' See 'Mao Zedong a Hundred Years On: The Legacy of a Ruler', *China Quarterly*, 137 (Mar. 1994), 131.

placed by a desire to emulate the economic approach of its corporatist Asian neighbours from within an international capitalist economy.

The United States has, therefore, both negatively and positively, been at the centre of China's foreign policy concerns post 1949. Even at the height of hostility between the two countries there seemed to be an admission that it was US recognition that mattered above all because such recognition carried with it the desired acknowledgement of equality of status. It was also realized that the US position in the global system, its structural power, allowed Washington to keep Beijing relatively isolated. Despite concepts such as 'paper tiger' and the expressed belief that imperialism carried within it the seeds of its own destruction, it was the United States that was seen as 'militarily the most powerful, economically the most prosperous, technologically the most advanced, scientifically the most inventive and culturally the most accomplished'. Moreover, when veteran Chinese leaders such as Deng Xiaoping considered the nature of alternative political systems based on liberal democratic principles, it was the United States and its division of powers that was always chosen as the example, despite Deng having spent six years in France.[25] As Chinese after 1979 began to visit the United States in their tens of thousands, their writings also depicted a fascination with a country viewed as modern, technologically advanced, efficient, and enlightened. Such visitors sought the 'clues to wealth and power in a post-industrial and post-modern American society'.[26] Americans as individuals appeared to many of these Chinese as dynamic, vigorous, and independent. When Fei Xiaotong, the renowned Chinese sociologist, returned to the

[25] Michael Yahuda, 'China's Future: Peaceful Evolution?', paper presented at the British International Studies Association Conference, Swansea, Wales, Dec. 1992, 5. Writing in 1991, Li Shenzhi, former vice-president of the Chinese Academy of Social Sciences and president of the Chinese Association for American Studies, stated: 'The United States is one of the most important countries in today's world; its strength in science and technology, as well as its economic and military power, has been the number one in the world for over half a century; and it has played so important a role (be it good or bad) in international politics that no other country could ignore it.' Quoted in Chen Jian, 'Sino-American Studies in China: A Historiographical Review', in Warren I. Cohen, ed., *Pacific Passage: The Study of American–East Asian Relations on the Eve of the 21st Century* (forthcoming).

[26] Yuan Ming, 'Chinese Intellectuals and the United States: The Dilemma of Individualism vs. Patriotism', *Asian Survey*, 29, no. 7 (July 1989).

United States in 1979—his first visit in over thirty years—he noted particularly the spread of electronic technology which he saw as an 'important part of the material basis for America's high speed high efficiency society'.[27] In the mid-1990s, the United States is still seen as central to China's efforts, the argument being that a good relationship with the United States is essential to the success of China's drive for 'comprehensive national strength'. In the absence of a productive relationship with Washington, the perception—rightly or wrongly—is that that objective will be more difficult to attain.

Aspects of power have similarly suffused America's relations with China, also a condition that has long historical roots. Nineteenth- and early twentieth-century unequal encounters encouraged the United States in its paternalism and in its desire to make the Chinese behave or reform in ways that Americans found compatible with their vision of a modern and civilized country.[28] With the communist victory on the mainland in 1949, the American way appeared to have been rejected, and the Sino-Soviet alliance seemed to confirm it. When the 'ungrateful' Chinese added to that ideological opposition by engaging directly in military conflict against US forces in Korea, attacking America's ally on Taiwan, and marching into democratic India in 1962, it was a relatively easy task to depict China as powerful and menacing. In his study of American images of China, Harold Isaacs noted that the most pervasive image his respondents offered was that of China as a sleeping giant awakening, a civilization that had been 'bottled up' for so long 'now bursting forth with tremendous energy'.[29]

In the 1950s American officials watched the improvement in China's capabilities closely and assumed its malevolent intentions and desire to challenge the international *status quo*. Its alliance with the Soviet Union, although evidently difficult for the

[27] Fei Xiaotong, 'America Revisited', in R. David Arkush and Leo O. Lee, eds., *Land without Ghosts: Chinese Impressions of America from the Mid-19th Century to the Present* (Berkeley: University of California Press, 1989), 276.

[28] Michael H. Hunt, *The Making of a Special Relationship: The United States and China to 1914* (New York: Columbia University Press, 1983). For a discussion of the reformist strand in the US approach to international relationships see David Armstrong, *Revolution and World Order: The Revolutionary State in International Society* (Oxford: Clarendon Press, 1993), esp. ch. 2.

[29] Harold R. Isaacs, *Scratches on our Mind: American Images of China and India* (Westport, Conn.: Greenwood Press, 1977), 221.

two socialist allies to manage, added to China's security, and increased its access to economic and military assistance and advanced technology. The Sino-Soviet bloc then ruled over 850 million people in the 'strategic "heartland" of Eurasia',[30] as one analyst depicted it. China also began to appear to the United States to be a potential model developing country to parts of Asia and Africa, in competition with the main alternative offered in India.

But as the alliance with Moscow foundered, as China's economic programme revealed serious weaknesses, and the limited nature of its military capabilities became better understood, the assessment of the resources available to the Chinese government significantly altered. Certainly, Beijing still retained the ability to project itself as the source of support for those engaged in anti-imperialist struggles. With the explosion of its atomic device in 1964, Beijing could attack the non-proliferation norm, and claim that advanced technology was not solely the privilege of the industrialized world, thus renewing interest in its development strategy. Nevertheless, China did not appear to be establishing the broad industrial base necessary to the development of a powerful and prosperous country; thus, did not seem as comprehensively menacing as it had in earlier years. In these circumstances, it might be more willing to be drawn into support of the contemporary world order.

In the 1950s, when the PRC did appear to be advancing rapidly, Washington believed that the most prudent policy to adopt was one that did not further empower but instead diminished and held back that 'awakening giant'. China was a state that appeared to challenge many of the world-order policy goals that the United States and its allies had tried to build post-war. Where America wanted to establish a liberal, multilateral economic order, China adopted policies of collectivized control and was reliant on centralized economic planning. Where the USA wanted to prevent revolutionary change in the Third World and to contain communism, China represented the first post-war revolutionary movement to come to power. Moreover, it could widen its appeal

---

[30] A strategist's nightmare conjured up in one of the most thoughtful books to be published on China under the auspices of the Council of Foreign Relations at a very early stage in the debate: A. Doak Barnett, *Communist China and Asia: Challenge to American Policy* (New York: Harper, 1960), 337.

through the projection of its own struggle before 1949 as an anti-colonialist fight for independence.

The ability of the United States to empower others derived from what has been described earlier as its hegemonic position in the global system. The United States enjoyed much influence in international institutions, in the global economy, and within the diplomatic community. Its allies were generally reluctant to thwart the broad thrust of its China policies, although they often adjusted in terms of timing and detail. US administrations believed that if they gave way on issues such as diplomatic recognition and trading, other governments would quickly follow suit, and China's position would thereby quickly be transformed.

But, as has been argued earlier, the maintenance of Washington's hegemonic position depended on a normative element: to be fully effective America's China policies had to be regarded as legitimate, and over time they were not so regarded. It made no sense to some allied governments that the trading embargo the West imposed on the PRC continued to be harsher than the one imposed on the Soviet Union, or that Moscow was recognized and Beijing was not. Washington blocked Beijing's entry into the United Nations for two decades, despite the institutional norm of universality, and it frequently threatened China with nuclear attack at a time when Beijing was a non-nuclear state. In these circumstances, US administrations had to devote considerable resources to maintaining international support for their policies—in the UN, at meetings of multilateral trading bodies, and in bilateral talks with allies—to undercut the perception that hegemony was more an exercise in command rather than leadership on behalf of a widespread consensus where China policy was concerned.

The explanation for the harshness in the stance of successive administrations towards Beijing relates to points made earlier concerning China's challenge to world-order goals and also to the direct contact on the Korean battlefield. But administrations also needed to respond to US domestic attitudes towards China. In the late 1940s and early 1950s, the China bloc within Congress—supporters of the Nationalist regime of Chiang Kai-shek—enjoyed a strength well beyond its actual numbers, in those early years drawing additional succour from Senator McCarthy and his attacks on the State Department for being 'soft on communism'. The fact that American and Chinese troops fought each other to a bloody standstill on the Korean peninsula gave a particular resonance to the bloc's depiction of China as a hostile, malevolent state. The United States, as a pluralist state that allocated a role for public opinion in the formulation of foreign policy—even if US officials have been highly selective and manipulative where opinion is concerned[31]—and with an adversarial domestic political system based on separation of powers, depended for the credibility of its China policy on there being a close fit between the policy enacted and the views articulated by domestic opinion leaders.

In the 1950s that fit was reasonably close, but during the early to mid-1960s the ground quietly shifted as a result of the longevity of the Chinese regime, its developing nuclear capability, and a perception that internationally America's China policy had begun to be counter-productive. In 1965 and 1966, the US Congress launched its own investigations into the country's policy towards Beijing, and the influential Council on Foreign Relations sponsored a series of studies on China designed to generate a debate. Within the executive branch, bureaucratic reorganization and the introduction of new expertise, coupled with the Sino-Soviet rift and abject failure of the Great Leap economic strategy, led to new assessments of the Beijing regime. These developments also produced certain policy recommendations, a few of which were taken up to include limited trading and travel. By 1967, Richard Nixon, a presidential candidate in the 1968 election, could contemplate publishing an article in *Foreign Affairs* cautiously worded but nevertheless arguing that the United States could not 'afford to leave China forever outside the family of nations'; it could not be left to 'live in angry isolation'. Even more bravely, a Democrat—Senator Edward Kennedy—would take a strong stand in March 1969 on the need to liberalize China policy, calling for UN recognition, opening of consular offices, removal of US military forces from Taiwan, and the withdrawal of restric-

---

[31] Bernard Cohen, *The Public's Impact on Foreign Policy* (Boston: Little, Brown, 1973). See also Michael Leigh, *Mobilizing Consent: Public Opinion and American Foreign Policy* (Westport, Conn.: Greenwood Press, 1976).

tions on travel and trade, and all this well before he had given up
his presidential aspirations.[32]

It could be argued, therefore, that the Nixon–Kissinger change
of policy towards China was prompted by the divergence of
views over that policy that had begun to be articulated in the early
to mid-1960s and by the reassessment of Chinese capabilities
that had taken place about the same time. It was not only an
international consensus that was regained with the shift of stance
that came with the first Kissinger visit to Beijing in July 1971, but
also a domestic consensus that was re-established, at least in
terms of a broad understanding that Beijing could not be ignored,
would be better dealt with directly, and was neither as menacing
nor as potentially all-powerful as had been thought to be the case
in the 1950s. That leaders in Washington perceived probable benefits in terms of policy towards the Soviet Union is undeniable,
but there is a far wider context to that decision that ought to be
exposed.

Exposure of that wider context does, however, require some
explanation of the reason why the Nixon–Kissinger initiative generated such intense levels of surprise and excitement. Perhaps
attention had been too sharply focused on Vietnam developments
and only indirectly on China. More likely, it was because the steps
taken by the Johnson and Nixon administrations up to that point
had been essentially minor, incremental ones, involving certain
changes in rhetoric, and the lifting of some travel and trading
restrictions to include, about three months before Kissinger's first
stay in Beijing, the visit of a US table tennis team. The rapid shift
to contacts at the highest political level, in Beijing itself, and
between a former McCarthyite—Nixon—and leading revolutionary—Mao—marked a dramatic advancement in relations. So too
did the change in the focus of containment, from one which had
emphasized the containment of communism to one which
stressed the need to balance the power of America's main strategic enemy, the Soviet Union, whose global reach and influence
had grown from the late 1960s.[33]

[32] Kennedy in July 1966 had responded positively to President Lyndon
Johnson's call for 'reconciliation' with China, offering then a suggestion for resolving the UN recognition issue. Such developments are discussed in Ch. 4.

[33] For one explanation of these conceptual shifts see John Lewis Gaddis, *Strategies of Containment: A Critical Appraisal of Postwar American National Security Policy*
(New York: Oxford University Press, 1982), esp. ch. 9.

The chapters that follow all illustrate the various aspects of power, identified above, in America's relationship with China. The analysis in the first three chapters points up the connections between legitimacy and power and seeks to demonstrate the erosion of international and domestic support for America's China policy. The next four chapters focus on America's perceptions of China's capabilities and dwell on the correspondence between those perceptions and projected consequences. They show that over time the United States had a better appreciation of China's strengths and—crucially—of its weaknesses, of its hard and soft power attributes, the overall conclusion being that China seemed less menacing in certain respects from the early 1960s than it had in the 1950s. China came to be viewed as a regional power, of some significance militarily in a conflict of limited duration, and because of its nuclear capacity, which had a greater psychological than military impact; but it had diminished as a model politically, ideologically, and economically. If from the Nixon era it was regarded as enhancing Washington's leverage over Moscow, that resulted less from China's objective capabilities and more from its envelopment in an alignment with the United States, and secondarily with Japan.

Chapter 8, which dwells primarily on China's perceived soft power attributes, raises directly questions relating to China's decline as an alternative politico-economic model and provides the setting for an understanding of why and how Beijing lessened its challenge to the norms of the international system. Chapter 9, which charts aspects of the relationship from the normalization of 1979 to the current day, develops these points further. Its emphasis is on US structural power and on China's responses to the norms and rules of behaviour in an international order that many have seen as having been promoted largely by the United States. This was particularly important to US administrations because, as all Presidents after Nixon were constantly to reiterate, it meant the prospect of co-operation and friendship with a government representing one-quarter and more of the world's population,[34] as though sheer numbers in themselves reinforced the universal quality of the norms America wished to see bolstered. The Chinese, not always willingly and certainly not uncontroversially

---

[34] *Public Papers of the Presidents* (Washington, DC: Government Printing Office) is a good source for the numerous statements stressing this point.

in terms of Beijing's domestic politics, appeared after 1979 and especially in the mid-1980s to have adopted certain world-order principles. The language of their diplomacy changed as they eschewed their revolutionary rhetoric. They became active in a United Nations once reviled as being in the grip of the superpowers; they participated in an anti-Soviet containment coalition for as long as it was necessary; they joined keystone economic institutions that espouse the norms of liberal capitalism and that once were seen as oppressive; and they openly accepted that they had much to learn from advanced capitalist states. Participation in international institutions seemed to confirm that such bodies did have a role in shaping behaviour and in altering the pattern of costs facing the Chinese state.[35]

The transition to this era has not been a smooth one, however, either in terms of Chinese domestic politics or its foreign relations. In the post-cold-war era, it has proved to be especially problematic. The Tiananmen bloodshed, and the sanctions that were imposed on China immediately after it, demonstrated anew America's power in the global system. The United States—coordinating policies with Western Europe and Japan—for a time barred high-level exchanges, military sales, World Bank loans, IMF projects, and delayed China's GATT application. The nature of those policies after Tiananmen owed much to the coincidence of Chinese repression with the collapse of communism in Eastern Europe and then in the Soviet Union itself. Such a transformation in the global system undermined American need for a tacit alignment with China.

In undermining this need, however, the global transformation resulted in a focus on important areas in the bilateral relationship that have been more difficult to resolve and for which there is a narrower basis of agreement. The focus also shows how difficult it is to exercise power in a world where states are interdependent, power is diffused, and the range of issues has broadened. American actions post-1989 demonstrated a desire to remain engaged with a country now frequently depicted as significant to the healthy development of the world economy and to regional

---

[35] Such an argument is suggested in the work of Robert Keohane among others. See e.g. *International Institutions and State Power* (Boulder, Colo.: Westview Press, 1989); Ernst B. Haas, *When Knowledge is Power* (Berkeley, Calif.: University of California Press, 1990).

security, and with a vital role to play in the maintenance of global norms connected with weapons proliferation questions, the environment, and human rights, to name but three. A basis for agreement on such issues would be difficult for any two states with widely divergent political cultures to determine; it is doubly the case at a time of leadership transition in Beijing when each potential candidate seeks to establish that he would best protect China's freedom of action. Chinese leaders still show by their statements that they veer between the temptations of integration and the fear of dependency, still seek a balance between learning from outsiders and retaining a Chinese essence, still seek to retain national autonomy while adopting policies that demonstrate global interdependence. Although we might conclude that China in the 1980s and 1990s has reduced the level of its challenge to the state system compared with the Maoist era, nevertheless its level of support to that order remains in doubt.

For the United States, the period since 1979 has been one of considerable gain if one measures that in terms of China's re-entry into the world economy and the broad change in Beijing's foreign policies.[36] Since 1989, moreover, with the collapse of the Soviet empire and then of the Soviet Union itself, the United States faces a much improved strategic environment. This is not to deny that there are indeed serious security issues to be faced and that domestically the United States has much to attend to. But on a number of international issues the United States retains a capacity to lead; and the temptation in these circumstances to attempt to pressure China to behave, to further transform itself, to move more speedily towards an American vision of political and economic reform, is great. This presages much tension in the uncertain future we as yet have no better label for than the post-cold-war era.

[36] A point made in Russett, 'The Mysterious Case', 219.

2

US Hegemony and International Legitimacy: The Chinese Representation Issue at the United Nations

> We are in no hurry to take our seat in the United Nations, just as we are in no hurry to establish diplomatic relations with the United States. We adopt this policy to deprive the United States of as much political capital as possible and put it in the wrong and in an isolated position . . . The longer you stall, the more you will be in the wrong and the more isolated you will become in your own country and before world opinion.[1]
>
> Mao Zedong, Jan. 1957

> For eighteen years the General Assembly of the United Nations has discussed the representation of China in the United Nations. This Assembly has almost been beaten into insensibility by the arguments, reiterated with monotonous and predictable regularity, for and against the restoration of the lawful rights of the People's Republic of China in the Organization.[2]
>
> UN Representative of Ceylon, 1968

The United States emerged from the Second World War as the most powerful state in the global system, ready to use its resources to help shape a post-war order conducive to the satisfaction of its interests and those of its major allies. The United Nations was viewed as an essential part of that order, and Washington, with its disposition to lead, its diplomatic influence, and the widespread realization that without its full participation the organization would be stillborn, managed to secure 'the adop-

---

[1] Mao Zedong, 'Talks at a Conference of Secretaries of Provincial, Municipal and Autonomous Region Party Committees', January 1957, in *Selected Works*, v (Beijing: Foreign Languages Press, 1977), 363.

[2] UN Archives, Dept. of Political and Security Council Affairs (PSCA), DAG 1/ 5.2.2.13, Box 2, 'General Debate: 23rd Session of the General Assembly', 23 Dec. 1968.

tion of a Charter which was fundamentally based upon principles advocated by the United States'.[3]

One of those principles was universality. Thus, when the Chinese Communists had won the civil war on the mainland and had proclaimed in October 1949 an independent state, they among others believed it would not be long before they took their rightful place in this most important of all post-war international organizations.

The matter of entry was never to be as straightforward as that, however. An initial reluctance on Washington's part to see Beijing take up the seat and expel the Nationalists was replaced in early 1950 with a position of neutrality on the issue, became harder with the outbreak of the Korean conflict, and then with Chinese entry developed into a firm desire to exclude the PRC and maintain the pro-American Republic of China (ROC) in the organization. Between 1951 and 1960 the United States managed to block a UN debate on the question of representation through the so-called 'moratorium' procedure. When this method could no longer be sustained, the United States worked to have the matter declared an 'important question' under Article 18 (2) of the Charter which required a two-thirds majority in the General Assembly for any resolution on seating to pass. This basic policy of excluding the PRC and maintaining the ROC in the United Nations remained in place for two decades, even as the composition of the organization underwent significant change. A UN of 59 states in 1950 had been transformed into one of 131 by 1971, many of the new members declaring themselves to be non-aligned. Specific US interests steadily came to be less well guarded in this larger body. Whereas Washington cast no vetoes between 1946 and 1965—compared with the Soviets who cast 101—between 1966 and 1975 it cast 12 to the Soviets' 7.[4]

In 1971, having gained the required two-thirds majority, the PRC did finally enter the UN and the Chinese Nationalists walked out as they had earlier threatened to do. The US failure to prevent this outcome has been cited as evidence of America's hegemonic decline, as significant as the other indices that showed that a

[3] Inis L. Claude, Jun., *Swords into Plowshares* (New York: Random House, 1971), ch. 4, esp. p. 62.

[4] Adam Roberts and Benedict Kingsbury, eds., *United Nations, Divided World*, 2nd edn. (Oxford: Clarendon Paperbacks, 1993), 10.

redistribution of power and wealth had taken place in the global system. Indeed, it could be taken as evidence that Mao Zedong's remarks, quoted at the start of this chapter, were remarkably prescient. Yet, PRC entry in 1971 was not an outcome that was unwelcome to the US administration, and the assumption of decline obscures our understanding of the many types of power the United States has exercised in the post-war era. It also neglects consideration of the relationship between legitimacy and power and the extent to which US policies at the various phases of the representation debate generated dissent or consensus. This perception of decline also gives priority to the relational rather than the structural aspects of US power. An examination of Chinese behaviour, once it became a member of the UN, allows greater insight into the degree to which PRC entry truly represented a loss for the United States.

The PRC's Objectives

The exercise of US power can be thrown into sharper relief if it can be established that between 1949 and 1971 the PRC did indeed wish to enter the United Nations: that its application for membership was thwarted predominantly by Washington and not by a cavalier and dismissive attitude on the part of the new revolutionary government in Beijing to this post-war institution.

Notwithstanding the quotation from Mao at the start of this chapter, evidence suggests that the PRC had a desire to participate in the work of the United Nations from its inception. In 1945, Mao Zedong declared that the Chinese Communist Party 'fully agrees with the proposals of the Dumbarton Oaks conference and the decision of the Crimea conference on the establishment of an organization to safeguard international peace and security after the war'.[5] In the period between October 1949, when the PRC was established, and June 1950, when the Korean fighting broke out, Beijing sent some eighteen telegrams to the UN and its specialized agencies calling for the removal of the Chinese Nationalist delegation, which had in Beijing's view 'lost all de jure and de facto grounds for representing the Chinese people'. In

[5] Samuel S. Kim, *China, the United Nations and World Order* (Princeton, NJ: Princeton University Press, 1979), 100.

January 1950, the Chinese Premier, Zhou Enlai, appointed Zhang Wentian to head the PRC's UN delegation. Zhang had the twin credentials of having studied at the University of California, at Berkeley, and having been a veteran of the Long March. When he failed to become the first Permanent Representative, he became instead ambassador to the Soviet Union, a mark of the esteem in which he was held.[6] Beijing clearly saw membership in the United Nations as a matter to be taken seriously and as a significant mark of its legitimacy as the proclaimed new government of China.

Indications that support for its membership was widespread at this stage encouraged China's favourable attitude to the world body. The then UN Secretary-General, Trygve Lie, released a special memorandum on the legal aspects of Beijing's representation in March 1950 which gave strong support to Beijing's position.[7] Lie also made it known that he was particularly concerned about the Soviet boycott over the question of the China seat, fearing that Moscow and Beijing might proceed to set up a rival organization, thus destroying the UN principles of unity and universality.[8]

The British, who had extended diplomatic recognition to the PRC on 6 January 1950, were also moving forward cautiously with a policy aimed at securing the UN seat for Beijing. With five members of the Security Council—the Soviet Union, the United Kingdom, India, Norway, and Yugoslavia—already having recognized Beijing, and two others that London believed could be influenced to support PRC membership (France and Egypt), PRC entry seemed only a matter of time. Cognizant of such trends in opinion, the United States retreated—if only temporarily—from its obstructive stance. While making it clear that it would vote against the Soviet proposal to seat the Communists and expel the Nationalists, Washington also made it known that it considered the matter procedural and not substantive. This implied that it

[6] Xue Mouhong and Pei Jianzhang, eds., *Diplomacy of Contemporary China* (Hong Kong: New Horizon Press, 1990), 19–20; UN Archives, PSCA, DAG 1/5.2.2.13, Box 2, 'Survey of Attitudes of the People's Republic of China Toward the United Nations', 9 June 1969.

[7] Byron S. Weng, 'Communist China's Changing Attitudes Toward the United Nations', *International Organization*, 20, no. 4 (Autumn 1966), 679.

[8] June M. Grasso, *Truman's Two-China Policy* (Armonk, NY: M. E. Sharpe, 1987), 151.

would adopt a position of neutrality on the issue, would accept the decision of a majority of the Security Council, and not use its veto. Thus, expectations were that the UN subsidiary agency—the Economic and Social Council—would at its forthcoming meeting in Geneva in July 1950, vote affirmatively for PRC entry.[9] Full membership would follow shortly after that.

Beijing's positive attitude towards the United Nations was, however, to be put under severe strain as a result of the organization's role during the Korean war. The North Korean attack on South Korea and the UN decision to interpret this as an act of aggression requiring action under its collective security provisions immediately complicated the representation issue for all concerned parties. UN embroilment in the conflict under US command forced Beijing to take a new look at the world organization. It reached the conclusion that China needed to make a distinction between 'the UN of the Charter and the UN under United States control'.[10] When Beijing took its decision to enter the fighting—an eventuality that the United States had deemed unlikely in part because of Washington's belief that the PRC did not want to jeopardize its entry into the UN[11]—it found itself to be at war with that body. Nevertheless, Beijing still tried to avoid direct criticism of the organization and constantly depicted the war as one between the North Koreans and its allies and the United States and its 'lackeys'. Yet, it was difficult to ignore the force or the consequences of a UN resolution that declared Beijing and Pyongyang aggressors, one that passed by an overwhelming majority of 44 to 7 with 9 abstentions. Its disillusion with the 'UN under US control' was further deepened in May 1951 when the General Assembly adopted another resolution embargoing the sale of materials of strategic value to the two communist states.

Membership remained, however, an objective of policy. When consideration was given in December 1950 and January 1951 to a

---

[9] Robert Boardman, *Britain and the People's Republic of China 1949–74* (London: Macmillan, 1976), 50–3; Qiang Zhai notes British approaches also to Ecuador and Cuba. See his *The Dragon, the Lion, and the Eagle: Chinese–British–American Relations, 1949–58* (Kent, Ohio: Kent State University Press, 1994), 100, and more generally 98–104.

[10] Weng, 'Communist China's Changing Attitudes', 681.

[11] *Foreign Relations of the United States*, 1950 (Washington, DC: Government Printing Office, 1976), 7: 765, 22 Sept. 1950.

ceasefire in the conflict, China made UN representation one of its conditions.[12] Moreover, throughout the 1950s, its legal agreements with other states frequently embodied language taken from the UN charter: it tried, for example, to tie the doctrine of the five principles of peaceful coexistence to the charter; and its treaties of friendship and co-operation signed in that decade all alluded to the aims and principles of the United Nations. During the first phase of the Sino-American ambassadorial talks held in Geneva, the Chinese response to the American demand that they renounce the use of force in general and particularly in the Taiwan area, was to draft a reply that referred to Article 2 (4) of the UN Charter and which required US adoption of a statement that read in part: 'The People's Republic of China and the United States agree that they should settle disputes between their two countries by peaceful means without resorting to the threat or use of force.'[13] And when the UN Secretary-General, Dag Hammarskjold, visited Beijing in January 1955 in an attempt to secure the release of American fliers shot down over China, Zhou took the opportunity to argue that his government supported the 'purposes and principles of the UN Charter', and believed that it was an injustice that his government, representing one-quarter of the world's population, should be deprived of its rights and status.[14]

When the United Nations shifted from its use of the moratorium device to the 'important question' (IQ) resolution in 1961 (explained below), admittedly China's interest in entering into the United Nations appeared to wane, leading one author to argue that between December 1961 and June 1965, China was engaged in a search for a substitute for the UN.[15] Certainly, it became disillusioned with the body, disappointed that changes in its composition after 1960 could not prevent the introduction of the IQ

[12] Rosemary Foot, *A Substitute for Victory: The Politics of Peacemaking at the Korean Armistice Talks* (Ithaca, NY: Cornell University Press, 1990), 29.

[13] James Chieh Hsiung, *Law and Policy in China's Foreign Relations: A Study of Attitudes and Practice* (New York: Columbia University Press, 1972), 89–98.

[14] UN Archives, microfilm of Andrew Cordier Papers, Political Matters, series 3, meetings 7 and 8 January 1955. The UN Secretary-General confirmed while in Beijing that he supported universality and 'it being so, I consider it a weakness and an anomaly that this people, one fourth of mankind, is not represented in our work'.

[15] Weng, 'Communist China's Changing Attitudes', 694.

resolution[16]. Nevertheless, its criticism of that resolution implied it retained an interest in membership. As a major editorial in December 1964 succinctly put it: 'Since 1949 revolutions or *coups d'état* have taken place in many of the UN member states, and the new regimes, irrespective of their character, have immediately and legally replaced the old regime as representatives of their countries at the UN . . . why should the question of the legitimate rights of the People's Republic of China be the only exception and even be described as an "important question"?'[17]

Only briefly did China suggest it was considering organizing an alternative UN or try to impose unrealistic conditions before it would even consider entry. At the time of the withdrawal of Indonesia from the organization in 1965, Premier Zhou gave a warning that 'another UN, a revolutionary one, may well be set up so that rival dramas may be staged in competition with that body . . . which is under the manipulation of United States imperialism'.[18] And in September 1965, in the course of a rambling four-hour press conference, Foreign Minister Chen Yi put forward several demands that had to be met before Beijing would be prepared to enter the UN, including the cancellation of the aggressor resolution and the adoption of one labelling the US an aggressor, the revision of the charter, and the expulsion of the 'imperialist puppets', that is, the Chinese Nationalists.[19] But such negative statements have also to be seen in the context of China's radical shift in its domestic policy. In 1966, in the context of the Cultural Revolution and Mao's claimed desire to train worthy revolutionary successors, China sought not only to spurn the UN but also most other forms of formal diplomatic contact, as shown by its decision to withdraw all but one of its ambassadors from abroad.

As soon as the worst excesses of the Cultural Revolution were over and a new assessment made of China's foreign policy needs, Beijing evinced once again a strong interest in entering the United Nations. In discussions with Canada in 1969 and with several other UN members in 1970, China stressed its intent to join the

---

[16] This was partly as a result of ROC provision of technical assistance to a number of states, which swayed their votes, and also of active US lobbying on the matter.

[17] Weng, 'Communist China's Changing Attitudes', 696.

[18] Ibid. 699.   [19] Ibid. 703.

organization.[20] This was part of a more general diplomatic offensive that had begun in 1969, and had accelerated in 1970 and 1971. In 1971 alone, some 290 delegations from 80 countries were invited to China. Aid disbursements also increased dramatically from $13 million in 1969 to $728 million in 1970, representing 71.1 per cent of all PRC aid extended to non-communist states between 1954 and 1969.[21] African states were major beneficiaries of this aid, eleven of the twelve that received disbursements voting for the PRC to enter the UN, leading one author to argue that Beijing's efforts in this area 'made the difference in the U.N. vote'.[22] China also moved quickly to improve its relations with the developed world, establishing diplomatic relations with Canada and Italy in 1970, with Austria and Belgium in 1971, and upgrading its relations to ambassadorial level in 1972 with the United Kingdom and The Netherlands.

It seems reasonable to conclude, therefore, that apart from a period of intense pessimism over the possibility of entry between 1961 and 1965, and during the height of the Cultural Revolution when all formal channels of diplomatic intercourse were interrupted, the Chinese leadership did want to take up the seat in the UN provided the Nationalists were expelled. As the UN's department of political and security affairs noted in its survey of the PRC's attitude, each year certain socialist and developing countries had seen fit to include the question in the agenda of the General Assembly, but only 'after consultations with the PRC Government and with its endorsement'.[23]

The American Attitude and the Impact of Korea

As stated earlier, America's initial intentions with respect to the representation issue were to delay the transfer of status from Taiwan to Beijing for as long as possible, but when the transfer became inevitable, to accept the will of the majority of the Security

[20] UN Archives, PSCA, DAG 1/5.2.2.13, Box 2, China, 12 Dec. 1969 and 4 Dec. 1970.
[21] Kim, *China*, 103.
[22] John Franklin Copper, *China's Foreign Aid: An Instrument of Peking's Foreign Policy* (Lexington, Mass.: D. C. Heath, 1976), 85.
[23] UN Archives, PSCA, DAG 1/5.2.2.13, Box 2, 'Survey of Attitudes of the People's Republic of China Toward the United Nations', 9 June 1969.

Council. With the outbreak of the Korean war, however, that policy of neutrality came under scrutiny. The close votes on the UN Security Council in the opening stages of the war convinced certain US officials of the importance of having the ROC as a supporter of the Western position. (The crucial resolution of 27 June was supported by 7 votes to 1 (Yugoslavia), with India and Egypt not participating and the Soviet Union still boycotting the Council.) As Ruth Bacon, an adviser on UN affairs in the State Department, argued on 29 June, the vote in the Security Council demonstrated that the United States possessed 'no margin of dependable votes on this question' of UN enforcement, and without the affirmative Chinese Nationalist vote, the resolution would apparently have failed. Thus, the need for a 'dependable majority in the S[ecurity] C[ouncil] would appear to be the overriding consideration. Accordingly, it is suggested that we should inform other friendly powers that for the present we believe that any change in Chinese representation would be undesirable.' A few days later, and in the light of the developing situation in Korea, the US Secretary of State, Dean Acheson, informed the US ambassador to the United Nations that in Washington's view the Chinese representation issue should not be raised and that he should indicate 'as appropriate . . . that during Korean crisis we w[ou]ld be even more disinclined see change [in] Chi[nese] representation'.[24]

With China's entry into that conflict, the exclusion of Beijing became an overwhelming priority for Washington, for both domestic and international reasons. Administration support for Chiang helped to ward off the attacks of those in Congress claiming that the Nationalists were to be sold down the river. Maintenance of the ROC's position not only helped the voting majority on the Security Council but allegedly it also helped bolster Taipei's prestige and legitimacy internationally at the same time that it diminished that of the Chinese Communists.

Nevertheless, maintaining international support for this policy of excluding the PRC was problematic: the UN had an existence of its own outside of the country that had played the major role in shaping it, and UN officials were concerned about its credibility. Moreover, attitudes differed as to the best means of dealing with

[24] *Foreign Relations*, 1950 (Washington, DC: Government Printing Office, 1976), 2: 246, 29 June 1950; 2: 247, 3 July 1950; Grasso, *Truman's Two-China Policy*, 156.

the PRC: some states, such as the UK, believed fundamentally, and despite the Korean fighting, that China should be integrated into the international society of states, there to have its behaviour modified. The United States, however, showed a marked preference for isolating and shunning Beijing until that revolutionary regime had learned to 'behave'. This difference was as much a consequence of national style where foreign relations were concerned as a policy directly connected with the Chinese Communists.

Such tensions between the US and its major allies were apparent at the time of the passage of the aggressor resolution in February 1951. A finding of aggression would put China (and North Korea, too) in direct contravention of the UN Charter, thus making entry even more difficult to effect. But what immediately concerned the UK, France, Canada, India, and others was that a resolution of this kind made it likely that, in the UN's name, the war on the Korean peninsula would be extended to China itself. Moreover, many of these same states had been uneasy about the UN resolution which had authorized US–UN forces to cross the 38th parallel to prosecute the war in North Korea. Such governments tended to believe that this action had been responsible for bringing Beijing's 'volunteers' directly into the fighting for what China described as defensive reasons. Arguments of these kinds led certain states—especially the British, and Canadians—to work first to delay the passage of the aggressor resolution and, when it could be delayed no longer, to place a brake on the implementation of additional measures against China, thus allowing further opportunity for a negotiated outcome to the conflict.[25]

In order to ensure that its major allies would give their support to the tabling and passage of this resolution the Truman administration voiced three arguments, all of which raised questions about Washington's intended international role and about its future support of the United Nations. It reminded the allies that without UN action there would be demands in the USA for unilateral action and a regeneration of isolationist sentiment sufficient to jeopardize all that Washington was trying to do 'with

[25] For further details on this resolution see, Rosemary Foot, 'Anglo-American Relations in the Korean Crisis: The British Effort to Avert an Expanded War, December 1950–January 1951', *Diplomatic History*, 10, no. 1 (Winter 1986), esp. 53–7.

and for the Atlantic Pact countries'. The administration also claimed that a failure to label China an aggressor would mark the beginning of the end of the UN as a collective security organiza- tion. Washington would compromise somewhat on wording in order to 'preserve the greatest degree of free world unity', but it would not give up its basic goal of a finding of aggression.[26]

With the passage of this modified resolution, it was a relatively easy step for the United States to gain support for what came to be known as the 'moratorium' procedure on the representation issue—a device whereby the General Assembly agreed annually not to make any changes in China's representation and not to debate the issue. However, with the signature of the Korean armistice agreement in July 1953, the gradual withdrawal of Chi- nese forces from the north of that country, together with Beijing's adoption of a policy of peaceful coexistence, many states became increasingly uncomfortable with a position that denied the reality of Beijing's existence.

Shifts in International Attitudes

At the end of the Korean war, the US Secretary of State, John Foster Dulles, had sought refuge in the UN charter as a means of maintaining allied support for the moratorium. He argued that Beijing was both an 'aggressor in Korea' and a 'promoter of ag- gression in IndoChina', which proved an unwillingness 'to be peace loving and faithful to the obligations of the United Nations Charter'.[27] Some years later, in his oft-quoted speech on China in San Francisco, June 1957, he again stated that the UN was 'not a reformatory for bad governments' but 'supposedly an association of those who were "peace loving" '.[28] At other strategic moments,

[26] Rosemary Foot, *The Wrong War: American Policy and the Dimensions of the Korean Conflict, 1950–1953* (Ithaca, NY: Cornell University Press, 1985), 112.

[27] Dwight D. Eisenhower, Papers as President of the United States, Ann Whitman File, International Meetings Series, Box 1, Bermuda—State Department Report, 7 Dec. 1953, DDEL.

[28] *Foreign Relations*, 1955–7, 3: 561, June 28, 1957. For an argument that Dulles in fact was not as rigid on the matter of UN entry see Nancy Bernkopf Tucker, 'John Foster Dulles and the Taiwan Roots of the "Two Chinas" Policy', in Richard H. Immerman, ed., *John Foster Dulles and the Diplomacy of the Cold War* (Princeton, NJ: Princeton University Press, 1990), 255–6. Nevertheless, the weight of his argu- ments suggested change in the US position was unlikely in the 1950s.

members of the Eisenhower administration warned that, if Chiang Kai-shek's delegation was unseated, influential political leaders in the USA would demand American withdrawal from the organization altogether, including the withdrawal of financial support, or would urge that its headquarters be removed from New York.[29] Dulles repeated these arguments to his British counterpart, Anthony Eden, in July 1954, pointing out that he 'did not think he could exaggerate the [domestic] difficulties for us inherent in such a proposal' to seat Beijing. Although he acknowledged that the policy of PRC exclusion from the UN was not immutable, he noted that, beyond the domestic constraints, there was also the fact that the Chinese Communists constantly challenged the US position in the Pacific area. Moreover, 'so long as the Chinese Communist regime continues its campaign of venom against the United States, we would have to oppose any policy that would add to its power. If and when the Chinese Communists became decent and respectable in deeds not just in words, then it would be time for us to take another look at the situation.'[30] President Eisenhower also tried to convince the British and the Canadians that he too sympathized with, or at least understood, the strong feeling of the American public against seating Beijing, claiming that it was 'more aroused about the casualties in Korea than about the far greater casualties in World War II'.[31]

[29] For one example, see RG 59, Policy Planning Staff Office Files, 1956, Lot 66 D 487, Box 75, 'Summary Conclusions and Recommendations of Chiefs of Mission Conference, Tokyo, March 1956', National Archives, Washington, DC; and see Dulles's discussions with Eden, note 30 below, and Pearson's discussions with Eisenhower described in note 31.

[30] *Foreign Relations*, 1952–4 (Washington, DC: Government Printing Office, 1979), 3: 733–4, 2 July 1954.

[31] *Foreign Relations*, 1955–7 (Washington, DC: Government Printing Office, 1992), 27: 707–8, 20 Mar. 1957; Rosemary Foot, 'The Search for a Modus Vivendi: Anglo-American Relations and China Policy in the Eisenhower Era', in Warren I. Cohen and Akira Iriye, eds., *The Great Powers in East Asia, 1953–1960* (New York: Columbia University Press, 1990), 144–6. In a conversation with Prime Minister Lester Pearson, for example, Eisenhower explained the 'very deep-seated feeling of the American people against the Chinese Communists . . . He said that this was not anything superficial or reflective merely of extremist views, such as those of Senator Knowland, but that it was very general throughout the country. A successful effort to bring the Chinese Communists into the United Nations, would, the President said, lead to very strong reactions—certainly a resolution in both Houses to withdraw the United States from the United Nations, or at least to exclude the United Nations from the United States . . . the Chinese Communists would, through their own conduct, have to supply a reason for a change of United

But if Eisenhower had his domestic opinion to consider so too did the North Atlantic allies. The British government found the moratorium policy increasingly difficult to defend to its domestic audience. It was not a sense of 'real agreement' that kept London and Washington together on the matter, 'only a sense of comradeship', Selwyn Lloyd affirmed in 1955. In 1956, Anthony Eden, a Prime Minister less solicitous of American good opinion, recommended overturning the moratorium procedure after the 1956 UN session (and after the presidential election in the United States). He was only dissuaded from this course by strong representations from the Foreign Office, including the Foreign Secretary.[32] The Canadians also found it an awkward policy to maintain. Lester Pearson, Secretary of State for External Affairs, told Dulles and Eisenhower in 1956 that the 'feeling in Canada was that it would be better to have contact with the Chinese Communists and find out what they were like and why they acted as they did rather than keep them at a distance'.[33] Officials in London believed that keeping China at a distance tended to work to Beijing's advantage giving both the 'glamour of forbidden fruit' and allowing it to avoid taking positions on Asian questions that could alienate its neighbours.[34]

America's willingness to compromise in other policy areas demonstrated the centrality to Washington of this matter of representation. When the British offered support for the US position in the UN if the USA gave ground on the question of trade controls, the Americans reluctantly acquiesced. At the Washington summit in October 1957, a somewhat astonished Macmillan readily agreed to Eisenhower's suggestion that, in exchange for the sharing of information on developments in nuclear weapons' technology, London would not press for PRC representation.[35]

States attitude.' Dulles Papers, White House Memorandum Series, Box 4, memo of conversation, 27 Mar. 1956, DDEL.

[32] Foot, 'Search for a *Modus Vivendi*', 145.

[33] Dulles Papers, White House Memo Series, Box 4, memo of conversation, 27 Mar. 1956, DDEL.

[34] RG 59, Records of Office of Chinese Affairs, Box 4, 9 Oct. 1957, National Archives (NA).

[35] Jan Melissen, 'The Restoration of the Nuclear Alliance: Great Britain and Atomic Negotiations with the United States, 1957–58', *Contemporary Record*, 6, no. 1 (Summer 1992), 85. Macmillan recorded that he could hardly believe the offer. See Alistair Horne, *Harold Macmillan*, ii. *1957–1986* (New York: Viking, 1989), 56. See also *Foreign Relations*, 1955–7, 27: 733 and Mar. and Oct. 1957.

But the kinds of negotiations that were possible with close allies were not always available with other governments. Neither could the United States prevent the UN from changing its political complexion from the mid to late 1950s. The numbers voting against the moratorium resolution rose slowly but steadily. Without the staunch support of the Latin American group, which had 20 votes, the US would already have been in the minority. In the 1958 vote, only 5 of 12 Asian states, 4 of 14 Middle Eastern, 7 of the non-communist European members, and 8 of the 13 NATO partners voted in support of the US position.[36] In 1960 alone, 15 African states plus Cyprus were admitted to the world body, and it was not thought likely that they could be persuaded to support the *status quo* on Chinese representation. The US did make efforts to ensure the compliance of these new states: in anticipation that the 1960 vote would be a close one, the Eisenhower administration requested that London explain the moratorium procedure to colonies approaching independence, such as Nigeria. The British agreed to do this, but they were not willing to expend many of their political resources in lobbying for a policy in which they did not believe.[37]

The Japanese, who constantly tried to strike some kind of balance between US and Afro-Asian opinion, found themselves under domestic pressure in 1960 at a minimum to abstain on the moratorium resolution.[38] Even as Sino-Indian relations deteriorated, this did not dent Indian support for China's admission, one argument being that entry into the UN might serve to moderate Beijing's behaviour.[39] Such restiveness among UN delegations of various hues led the UN Secretary-General to remark that it would be far better if the Americans could be 'brought to face realities ahead of pressure'.[40]

The realities were made known soon enough. In the autumn voting round, of the 15 new African states, twelve abstained on

---

[36] A. Doak Barnett, *Communist China and Asia: Challenge to American Policy* (New York: Harper, 1960), 451–2.

[37] FO 371/150418 and FO 371/150526, 21 Feb. 1960 and 1 Aug. 1960, Public Record Office (PRO).

[38] Reported by British embassy, Tokyo, FO 371/150426, 14 Oct. 1960, PRO.

[39] Don Page, 'The Representation of China in the United Nations: Canadian Perspectives and Initiatives, 1949–1971', in Paul M. Evans and B. Michael Frolic, eds., *Reluctant Adversaries: Canada and the People's Republic of China 1949–1970* (Toronto: University of Toronto Press, 1991), 85.

[40] FO 371/150525, 6 June 1960, PRO.

the moratorium resolution and three voted against it. If only five of the abstainers changed their vote in 1961, then a debate would ensue on the substantive question. The Americans were made aware that those nominally supporting them on the question had proved very reluctant to speak in 1960, a trend that was unlikely to be reversed. Furthermore, if the mood to break the deadlock on the matter was hardening in 1960, the US administration was also about to change, whatever the result of the 1960 presidential contest. Dulles, who had been closely identified with keeping China out of the UN, had died in office in 1959 and Eisenhower, publicly identified with the policy, was shortly to come to the end of his second term. Such political developments reinforced the sense that the UN was about to enter into a new era where this question of Chinese representation was concerned.

Certainly, the Democratic presidential candidate did suggest that a Kennedy administration would alter America's stance towards China, in a speech delivered in June 1960 hinting at greater flexibility. Although he drew back from UN admission for Beijing 'without a genuine change in [China's] belligerent attitude toward her Asian neighbours and the world', he did argue for improved communications with the mainland, via the test-ban talks at Geneva.[41]

Other prospective members of a Kennedy administration took up the theme of increased cultural, economic, and selected political contact with the PRC. Adlai Stevenson, a Democratic contender for the nomination who later became Kennedy's UN ambassador, went further and argued in *Foreign Affairs*, January 1960, for an end to Beijing's exclusion from the UN, although he coupled this with UN supervised elections in Korea, and self-determination for Taiwan. In his view, China, 'with a quarter of the world's population, would be more accountable to world opinion than as an outcast'.[42]

The British eagerly watched these developments, seeing in these views the opportunity of bringing American policy closer to their own objectives and, in consequence, easing the strain of their position not only with Washington but also with the new Com-

---

[41] FO 371/148589, 17 June 1960, PRO.
[42] Adlai E. Stevenson, 'Putting First Things First: A Democratic View', *Foreign Affairs*, 38, no. 1, Jan. 1960.

monwealth states. Further cause for London's optimism was given when the designated Secretary of State, Dean Rusk, described Washington's UN policy in December 1960 as 'unrealistic', stating that he would like to see the new administration get itself 'off the hook'.[43]

Devising a workable means of achieving that once in power was another matter, however. It was one thing to report that leading Latin American states, such as Brazil, had publicly announced that they would vote against the moratorium in the autumn of 1961, that the old Commonwealth was unenthusiastic, that British support could no longer be counted upon, and that without it Canada, Australia, New Zealand, together with The Netherlands, Luxembourg, and Belgium, would probably withhold their affirmative votes;[44] but it was quite another to find an alternative device that would satisfy these criticisms, the Kennedy administration's obligations to Chiang Kai-shek, and the Nationalists' political supporters in the United States. Kennedy's mandate in November 1960 had been less than convincing, precluding bold steps. Rusk told his British counterpart in April 1961 during discussions on the UN matter, that 'the President had been much impressed by Mr. Eisenhower's warning that China was the only issue which might bring him back into politics'.[45] The new President's priorities were elsewhere, and in the foreign policy field this included getting the foreign aid bill through Congress and advancing relations with the Soviet Union. The dilemma was to find a policy for the UN that would prove more acceptable to world opinion and that domestic opinion would not find either controversial or unacceptable. Options canvassed included a 'two Chinas' or successor states' resolution—that is, the General Assembly would affirm the continuing membership of the ROC while also supporting membership for Beijing—or that the matter of representation be considered an important question to be taken under Article 18 (2) of the Charter.

[43] FO 371/158442, 12 Dec. 1960, PRO.

[44] John F. Kennedy, Papers as President, National Security File (NSF) Country File, China, General, Box 22, 6 July 1961, JFKL.

[45] FO 371/158445, 4 Apr. 1961, PRO. Warren Cohen has argued that there is no direct evidence that Eisenhower said this, but it is hard to credit the idea that Rusk would have fabricated the statement. For further details on this and other aspects of the domestic environment, see my Ch. 4.

This latter option might or might not be coupled with the establishment of a study committee that would look into the whole matter of UN representation.

How seriously the Kennedy administration considered 'two Chinas' as a solution is a debatable point. In March 1961, Averell Harriman told the British Prime Minister that the US was reconciled to the seating of both delegations.[46] In May, Rusk proposed to Kennedy that Chiang and his supporters be persuaded to support such a 'two Chinas' course. Then, when Mao refused this solution, Beijing rather than Taipei or Washington would be blamed for the PRC's exclusion.[47] But when faced with the prospect of actually voting to seat the PRC, ardour for this proposal cooled. The lesser evil of abstaining on a successor-state-type resolution was only slightly more palatable for, if it was successful despite the US abstention, then this could be portrayed as a defeat for Washington; additionally, it would make it appear that the US was out of step with majority UN opinion.[48] It seems unlikely that the Kennedy administration expected the PRC to take up its seat under these conditions—indeed, both Chinas had made it known that they would not tolerate any kind of two-Chinas solution—nevertheless, the problem was how to explain to US domestic opinion that the successor state format was a way of keeping the PRC out of the UN, without losing the support of the developing countries.[49]

When news of the contemplated successor-state resolution leaked, the expected outcry in the United States quickly materialized. A Senate Resolution constrained Kennedy still further when it stated, not that the administration should support the position of the Nationalist government in the UN, but that it should support it as the 'representative of China' in that body.[50] With 76 Senators voting in favour of this resolution and none against, together with the unequivocal statements by Senators Cotton,

[46] FO 371/158444, 10 Mar. 1961, PRO.
[47] Warren I. Cohen, *Dean Rusk* (Totowa, NJ: Cooper Square Publishers, 1980), 166. Cohen argues that this was Rusk's attempt to 'muzzle the China Lobby so that Rusk, Stevenson and Cleveland could work toward a two China solution in the UN'. But Chiang's and Mao's known aversion to two-Chinas makes this scheme either an unrealistic proposition or more likely one designed to gain a PRC veto, as Cohen also suggests.
[48] NSF, Country File, China, Box 22, 15 June 1961, JFKL.
[49] NSF, Country File, China, Box 22, 24 May 1961 and 15 June 1961, JFKL.
[50] FO 371/158450, 1 Aug. 1961, PRO.

Hickenlooper, and Dirksen that such a resolution left no room for a two-Chinas policy, the 'important question' option began to take firm precedence. Building support for that option was not necessarily straightforward, however. In a somewhat bizarre development, African states' support partly depended on a sensible policy on the part of the Chinese Nationalists towards the matter of UN representation for the Mongolian People's Republic. Chiang was not reconciled to the independence of that country and threatened to veto its application for membership; but if he did so the Soviets had said they would veto the application of Mauritania, which in turn would cause the French African states to turn against Taiwan. Exasperated with Nationalist intentions over this matter, US officials believed Chiang had to be made aware of the real issues at stake: that US policy was part of a plan to keep the PRC out of the UN, that Nationalist standing in the world largely rested on its UN membership, and that for more than a decade the United States as the Nationalists' main ally had expended much political capital in keeping Taiwan in and Beijing out.[51] Despite the power of this case, Kennedy assumed that the only thing that would ensure Nationalist co-operation was the guarantee of a US veto of any resolution recommending membership for the PRC in exchange for Chiang's promise not to veto Mongolia's application.[52]

To generate allied support for the important question resolution required resort to the familiar range of threats and blandishments. As Rusk told the British Foreign Secretary, Lord Home, in August 1961, if America's friends voted against the important question resolution then Washington 'would feel that the United Nations had "gone insane" and would walk out' of the organization. Although the British seriously objected to this new policy as a 'transparent device for delay', the Prime Minister was nevertheless loath to cross the Americans over a subject that they apparently felt so deeply about and especially on the 'eve of great perils in Europe' connected with Berlin.[53]

[51] NSF, Country File, China, Box 22, 5 Sept. 1961, JFKL.
[52] This and other aspects of UN policy are discussed in James Fetzer, 'Clinging to Containment: China Policy', in Thomas G. Paterson, ed., *Kennedy's Quest for Victory: American Foreign Policy, 1961–1963* (New York: Oxford University Press, 1989), esp. 188.
[53] FO 371/158451, 12 Aug. 1961, PRO.

Washington also drew on the UN Charter as a source of support for its position. To some extent, however, Washington overplayed its hand and its rhetoric in this respect when it stressed the dictatorial and violent nature of the rulers in Beijing. Adlai Stevenson's speech in December 1961 in which he argued that the UN would be making a tragic mistake if it 'yielded to the claim of an aggressive and unregenerate "People's Republic of China" . . . would be ignoring the warlike character and the aggressive behaviour of the rulers who dominate 600 million people', prompted the Sinhalese ambassador to retort: 'Dictatorship indeed! If the United Nations in 1945, and thereafter, had kept out all the peoples who lived under one dictatorship or another, who but a handful of nations would be here today?'[54]

But when the US ambassador pointed to the fact that the Chinese Nationalist government's effective control extended over 'more people than does the legal jurisdiction of two-thirds of the Governments represented here'[55] he found an argument with somewhat wider potential appeal, based on the concept of self-determination, and one that also offered a way out for those countries that did not want to cross the United States over this matter. The British government, for example, having voted for the resolution to seat Beijing, explained that this did not prejudice its opinion that sovereignty over the island of Taiwan still remained to be determined. Canada, Malaya, and Nigeria among others argued unequivocally that Taiwan must preserve its right to self-determination. Japan stated that, while it was cognizant of the principle of universality and of the fact that the PRC was in effective control of the mainland, it was also the case that the Nationalists were in 'solid and effective control of Taiwan and the adjacent islands'.[56] It was these kinds of arguments that gave some credibility to the position that the question of Chinese representation was an important matter deserving of a prudent and deliberate approach. The appeal of this argument helped to ensure that in 1961 the Soviet resolution to seat the PRC and expel the Nationalists failed 36 to 48 with 20 abstentions, and

---

[54] UN General Assembly (UNGA), 16th Session, 1069th meeting, 1 Dec. 1961, p. 903 and 1070th meeting, 4 Dec. 1961, p. 918.

[55] UNGA, 16th Session, 1069th Meeting, 1 Dec. 1961, p. 905.

[56] These views are to be found in the verbatim reports of the 16th Session, *passim*.

that 61 states voted for the important question resolution requiring a two-thirds majority to change representation, with 34 against.

Voting in the next two years indicated the degree to which the important question device had served to shape a new debate on the issue of representation. In order to maintain the unity over the issue that had emerged, the Under-Secretary of State, Chester Bowles, recommended that US opposition to PRC entrance into the UN be tied more closely to Beijing's refusal to accept the independence of Taiwan. He even suggested in 1962 that in the following year the US should publicly forgo opposition to Communist China's membership, provided Beijing accepted Taiwan as an independent government entitled to UN representation.[57] Although the administration did adopt Bowles's first recommendation, there was no requirement for Washington to adopt the second, more politically dangerous, course. A number of states, as noted earlier, such as the UK, Canada, and Japan, were willing to advance this argument anyway.

Yet, the weakness of allowing the two-Chinas argument to flourish was apparent over the longer term, for if both Taipei and Beijing continued to reject it then governments at some point if they wanted to resolve the issue would have to make a choice of which China should be in the United Nations. Moreover, a growing number of states wanted Beijing to be subjected to the moderating influence of that body.[58]

1964 proved to be another crucial year for the policy not only because of the Chinese nuclear explosion but also because in January 1964 the French recognized the PRC, largely to affirm their independence of Washington.[59] Washington feared that others would soon follow, if not with recognition, then at least with the dropping of their support for the important question resolution. Rusk pleaded with the Canadian government, for ex-

---

[57] James C. Thomson Papers, Chester Bowles, 1961–3, Box 7, 4 Apr. 1962, JFKL.

[58] The Canadian Prime Minister, Lester Pearson, was clearly of this view. As he stated in an address to the Atlantic Treaty Association in Ottawa on 14 Sept. 1964: 'If we exposed them more to the views of the rest of the world, we might some day expect a more realistic policy from them. The present isolation of China encourages recurring crises.' John W. Holmes, 'Canada and China: The Dilemmas of a Middle Power', in A. M. Halpern, ed., *Policies Toward China: Views from Six Continents* (New York: McGraw Hill, 1965), 120.

[59] For further details see Francois Fejto, 'France and China: The Intersection of Two Grand Designs', in Halpern, ed., *Policies Toward China*.

ample, not to follow the French lead; but the new Liberal government in Ottawa was not to be so easily cowed this time and
vowed that it would only support the IQ resolution in return for
a 'very specific promise at the highest level' in Washington that a
new look would be taken at the representation policy.[60] The Ital-
ian government was also known to be impatient to get on 'some
new track that is not vulnerable to the political charge they are
ignoring the world's most populous nation'; the Africans were
said to be 'increasingly wobbly' and 'even so strong an opponent
of CHICOM admission as Paul-Henri Spaak has now told us this
Assembly [1964] is the last time around for him in the face of
mounting public and parliamentary pressure at home'.[61]

    With China's atomic test, media opinion in nearly every
country of concern to the United States—the UK, Canada, France,
Italy, West Germany, Japan, Brazil, Nigeria—indicated widespread support for China's entry.[62] Some in the Johnson administration were of a similar mind, the Asia specialist on the White
House staff, R. W. Komer, arguing in a memorandum to the
Special Assistant for National Security Affairs, McGeorge Bundy,
that Johnson's new mandate gave him room for manœuvre domestically because it was 'partly a vote for cautious responsibility
in a nuclear world'.[63] And if the argument against flexibility in
policy was that Vietnam made it the wrong moment to appear
soft—apparently Dean Rusk's view—could that argument not be
reversed by claiming that increased pressure in Vietnam provided the opportunity for greater flexibility on the UN representation issue?[64]

    No vote on the matter was in fact taken in 1964 because of the
crisis over the funding of UN peacekeeping operations that year;
but the momentum behind the position of allowing China to enter
continued to gather. In addition to shifts among the Atlantic
allies, Washington was well aware prior to the 1965 debate that
the Latin American vote was fragmenting, and that these states
felt uneasy at being the only solid bloc left that supported the

    [60] Norman St Amour, 'Sino-Canadian Relations 1963–1968: The American
Factor', in Evans and Frolic, eds., *Reluctant Adversaries*, 113.
    [61] Lyndon Baines Johnson, Papers as President, NSF, Country File–United
Nations Charter Representation, Box 290, 31 Oct. 1964, LBJL.
    [62] NSF, Country File—UN Charter Representation, Box 290, 19 Oct. 1964, LBJL.
    [63] NSF, Country File, China Memos, vol. 3 , Boxes 237–8, 23 Nov. 1964, LBJL.
    [64] Ibid.

United States. Expectations were that Chile would change its vote and neither Peru, Brazil, Colombia, Venezuela, nor Costa Rica could be counted on to speak in the General Assembly in opposition to Chinese Communist membership.[65] Worse was to come when the 1965 debate itself got underway. The UN Secretary-General's report on the work of the United Nations argued that the Vietnam war and the impasse over disarmament pointed 'once again to the imperative need for the United Nations to achieve universality of membership'. New Zealand hinted at a future change in its policy and warned against the 'dangers and the illusions' of attempts to solve international problems without China. When the US ambassador argued that the PRC in fact did not want to enter the UN, as Zhou Enlai's recent statement had indicated, the French delegate directly undercut his remarks: 'What Government, if it found itself in the same circumstances, kept out of the United Nations for so many years, could be expected to show kindly feelings towards the United Nations?'[66] Perhaps it was this sense of the basic lack of realism in the UN's position that led several delegations to ignore the rhetoric of Chen Yi and Zhou's statements (quoted earlier) and to vote for the Albanian resolution to seat the PRC and expel the Nationalists. For the first time, that resolution produced a tie vote, 47 to 47 with 20 abstentions.

Not surprisingly, such an outcome produced much 'soul searching' within the US State Department, and this result, together with the belief that 1966 would see the Albanian resolution gain a simple majority, sparked a further debate on the prospects of a new representation policy, but again one that incorporated a two-Chinas solution. In speeches in Chicago and California in the spring of 1966, the Assistant Secretary of State for International Organization, Joseph Sisco, and the US Ambassador to the UN, Arthur Goldberg, both attempted to draw attention away from PRC exclusion and towards the prevention of ROC expulsion. The Assistant Secretary of State for Far Eastern Affairs, William Bundy, Sisco, and Goldberg, meeting with a sceptical Dean Rusk on 6 May 1966, also recommended that Washington support countries such as Canada who were ready to argue openly for two Chinas at the 1966 UN General Assembly session.

[65] NSF, Country File—UN, Box 290, 12 Nov. 1965, LBJL.
[66] UNGA, 20th Session, 1369th–1372nd meetings, Nov. 1965.

The three US officials sought to enlist directly the help of the Canadians, putting it to Lester Pearson and Paul Martin that, if Ottawa offered to discuss its proposal with the Johnson administration, this was the moment when they would be able to exert most influence on Washington's China policy. This suggestion bore fruit and Johnson authorized a meeting in Ottawa between Martin, Goldberg, and Sisco. However, Martin was clearly ahead of US thinking on the issue: whereas he contemplated a resolution that would bring the PRC into the Security Council immediately and leave the Nationalists in the General Assembly, the furthest the US administration was prepared to contemplate going was a two-Chinas initiative or a resolution advocating setting up a study committee to consider the whole question of representation.

When the terms of the proposed Canadian resolution were made known to the US administration, Johnson and Rusk were, according to William Bundy, 'absolutely dumbfounded' by it, and Ottawa was warned that Washington would work actively to oppose it. In a personal letter to Lester Pearson, Rusk stated baldly: 'If your resolution is introduced, we shall not merely have to oppose it, but [shall] have to go to great lengths to see that it is defeated by the heaviest possible margin.' To further ensure Canadian compliance, Rusk warned: 'I need not underscore the seriousness of such a split between our two nations.'[67]

Aware of intense Canadian dissatisfaction over the issue and suspecting that the Albanian resolution would receive a simple majority in 1966, the Johnson administration plumped for one calling for a study committee that would make appropriate recommendations on representation to the 1967 session. Canada, unwilling to put its name to what it saw as yet another delaying tactic, refused to co-sponsor, but Italy, Belgium, and Chile all agreed to do so. As it turned out, the study committee resolution

---

[67] The full details of this extraordinary episode in US–Canadian relations are given in St Amour, 'Sino-Canadian Relations', esp. 117–21. The Chilean Foreign Minister and the country's UN ambassador were also advocating a Chilean vote in favour of the Albanian resolution in 1966. In this instance, the US ambassador in Santiago recommended 'representations by Secretary Rusk or Ambassador Goldberg . . . I also wish to underscore that this cannot be done in a polite way. It has to be done in a manner which is unmistakably clear.' President Johnson followed up this suggestion by asking Walt Rostow for a report on what Rusk and Goldberg had done. NSF Country File, China, vol. 7, Box 240, 29 Sept. and 30 Sept. 1966, LBJL.

was rejected (34–62–25) as was the Albanian resolution, despite there having been a tied vote in 1965. Perhaps this result reflected the fact that the study committee resolution allowed some delegations to vote with more enthusiasm for the IQ resolution. More probably, the voting pattern reflected the deterioration in Chinese Communist relations with a number of countries as the Cultural Revolution got underway. Beijing itself had helped rescue the United States from its growing isolation over the matter.

Indeed, the vote against the Albanian resolution stayed high in 1967 and 1968, suggesting that the violence and disruption associated with the Cultural Revolution were undermining China's case for entry. It was not until 1969 and especially 1970 that voting patterns began to shift in the PRC's favour once again, a time when Beijing had begun to exhibit greater moderation and flexibility in its dealings with other states. As noted earlier, diplomatic contact including UN membership had once again become a high priority for the PRC and it set out deliberately to woo the West, Japan, and the non-aligned.

Such a moderation in Beijing's approach quickly showed results in the UN General Assembly votes on Chinese representation. In 1970, the Albanian resolution for the first time gained a simple majority, with both Canada and Italy voting in favour of it even as they continued to support the IQ resolution. The United States itself finally formalized the position it had articulated earlier, no longer questioning the right of the PRC to be represented, but focusing still on Washington's opposition to the expulsion of the ROC.[68] The UK and Canada determined that in 1971 they would cast their first votes against the IQ resolution; indeed, Canada, in 1971, voted for the Albanian resolution even with its clause expelling Taiwan, and explained that it did so because it was clearly the will of the majority of UN members that the PRC be represented in that body.

This was the first year that the United States and both of its major allies had taken a public and entirely different route. Washington nevertheless made some effort in 1971 to mobilize its political capital in order ostensibly to defeat the Albanian resolution. Its UN ambassador, George Bush, introduced a variant which argued, much as Ottawa had in 1966, that the PRC should

[68] UN Archives, DAG 1/5.2.2.13, Box 2, 'Chinese Representation', 4 Dec. 1970.

hold the Security Council seat, but that both Chinas should be in the General Assembly. The US mission to the UN contacted over ninety delegations in New York in order to gain the necessary support for this position, the State Department undertaking a similar effort with various governments. Despite such efforts, the 'dual representation' resolution, which included Japan, Australia, and New Zealand as co-sponsors, failed to pass, apparently much to the astonishment of the US delegation. When Bush rose on a point of order to try to have the expulsion clause deleted from the Albanian resolution, this too was blocked. Once the IQ resolution was overturned, the Chinese Nationalists declared that they would no longer 'take part in any further proceedings of the General Assembly', which left the way open for the Albanian text. It passed by the healthy majority of 76 to 35 with 17 abstentions.[69]

The Impact of China's Entry

One author has interpreted this US defeat as a 'vivid reminder of the end of Pax Americana in the world organization'.[70] Clearly, Washington's inability to prevent Taiwan's expulsion from the United Nations on the surface at least suggests an erosion of its ability to coerce or persuade most of its major allies together with other states of the wisdom of its policy. Nevertheless, it is also necessary to remember that Washington itself had been encouraging, if not this particular outcome, certainly one very similar to it, and that in many respects its new China policy had already indicated that US support for Taiwan's representation in the United

---

[69] UNGA, 26th Session, 1967th–1976th meetings, Oct. 1971; UN Archives, DAG 1/5.2.4, Box 5, 25 Aug. 1971, and DAG 1/5.2.2.13, Box 2, 'The Chinese Representation Decision', 28 Oct. 1971. An indication that the Chinese Communists themselves were surprised at the voting in 1971 is suggested in the report of the first meeting of the Chinese delegation with Chef de Cabinet, C. V. Narasimhan, and other UN officials. Faced with a series of specific questions, it was plain that Beijing was unfamiliar with some of the practices of the organization and had not formulated its position on a variety of matters, including ROC debts to the UN of some $30 million and what would actually be inscribed on delegation nameplates ('China, People's Republic of', or simply 'China'). UN Archives, DAG 1/5.2.4, Box 5, 'Report on the Meeting with the Delegation of the People's Republic of China held at Headquarters on 12 November 1971'.

[70] Kim, *China*, 104.

Nations had been seriously eroded.[71] Small US steps to improve relations with China had been apparent to all since the Johnson era and became clearer under Nixon as he decided in 1969 to withdraw the Seventh Fleet from the Taiwan Straits, and to remove US air force squadrons and troops from the island. At the 1970 UN General Assembly, the US ambassador reminded Assembly members that the accusation that Washington was ignoring the reality of the PRC did not stand up to inspection, since representatives from his government had met twice that year with officials from Beijing. Like many other delegations, he said, the US wanted to see the PRC 'play a constructive role in the family of nations'.[72] But the most decisive move of all came with Kissinger's decision to visit Beijing in July 1971, which signalled that the old UN policy was now moribund. This signal was further underscored by Kissinger's second visit to Beijing in October at the precise time that the 1971 vote was taking place. Moreover, it had also been announced that Nixon himself would be going to China in early 1972.[73]

Thus, as the Pakistani delegate put it, the 1971 vote took place in the most extraordinary of circumstances, suggesting that while the State Department and the US UN delegation may well have been genuine in their efforts to find a dual representation formula, Nixon and Kissinger were engaged in something of a 'diplomatic charade'.[74] The administration was in fact simply going through the motions for Taiwan's sake, and because it wanted to convince certain potential critics of its policy that it remained a staunch and loyal ally of the Chinese Nationalist. However, the direct contact with Zhou Enlai and Mao Zedong made plain that

[71] At least one and probably more delegations at the United Nations were confused, however, as to the kind of voting result that Washington actually desired. As one representative remarked, 'Washington, having placed itself in an extremely untenable position from which it could not gracefully extricate itself, left us with only one option, that of rescuing it from its difficulty.' UN Archives, DAG 1/5.2.2.13, Box 2, 'The Chinese Representation Decision', 28 Oct. 1971.

[72] UNGA, 25th Session, 1902nd meeting, 12 Nov. 1970.

[73] According to Chinese sources, Kissinger at that first meeting acknowledged that Taiwan was a part of China and no longer considered its status to be undetermined. Xue and Pei, eds., *Diplomacy*, 272.

[74] A point made by the Washington journalist Tad Szulc. See his *The Illusion of Peace: Foreign Policy in the Nixon Years* (New York: Viking Press, 1978), 497. Kissinger discusses the episode, emphasizing his differences with the State Department over the matter, in *White House Years* (Boston: Little Brown, 1979), esp. 770–4.

China was no longer being viewed as an outcast but had come to be perceived as a strategic partner, and one of far greater significance to Washington than Taipei. The 'defeat' of 1971 was hardly that, therefore, and was certainly a more complicated matter than that description implies. The outcome served to bolster Washington's efforts to normalize relations with the PRC, to bring US interests into line with majority world opinion, and more broadly reinforced a view that the United Nations would henceforth be in a better position to fulfil its mission, and would better reflect the realities of power in the global system. By attempting to 'save' Taiwan, the administration, at the same time, could try to claim that it had made some effort to reflect a domestic opinion that, while it favoured PRC entry, did not support the expulsion of the Chinese Nationalists.[75]

The relationship of the 1971 vote to the debate on US hegemonic decline also needs to be interpreted in the context of Chinese behaviour once it joined the UN. Developing countries jubilantly greeted China's assumption of the UN seat, and China's swift identification with Third World causes could be seen as a further blow to Western interests in the organization. However, in many respects, China's UN behaviour was of some benefit to the West. For the rest of the decade, its attitude was modest and cautious and its role generally passive. In terms of its support for the developing world it adopted what has been described as a 'championship' rather than a 'leadership' role. It did not join the Group of 77, nor indeed any bloc or alliance grouping. Beijing almost never sponsored a draft resolution and only used its veto twice, once in support of its ally Pakistan (at a time when Washington had better relations with Islamabad than it did with New Delhi). Beijing preferred instead to demonstrate its 'non-hegemonic' behaviour on the Security Council frequently by not participating in the vote.[76]

Throughout the 1970s China's annual 'state of the world' report during the General Debate of the opening plenary session tended to treat the Soviet Union and not the United States as the primary

---

[75] It was unsuccessful with domestic opinion, many in Congress criticizing Kissinger for timing his visit to Beijing to coincide with the UN vote. Kissinger, *White House Years*, 785.

[76] Kim, *China*, *passim*; Kim, 'Behavioural Dimensions of Chinese Multilateral Diplomacy', *China Quarterly*, 72 (Dec. 1977); Kim, 'Whither Post-Mao Chinese Global Policy?', *International Organization*, 35, no. 3 (Summer 1981).

threat to the international system.[77] At the level of policy performance, Moscow was 'targeted as being more insidious, more aggressive, more hegemonic, and more dangerous to genuine world power than the capitalist superpower'.[78] Indeed, it is probable that China's obsession with Moscow served to irritate other developing countries. Certainly, it served to estrange Beijing from its erstwhile socialist allies, Albania, North Korea, and Vietnam.

The representation question can be seen, therefore, as an area where the United States used its command power to maintain a policy reflecting its interests, utilizing both coercive as well as persuasive means. A heavy investment of political capital was needed at almost every stage of the policy between 1951 and 1971, largely because Washington's positions on representation did not generate willing consent. As has been argued elsewhere, when legitimacy is absent or has eroded, 'power does not necessarily collapse, or obedience cease, since it can continue to be kept in place by incentives or sanctions. However, coercion has to be much more extensive and omnipresent, and that is costly to maintain.'[79]

Although large numbers supported the aggressor resolution when it was tabled in 1951, few were entirely at ease with their position. Governments, which may have viewed China as an aggressive power, did not necessarily perceive it as the aggressor in this instance because it had only entered the Korean fighting when UN troops had crossed the 38th parallel into North Korea, a move that many saw as going beyond the UN's original intentions. The USA managed to gain support for this resolution, for the subsequent moratorium procedure, and then the 'important question' resolution not so much because the United States had the willing consent of its major allies, but because these same Western allies realized that this was a far bigger issue for Washington domestically and internationally than it was for other governments; because they believed that the future of the United Nations depended significantly on US support for the organization; and because they wanted the United States to play a major international role in other arenas of importance to them, such as in the NATO alliance.

[77] Kim, *China*, 117.   [78] Ibid. 162.
[79] David Beetham, *The Legitimation of Power* (London: Macmillan, 1991), 28.

China, as the subordinate actor in this power relationship, drew strength from two interpretations of the UN charter: that it was a body that was intended to be universal in membership; and that it should contain those governments that were in control of territory and people. Beijing and other governments' frequent references to the fact that the PRC government represented one-quarter of humankind, was indeed the most populous state in the world, highlighted the belief that the UN without China would never be entirely credible as an international organization. Moreover, China became an even more obvious candidate for Security Council membership when it exploded its nuclear device in 1964. As the numbers voting for China's entry increased over the years, and UN officials repeated their dismay at the PRC's absence, Beijing derived added strength from being the object of US exclusion. Its foreign policy behaviour was probably treated more leniently as a result of this victimization. Although US officials believed—at least in the 1950s—that it would add significantly to the prestige of the PRC if it were to gain the China seat, in a curious way, exclusion gave it another kind of prestige as year after year it was the focus of attention and debate.

The Canadian Prime Minister, Lester Pearson, believed that America's Chinese representation policy undercut the moral and political authority of the United States; the British were concerned that world confidence in US leadership had declined as a result of its stance over this matter; and others interpreted US policy as unrealistic and based on emotion. The struggle over maintaining a multilateral coalition in support first of the moratorium procedure and then the important question resolution, provided Washington with concrete evidence of its lack of legitimacy in this policy area and of the limitations of command power. Thus, it was a crucial part of the environment that encouraged change in America's China policy; crucial to the development of the understanding that Washington would have to accommodate the reality of a PRC presence.

Yet if we focus on US structural or co-optive power, we might note that China entered into a United Nations 'fundamentally based on principles advocated by the United States'[80] at a time when Beijing had visibly become a strategic ally for the United

---

[80] Claude, *Swords into Plowshares*, 62.

States, of presumed value in the task of containing a more assertive and powerful Soviet Union. Moreover, China had finally come to New York in the period when Beijing had turned away from the most radical phase of its domestic and foreign policies, putting the emphasis on reform of the UN and the international system from within, rather than on its revolutionary overthrow. China's passive UN behaviour, lack of active militancy on behalf of Third World causes, anti-Soviet rhetoric during its first years of membership, and obvious support for establishing interstate relationships, were further reminders that, while Washington's policy of exclusion had led the United States to suffer a serious erosion of its international legitimacy, that erosion had now ceased. Instead, a PRC presence had begun to bolster certain American interests.

3

Trading with the Enemy: The USA and the China Trade Embargo

In 1949, as China's revolutionary army moved inexorably towards victory in the Chinese civil war, the United States and its allies were engaged in protracted and at times difficult negotiations to co-ordinate export restrictions on trade with the Soviet bloc. By the winter of 1949–50, the United States, Canada, and countries in the Organization for European Economic Co-operation had established an international organization, with a co-ordinating committee (COCOM) and a decision-making group that met quarterly in Paris. By 1952, through the deliberations of these bodies, three international control lists had been established. The first (IL/I) contained strictly embargoed items that could directly contribute to the military capacity of enemy states; the second list (IL/II) comprised items under quantitative control: that is, those items such as machine tools, raw materials, and industrial equipment, 'which if shipped in substantial quantities may contribute to the war potential of the Soviet bloc'. The third group (IL/III)—a watch or surveillance list—included goods that could be exported freely provided details were reported to COCOM.[1]

The imposition of export controls developed more slowly in East Asia but from the start included a determination to impose restrictions on the new Chinese government. After China's entry into the Korean conflict, however, controls advanced rapidly and

[1] For further detail see Alexander Eckstein, *Communist China's Economic Growth and Foreign Trade* (New York: McGraw Hill, 1966), 184–5; Michael Mastanduno, 'Trade As a Strategic Weapon: American and Alliance Export Control Policy in the Early Postwar Period', *International Organization*, 42, no. 1 (Winter 1988); Yoko Yasuhara, 'Japan, Communist China, and Export Controls in Asia 1948–52', *Diplomatic History*, 10, no. 1 (Winter 1986); Tor Egil Forland, '"Selling Firearms to the Indians": Eisenhower's Export Control Policy, 1953–54', *Diplomatic History*, 15, no. 2 (Spring 1991); Robert Mark Spaulding, Jun., 'Eisenhower and Export Control Policy, 1953–1955', *Diplomatic History*, 17, no. 2 (Spring 1993).

with striking intensity. Until December 1950, the United States had been China's major post-war trading partner. Thereafter, and unlike its allies, it placed a total embargo on its trade with the PRC; controlled all of Beijing's foreign assets; prohibited US carriers from calling at PRC ports; and all US-flag, air or sea carriers from loading or in any way transporting goods destined for the country. It also denied bunkering facilities to all vessels that had called at Chinese ports. In May 1951, the United States was instrumental in putting through the UN General Assembly a resolution that embargoed trade in strategic items with the PRC and North Korea. By 1952, the United States and its allies, including Japan, had provided for a complete embargo on all of the goods appearing on the lists described earlier, together with a further 200 items, and had established the China Committee (CHINCOM) as a subcommittee of COCOM.

Trade controls with China were, therefore, harsher than those imposed on the Soviet Union and Eastern Europe. Known as the 'China differential', this embargo policy became a matter of public disagreement between the United States and its allies after the close of Korean hostilities. Britain, Japan, West Germany, and France, among others, sought what opportunities they could to breach the differential and then finally worked to overturn it in 1957, in the knowledge that the United States would maintain its total embargo on commercial contact. After 1957, the Western allies continued to take commercial opportunities as they arose, for straightforward economic reasons certainly, but also to placate some domestic interest groups. In addition, economic contact could help demonstrate to the United States that a form of coexistence with China was possible without dire political repercussions; and for governments that increasingly would have preferred to normalize their relationships with the PRC, trade proved less disruptive of their ties with their most significant ally. Although certain US officials and members of Congress were concerned first about allied attempts to remove the China differential, and then about the further development of trading contacts with Beijing, trade could be undertaken in the absence of formal diplomatic recognition, and this provided a means of striking a compromise with allies over that more serious political issue. As Dulles told Eden in July 1954, 'trade . . . was a bad problem [for the US administration] but it did not have the same degree of gravity as U.N. admission'.[2] Thus, US acquiescence to allied commercial exchange with China was one means by which Washington could obtain allied acceptance of a harder stance in other areas of China policy. But it could do little to protect the United States from the understanding that it stood alone among major states in refusing to trade with the PRC, and that its China policy could not be carried through internationally.

The Fate of the Embargo: 1950–1958

Even before the Chinese Communists had come to power, the Truman administration determined that it would use its trade policy as a means of signalling that it could 'deal drastically with China's foreign trade if necessary'. At that stage, however, it was decided not to cut off all economic contact with the newly emerging government because of the probable refusal on the part of America's allies to follow suit, and because limited trading might have the added beneficial effect of reducing Moscow's influence with the Chinese.[3]

Once China had entered the Korean fighting, however, restrictions were quickly established. As far as Washington was concerned, its own total embargo and the attempt to maintain a strict multilateral embargo on trade with the PRC served the primary economic purpose of delaying the country's modernization and thus the development of its military capacity. Economic warfare also fulfilled several political purposes: it placated domestic supporters of the Chinese Nationalists and it sent a signal to such Asian allies that the United States intended to support them through all means at its disposal. Moreover, the China differential reinforced the special pariah status Washington had accorded Beijing after the latter's decision to intervene in the Korean war and to fight against US-led United Nations forces. The multilateral element to the embargo served to legitimize and to universalize this perception of Beijing as pariah. With respect to Sino-Soviet relations, the policy made China more dependent on

[2] *Foreign Relations of the United States*, 1952–4 (Washington, DC: Government Printing Office, 1979), 3: 733, 2 July 1954.
[3] See *Foreign Relations*, 1949 (Washington, DC: Government Printing Office, 1974) 9: 826–34, NSC 41, 28 Feb. 1949.

the Soviet Union, thus hastening the day—so US officials now hoped or believed—when strains in the relationship would develop to the point of forcing a breach between the two. Thus, the embargo sent several clear signals to the PRC of the costs involved with its resolve in 1949 to 'lean to one side', and more particularly its decision in October 1950 to enter the Korean fighting.

Mao Zedong made his 'lean to one side' statement in June 1949 for a variety of domestic and international reasons.[4] The statement was a logical outcome of the Chinese Communist Party's (CCP) ideological linkage with Moscow; it was also a response to the security threats that the Chinese leaders believed emanated from Washington; it was designed to answer the criticism of domestic groups within China who doubted the wisdom of the foreign policy course that Mao had chosen to pursue; and it was intended to respond to Stalin's doubts, on the eve of a high-level visit to Moscow, with regard to new China's commitment to the Moscow-led socialist bloc.[5]

Mao also argued in that document that expecting genuine help from the British and American governments was naïve: 'Would the present rulers of Britain and the United States, who are imperialists, help a people's state? Why do these countries do business with us and, supposing they might be willing to lend us money on terms of mutual benefit in the future, why would they do so? Because their capitalists want to make money and their bankers want to earn interest to extricate themselves from their own crisis—it is not a matter of helping the Chinese people.' Moscow, on the other hand, as the head of the anti-imperialist front, could be expected, Mao stated, to give 'genuine and friendly help'.[6] The supposedly more moderate Zhou Enlai repeated these arguments, concluding that the United States had never traded with China on the basis of equal advantage, and had only been interested in relieving its surplus production. As a direct counter to the US attempt to use trade as a weapon to

---

[4] Mao Zedong, 'On the People's Democratic Dictatorship', 30 June 1949, *Selected Works*, iv (Beijing: Foreign Languages Press, 1969), 411–24.

[5] Chen Jian, 'The Sino-Soviet Alliance and China's Entry into the Korean War', Working Paper no. 1, *Cold War International History Project* (Washington, DC: Woodrow Wilson Center, 1992). For further discussion of Sino-Soviet relations see my Ch. 5.

[6] Mao, 'On the People's Democratic Dictatorship', 417.

enforce compliant behaviour, Zhou claimed: 'I do not depend on you, you depend on me.'[7]

This decision to 'lean to one side' and the subsequent Western embargo, resulted in a dramatic shift in the direction of China's trade when compared with the pre-war era. The total turnover in trade between the PRC and the USSR, 1950–9, was $13.16 billion, representing 47.8 per cent of China's total trade.[8] At the height of their commercial relationship in 1959, China rivalled East Germany as the Soviet Union's principal trading partner, with two-way trade of $2.09 billion. Beijing supplied one-fifth of Moscow's total imports including two-thirds of its food imports, and three-quarters of its textiles. In exchange, China imported machinery and equipment for complete plants, financed in part by long-term credits totalling $1.405 billion.[9] By the end of the decade, some 65.3 per cent of Beijing's total trade was with the Soviet Union and eight Eastern European states.

Economic relations with other states consequentially declined sharply, especially between 1950 and 1954. Whereas the non-communist world accounted for over 70 per cent of total trade in 1950, it represented only about a third of that in 1954. And although trade with such countries revived after that date, this vast area still accounted for only one-third of China's total foreign trade in 1959. To break these figures down still further, between 1950 and 1959, trade with Japan represented only 1.9 per cent of China's total; less than 1 per cent with respect to Italy, France, Canada, Australia, and Switzerland; 2 per cent of China's total with West Germany; and 3.7 per cent with the UK.[10]

In the first decade of the Chinese government's existence, therefore, given CHINCOM restrictions and Beijing's ideological orientation, there were relatively few opportunities for the Western allies and the PRC to trade. Nevertheless, despite China's

---

[7] Zhou Enlai is quoted in Ronald McGlothlen, *Controlling the Waves: Dean Acheson and U.S. Foreign Policy in Asia* (New York: Norton, 1993), 146.

[8] James T. H. Tsao, *China's Development Strategies and Foreign Trade* (Lexington, Ky.: Lexington Books, D. C. Heath, 1987), 83–4.

[9] Robert L. Price, 'International Trade of Communist China, 1950–1965', Joint Economic Committee of the United States Congress, *An Economic Profile of Mainland China* (New York: Praeger, 1968), 593; Xue Mouhong and Pei Jianzhang, eds., *Diplomacy of Contemporary China* (Hong Kong: New Horizon Press, 1990), 37–9.

[10] Tsao, *China's Development Strategies*, 84 ff.; Price, 'International Trade of Communist China', 598–9.

decisive break with its former trading partners, these same partners wished to maintain some level of economic contact for commercial and political reasons. The UK, for example, in view of its
previous sizeable stake in the country, wanted to keep a 'foot in
the door', and was additionally concerned about the economic
health of Hong Kong, and continuing its access to mainland food
resources. Moreover, it also believed that Beijing should not be
forced into a position of total reliance on Moscow, but should be
weaned away from that relationship. Despite China's deliberate
turn towards the socialist bloc, it too was not entirely averse to
establishing some trading contact, either to gain access to goods
not available from Moscow, or to lessen dependence on the Soviet
bloc, or to drive a wedge between the United States and its
allies. In April 1952, for example, at an international economic
conference held in Moscow, trade agreements were concluded
with European firms from the UK, France, Belgium, The
Netherlands, Switzerland, Finland, and Italy to the tune of $223
million[11]—an indication that America's allies were already
anxious to push the embargo to its limits, and that China wanted
to encourage that.

The strictness of the controls imposed on the PRC particularly
exercised the Japanese. Indeed, the United States had pressured
Japan through a bilateral agreement signed September 1952 ('Understanding Between Japan and the United States concerning the
Control of Exports to Communist China') to impose even tougher
restrictions than those already operating against Beijing. These
were to include 'all commodities on international control lists, all
items on U.S. security lists, and additional items upon which the
two governments would agree'. Of a list of 400 additional items
that the US submitted to Japan, Tokyo swiftly agreed to the control of about 280 of them.[12] Sino-Japanese trade plummeted: in
1952, it accounted for only 0.04 per cent of Japan's total exports
and 0.7 per cent of its total imports, compared with an average of
20 per cent of its pre-war exports, and 10 per cent of its pre-war
imports.[13] Despite Japan's acquiescence to these controls—hardly
surprising in that future American assistance had been made

---

[11] Michael B. Yahuda, *China's Role in World Affairs* (London: Croom Helm, 1978),
57–8.
[12] Yasuhara, 'Japan, Communist China and Export Controls', 88.
[13] Ibid. 85.

conditional on Japan's participation in these restrictions[14]—it was not a satisfactory position as far as most Japanese were concerned. In 1950, Prime Minister Yoshida had told the Japanese Diet that he was ready to send a trade representative to Beijing as soon as allied headquarters would allow it. A year later, he went on record as stating: 'Red or White, China remains our next door neighbor. Geography and economic laws will, I believe, prevail in the long run over any ideological differences and artificial trade barriers.'[15] Subsequent Japanese leaders differed over the depth of their commitment to the Nationalists on Taiwan, but neither Yoshida nor those who came after him wavered substantially from the position that trade and other contacts with the PRC were inevitable. Despite the signature of that agreement with the United States in September 1952, in 1953, both Houses of the Japanese Diet passed resolutions calling for the promotion of Sino-Japanese trade.[16] Japan had to be content, however, with the signature of various non-official trade agreements with the PRC, the first being signed in June 1952.

The signature of the Korean armistice agreement in July 1953 marked the start of more vigorous efforts by America's allies to remove the China differential. The UK took the lead in this for the reasons noted earlier. As early as December 1953 at a summit with the Americans in Bermuda, British ministers argued that trade was important to the country, not only for its own economic health, but also to help maintain its influence in the Far East. Malaya, for example, Eden argued, could not find a ready market for its rubber, and its resentment about the restrictions on China trade could lead to a loss of Western influence in Kuala Lumpur.[17]

London focused on improving its own trading position with China at the Geneva Conference on Korea and Indo-China held in mid-1954. Contacts there between Premier Zhou Enlai and Foreign Minister Anthony Eden, as well as between lower-level

[14] John Dower, *Empire and Aftermath: Yoshida Shigeru and the Japanese Experience, 1878–1954* (Cambridge, Mass.: Harvard University Press, 1979), 400–14.

[15] A. Doak Barnett, *Communist China and Asia: Challenge to American Policy* (New York: Harper, 1960), 259; Yoshida quoted in Wolf Mendl, *Issues in Japan's China Policy* (London: Macmillan, 1978), frontispiece.

[16] Kurt Werner Radtke, *China's Relations with Japan, 1945–1983: The Role of Liao Chengzhi* (Manchester: Manchester University Press, 1990), 102.

[17] International Meetings Series, Bermuda—State Department Report, Box 1, 7 Dec. 1953, DDEL.

Chinese and British officials, not only facilitated the resolution of matters concerning diplomatic representation with the appointment of chargés d'affaires, but also led to important developments in commercial relations: for example, the two sides agreed that inventories of goods for sale should be exchanged on a regular basis; and that a Chinese trade mission should come to the UK as early as the end of 1954. The subsequent success of this visit led to an invitation for a British trade delegation to go to China. Some sixty-two firms applied to join it, causing the delegation to be split into two groups, the first to go in late 1954 and the second in early 1955.[18]

But despite this intensification of the economic relationship, the formal restrictions on trading with China remained in place. Indeed, the Chinese complained at Geneva that the inventories the British had provided were narrow in scope and made no mention of 'industrial electrical equipment, vehicles, non-ferrous metals, train engines and vessels'.[19] These conversations in Geneva and the trade visits encouraged the British to press more firmly for a reduction in trade controls: in 1955, Eden warned Washington that London was prepared to act unilaterally, and in 1956 the Conservative government stepped up the pressure further, announcing publicly that it intended soon to start ignoring the differential entirely.[20]

Other US allies also worked for a reduction in trade controls. Like London, they were interested in taking advantage of China's turn towards a policy of peaceful coexistence and its post-Korean war determination to fulfil the objectives of its first five-year plan. Hatoyama had replaced Yoshida as Prime Minister in December 1954 and seemed determined to normalize relations with both the PRC and USSR, in part to illustrate that Japan henceforth would strive to become more politically independent. He made sure the American administration was fully aware of the heavy domestic pressure on his government to reduce the China trade embargo, especially in the light of the current recession in Japan, and also let it be known that, like London, Tokyo was considering acting

[18] Su Lumin, 'Peaceful Coexistence and Anglo-Chinese Relations: The British Government's Policy Towards China July 1953–July 1954', M. Litt. thesis, Oxford University, 1991, 162–8.

[19] Ibid. 162.

[20] Shao Wenguang, *China, Britain and Businessmen: Political and Commercial Relations, 1949–1957* (London: Macmillan, 1991), 108.

unilaterally on the differential. In the absence of an economic welcome for Japan in South-East Asian markets, and in response to US Commerce Department fears for certain of America's domestic industries should it open its markets further, the Eisenhower administration decided to 'release Japan gradually from its obligation "to maintain export controls at a higher level than the CHINCOM levels"'.[21]

Tokyo wanted speedier progress than this, however. In 1955 and 1956, Japan and China held trade fairs and at the Bandung Conference in April 1955, Takasaki Tatsunosuke, director of the Economic Rehabilitation Agency (ERA) in Japan, held a private meeting with Zhou to discuss the normalization of relations and the furtherance of economic contact. Acknowledging the difficulties surrounding the issue of formalizing relations, the director of the ERA nevertheless pledged to expand trade ties. In fact, imports from the PRC had already doubled in value that year and some 800 Japanese had visited the country, half of all China's foreign visitors. They represented an impressive cross-section of the Japanese élite, including more than 100 non-Communist Diet members, 200 prominent educators, publishers, labour leaders, scientists, and municipal assembly-persons.[22]

West Germans also agitated for increased contact in the mid-1950s. There had been a long history of trading between China and Germany and a business lobby remained interested in reactivating ties. In 1956, a Chinese trade delegation visited the Hanover Fair and was entertained at an official reception at the Federal Economics Ministry. In 1957, the first trade agreement was signed in Beijing, resulting in a tripling in the value of West Germany's exports over the 1956 figure.[23]

1957 turned out to be a crucial year for the differential. At another summit in Bermuda in March 1957, London again pushed

[21] Qing Simei, 'The Eisenhower Administration and Changes in Western Embargo Policy Against China, 1954–1958', in Warren I. Cohen and Akira Iriye, eds., *The Great Powers in East Asia, 1953–1960* (New York: Columbia University Press, 1990), 127–8.

[22] RG 59, Bureau of Far Eastern Affairs, Subject Files, Lot 58D3, Box 1, 3 Mar. 1956, NA; Chihiro Hosoya, 'From the Yoshida Letter to the Nixon Shock', in Akira Iriye and Warren I. Cohen, eds., *The United States and Japan in the Post War World* (Lexington, Ky.: The University Press of Kentucky, 1989), 28.

[23] Heinrich Bechtoldt, 'The Federal Republic of Germany and China: Problems of Trade and Diplomacy', in A. M. Halpern, ed., *Policies toward China: Views from Six Continents* (New York: McGraw Hill, 1965), 91–2.

for the reduction of controls and thus for the maintenance of a multilateral Western position. Indeed, it pressured to bring China controls into line with those for the Soviet Union in terms that were surprisingly direct given London's desire to use this occasion to repair relations with Washington after the Suez débâcle. The British Foreign Secretary impressed upon Dulles and Eisenhower that there was 'virtual unanimity' across the party-political spectrum on the need to trade with the PRC, adding that it was becoming 'extremely difficult to explain the "China Differential" in Parliament', in part because the 'British people regard the Russians as their principal enemies rather than the Chinese'. The existence of the differential, Lloyd argued, brought the 'whole system of trade controls into disrepute, making it harder to maintain them against the USSR and increasing the possibility of the disintegration of the whole system'. The British government had had, in fact, to answer some 200 parliamentary questions on China trade and been forced to respond to a 'flood of political and commercial criticism' on the subject of the differential.[24] Dulles offered Lloyd something of a bargain: if Britain remained steadfast on the question of Chinese representation in the United Nations, the United States would temper its criticism of London if it moved to remove the differential.[25]

Despite this offer of a bargain, at the official meeting in Paris in May 1957 to discuss China controls, the US delegation came prepared to offer some relaxation in its position, but remained determined to maintain certain parts of the differential. At that meeting, however, the French proposed the immediate abolition of all special restrictions on China trade except for 25 items then still under quantitative control to the Soviets and Eastern Europeans, a position that twelve of the sixteen nations voted for. The USA countered with a second proposal which offered a further relaxation in its original position and this fared better; but it

[24] White House Office, office of the Staff Secretary, International Trips and Meetings, Bermuda Trip, Box 2, 22 Mar. 1957, DDEL; Shao, *China, Britain and Businessmen*, 110–13.

[25] Tracy Lee Steele, 'Allied and Interdependent: British Policy during the Chinese Offshore Islands Crisis of 1958', in Anthony Gorst, Lewis Johnman, and W. Scott Lucas, eds., *Contemporary British History, 1931–61: Politics and the Limits of Policy* (London: Pinter, 1991), 232. Note that Washington also offered in October 1957 co-operation in the atomic field provided Britain did not seek any change in Chinese representation in the UN. (See Steele, and my Ch. 2.)

was still rejected by six of America's allies—the UK, France, Japan, Norway, Denmark, and Portugal. 'Determined [US] efforts to sway these countries were unsuccessful', the US delegates reported, the outcome being the British declaration in Parliament on 30 May that the government intended to act unilaterally to bring the controls into line with those operating on the Eastern bloc.[26] Within a few months, Belgium, Denmark, France, Japan, and The Netherlands followed the UK's path. Multilateral adherence, already crumbling privately through extensive use of the exceptions procedure, was officially and publicly dead.

According to Douglas Dillon (US ambassador in Paris) and Clarence B. Randall (Chair of the US Council on Foreign Economic Policy), it was the administration's failure to act on the question in 1956 that had led the British to assume that Washington was not prepared to offer any serious modifications, and to prepare themselves to act unilaterally. In the view of James Reston of the *New York Times* Eisenhower was to be criticized for allowing the continuance of a policy that he knew did not have allied support, and in which he himself did not believe.[27]

That Eisenhower did not believe in enforcing a strict trade embargo with the Communist bloc, nor in the China differential, was made plain on a number of private and public occasions. This knowledge probably encouraged the British and the Japanese to push ahead with their plan to overturn the differential, perhaps in the expectation that the Americans would gradually ease their own restrictions and in the knowledge that they would temper their criticism of these two governments. Eisenhower's statements may also have encouraged the Chinese Communists at the Sino-American ambassadorial talks in Geneva to put the issue of the trade embargo on the agenda. If Beijing succeeded in reducing the economic restrictions, this would be to the Chinese advantage; but even if they failed such an attempt would still alarm the Nationalists and aggravate America's allies.

The US President's views rarely appeared to prevail, however, which explains Reston's reaction, among others. One of his most

[26] White House Office, office of the Staff Secretary, subject series, State Department Subseries, Box 2, 'Memorandum on China Trade Control Negotiations', 4 June 1957, DDEL.

[27] Warren I. Cohen, 'China in Japanese–American Relations', in Iriye and Cohen, eds., *The United States and Japan*, 49. The reasons for some of the indecision in US policy are discussed in Qing, 'The Eisenhower Administration', 131–2.

successful interventions came when he overruled Dulles in 1958 to allow Canadian subsidiaries of American firms to fulfil PRC orders for non-strategic goods. A more typical response was to accept Dulles's advice, as he did when he wrote to the British Prime Minister on 16 May 1957 urging him not to eliminate the China differential.[28] His administration's failure to move away from the total US embargo on trade with the PRC, or the fact that his administration appeared to do little more than fight a rear-guard action against the allied attempts to reduce restrictions, could be viewed as the triumph of political over economic arguments, of the victory of Dulles over Eisenhower, or of the residual power of the China bloc in Congress over those who began to see some relaxation in US–China relations as desirable. Eisenhower had employed four main arguments to support a compromise over the embargo: first, that those items denied China on the differential list could still be supplied by the Soviet Union; second, that efforts to stop trade were always doomed to failure; third, where Japan was concerned, that the Chinese market had always been deemed important to it and might serve in the short term to ease Japan's export problems (otherwise, Eisenhower warned, the 'American taxpayer' would be drawn into 'endless subsidy of the Japanese economy'); and, finally, he argued that a trade embargo would not defeat the Communist regime but instead would force it to rely totally on the socialist bloc to the detriment of Western interests.[29]

Eisenhower had a number of supporters within his administration: the Treasury Secretary, George Humphrey, also believed that attempting to treat China differently from the Soviet Union was 'seeking to lock the barn door after the horse was gone'. Clarence Randall argued that US attempts to block Sino-Japanese trade in all but a narrow list of strategic items was based on emotion and not logic. Nevertheless, despite the support from these two officials, Eisenhower failed to back them at crucial moments in the debate, leaving the field to those who for domestic and international reasons wanted to maintain as hard a line as possible.[30]

[28] Ibid. 133, 135.

[29] Ibid. *passim*; Cohen, 'China in Japanese–American Relations', 45.

[30] Burton I. Kaufman, 'Eisenhower's Foreign Economic Policy with Respect to Asia', in Cohen and Iriye, eds., *Great Powers*, 110–12; at a press conference on 5

To take the international consequences first, Eisenhower's opponents argued that forcing Beijing into Moscow's embrace, so that it would more quickly discover the drawbacks of its alliance, had been part of the so-called 'wedge strategy' that his administration had purportedly been committed to since 1953. Moreover, because any breach in Sino-Soviet relations would take some time to emerge, Dulles argued that the administration had to be concerned about the question of gains for China in the interim period. An easing of trade restrictions would represent an advance because it would be seen as the start of a normalization process that might lead eventually to diplomatic and UN recognition, including by the United States.

This question of recognition seriously disturbed Dulles because of its implications for Taiwan's status in the global system, and because it would confer a degree of legitimacy upon the PRC that the administration was unwilling to see established while Beijing appeared committed to fomenting revolutionary upheaval.[31] Presumably, Eisenhower recognized the power of these internationalist arguments as he clearly recognized the divisions within his own Cabinet, and the strength of feeling among certain groups within Congress who could be relied upon to attack the administration for any policies that appeared to undermine Chiang Kai-shek, or that showed too great a willingness to appease America's Western allies over China policy.[32] In press conferences and in private he made it known that he believed that trade with communist countries could not be stopped. This undoubtedly helped reduce the domestic criticism of America's primary allies and reinforced their belief that they would be reasonably safe in pressing for the removal of the differential. But, beyond that, Eisenhower was unwilling to make the necessary effort to bring about a modification in Washington's own embargo policy, even as the allied governments adopted a quite contrary stance.

June 1957, for example, Eisenhower argued that there was not much advantage to be had in maintaining the differential. This statement may have served to temper US domestic criticism of London's decision to overturn the differential, but it still did not carry the day. See *Foreign Relations of the United States*, 1955–7 (Washington, DC: Government Printing Office, 1992), 27: 775, 12 June 1957.

[31] These arguments are taken up more fully in my Ch. 8.

[32] For a discussion of domestic criticism of trade with China see Qing, 'The Eisenhower Administration', 136–7; Kaufman, 'Eisenhower's Foreign Economic Policy with Respect to Asia', 110–11, and my Ch. 4.

Chinese Policy and Consequences for Trade: 1958–1971

Trade with China was not simply subject to changes in the embargo policy, it was also subject to policy decisions made within China itself. Quite clearly, after the Korean war, as Chinese diplomatic sources have acknowledged, 'a new period had come for our country to launch a full-scale diplomatic initiative'. The ceasefire had 'created a necessary precondition for the Chinese people to pay more attention to carrying out their first five year plan for the development of their national economy'.[33] Increasing trade with the West and with Japan was one logical outcome of this assessment.

However, by 1958, the year after the China differential was removed, Beijing's foreign and domestic policies were at another crossroads. Chinese leaders had been stung by the criticism that had resulted from 'letting a hundred flowers bloom', and quickly moved to launch an anti-rightist movement in China designed to silence these domestic critics. Mao had also become concerned about China's high levels of dependence on the Soviet Union. Coinciding closely with these developments was a notable hardening in China's foreign policy line. Where the United States was concerned, Chinese leaders had become disillusioned with the lack of progress in the ambassadorial talks with the Americans in Geneva, were concerned about the US decision to station Matador missiles on Taiwan, and abhorred Dulles's speech in San Francisco in June 1957, where he appeared to rule out any chance of improving relations with the PRC for the foreseeable future. In these circumstances, Beijing began to draw sharper distinctions between so-called progressive and reactionary states, and to pressure governments to take a firmer stand against imperialist nations, especially the United States. Moscow, on the other hand, had committed itself to a policy of peaceful coexistence, and to the search for a *détente* with Washington, policies which America wished to reciprocate. While China viewed the 1957 Soviet technological achievements in satellite systems and in nuclear weaponry as permitting the socialist bloc to adopt a more confrontational stance, Moscow treated these developments more cautiously, seeing them as potentially opening a new era in inter-

---

[33] Su, 'Peaceful Coexistence', 178.

national relations in which a strategic understanding with Washington might prove possible. These differing perceptions of the most appropriate policy line to be adopted towards the United States proved to be a fundamental spur to the eventual split between Beijing and Moscow, a breach that had dramatic economic consequences.

Japan was an early casualty of China's more militant stance and of its intention to make a greater distinction between 'friends and enemies'. In March 1958, Beijing and Tokyo had signed their fourth unofficial trade agreement, but this time the two sides had agreed to seek semi-official privileges including the right for visiting missions to fly national flags. The Republic of China instantly protested this aspect of the agreement, organizing anti-Japanese boycotts and making moves to cut its trade with Japan. Washington officials joined in the protest, seeing in these proposals further indication that Japan planned to normalize relations with the PRC. Under this combined onslaught, Prime Minister Kishi, already more sympathetic than his predecessors towards the Taiwan government, ensured Beijing was denied the right to fly its flag. In retaliation, the Chinese delayed the implementation of the trade agreement, then cancelled it entirely when two Japanese tore down a Chinese flag that had been raised at a postage stamp exhibition.[34]

The causes for the abrogation of this agreement, together with the emphasis China had begun to place on a self-reliant path to development, demonstrated the intertwined nature of political and economic considerations in trade policy. Nevertheless, other political developments involving Beijing's relationship with Moscow, which led to the abrupt withdrawal of Soviet technicians in July 1960, and the severe economic dislocation caused by Great Leap Forward policies, forced China to temper the unforgiving nature of its foreign policy stance. Great Leap policies had been developed in part out of the distaste the Chinese experienced as a result of having become so dependent on the Soviet Union. As noted earlier, something like two-thirds of China's

[34] F. C. Langdon, *Japan's Foreign Policy* (Vancouver: University of British Columbia Press, 1973), 97. West Germany seemed to be the beneficiary, its exports to China rising to DM 681.9 million in 1958 from DM 173 million in 1957. See Heinrich Bechtoldt, 'The Federal Republic of Germany and China: Problems of Trade and Diplomacy', in Halpern, ed., *Policies Toward China*, 92.

trade was being conducted with Eastern Europe by 1959 and Moscow was heavily committed to China's development drive. It had agreed to build some 291 major industrial plants in China by 1967, and by 1959 about 130 of these had been finished. However, about 20 per cent of those started under agreements signed earlier in the 1950s were incomplete, and 125 contracted for in August 1958 and February 1959 were still in the process of being designed. With the deterioration in Sino-Soviet relations, these projects became vulnerable, and with the sudden removal of all Soviet technicians many were doomed to lie idle for many years to come. Soviet withdrawal was like, as one Chinese economic planner put it, 'taking away all the dishes when you have only eaten half a meal'.[35]

The disasters encountered as a result of Great Leap agricultural policies, evident particularly between 1959 and 1962, far surpassed the disruption encountered in China's industrialization programme. Widespread dislocation in rural areas led to wholesale famine—between 15 and 30 million Chinese have been estimated to have died[36]—and China was forced to enter the world grain market. Faced with the stark realities of the consequences of that ill-conceived policy, together with the break with Moscow, China was forced to rethink the nature of its modernization plans and the orientation of its economic relationships. Japan was to be a willing and major beneficiary of these changes, but so too were Western Europeans in their supply of machinery and equipment,[37] and Australia and Canada through their sales of grain.

With respect to Japan, renewed signs of flexibility on the Chinese side began to emerge when Zhou Enlai, in August 1960, told Kazuo Suzuki, director of the China–Japan Trade Promotion Council (TPC), of the three political principles that should act as a guide to the trading relationship: first, that Tokyo should not adopt a hostile attitude towards Beijing; secondly, it should not

---

[35] Price, 'International Trade of Communist China', 591–2.

[36] Carl Riskin, *China's Political Economy: The Quest for Development since 1949* (Oxford: Oxford University Press, 1987), 136.

[37] For example, using medium-term credits China began the purchase of complete industrial installations—including chemical plants—and accepted the services of Western technicians. It also negotiated with West Germany for a steel mill complex valued at between $125 and $175 million. See Price, 'International Trade of Communist China', 602.

promote a 'two-Chinas' policy; and thirdly, it should not obstruct the normalization of relations. Negotiations over these principles led the TPC to suggest that China deal solely with 'friendly' companies that agreed to abide by these strictures, and indeed throughout the 1960s most trade was conducted through such companies.[38]

One drawback to this arrangement was that these firms did not have access to credit; neither could they guarantee stability of supply. Thus, Kenzo Matsumura—a Liberal Democratic Party (LDP) leader—and Zhou negotiated something more substantial and reliable in 1962: a semi-official five-year trade agreement which involved deferred payments, medium-term credits, and the establishment of trade liaison offices in Tokyo and Beijing. Known as the Liao–Matsumura trade agreement, after the two individuals who signed the final document, the communiqué which accompanied it pledged that 'both sides [would] agree to strive for the normalization of relations between both countries including political and economic relations by (a series of) gradual and cumulative measures'.[39] Although such trade was never as high as that with 'friendly' companies, the agreement was symbolically important because of its semi-official nature, its intended duration, and because it guaranteed that contracts could not be annulled arbitrarily.

Not surprisingly, neither Chiang Kai-shek nor the Kennedy administration were enamoured of this enhancement in the Beijing–Tokyo relationship. And when the Ikeda government in August 1963 decided to permit the export of a vinylon plant to the PRC under a deferred payments plan and with Export–Import Bank funding, Taiwan's protests reached fever pitch, and included a threat to break diplomatic relations. The US administration found itself in a mediating position, on the one hand trying to persuade Chiang that any break in relations could have wide-ranging and negative consequences for the ROC at a time when many states were arguing that the PRC should be brought

[38] Langdon, *Japan's Foreign Policy*, 97–8. Xue and Pei, eds., *Diplomacy of Contemporary China*, covers these developments in Sino-Japanese relations in some detail. See esp. 252–8.

[39] Kurt Werner Radtke, *China's Relations with Japan, 1945–1983: The Role of Liao Chengzhi* (Manchester: Manchester University Press, 1990), 142.

into the United Nations, and on the other putting pressure on Japan to reverse the decision. Former Prime Minister Yoshida, was sent to Taiwan to work out a solution, and on his return produced another 'Yoshida letter', this one promising that Export–Import Bank loans would not be used to support the vinylon deal and that in future purely private credit arrangements would be worked out in support of plant exports.[40]

As one analyst has written, trading with the PRC was 'hardly an issue in Japan. The real question was the extent to which various advocates were willing to offend the ROC and the United States.'[41] Japan trod a careful path, generally using pro-PRC members of the LDP to open various channels of communication with Beijing, while simultaneously having Party leaders take pro-Taiwan positions[42] (Prime Minister Ikeda's agreement to co-sponsor the 1961 'important question' resolution with respect to Chinese representation in the United Nations is but one significant example). Yet, despite this sensitive manœuvring through dangerous waters, Tokyo's policies managed to anger all parties at various times—the PRC, ROC, the United States, and various domestic political and economic groups within Japan itself—rendering it surprising that trade between Japan and the PRC continued to grow as rapidly as it did. Between 1963 and 1967, bilateral trade amounted to $2.03 billion, much higher than the amount set in the 1962 trade agreement. By 1965, Japan had become China's leading trade partner, and for Japan China was fourth in line after the United States, Australia, and Canada.

Australia and Canada were to benefit directly as a result of the failure of Great Leap Forward agricultural policies. China's inability to feed its population led it in 1960 into an urgent search to make up for the shortfall in grain production. Fortunately for China, Australia in 1960 was seeking new markets for its grain surpluses. An initial sale to the PRC—representing one-quarter of Australia's total wheat sales—was made for cash but thereafter short-term credits were made available.[43] Trade levels grew

[40] Langdon, *Japan's Foreign Policy*, 102–3; Cohen, 'China in Japanese–American Relations', 53–4.

[41] Ibid. 54.

[42] Chalmers Johnson, 'The Pattern of Japanese Relations with China, 1952–1982', *Pacific Affairs*, 59 (1986), 405.

[43] China scrupulously repaid its loans ahead of schedule and in sterling. Terms

quickly, from a two-way total of $26.7 million in 1960 to $192 million in 1961 and $256 million in 1963, with a balance that was highly favourable to Australia. China, in the early 1960s, became Australia's fourth-largest trading partner after the UK, Japan, and the United States. Not surprisingly, interest in the country began to grow as trade and labour delegations were exchanged and some tourist visas permitted. Public support for the recognition of the PRC also steadily advanced and the wheat sales themselves were extremely popular, with between 69 per cent and 73 per cent of those polled registering their approval.[44]

Canada had a similar experience in the 1960s. Until then Canada's trade with the PRC had been very small and generally in balance. There had been a purchase of Canadian wheat—some 45 tons—in 1958, but no reason at that stage to believe that this would necessarily be repeated. However, the newly appointed Canadian Agriculture Minister, Alvin Hamilton, had been charged to find new markets, and he sent a two-person team to Beijing in 1960. They returned clear in their minds that China would be facing an acute food crisis within six months, and when two Chinese negotiators arrived unexpectedly in Montreal later that year, the Canadians were predisposed to make a deal.

This first agreement, for cash, was signed in mid-December 1960; but it was plain that the Chinese would need credits to finance the huge amounts that they were seeking at this time. Although the Canadians were nervous about extending credit, when the Chinese informed them that they wanted to purchase wheat and barley worth $362 million over the next two and a half years, the doubts were overcome and the opportunity grasped. Two-way trade, involving a heavy surplus for Canada, rose from $7 million in 1959 to $170 million in 1961. In October 1965, Canada signed a contract with the PRC which guaranteed the purchase of between 5 and 12.5 million tons of grain over the next three to five

offered were 10 per cent cash on shipment, 20% in 6 months, 20% in 9 months and the balance in 12 months. See Edmund S. K. Fung and Colin MacKerras, *From Fear to Friendship: Australia's Policies towards the People's Republic of China, 1966–1982* (St Lucia, Queensland: University of Queensland Press, 1985), 83–6.

[44] Coral Bell, 'Australia and China: Power Balance and Policy', in Halpern, ed., *Policies Toward China*, esp. 190–1; Timothy P. Maga, *John F. Kennedy and the New Pacific Community, 1961–63* (London: Macmillan, 1990), 37; Fung and MacKerras, *From Fear to Friendship*, 71–2.

years, despite the revival of China's own agricultural production after 1963.[45]

As had occurred in Australia, there was a rise in the number of those favouring recognition of the PRC. Those concerned about the issue enquired how one could conduct such profitable business with a country Ottawa officially ignored. A Gallup poll conducted in 1961 indicated for the first time a majority in favour of seating China at the United Nations. In 1964, 51 per cent of those polled favoured diplomatic recognition, and a substantial 63 per cent gave their blessing to the trading relationship.[46]

US reactions to allied activity were mixed. On the one hand, controlling trade in non-strategic items was against the free-trade philosophy that successive administrations had been espousing, at least since Bretton Woods, if not earlier, given Wilsonian ideas about the relationship between unfettered trade and world peace. Washington also had sympathy for the argument that, for many of these countries, trade was a vital part of remaining a healthy economy: as Macmillan had put it to the sympathetic Eisenhower in May 1957, 'the commercial interests of our two countries are not at all alike. We live by exports—and by exports alone.'[47] Moreover, it was also understood that, when it came to the crunch, these same countries in these years would not go beyond a certain point in antagonizing the United States: for the UK, Canada, Australia, and Japan, among others, that relationship with Washington was just too important to risk. Yet, the United States also believed it had good reason to fear for the economic and political future of Taiwan; so much of this economic contact with the PRC seemed to presage a move towards the normalization of relations—diplomatic recognition and UN entry for the PRC, isolation and increased vulnerability for Taiwan.

A 1964 CIA report entitled 'The China Problem in Japanese Politics', reflected well US understanding of the dilemmas the

[45] Patrick Kyba, 'Alvin Hamilton and Sino-Canadian Relations', in Paul M. Evans and B. Michael Frolic, eds., *Reluctant Adversaries: Canada and the People's Republic of China, 1949–1970* (Toronto: University of Toronto Press, 1991); Price, 'International Trade of Communist China', 601.

[46] Don Page, 'The Representation of China in the United Nations: Canadian Perspectives and Initiatives, 1949–1971', in Evans and Frolic, eds., *Reluctant Adversaries*, 86; John W. Holmes, 'Canada and China: The Dilemmas of a Middle Power', in Halpern, ed., *Policies Toward China*, 115.

[47] Harold Macmillan, *Riding the Storm* (London: Macmillan, 1971), 317–18.

trade issue caused America's allies, as well as the uncertainties the US itself faced in terms of its China policy. The report recognized that, for the Japanese, trade with its large Asian neighbour was the 'most immediate real attraction', and that they were anxious 'lest Western commercial rivals beat them to China's door'. Yet, although trade with the PRC was growing rapidly, it was understood that for Tokyo a commercial relationship with the West and the United States in particular was far more important to it and not worth jeopardizing. Prime Minister Ikeda might believe that the future lay with the mainland, but 'one major factor restraining [him] from leaning forward too rapidly [was] the tacit but general recognition of the importance of relations with the US, particularly for trade and finance'. Despite Japan's recognition of the importance of Washington to its economic well-being, the report still saw, for cultural and historical reasons, an 'inevitable approach' to the PRC which was just a matter of 'manner and timing'.[48]

The Kennedy administration contained those willing to contemplate a change in Washington's own position on trading with the PRC, although mainly on the negative basis that the expected refusal on Beijing's part could be turned against it. Whereas during the Eisenhower era the argument that prevailed had been that any relaxation of the US embargo ought to be avoided because it carried too many domestic political risks, undermined the strategy of driving a 'wedge' between Beijing and Moscow, and might also make it appear as though Beijing had gained an undeserved reward, in the Kennedy period, Chester Bowles advocated a more devious strategy, involving the private sale of grain to China in US dollars or pounds sterling. Such a policy would reduce criticism of the United States on moral grounds, but would also use up China's stocks of hard currencies. He additionally suggested putting forward the position that US sales of wheat on the basis of local currencies would only be forthcoming if Beijing offered a 'private or public agreement: (a) to cooperate in ending the wars in Laos and Vietnam, and (b) to cease pressures aimed at Southeast Asia, Taiwan, South Korea, and India'[49]—a highly unrealistic

---

[48] National Security File (NSF) Country File, China Cables vol. 1, Box 237-8, CIA Special Report, 1 May 1964, LBJL.

[49] James C. Thomson Papers, Chester Bowles, 1961–3, Box 7, 'U.S. Policies in the Far East', 4 Apr. 1962, JFKL.

proposal in itself, and also because China by then had worked out purchasing agreements with Australia, Canada, France, and Venezuela. Bowles also argued that the time had come to tackle the central illogicality in America's embargo policy: beginning with the sales of medicines and foodstuffs, he recommended that trade controls with the PRC be brought into line with those operating against Moscow.

Despite extensive discussions within the State Department on the food sales question, it was left that, if China itself asked the United States for food, Washington might then respond. Kennedy was no longer concerned about the wedge strategy given the Sino-Soviet breach and the decision to cultivate Moscow at China's expense,[50] but he was concerned about potential domestic criticism, and about contributing to the recovery of the PRC. Thus, with extreme caution, at a press conference on 23 May 1962, Kennedy stated that there had been 'no indication of any expression of interest or desire by the Chinese Communists to receive any food from us', adding that the administration 'would certainly have to have some idea as to whether the food was needed and under what conditions it might be distributed'. This highly qualified statement evoked a not entirely unexpected reply from China's Foreign Minister, Chen Yi, six days later. In an interview with Japanese journalists he stated, 'American traders, Rusk and President Kennedy say they will supply China with food if China makes a gesture, but we will never make any gesture to this bid ... Even if we receive aid from somewhere, we will refuse American aid.'[51] The matter appeared closed.

Yet, despite the unproductive nature of this dialogue, it represented a degree of forward movement in the argument within the United States concerning trade relations at a time when America's allies were preparing to move ahead strongly. It inevitably resurfaced even more forcefully among East Asian specialists in the Johnson administration. James Thomson, for example, among others,[52] recommended in October 1964 that US policy should move away from 'containment plus moral preachment',

[50] Gordon H. Chang, *Friends and Enemies: The United States, China, and the Soviet Union, 1948–1972* (Stanford, Calif.: Stanford University Press, 1990), esp. chs. 7 and 8.

[51] Thomson papers, Far East 1961–6, Comm. China General, Box 14, 'China Speech Material', undated, JFKL.

[52] See my Ch. 4 for further details.

and towards 'modified containment . . . plus subversion', through the 'careful use of free world goods, people, and ideas'.[53] That such a policy could help to deflect the dismay that many countries felt about America's China policy was confirmed in various memoranda, including one from the American Consul General in Hong Kong, who argued that sensitive and limited changes in policy 'would ease criticism [of it] by third countries, and, more important, restore some flexibility in our policy'. And if China failed to respond, then it would convince many that it was no longer the United States that was isolating China, but Beijing that had chosen to isolate itself[54]—an argument that would have considerable resonance internationally the following year as Chinese leaders turned inwards and embarked on the Great Proletarian Cultural Revolution. One result of this turn was that Chinese trade was cut back by some 13 per cent over the period 1966 to 1969.[55]

A modification in the containment policy (to become known as containment without isolation) was called for in Congressional Hearings in 1965 and the spring of 1966,[56] but was not to be taken up publicly at the highest level until July 1966, when President Johnson, in a major TV address, and matching Thomson's earlier words, advocated reconciliation through the 'free flow of ideas and people and goods'. In April 1967, the administration launched a limited trade initiative with the decision to license for sale to the PRC pharmaceuticals and medical supplies.[57] The Cultural Revolution in China and the absorption of the US administration with the Vietnam war prevented further development of these ideas. And Presidential candidates of the future, such as Richard Nixon, did not at that stage suggest that they were willing to go much beyond Johnson's statement. Although Nixon stated in 1967 that, taking the long view, 'we simply cannot afford to leave China forever outside the family of nations', he also reiterated that 'this did not mean rushing to grant recog-

---

[53] NSF Country File—China, China Memos vol. II, Box 237-8, 28 Oct. 1964, LBJL.
[54] NSF Country File, China Cables, vol. I, Box 237-8, 6 Nov. 1964, LBJL.
[55] Harry Harding, *China's Second Revolution: Reform After Mao* (Washington, DC: Brookings, 1987), 131.
[56] See my Ch. 4.
[57] Administrative History of the Department of State, vol. 1, ch. 7, East Asia, LBJL.

nition ... to admit it to the United Nations, and to ply it with offers of trade'.[58]

As President, however, Nixon did take that further step, deciding to use the lifting of trade restrictions as one means of demonstrating the seriousness of his intent to improve relations with Beijing, and responding too to US business pressures to explore the possibilities of the China market. In 1969, he lifted the ban on travel to the PRC, removed a previously imposed ceiling of $100 on tourist purchases, and signed an order allowing foreign subsidiaries of American firms to trade with the PRC.[59] More significantly, in April 1971, the President announced the ending of the embargo on non-strategic sales to China, stating that he had requested a list of such items that could be placed under general licence for direct export. The Shanghai Communiqué signed in February 1972 at the close of Nixon's historic visit to the PRC sealed this aspect of the new relationship in its promise to 'facilitate the progressive development of trade between their two countries'.[60] US trade policy towards China at last had the opportunity to come into line with that of its allies. Nixon's move in April 1971 could be viewed as an admission that its earlier attempt to ostracize Beijing was unrealistic, a policy that could not generate an international consensus.

Trade Patterns 1972–1979

The Chinese government's more open trading policy from 1970 and the shifts in the US diplomatic position towards China led to an enhancement of Beijing's economic relations not only with the United States but also with other capitalist countries. The United States moved speedily from a position of virtually no trade at all, to being China's third-largest partner in 1973, with trade valued at $803 million, mainly through China's purchase of large quantities of grain and cotton. (In 1972, grain accounted for 95 per cent

[58] Richard M. Nixon, 'Asia After Vietnam', *Foreign Affairs*, 46, no. 1 (Oct. 1967), 121.
[59] Kissinger, *White House Years* (Boston: Little Brown, 1979), 180 and 191.
[60] Tsao, *China's Development Strategies*, 93; Joint Economic Committee, *Chinese Economy Post-Mao* (Washington, DC: Government Printing Office, 1978), 76.

of China's total imports from the United States.)[61] Over the seven-year period, China imported a total of $1.94 billion in goods from the United States and exported $887.4 million.[62] Key Western states also increased their sales. Together with the United States, two-way trade between these countries and China increased 289 per cent between 1972 and 1978, representing some 28.5 per cent of China's total trade.[63] These developments in themselves further underlined the perception of the importance of the breakthrough that had been made in 1971 and 1972.

Nevertheless, though the relationship between Beijing and Washington did develop rapidly, there was not steady advance-ment, the US dropping to fifth place as a trading partner in 1975 and eighth place in 1976 and 1977. In 1973 liaison offices had been established in the two capitals, in part to institutionalize and stabilize the relationship, and to facilitate various forms of ex-change in the absence of formal diplomatic ties. That year, the National Council for United States–China trade made its first visit to the PRC, but disappointingly it took until 1975 before the first return visits were made to the United States.

The United States, compared with Japan and other Western countries, was paying a price for the long delay in establishing economic ties. In contrast to Washington, Tokyo's trade con-tinued to advance rapidly. It had become China's leading trading partner in 1965 and maintained that position in the 1970s. Its exports surged from $627.4 million in 1972—the year when full diplomatic relations were established—to $13.11 billion in 1978. China's exports to Japan over the same period rose fourfold from $411.8 million to $1.72 billion.[64] Of the West European countries, the Federal Republic of Germany became China's most significant partner, especially in the light of Beijing's earlier decision to im-port a German steel plant and German mining equipment. The UK made a breakthrough of a different kind, however, when London agreed in December 1975 to sell China Rolls Royce Spey jet engines, which are strictly for military aircraft. Concerned to support the strategic alignment with Beijing directed at Moscow,

---

[61] A. Doak Barnett, *China's Economy in Global Perspective* (Washington, DC: Brookings Institution, 1981), 507.

[62] Tsao, *China's Development Strategies*, 92–4.

[63] Richard E. Batsavage and John L. Davies, 'China's International Trade and Finance', in Joint Economic Committee, *Chinese Economy Post-Mao*, 712.

[64] Tsao, *China's Development Strategies*, 95.

and ignoring COCOM restrictions, Washington acquiesced in this deal. Also about this time, West Germany and France moved to sell Beijing helicopters, radar, and missile-tracking equipment. Soon after, Washington moved to sell computers with a military application, sales that had been previously denied to the Soviet Union: the start of the Soviet differential.[65]

As suggested above, the economic relationship between the United States and China in the 1970s lacked a stable basis. High US expectations regarding the China market remained unfulfilled, America accounting for only 2.6 per cent of China's imports and 2.5 per cent of its exports in 1977. The causes related to America's late start in trading when compared with Western Europe and Japan, the inadequacy of the legal and institutional framework for the development of relations, and the failure to resolve the assets and claims issue between them until after the full normalization of relations.[66]

The relationship was also difficult to manage in the context of China's domestic politics. As far as the Chinese were concerned, trading with the United States and with other capitalist states was still controversial, and the radical critique of it reached a peak in 1974 and was renewed in 1976 and 1977 after Zhou Enlai's death. One fear was that such contact would undermine the authority of the Communist system, but in addition for a country that feared dependency of any kind there was also the enormous trading deficit—$1.2 billion in 1974—to contemplate.[67]

The world recession in 1974–5 had led to a sharp decline in the demand for Chinese products. Beijing's solution was to cancel contracts and postpone delivery dates. As this behaviour demonstrated, in many respects China's view of trade in the 1970s conformed with its earlier perspectives: exports were to pay for

---

[65] A. Doak Barnett, 'Military-Security Relations between China and the United States', *Foreign Affairs*, 55 (Apr. 1977); Banning Garrett, 'China Policy and the Strategic Triangle', in Kenneth Oye, Donald S. Rothchild, and Robert J. Lieber, eds., *Eagle Entangled* (New York: Longman, 1979), 234–7.

[66] The Chinese Communists had taken over US property without compensation shortly after the establishment of the PRC, and the United States had frozen Chinese assets after the outbreak of the Korean war. Barnett, *China's Economy*, 519, and see also 514–20.

[67] For discussion of this point see e.g. Ann Fenwick, 'Chinese Foreign Trade Policy and the Campaign against Deng Xiaoping', in Thomas Fingar, ed., *China's Quest for Independence: Policy Evolution in the 1970s* (Boulder, Colo.: Westview Press, 1980).

imports and as little use as possible was to be made of credits. Above all, imports were to be seen as filling shortfalls or gaps in domestic production: the whole plants that were purchased were designed to allow China in later years to produce the goods that in the meantime were to be imported from abroad—steel, ferti- lizers, synthetics, and petrochemicals.[68] Grain purchases were also to make up for shortfalls, and thus demand for grain fluctuated from one period to the next.

It would take the consolidation of Deng's position after 1978 and of his reform programme before a new attitude towards trade could be introduced. This inaugurated a period in China when trade would no longer be conducted solely to make up for dom- estic shortfalls or for political purposes, but because it was recog- nized by most reformers as being an important component in the engine of growth. Deng's consolidation coincided with the pres- ence in the United States of a President who was determined to normalize relations partly in the belief that economic and cultural ties had suffered in the absence of such normalization. As the log- jam in the US–China negotiations showed signs of being over- come in 1978, trade between the two countries tripled, whereas, overall, China's trade rose by some 40 per cent.

As Carter had predicted, after the normalization of relations in January 1979, economic relations deepened further. Although strategic matters formed a central feature of Deng's visit to the United States in late January 1979, the signing of new agreements in economic, scientific, and technical areas signalled that econ- omic objectives were also prominent.[69] By the end of the year, some sixty Chinese delegations a month were visiting America, most of them trade or technical,[70] and trade had quadrupled over the 1978 level.

[68] Batsavage and Davies, 'China's International Trade', 713–14, 722.

[69] During a background briefing for the American media, a 'Senior Adminis- tration Official' explained: 'clearly, over a period of time we wish to establish a more normal economic relationship with the People's Republic of China. At the present time American firms are somewhat handicapped in their competition with Japanese and Western European firms in their access to the Chinese market. And so, on this trip, as well as on Secretary Blumenthal's trip to China at the end of February and Secretary of Commerce Kreps' trip to China [May 1979] . . . we hope to move forward toward establishing the basis for a normal economic relation- ship.' Staff Offices, Press, Powell, Box 81, Visit to US by China's Vice Premier Deng Xiaoping, 'Background Briefing on the visit of Chinese Vice Premier Deng Xiaoping to the United States', 27 Jan. 1979, JCL.

[70] Barnett, *China's Economy*, 515.

Normalization also prompted both sides to explore the establishment of a general trade agreement, to include Most Favoured Nation (MFN) status. Difficulties arose over such matters as market protection and China's emigration policy, the latter potentially an issue because of the provisions of the Jackson–Vanik amendment to the US Trade Act of 1974. Reportedly, on the Chinese side, it took an intervention by Deng himself before certain of the outstanding problems could be overcome,[71] a sign that for the paramount leader the American connection had come to be viewed as crucial to China's development programme.

On the US side, Congress still had to be won over to the trade agreement. Congressional concerns mirrored those in some parts of the Executive about preferential treatment for China when compared with the Soviet Union, and, more parochially, about the fortunes of US textile producers. However, Congress finally gave support to the trade agreement in late January 1980, the House voting 294 to 88 in favour, and the Senate 74 to 8, probably having been spurred on by the Soviet intervention in Afghanistan in December 1979.[72] The economic relationship had been fully normalized and US businesses could compete on equal terms with the rest of the industrialized world, at a time when the Chinese attitude towards foreign trade and the international economy had also begun to change substantially.

As with the UN recognition policy, US administrations in the 1950s and 1960s adopted a stance on trade with the PRC that was far tougher than that of their primary allies; and as with that recognition issue the United States found itself having to negotiate hard to maintain a degree of unity on the question of economic contacts. But as America's allies took what opportunities were available to develop trade ties with Beijing, their actions stood in stark contrast to a United States that enforced a strict embargo. Indeed, more than the question of recognition or travel, it was the absence of any kind of commercial contact between Washington and Beijing in these years that distinguished the United States most clearly from its allies, contributing further to a sense that its China policies were unrealistic, could not be carried through in the international arena, and would have to be changed.

[71] Ibid. 522.
[72] This formed a prominent part of the debate in the House. See ibid. 532.

Attempts to maintain the China differential were successful over the duration of the Korean conflict, but with the signature of the armistice agreement it became more difficult to hold it in place. It was undermined by the illogicality of the attempt to make a distinction between Beijing and Moscow, the fact that the NATO allies and Japan viewed Russia and not China as the greatest threat, the obvious sympathy of Eisenhower for reducing trade controls, and China's own desire and then necessity to increase economic and political ties. Thus, while many in Washington were exercised by the moves its allies made to relax trade controls, they realized that US governments would have to expend much in the way of their own political and economic resources in order to put a stop to such economic contact. Moreover, some US officials saw in their agreement to the reduction of trade restrictions, or the acceptance of informal economic ties, the makings of a bargain whereby commercial contact with the PRC was accepted in exchange for adherence to a policy seen as more vital—that of non-recognition and support of Taiwan in the United Nations. With the major exception of France in 1964, (London had recognized Beijing in January 1950) it was a bargain that was adhered to. Allies might have disagreed with the policy, but they feared congressional retaliation in the economic field, and weighed the political and security costs of administration displeasure against the less direct and longer-range benefits of formal political linkages with the PRC or support for its UN entry.

In the 1960s, this bargain came under renewed strain as trade levels with China increased, partly as a consequence of the Sino-Soviet split, but also because of China's domestic needs. This prompted opinion formers in allied countries to question the logicality of trading with a country governments had failed to recognize. New currents of opinion were also evident in the US executive and legislative branches, as the realities of the Chinese Communist hold on the mainland—even after a débâcle of the size of the Great Leap—came grudgingly to be admitted. Moreover, the terms of the debate within Washington shifted, with a willingness to acknowledge that it was the United States and not China that in many eyes appeared isolated and intransigent. The trick for some was to find a means of reversing that perception: of re-establishing the legitimacy of the US stance through placing the blame for that isolation on China instead of on the United States.

In the Johnson era, the policy that developed came to be termed 'containment without isolation', but it was a difficult policy to enact, not least because the timing always seemed to be inappropriate: Vietnam, China's virulent anti-Soviet behaviour, and then its embarkation on the Cultural Revolution made it especially problematic. Nevertheless, Johnson did advance calls for reconciliation using the exchange of certain goods as a first step. But it took until 1969 before more concrete moves were made, and with the new Sino-American strategic alignment cemented in 1972, Washington hoped to make up for lost time in the economic sphere. Unlike the West Europeans and Japanese, however, US business was relatively inexperienced in the China market, lacked the legal and institutional support for trading, and still represented a more controversial partner than firms from other countries. In these circumstances, normalization of ties could help solve some of these difficulties.

Carter and Deng were firmly committed both to China's modernization with outside assistance and to the United States playing a central role in that formidable undertaking. By 1979, diplomatic relations and a trading agreement were in place. A year later, trade was some four times higher than it had been in 1978, and the two countries signed four agreements that Washington described as having completed the political and legal framework of normalization.[73] The United States was finally in a position to compete actively in the China market, some twenty-two years after most of its major economic rivals. Over that period, it had been in an isolated position, which had encouraged *rapprochement*, followed by one of relative disadvantage, which had encouraged normalization. Finally, it was set to become a major economic partner of China, as Beijing itself was poised to enter more fully into a global political economy whose central norms largely had been promoted by the United States.

[73] Staff Offices, speechwriters—chronological file, Box 80, 'text of President's remarks at signing ceremony for United States–People's Republic of China Agreements', 17 Sept. 1980, JCL. Carter described this final stage of the normalization process as 'one of the most important achievements of my Presidency'.

4

'We the People': US Public Opinion and China Policy

All forms of government are concerned to relate power with authority, and prefer to exercise power legitimately. Because power is difficult to exercise, those who hold it seek to justify their place, to show they have a right to issue orders, and that subordinates have an obligation to obey. For power to be legitimate, it has to be seen to serve the general interest: to reflect the beliefs and values prevalent in the society, rather than simply the narrow interest of the power holder.[1]

In communist political systems, leaders try to justify rule by reference to the existence of objective laws of social development. The Party's role is to interpret those laws on behalf of a proletariat which may not be reliably aware of what its authentic consciousness ought to be at any one time. Liberal-democratic theory, on the other hand, implies a less elitist view: that wisdom is reposited within the public and that those officials in a position of public trust are in power in order to convert public preferences into policy.

Few of those with an interest in the relationship between public opinion and foreign policy within liberal-democratic societies would accept, of course, that the relationship and the causal direction it implies can be quite so simply depicted. Indeed, empirical investigation has often shown that the direction of influence is the reverse of this: policy is first determined and then opinion is shaped in order to support it. Furthermore, in the case of the United States, some have argued that such shaping or manipulation is justified because mass public views are dangerously volatile and uninformed. Gabriel Almond's oft-quoted position

[1] The classic statement of this argument is contained in Max Weber's *Wirtschaft und Gesellschaft*, 4th edn. (Tübingen: J. C. B. Mohr, 1956), but see also the critique of Weber's position developed in David Beetham, *The Legitimation of Power* (London: Macmillan, 1991).

that public opinion in the United States is no more than a mood, a 'superficial and fluctuating response' to particular events, has mirrored the attitudes of those at the highest levels in American administrations. In 1963, Theodore Sorensen, an aide to President Kennedy, contended that 'public opinion is often erratic, inconsistent, arbitrary, and unreasonable . . . It rarely considers the needs of the next generation or the history of the last . . . It is frequently hampered by myths and misinformation, by stereotypes and shibboleths, and by an innate resistance to innovation.' John Foster Dulles, Secretary of State in the Eisenhower administration, once wrote to a critic of some aspects of the administration's China policy, 'United States foreign policy inevitably involves the acceptance of certain restraints by the American people . . . Foreign policy and diplomacy cannot succeed unless, in fact, it channels the activities of our people': a more benign view of the public perhaps than Sorensen's, but a suggestion too that the public needs to be guided lest its emotions lead it onto an incorrect path.[2]

More systematic investigation into the nature of American public opinion has tended to conclude that the mass public is generally indifferent to most foreign-policy issues, and that the attentive public represents at best some 15 per cent of the population. One corollary or consequence is that the press tends to devote no more than 10 per cent of its coverage to foreign events, and that most people are content to leave this domain to the President, Congress, and bureaucracy.[3] This does not mean that Americans do not hold broad, structured beliefs: in 1985, for example, while only 65 per cent of those surveyed knew that the United States had supported South Vietnam during the Vietnam war, nevertheless there remained a strong conviction arising out of the Vietnam experience that American soldiers should not be sent to fight in potentially long, drawn-out conflicts.[4]

[2] Gabriel A. Almond, *The American People and Foreign Policy* (New York: Praeger, 1960); Theodore C. Sorensen, *Decision-Making in the White House* (New York: Columbia University Press, 1963), 45–6; John Foster Dulles Papers, Selected Correspondence, Box 114, letter to Arthur H. Sulzberger, 30 Apr. 1957, SGML.

[3] See e.g. Charles W. Kegley, Jun. and Eugene R. Wittkopf, *American Foreign Policy: Pattern and Process*, 4th edn. (New York: St Martin's Press, 1991), esp. chs. 8 and 9; and Ralph B. Levering, *The Public and American Foreign Policy, 1918–1978* (New York: William Morrow, 1978).

[4] Kegley and Wittkopf, *American Foreign Policy*, provide details of six such

Neither does indifference mean that foreign policy elites be-lieve they can disregard public opinion entirely. As one student of the subject has written: 'most American Presidents apparently have believed that although they have the right and perhaps the duty to seek to build support for their policies, they should not make foreign policy decisions which are too far in advance of public opinion'.[5] To that degree, then, opinion sets broad con-straints and leaders acknowledge that they derive strength—bar-gaining power with both domestic and external actors[6]—if they are able to demonstrate a close correspondence between the ar-ticulated policy and the public's passive or preferably active ac-ceptance of that policy. Considerable resources are thus often devoted to ensuring that close fit between the positions of leaders and led.

This chapter examines the relationship between government policy and articulated policy preferences with respect to the People's Republic of China. In common with much of the litera-ture on the topic, public opinion is here defined in its widest sense to include the views of the mass public, those of the attentive or informed public, and finally those of the policy elites with direct access to decision-makers. Broadly put, examination of these views will show that until the early 1960s images articulated at the highest levels within administrations closely corresponded with and at times helped to shape informed and mass public opinion; but that, conversely, at later stages public attitudes were in advance of policy and demonstrated a desire to see a change in approach towards the PRC. From this perspective, the *rapprochement* and then normalization of relations with the PRC could be said to have helped re-establish the authority relationship between the public and decision-makers in this policy area.

Between 1949 and 1979, domestic attitudes towards China went through four main stages. The indifference of the mass public, and a lack of consensus within informed circles, the bureaucracy,

findings that show the public to be ill-informed on the specifics of policy; but see too their discussion of 'politically relevant foreign policy beliefs', 283–4.

[5] Levering, *The Public*, 152.

[6] For an interesting argument about the entanglement of domestic politics and international relations see Robert D. Putnam, 'Diplomacy and domestic politics: the logic of two-level games', *International Organization*, 42 (1988).

and in Congress marked the first phase from the last stages of the Chinese civil war to October 1950. In the next phase, China's entry into the Korean conflict dramatically shaped attitudes, generating criticism of those in government who in an earlier period had failed to identify China as an implacable enemy. By the late 1950s to mid-1960s doubts about the rigid quality of America's policy towards the PRC surfaced, articulated most strongly within Congress, but also among the wider public and—if more mutedly—at various levels within the Kennedy and Johnson administrations. From then on through to the establishment of diplomatic relations in 1979, there was a widespread consensus that China should neither be left in 'angry isolation' nor diminished through a Soviet attack. Thus, for reasons of world order and American political and security interests, many in the United States came to believe that Beijing needed to be brought into the international community.

The Uncertain First Phase

Mass public attitudes towards the PRC in the latter stages of the Chinese civil war might best be summarized as indifferent. Both Communists and Nationalists were generally disliked, and a majority continued to oppose intervention in the domestic struggle, Truman's promise in January 1950 of non-intervention 'at this time' received an approval rating of 5 to 3. But beyond this, little was known about the new government in Beijing and little interest was shown in its or in the Nationalists' fate.[7] In August 1949, the US State Department published the China White Paper, designed to explain to supporters and critics alike the reasons for the Nationalist defeat on the mainland, and why the United States was unwilling to become directly involved in the final stages of the civil conflict. Despite major press coverage of the paper's launch, when polled, 64 per cent of those responding had neither heard nor read anything about it.[8]

[7] Levering, The Public, 101; Leonard A. Kusnitz, Public Opinion and Foreign Policy: America's China Policy 1949–1979 (Westport, Conn.: Greenwood Press, 1984), 31.

[8] Nancy Bernkopf Tucker, Patterns in the Dust: Chinese–American Relations and the Recognition Controversy, 1949–1950 (New York: Columbia University Press, 1983), 156–61.

Such lack of interest in China's fate was not matched within the opinion elite and within certain parts of Congress. The so-called 'China bloc' in the legislature was small, but, in the absence of arguments against continuing staunch support for Chiang, the bloc obtained a position of influence far beyond its size. Other groups outside of Congress, including business representatives, missionaries, and scholars, nevertheless continued to see recognition of the PRC as inevitable and to believe that contact and exchange with Beijing would develop at least to the level that existed with the Soviet bloc. Those within the bureaucracy with similar expectations—at least until the spring of 1950—included the US Secretary of State, Dean Acheson. With the Nationalist defeat looking ever more inevitable, the hope was that a weak and chaotic China would hardly represent a strategic asset to the Soviet Union, even if it was under Communist rule. Moreover, there was some justification for believing that in due course the Chinese—with their strong nationalist sense—would find the alliance with the USSR irksome, and would seek a more independent stance. It seemed reasonable, therefore, for the United States to develop policies designed to accelerate Beijing's disillusionment with Moscow.

Truman and Acheson would not grant recognition to the PRC, however, without Beijing satisfying certain conditions. Neither would recognition be given speedily, a decision that allowed a President somewhat doubtful of the merits of any positive move towards Beijing, the China bloc within Congress, and those concerned about the strategic consequences of the change of government, the opportunity to harden the policy stance. Chinese actions and statements in 1949 and early 1950, undertaken with the intention of convincing the waverers within the country that genuinely friendly support could only come from socialist countries, and of reassuring Stalin that Mao was not another Tito,[9] did not much help matters either. Thus, when Dean Rusk was appointed in March 1950 as Assistant Secretary of State for Far Eastern Affairs, and John Foster Dulles in April as State Department Consultant—both appointments designed to bolster biparti-

[9] See e.g. in Mao Zedong's *Selected Works*, iv (Beijing: Foreign Languages Press, 1969), 'On the People's Democratic Dictatorship', 30 June 1949; 'Cast Away Illusions, Prepare for Struggle', 14 Aug. 1949; and 'Farewell Leighton Stuart!', 18 Aug. 1949.

san support for Truman's Asian policy—the time had come for the development of a more active anti-communist role in Asia. Dulles and Rusk wanted to draw the line—to prevent further communist gains in the area—and that meant the development of a policy designed to 'guarantee by American armed forces the status quo of Formosa pending its disposition by peaceful means either through Japanese Peace Settlement or by the United Nations'.

Acheson, in receipt of Rusk's report on the topic on 30 May, probably found his arguments persuasive, given that the Secretary by that time had come around to the view that the balance of power had tipped in the Soviet favour, that Chinese Communist encroachments in South-East Asia had become more likely, and that the island of Taiwan had greater strategic significance than he was once willing to acknowledge. Thus, Acheson met with Rusk, Nitze, Jessup, and Dulles to discuss the report on 31 May, and the Secretary quickly took up the points with Truman. The difficult question of how far to go in aiding Taiwan to help keep the island out of Communist hands, and whether that would include support for a coup d'état against Chiang Kai-shek led by the supposedly more effective and amenable General Sun Li-jen, was still being deliberated when fighting broke out on the Korean peninsula on 25 June.[10]

The Korean War and its Domestic Legacies

With the outbreak of the Korean conflict, the administration's swift decision to interpose the Seventh Fleet in the Taiwan Straits, and to recommend the neutralization of the status of the island, intensified the hostility between the United States and China. Nevertheless, the subsequent Chinese entry into the fighting in October graphically confirmed for Washington the wisdom of those strategic moves.

The Truman administration's Seventh Fleet decision received endorsement in most major US newspapers, together with the

[10] Ronald McGlothlen, *Controlling the Waves: Dean Acheson and U.S. Foreign Policy in Asia* (New York: Norton, 1993), 119–25; Gordon H. Chang, *Friends and Enemies: The United States, China, and the Soviet Union, 1948–1972* (Stanford, Calif.: Stanford University Press, 1990), esp. 72–5.

enthusiastic support of those within Congress and the bureaucracy who had been attempting to draw such a line in Asia.
Although Truman and Acheson might well have preferred some
alternative to Chiang's rule, keeping their distance from him
proved difficult once the conflict erupted on the peninsula, and
they had acknowledged the strategic importance of the island he
presided over. With Chinese entry into the war and with the
'Volunteer' armed forces meeting their American counterparts on
the battlefield, public support for accelerating military aid to the
Nationalists increased to the point where in 1951 about 60 per
cent of those surveyed wanted the United States to give Chiang's
forces all the help they needed to attack the mainland, and 60 per
cent also urged the bombing of China's air bases. By 1953, four
out of five Americans favoured American aid for a Chinese
Nationalist attack on the mainland. Not surprisingly, such
hostility towards the PRC included public support for the policy
of non-recognition, denial of the UN seat, and the administration's submission that all allied trade with Beijing should be
stopped.[11]

China's direct entry into the fighting also hardened attitudes
within the US bureaucracy and reduced the room for policy
manœuvre. When the British Prime Minister, Clement Attlee,
tried in December 1950 to revive Acheson's interest in a policy
that had been designed to wean Beijing away from Moscow
through positive inducements, Acheson replied that it had now
become impossible to act in that way given that 'they have now
attacked us with their armies and have denounced us violently'.[12]
During the Congressional Hearings held to investigate the dismissal in April 1951 of General MacArthur from his positions as
UN and Far Eastern Commander, administration officials were
pressed to explain the longer-term objectives of their Asian strategy. The Secretary of Defense, General George C. Marshall, for
example, stated more categorically than he would probably have
wished that Taiwan would never be allowed to fall into the hands
of the PRC; and neither would Beijing be permitted to assume the
China seat at the United Nations. Also in mid-May 1951, Rusk

[11] See e.g. RG 59, Public Opinion Studies, Public Attitudes on US Policy
Towards China, Boxes 12, 27, 33, NA; Kusnitz, Public Opinion, esp. chs. 4 and 5.
[12] Foreign Relations of the United States, 1950 (Washington, DC: Government
Printing Office, 1976), 7: 1401–2, 5 Dec.

and Dulles made similarly uncompromising public statements, Rusk seeming to rule out any future accommodation with the current Chinese leaders and effectively calling for the overthrow of this 'colonial Russian government', this 'Slavic Manchukuo on a large scale'.[13]

China's initial stunning successes on the battlefield, the realization that this would be a long, drawn-out conflict, together with the steady reporting of information about the treatment of Americans taken prisoner, helped solidify anti-Communist sentiment in the country at large. Even if President Eisenhower had wanted to alter these attitudes, he would have been hard-pressed to do so. As it was, having witnessed the loss of authority of his Democratic predecessors, partly as a result of their having been labelled 'soft on communism', and having promised to be steadfast in his support of the Chinese Nationalists, change in China policy under Eisenhower was rendered unlikely.

Adjustments in policy post-Korea were further constrained when those favoured by the right wing of the Republican Party were placed in positions of power within the Eisenhower administration. Walter Judd, a leading figure in the China bloc, recommended Walter S. Robertson as the Assistant Secretary of State for Far Eastern Affairs, and a known tough opponent of the Beijing regime, Walter P. McConaughy, was appointed as Director of the Office of Chinese Affairs. Two staunch supporters of Chiang Kai-shek were also appointed to the ambassadorship to Taipei: first, Karl Lott Rankin, then Everett F. Drumwright. These men may not have been part of Dulles's trusted 'inner circle' but their presence demonstrated the extent to which the President and his Secretary of State were responsive to right-wing opinion on China.[14] Moreover, they helped define the parameters of China policy, and contributed to the shaping of mass public and media opinion of the Communist government.

Eisenhower began his administration convinced that Congress had to take its rightful place in the policy-making process, perhaps, as has been suggested, so that 'it could share in the responsi-

---

[13] Rosemary Foot, *A Substitute for Victory: The Politics of Peacemaking at the Korean Armistice Talks* (Ithaca: Cornell University Press, 1990), 35.

[14] Nancy Bernkopf Tucker, 'A House Divided: The United States, the Department of State, and China', in Warren I. Cohen and Akira Iriye, eds., *The Great Powers in East Asia, 1953–1960* (New York: Columbia University Press, 1990), 36–7.

bility for the crack ups'. He fully intended to have weekly meetings with legislative leaders and was the first President to establish a congressional liaison staff. Dulles too 'was tireless in his efforts' to keep Congress informed. Indeed, William F. Knowland—known as the Senator for Formosa as a result of his staunch support for Chiang—gratefully acknowledged that levels of consultation far outstripped those reached in the previous administration. As Senate Majority leader he was never slow to take advantage of those opportunities where China policy was concerned.[15] During the Korean war itself, Knowland worked to ensure that acceptance of the truce was not traded for a policy of flexibility towards the PRC and, when the Chinese were invited to participate in the 1954 Geneva Conference on Indo-China and Korea, he warned that the administration 'would be held accountable if there were any "slips" that might lead' to formal recognition of Beijing.[16] Rumours in 1954 that UN recognition for the PRC might shortly be forthcoming led the Senator to state that in this eventuality he would leave the Senate in order to have time to lead the fight to take the United States out of the United Nations altogether.[17] His stance was reinforced by the activities of the 'Committee of one Million' which had been founded in 1953 to campaign against PRC admission to the United Nations. During the Geneva conference, the Committee sent a cablegram to Dulles claiming that, as of 26 April, 833,867 Americans had endorsed its organization's goals and signed its petition.[18]

With Korea out of the way, however, mass public opinion, despite Knowland and the 'Committee', had in fact softened on the UN and other questions. But on the UN issue it hardened markedly once again when Eisenhower made a speech underlining the extent to which Beijing's behaviour flagrantly opposed the ideals of that organization. Where 59 per cent in 1954 felt the United States should go along with UN majority opinion on this

[15] Anna K. Nelson, 'John Foster Dulles and the Bipartisan Congress', *Political Science Quarterly*, 102, no. 1 (Spring 1987); Eisenhower, Papers as President (Whitman File), Cabinet Series, Box 2, 23 Jan. 1953, DDEL.

[16] Foot, *Substitute for Victory*, 203; Henry W. Brands, Jun., 'The Dwight D. Eisenhower Administration, Syngman Rhee and the "Other" Geneva Conference of 1954', *Pacific Historical Review* (Feb. 1987), 67.

[17] FO 371/109101, Weekly Political Summary, 26 June–2 July, 1954, PRO.

[18] Stanley D. Bachrack, *The Committee of One Million: 'China Lobby' Politics, 1953–1971* (New York: Columbia University Press, 1976), 94–5.

matter, nineteen days after the speech was delivered Gallup found that 78 per cent opposed UN recognition of the PRC, with only 7 per cent in favour.[19] The administration stayed in step with Congressional views on this topic over the next few years, taking heed of the fact that both the Republican and Democratic Party platforms in 1956 endorsed the policy of exclusion, and House and Senate resolutions unanimously opposed the PRC's admittance to the body. It is not surprising that Eisenhower used these emphatic views as a means of bargaining with the British on the matter. Where London favoured a relaxation of UN recognition policy, Eisenhower claimed he sympathized with congressional opinion that if Chiang were to be thrown out it would be necessary for the United States to withdraw from that body, a position he reiterated at the Anglo-American conference in Bermuda in March 1957.[20]

This degree of domestic consensus did not mean, however, that there were no dissenting voices on trade, contact, and even recognition. There was a growing sense within and outside of the administration that the Communist Chinese were there to stay, and that a *de facto* 'two-Chinas' policy had come into being, given the unlikelihood of Chiang being able to gain a foothold on the mainland. As a result of the Sino-American ambassadorial talks at Geneva—negotiations that began in part out of contacts at the 1954 Geneva conference and then more formally as a means of resolving the crisis that had arisen between China and America over islands in the Taiwan Straits in 1954-5—large pluralities (74 to 82 per cent) came to view a meeting between Zhou and Dulles as not inconceivable. Within the business community, West-coast firms, together with individuals such as Henry Ford II, and John S. Coleman, President of the US Chamber of Commerce, all with the support of the *Wall Street Journal*, were responsive to allied arguments that recommended the reduction of controls on trade with China, at least to the level of those operating against the Soviet Union.[21] The PRC also offered during the Geneva negotiations to allow US news representatives to visit China. This evoked enormous interest within the US media much to the cha-

[19] Kusnitz, *Public Opinion*, 68–9.

[20] FO 371/127239, 23 Mar. 1957, PRO; *Foreign Relations*, 1955–7 (Washington, DC: Government Printing Office, 1992), 27: 707–8, 755–6, 20 and 23 Mar. 1957.

[21] Kusnitz, *Public Opinion*, 74–7.

grin of the administration. The first administration response had been to threaten to revoke the passports of those Americans who attempted to make such a trip; but Washington was forced somewhat to relent, partially because of the arguments of those such as Arthur H. Sulzberger of the *New York Times* who stated that he could not 'escape the feeling that the Administration [was] abridging the freedom of the press and using the press as an instrument in its diplomacy'.[22]

More significant were the isolated but nevertheless notable statements being made in the mid-1950s in Congress and by former and current administration officials. Arthur Dean, an international lawyer with Dulles's New York firm of Sullivan and Cromwell, who had previously headed the US team to negotiate arrangements for the post-armistice conference on Korea, went as far as to argue in April 1955 that Japan needed China as a trading partner, that the UN was 'being restricted' as a result of the exclusion policy, that US foreign policy elsewhere was in danger of becoming 'a mere adjunct' to the problems of Taiwan, and that Washington might 'simply have to accommodate to a hard fact [i.e. the PRC] that seems unlikely to change in the near future'.[23] Within the Senate, Theodore F. Green (Democrat, Rhode Island), as chair of the Foreign Relations Committee, remarked in mid-February 1957 that before too long the PRC would have to be recognized: 'We don't like their form of government, but the country is a great country and organized, and I do not myself see why we should recognize those other Communist countries and withhold recognition of China.'[24] Senator John F. Kennedy also published an article in *Foreign Affairs* in October 1957 calling for a reassessment of the administration's rigid China policy.

There were, too, differences of opinion within the bureaucracy with respect to the best means of promoting a successful China

[22] Dulles Papers, Selected Correspondence, Box 114, letter to Dulles, 23 Apr. 1957, SGML. Dulles did soften the policy on visits, but he also stated publicly that in allowing a limited number of correspondents to visit China, this did not imply that Washington would 'accord reciprocal visas to Chinese bearing passports issued by the Chinese Communist regime', a statement which in the media's view invited Beijing's subsequent refusal to receive Americans on this non-reciprocal basis. See *Foreign Relations*, 1955–7 (Washington, DC: Government Printing Office, 1986), 3: 584–5, 22 Aug. 1957, (editorial note); and ibid. 3: 600–1, 11 Sept. 1957.

[23] Arthur Dean, 'United States Foreign Policy and Formosa', *Foreign Affairs*, 33 (Apr. 1955), 360–75.

[24] Bachrack, *Committee of One Million*, 133.

policy. Robert Bowie, head of the Policy Planning Staff and a member of Dulles's 'inner circle' did not support the Secretary's unremitting efforts in 1957 to hold the line on policy towards Beijing. In response to a draft of Dulles's June speech, to be delivered in San Francisco and designed to undermine any notion that US policy towards the PRC was about to change, Bowie admonished Dulles for failing to consider either the costs of that policy or the chances of its success. In Bowie's view, the US effort to coerce other countries into withholding recognition of the PRC and excluding it from the United Nations would entail severe costs: 'In twisting arms, granting favors, and making deals to isolate the Chinese Communists, we will use up influence and leverage which is needed for other purposes.' Far better, Bowie argued, to move towards a two-Chinas policy which would eventually lead most states to recognize both Beijing and Taipei—although this need not include the United States—and might provide a means of complicating and delaying the resolution of the UN issue, disassociating Washington from the onus for delay.[25]

At this stage, however, although these comments were prescient, they were essentially isolated, and garnered little additional support and much Congressional and administration criticism. As Dulles stated in his 1957 San Francisco speech: 'If Communism is stubborn for the wrong, let us be steadfast for the right. The capacity to change is an indispensable capacity. Equally indispensable is the capacity to hold fast that which is good.'[26]

Transition

The year 1959 brought forth a number of indications that arguments for greater flexibility in China policy were gathering pace. Dulles's and Robertson's replacements in the State Department may not have been daring advocates of change but at least they were not tied quite so fixedly to the public line. Chiang Kai-shek's staunchest supporters in the Senate—Alexander Smith and William F. Knowland—had left, the latter's seat was taken over by Clair Engle, who rapidly staked out a position markedly differ-

[25] *Foreign Relations*, 1955–7, 3: 558–66, 'Our Policies Towards Communism in China', 28 June 1957; Bowie's comments in ibid. 3: 545–9, 19 June 1957.
[26] Ibid. 3: 566.

ent from Knowland's own. Engle, in May 1959, made a cautious yet brave speech decrying the 'Maginot line response' to China, a policy that tried to build a military, economic, and psychological wall around the country. Instead, he advocated limited contact to include the reciprocal exchange of news representatives; trade on the same basis as that with the Soviet Union; prevention of Chinese Nationalist attacks against the mainland; and negotiations at a level higher than that of ambassador.[27]

Two weeks later, Senator Byrd rose to defend the current policy but Senator Thomas J. Dodd (Democrat, Connecticut) congratulated Engle, and Congressman Porter of Oregon followed up with the suggestion of a trade mission. Perhaps in response to this mood, the incoming chair of the Senate Foreign Relations Committee, Alexander Wiley, proposed an examination of China policy. Conlon associates were commissioned to produce a report and their recommendations, penned largely by Professor Robert Scalapino, included many of those Engle had put his name to. It also proposed, however, enlargement of the Security Council to include seats for India and Japan as well as Communist China.

The report additionally took issue with some of the central arguments the Eisenhower administration had used over the years in explaining policy towards Beijing. Membership of the United Nations did not automatically increase the prestige of the state in question, the report stated, and it used the Chinese Nationalists as a case in point. Although it acknowledged that Taiwan, South Korea, and South Vietnam would object to any change of stance, it also predicted that such governments would adjust to this as they had adjusted to US policies they had disapproved of in the past. Elsewhere in Asia, it stated, the attractions of communism depended less on the United States holding the line on China policy and more on internal developments within the countries themselves.[28] The China specialist, A. Doak Barnett, agreed with much of this. In a work sponsored by the Council on Foreign Relations, begun in 1958 and published in 1960, Barnett advocated relaxation of trade restrictions,

---

[27] *Congressional Record*, 86th Congress, 1st Session, 21 May 1959.

[28] The British acquired a copy of this report and were pleased to discover that it mirrored many of the views they had expressed. FO 371/141216, 10 Nov. 1959, PRO.

Nationalist evacuation of the offshore islands, and a 'two-Chinas' position in the United Nations and over the question of diplomatic recognition.[29]

Personnel changes within Congress obviously explain much of this willingness to re-evaluate the position, but public reaction to the 1958 Offshore Islands crisis also prompted it. The fact that Eisenhower had publicly nailed his administration's colours to the mast by supporting Chiang's retention of the islands, and the expectation that atomic weapons might have to be used in their defence, aroused intense opposition. In telegrams, letters, and telephone calls to the White House and to Capitol Hill, Americans showed themselves to be overwhelmingly opposed to a potential war of this magnitude for the sake of two small islands. Some 80 per cent of the mail into the State Department was against administration policy, a fact revealed in the Sunday *New York Times*. All major newspapers such as the daily *New York Times, Washington Post, St. Louis Post-Dispatch*, and *Christian Science Monitor* expressed strong doubts about the administration's stand, and many blamed Chiang for tying the United States to such an unrealistic policy. Research undertaken by the US Information Agency led it to state categorically that US public opinion could not be brought around to supporting the policy, despite administration efforts to explain why such a tough stance was necessary.[30]

The informed public was equally dismayed. Professor Edwin Reischauer, writing to Dulles from Harvard, provided some indication of the views of many of his colleagues when he noted: 'In my experience at Harvard during the past 20 years, I cannot remember any important foreign policy problem on which a similar group would have been so unanimously out of sympathy with important aspects of our government's position.'[31] Senator Green wrote to the President in his capacity as chair of the Senate Com-

[29] A. Doak Barnett, *Communist China and Asia: Challenge to American Policy* (New York: Harper, 1960), esp. chs. 14 and 15.

[30] Kusnitz, *Public Opinion*, 80; George C. Eliades, 'Once More Unto the Breach: Eisenhower, Dulles and Public Opinion during the Offshore Islands Crisis of 1958', *Journal of American East-Asian Relations*, 2, no. 4 (Winter 1993), 356–61.

[31] RG 59, 611.93, China, 29 Sept. 1958, Box 2569, NA. Dulles replied: 'The feeling I had was that there were persons there who were experts on small parts of the problem', but were not expert on the 'free world' position in the Western Pacific as a whole.

mittee on Foreign Relations, and described possible military action in the Far East as being involvement 'at the wrong time, in the wrong place, and on issues not of vital concern to our own security, and all this without allies either in fact or in heart'. Moreover, such involvement, as Green's post-bag and the press had shown, would not command the support of the American people.[32] Such views had their impact on Eisenhower, who noted when the worst of the tension had subsided that he disliked waging 'a fight on the ground of someone else's choosing', that he realized that the United States was 'at a great disadvantage in terms of world opinion,' and that the alliance with Chiang would be far stronger if it were based on a 'unified public opinion at home'.[33]

This second crisis over the offshore islands reinforced sentiment in favour of an explicit two-Chinas policy and additionally became an issue in the presidential election race of 1960. But despite Kennedy's expressed desire for greater flexibility and the appointment of advisers who were similarly inclined, none of these individuals—once in power—were willing to argue for significant change. The domestic signals still were not seen to be strong enough, especially in the light of Kennedy's narrow electoral victory, Eisenhower's apparent warning that he would come out fighting if the new President moved to change China policy,[34] and votes in Congress in July 1961 (despite the signs of flexibility indicated earlier) demonstrating a blanket unwillingness to contemplate UN or diplomatic recognition for the PRC at that time. For these reasons, and because Kennedy personally seemed to view China as a more aggressive and dangerous foe than a Soviet Union increasingly interested in *détente*, the President did relatively little to enlarge his own freedom of manœuvre.[35]

---

[32] Dwight D. Eisenhower Diary, (Ann Whitman File), Box 36, 29 Sept. 1958, DDEL.

[33] DDE Diary, (Ann Whitman File), Box 36, 30 Sept. 1958 and 7 Oct. 1958, DDEL; Eliades, 'Once More Unto the Breach', covers well the impact of these negative views on Eisenhower and others within the administration.

[34] Rusk reported this to his British counterpart in 1961: see FO 371/158445, 4 Apr. 1961, PRO.

[35] Dean Rusk, *As I Saw It*, as told to Richard Rusk and ed. by Daniel S. Papp (New York: Norton, 1990), 283–5; James Fetzer, 'Clinging to Containment: China Policy', in Thomas G. Paterson, ed., *Kennedy's Quest for Victory: American Foreign Policy, 1961–1963* (New York: Oxford University Press, 1989), 185; Gordon H. Chang, *Friends and Enemies: The United States, China, and the Soviet Union, 1948–1972* (Stanford, Calif.: Stanford University Press, 1990), 229 ff. For a Chinese

Nevertheless, despite these constraints, certain decisions were taken that made a difference in terms of the level of understanding of the PRC and in the range of policy options that could be considered. Personnel changes in the bureaucracy from November 1961 brought Averell Harriman in to replace Walter McConaughy as Assistant Secretary for Far Eastern Affairs and he, in turn, brought in the China specialist, Edward Rice, as Deputy Assistant Secretary for Economic Affairs. The latter joined James Thomson, a special assistant on Far Eastern affairs, and a colleague of Chester Bowles, the former Under-Secretary of State who now had a roving ambassadorship within the administration. This represented a critical mass who all favoured greater flexibility in China policy. Indeed, Rice had produced in early 1961 a long paper when at State's Policy Planning Council which argued for a raft of initiatives to include the lifting of the passport ban, trade in non-strategic goods, China's involvement in arms control and disarmament discussions, more productive use of the Sino-American ambassadorial talks (now in Warsaw), some form of UN representation for Beijing, and Nationalist evacuation of the offshore islands.[36] Harriman was also instrumental in creating a separate 'mainland China affairs' desk in the Far Eastern bureau, a change which gave specialists greater access to upper levels of the bureau and State Department, and provided greater visibility to the excellent reports from the US consulate general in Hong Kong. Allen Whiting was also added later to the Far Eastern section of State's intelligence and research bureau. He injected a vision of China at odds with that which had prevailed up to this point, emphasizing its cautious rather than its reckless attitude to the use of force.[37]

Policy discussion crystallized around three major issues in 1962: modification of the trade embargo; an offer of grain sales to the Chinese in light of severe agricultural shortages after the failed Great Leap Forward; and the partial lifting of the ban on

analyst's view, published in the PRC, see Gu Ning, 'Kennedy zheng fu de dui hua zheng ce' [Kennedy Administration Policy Towards China], *Journal of World History*, 6 (1991).

[36] James C. Thomson, Jun., 'On the Making of U.S. China Policy, 1961–9: A Study in Bureaucratic Politics', *China Quarterly*, 50 (Apr./June 1972), 223.

[37] Allen S. Whiting's excellent *China Crosses the Yalu: The Decision to Enter the Korean War* (Stanford, Calif.: Stanford University Press), was published in 1960. It emphasized China's defensive objectives in entering the war.

travel to China. Such discussion basically got nowhere, however, given the violent reaction from the Chinese Nationalists, the Sino-Indian border war, the Cuban missile crisis, and Kennedy's basic animosity towards Beijing and preference for dealing with Moscow. As James Thomson was to write subsequently, Cuba eventually brought Soviet–American *détente* to 'the forefront, while the Himalayan war temporarily put China into the role of trouble-maker'.[38] True, the offer to sell food was made, but in a way that did not invite agreement.[39] The one positive move during the period was the reassurance given to Chinese officials at the Sino-American ambassadorial talks, now in Warsaw, that the United States would give no support or encouragement to Chiang if he were to launch an attack on the mainland that year.[40]

With the Soviet–American relationship given precedence, Kennedy's particular distaste for the Beijing regime, and the possible use that could be made of the Sino-Soviet rift to move closer to Moscow (now the 'wedge' was in place, the next moves were the opposite of the original intention), there were few reasons to expect the establishment of an alternative China policy. Certainly, in November 1963—a week before his assassination—Kennedy responded to a question regarding trade to the effect that the United States was 'not wedded to a policy of hostility to Red China'.[41] But it was not until after Kennedy's death and possibly as a result of a failure properly to clear the text that Roger Hilsman's so-called 'watershed' speech came to be made.[42] In that speech the new Assistant Secretary for Far Eastern Affairs tried to convey two main points: that, unlike the view that had supposedly been held in the Dulles era, the administration no longer believed the Chinese Communist government to be a passing phenomenon; and that if Beijing gave up its preference for 'for-

---

[38] Thomson, 'On the Making of U.S. China Policy', 228.

[39] See my Ch. 3 for details.

[40] See Fetzer, 'Clinging to Containment', and Wang Bingnan, 'Nine Years of Sino–U.S. Talks in Retrospect', tr. in JPRS-CPS-85-079, 7 Aug. 1985, 49.

[41] James C. Thomson Papers, Box 15, Comm China—General, 'President Kennedy's press conference, Nov. 14, 1963', JFKL.

[42] Not regarded as a watershed in China, it seems. During interviews at the Chinese Academy of Social Sciences, Institute of American Studies, Sept. 1993, I was assured that Hilsman's speech was interpreted negatively because it seemed to be a further indication that the administration favoured a 'two-Chinas' policy rather than a degree of accommodation with the PRC.

eign adventure' then it would find Washington to be flexible and willing to negotiate.[43]

As Hilsman and others have recounted, the press—including the more conservative journals—widely approved of his statement, and there was only a muted reaction in Congress despite the Committee of One Million's attempts to stir up Congressional passions by sending a critique of the speech to every member of that body. For the *New York Times*, Hilsman's prescriptions were barely enough, for it had advocated, on the fourteenth anniversary of the founding of the PRC, testing Beijing's reaction by offering trade and exploring recognition and admission into the United Nations—though it cautioned that this should be done 'without prejudice to the right and independence of Taiwan'.[44] Once out of government and installed as Professor at Columbia University, Hilsman was indeed more explicit, returning to the ideas urged in Rice's paper: that China be invited to the arms-control talks in Geneva; that travel restrictions to the mainland be eased; and that US trade policies be re-examined.[45]

But this time election-year preoccupations, consequent circumspection, and China's explosion of its atomic device intervened to prevent further movement. McGeorge Bundy, Johnson's Special Assistant for National Security Affairs, reminded the President two months after that explosion that now was 'not the time to give [the PRC] increased prestige or to reward her belligerence—at the UN or elsewhere'.[46] The time was still not ripe, it seemed, but nevertheless it was still ripening, for in August 1965 a new initiative emerged. Dr Paul Dudley White, the renowned heart specialist and Eisenhower's physician, offered himself as a possible means to break the travel ban to a country White wanted to visit. The initiative finally bore bureaucratic fruit at the end of the year, generating domestic applause. The press reported it widely and favourably and Congress took it in its stride.[47]

---

[43] Hilsman provided a rationale for the speech to Adlai Stevenson, US Representative to the United Nations. See Roger Hilsman papers, Box 1, China Policy Speech, 13 Dec. 1963, letter to Stevenson dated 19 Dec. 1963, JFKL.

[44] *New York Times*, 1 Oct. 1963.

[45] A.T. Steele, *The American People and China* (New York: McGraw Hill, 1966), 250.

[46] Bundy quoted in Chang, *Friends and Enemies*, 262.

[47] Thomson, in 'On the Making of U.S. China Policy', provides a detailed and entertaining description of how policy on this issue came to be modified.

Congress and the informed public had in fact been signalling their readiness for change for some months. In a speech to the Senate on 25 March 1964, J. William Fulbright, then chair of the Senate Foreign Relations Committee, called for greater flexibility in China policy, a call that elicited over 12,000 letters in response, two-thirds of which were favourable.[48] In March 1965, a House Sub-Committee headed by Clement J. Zablocki (Democrat, Wisconsin) issued a report on the Sino-Soviet conflict which urged that the United States give 'consideration to the initiation of limited but direct contact with Red China through cultural exchange activities with emphasis on scholars and journalists'.[49] Late in 1965, Yale students and faculty took out a full-page advertisement in the *New York Times* calling for a re-evaluation of policy in the light of the 1965 tied vote at the UN over the resolution calling for PRC entry and Taiwan's expulsion. Religious groups, most actively the Quakers, also proposed changes to include greater restraints on Taiwan, a *de facto* acknowledgement that the PRC was the government of China, discussions over problems of mutual interest, and an end to the special restrictions on trade and commerce. It too advocated that the PRC take the China seat in the United Nations, 'the major center for international communication'.[50]

By far the greatest attention was given, however, to the Senate Hearings held in the spring of 1966. It was during these, 'the most complete discussion of China policy ever given to the American people',[51] that the theme of 'containment without isolation' took shape, with several China specialists urging trade in non-strategic items, greater contact, and entry for Beijing into the United Nations.[52] Perhaps as a result of these hearings, a Lou Harris poll in June of that year found that 57 per cent of the American public favoured recognition of China, with 43 per cent against; 55 per cent wanted both Chinas in the UN, with 45 per cent against; and

[48] Steele, *American People and China*, 214.

[49] Thomson Papers, memo for Mr Bundy, National Security Staff, McGeorge Bundy, 1964–6, Box 11, 26 May 1965, JFKL. Thomson notes in this memo that the US Chamber of Commerce in its 1965 meeting also urged the opening of 'channels of communication with the people of Mainland China'.

[50] Bachrack, *Committee of One Million*, 228–9; *A New China Policy: Some Quaker Proposals* (New Haven: Yale University Press, 1965).

[51] Chang, *Friends and Enemies*, 273.

[52] United States, Senate, Committee on Foreign Relations, 89th Congress, 2nd Session, 1966.

only 8 per cent thought the USA should pull out if the PRC were to be admitted. As Harris was to conclude: 'the American people generally believe every effort should be made to begin a dialogue between this country and Red China to avert war'.[53]

The Harris summary of opinion neatly encapsulated the argument. It was not that the Chinese were no longer feared or no longer perceived as aggressive—after all, in a 1964 poll, the US public by two to one had seen China as the greatest threat to world peace;[54] what had happened was the widespread realization that the Chinese Communists were a hard fact of life and that the only means of reducing that sense of threat and foreboding was to engage Beijing in dialogue, to negotiate with it on specific issues, and gradually to draw it into the full range of international interaction. By the spring of 1966, the most senior members in the Johnson administration indicated their readiness to respond to these signs. In mid-March Vice-President Hubert Humphrey during an NBC interview took up the language of the Senate Hearing, advocating a policy of 'containment without necessarily isolation'.[55] Finally, the President himself gave the new terminology his seal of approval. In a nationwide TV address on Asia he offered 'reconciliation between nations that now call themselves enemies', and more specifically the 'free flow of ideas and people and goods'. To this end, he noted that recent steps had been taken to allow scholars, medical specialists, and others to travel to China, adding 'only today we have here in the Government cleared a passport for a leading American businessman to exchange knowledge with Chinese mainland leaders in Red China'.[56] But with the administration now increasingly absorbed by the Vietnam war; with Washington's articulation of a position that, although China might not have its own combat forces in that

[53] Fred Panzer files, China Hearings, Box 572, 11 July 1966, LBJL. The Harris survey also asked whether the US should try to negotiate an atomic test-ban treaty with the PRC (74 per cent in favour), and whether the government should allow visits (68 per cent in favour).

[54] W. I. Cohen, *Dean Rusk* (Totowa, NJ: Cooper Square, 1980), 168.

[55] *New York Times*, 14 Mar. 1966.

[56] Thomson Papers, FE—Comm. China General, Box 17, President Lyndon B. Johnson on Nationwide Radio and TV, 12 July 1966, JFKL. See also memo from Thomson to Bill Moyers explaining the significance of this speech, Thomson Papers, Speeches 1961–6, Box 11, 12 July 1966, JFKL. Senator Edward Kennedy also began to stake out his position on China, on 20 July applauding Johnson's TV address while advocating specific attention to the UN representation question.

conflict, nevertheless the efficacy of Beijing's model of revolutionary warfare was being tested; with a China that itself offered nothing in the way of reciprocation, indeed had entered into an internal battle during which a militant stance was adopted against both the United States and the Soviet Union—the time for fundamental change had still not come.

Beijing in fact had failed to respond to any of these American gestures in the 1960s. Hilsman's speech, for example, fell foul of the Chinese leadership's view that the Kennedy administration was worse than Eisenhower's, and was certainly more open in its support for two Chinas as Hilsman's statement showed. The fact that his speech acknowledged the permanence of the Communist regime seemed to cut little ice. All references to China in Johnson's TV address were ignored; instead the criticism focused on America's Vietnam policy. Anti-Soviet sentiment was rife in China at this time, of course, but anti-Americanism remained strong, especially given its deep roots within the Chinese leadership. Many of the targets in the Cultural Revolution were those intellectuals who had been denounced for their pro-American sentiment in the anti-rightist campaign in 1957 and singled out as 'waverers' by Mao on the establishment of the PRC in 1949. Such people were, he said, 'easily duped by the honeyed words of the U.S. imperialists as though these imperialists would deal with People's China on the basis of equality and mutual benefit without a stern, long struggle'.[57] In March 1957, when it became clear that the 'Hundred Flowers Movement' was endangering the regime, Mao again recorded his doubts about the degree of support the Party was getting from intellectuals and again noted their pro-American leanings: 'they generally endorse the socialist system, but they haven't completely accepted Marxism as a world outlook. I would say they are not serving the people wholeheartedly, but only halfheartedly. . . . when it comes to foreign countries, I'm afraid they would still say the United States is admirable. "Look, the United States has so much steel. Science in the United States is so advanced." . . . Some of our intellectuals still keep trumpeting how much steel the United States has. Steel! Steel! We must persuade them out of this.'[58]

[57] Mao Zedong, *Selected Works*, iv. 'Cast Away Illusions', 427.
[58] Roderick MacFarquhar, Timothy Cheek, and Eugene Wu, eds., *The Secret Speeches of Chairman Mao: From the Hundred Flowers to the Great Leap Forward*

Such anti-Americanism had been regularly promoted in mass mobilization campaigns, and in schools where children were taught from an early age to sing anti-American songs.[59] Mao's response to the China White Paper of August 1949 had been to pen five widely disseminated articles between 14 August and 16 September 1949 castigating the United States for its China policy.[60] He was not about to reverse this well-established line while his supposed preoccupations in the mid-1960s were with training 'revolutionary successors' and purifying the revolution. As Walt Rostow, the National Security Adviser, was to write in a memorandum to Johnson in February 1968, 'it takes two to play some games, and Peking does not see it in its interest to play, just now'.[61]

Direct Contacts

Richard Nixon was clearly not immune to these shifts in American conceptions of what needed to be done in terms of China policy, and in 1967 set out to articulate his vision of the future in an article in *Foreign Affairs*. 'Taking the long view,' he said, 'we simply cannot afford to leave China forever outside the family of nations, there to nurture its fantasies, cherish its hates, and threaten its neighbors. There is no place on this small planet for a billion of its potentially most able people to live in angry isolation.' It was a statement that in 1967 stood alongside one from Dean Rusk, who had spoken fearfully of a 'billion Chinese, armed with nuclear weapons'.[62] Rusk's statement drew the ire of

(Cambridge, Mass.: Harvard University Press, 1989), 'On Ideological Work', 19 March 1957, 333–4.

[59] It has been argued, for example, that the Chinese bombardment of Jinmen and Mazu in 1954 was accompanied by a 'strident anti-US campaign and a "Liberate Taiwan" campaign at home, which was one of Mao's main interests [in initiating the bombardment] in the first place'. See Gordon H. Chang and He Di, 'The Absence of War in the U.S.–Chinese Confrontation over Quemoy and Matsu in 1954–55: Contingency, Luck, Deterrence', *American Historical Review*, 98, no. 5 (Dec. 1993), 1517. There were many similar such campaigns, notably the 'Resist America and Aid Korea' campaign during the Korean war.

[60] See *Selected Works*, iv, 425–59.

[61] Johnson Papers, Ex-Co 50-2 Box 22, 'Memorandum for the President', 22 Feb. 1968, LBJL.

[62] Cohen, *Dean Rusk*, 280.

administration critics, perhaps prompting the Democratic candidate, Hubert Humphrey, during the election campaign itself to put matters more positively. He expressed the excitement of 'building peaceful bridges to the people of mainland China'. Nixon went further and spoke of the assumption of negotiations not just with the Soviet Union but also 'eventually with the leaders of the next superpower, Communist China'.[63]

Nixon continued to speak out after he had won the election, his inaugural address in January 1969 again referring to China as a large, populous, and nuclear country that could not be left alone. The Beijing leadership began to take notice: Chinese scholars have revealed that Nixon's *Foreign Affairs* article did attract Mao's attention,[64] but the 1969 speech unusually was published in full and entirely accurately in the theoretical journal *Hongqi*, and in the daily newspaper, *Renmin Ribao*. The complete text was also broadcast over the radio and subject to detailed if highly critical analysis for several days thereafter.[65]

Senator Edward Kennedy showed that some Democrats by this time were prepared to do more than simply keep in step with Republicans. He and other Democrats such as Senator Mike Mansfield since the mid-1960s had been identified with a more liberal position on Beijing, but in March 1969 Kennedy showed a willingness to pick up on the public mood more forthrightly. He called for recognition, admission to the United Nations, opening of consular offices, withdrawal of US military forces from Taiwan, the elimination of restrictions on travel and trade, and attempts to involve China in arms control talks. Some twenty-two editorials praised this speech and only four were against,[66] demonstrating how thoroughly the terms of the debate on China had altered by this period. The previous policy had come to be regarded as bankrupt.

[63] UN Archives, Archives of the Office of the Secretary General, PSCA, DAG-1/5.2.2.13, Box 2, 'The PRC', 21 Aug. 1968, p. 12.

[64] For a Chinese account see Zi Zhongyun, 'ZhongMei guanxi da kai zhi qian shi nian jian meiguo dui hua yulun de zhuanbian guocheng' [Gradual Thawing: The Process of Change in American Public Opinion During the Decade Prior to the Opening-Up of Sino–U.S. Relations], in *American Studies*, 1, no. 2 (Summer 1987), esp. 31–2.

[65] BBC Monitoring Reports, *Summary of World Broadcasts*, Far East, no. 2986i, 27 Jan. 1969 and ff.

[66] UN Archives, PSCA, DAG 1/5.2.2.13, Box 2, 'American Attitudes Toward the People's Republic of China', 4 Dec. 1969.

The Nixon administration itself began a series of concrete steps and positive statements which led to further relaxation of the trade and travel bans and termination of the regular Seventh Fleet patrols in the Taiwan Straits. In Nixon's first foreign affairs report to Congress in February 1970, the President described the Chinese as a 'great and vital people' having the 'longest unbroken history of self-government in the world'. A year later he signalled his full acceptance of the Beijing regime by referring to it as the People's Republic of China; and in July went so far as to describe it as becoming within his lifetime one of the 'five great economic superpowers'—a statement that caused enormous excitement among the Beijing leadership.[67]

The Chinese were by 1970 ready to reciprocate, signalling their agreement to the restarting of the ambassadorial talks in Warsaw, Mao appearing on the rostrum with Edgar Snow to review the parade on China's National Day in October 1970, and the Chairman telling Snow in December of his readiness to invite Nixon to China 'either as a tourist or as President'.[68] In April 1971, the Chinese were also willing to invite the US table tennis team to their country, along with news representatives who would not be restricted simply to coverage of the tournament.

Lin Biao, China's Defence Minister and Mao's designated successor, disapproved of the policy of *rapprochement*, which resulted in his attempt to launch a coup d'état and his subsequent death in a plane crash while trying to escape.[69] As Nixon edged

[67] UN Archives, PSCA, DAG 1/5.2.2.13, Box 2, 'Recent Developments in Sino-American Relations', 27 Mar. 1970, and 'Recent Developments in Sino-American Relations', 12 May 1971; Congressional Quarterly, Inc., *China: U.S. Policy Since 1945* (Washington, DC, 1980), 321–2. Interviews conducted in Beijing in Sept. 1993 confirmed that Nixon's July statement generated intense interest. Henry Kissinger also discusses Nixon's remarks in his memoirs: see *White House Years* (Boston: Little, Brown, 1979), 748–9.

[68] Edgar Snow, *The Long Revolution* (London: Hutchison, 1973), 172. This talk with Snow was widely distributed in China, but those examining it focused entirely on the sections reflecting Mao's irritation with those such as Lin Biao, Mao's designated successor, who kept calling him Great Teacher, Great Leader, Great Supreme Commander, and Great Helmsman. 'What a nuisance,' he told Snow in reference to the 'Four Greats' (see 169). Zi, [Gradual Thawing], 32. One specialist on the United States was called back from the May 4th Cadre School in early 1971 to help prepare for the Kissinger visit. This scholar was given Nixon's inaugural speech, his foreign affairs report of 1971, and the discussion between Mao and Snow to read. Interview in Beijing, 27 Sept. 1993.

[69] See e.g. Philip Bridgham, 'The Fall of Lin Piao', in *China Quarterly*, 55 (July–Sept. 1973). Bridgham argues that Lin opposed the *rapprochement* on ideological

towards the historic meetings of 1971 and 1972 he also suffered one major defection from within his circle, but with far less serious consequences. When Vice-President Agnew publicly voiced his opposition to the administration's policy, Nixon instructed Haldeman to tell Agnew to 'stay off this topic'.[70] Other officials saw the moves as being politically advantageous to Nixon: critics of the continuing US role in Vietnam would be thrown into some confusion, public attention would be captured, and the administration would be seen to be in firm command of the international situation.[71] One of the President's not wholly irrational fears was that Democrats such as Senators Muskie, McGovern, and Kennedy would visit Beijing before him: as Kissinger was *en route* from Pakistan to China Nixon told him that he must get a promise out of Premier Zhou that such political rivals would not be invited.[72]

Groups involved in the past in advocating change in China policy continued their activities during the Nixon era. While Catholic Church organizations remained opposed to a *rapprochement*, Protestant ones generally did not. The Committee for a New China Policy, established in October 1969, was chaired by Dr Carl Soule of the United Methodist Church and embraced Episcopalians and those from the United Church of Christ. Jewish organizations were similarly supportive of the development of new ties, and in 1970 the Central Conference of American Rabbis added its voice to those urging that the PRC be brought into the United Nations—this despite the PRC's close identification with the Palestine Liberation Organization.[73]

grounds, as shown by an accusation in *People's Daily*, 1 July 1971, that Mao's line on proletarian internationalism had been subjected to 'interference' from the 'Left'; and by a *Red Flag* article in August 1971 which criticized those opposing Mao's opening to the United States for their 'subjectivism, dogmatism and idealism' (p. 446). Richard Solomon also comments on Chinese hints indicating Lin's opposition. See his 'Chinese Political Negotiating Behaviour: A Briefing Analysis' (Santa Monica, Calif.: Rand, 1985), 7 n. 2.

[70] Uldis Kruze, 'Domestic Constituencies in Nixon's China Policy: A New Look from the National Archives', paper presented at the 1989 Asian Studies on the Pacific Coast Conference, Honolulu, Hawaii, 29 June–2 July 1989, 26.

[71] Robert D. Schulzinger, *Henry Kissinger: Doctor of Diplomacy* (New York: Columbia University Press, 1989), 86.

[72] Ibid. 89; and see Mao's comments to Edgar Snow: Mao did not expect anything to come of his invitation to Nixon before 1972, 'which is an election year'. In a review article by Allen S. Whiting, 'Sino-American *Detente*', *China Quarterly*, 82 (June 1980), 338.

[73] Kruze, 'Domestic Constituencies', 15–18.

Nixon clearly still feared a conservative backlash, however, and once he had announced his intended visit to Beijing he stepped up efforts to woo this group. Although some 67 per cent of the mass public who were polled approved his plan to go to China, Nixon gave high priority to the hosting of bipartisan briefings to include Republican Senators Barry Goldwater, John Tower, Paul Fannin, and Strom Thurmond; and Democratic Senators Robert Byrd, James Eastland, Russell Long, and Herman Talmadge. Former Congressman Walter Judd, one time a leading member of the 'China bloc' in Congress and active still in the 'Committee of One Million', was to be treated with 'firmness' but, if possible, not 'alienated'.[74] Other staunch members of the China bloc seemed to have mellowed somewhat: Knowland, now publisher of the *Oakland Tribune*, offered his 'hopes for the best'. The Veteran's organizations passed a resolution reaffirming their traditional support for Taiwan and their opposition to UN membership for the PRC, yet at the same time expressed their support for the President's trip.[75]

Such careful monitoring and preparation of opinion was damaged when at the time of Kissinger's second visit to Beijing in October 1971, the PRC finally replaced Taiwan in the United Nations. Nixon recorded his concern at Republican reactions: Ronald Reagan, for example, called the UN morally bankrupt, and Barry Goldwater argued that the organization had lost whatever 'small usefulness' it ever had.[76]

Sympathy for Taiwan's plight went well beyond the conservative wing of the Republican Party, however. Certainly Nixon's trip to China in 1972 generated great excitement and high levels of support with 98 per cent of those polled registering that the trip had taken place, the 'highest awareness score for any event within the history of the Gallup poll', and Nixon's own popularity rating rising to 56 per cent, the highest level in fourteen months. Yet, being supportive in these areas did not mean that the public believed Taiwan should be abandoned: as opinion polls continued to demonstrate, some 70 per cent wanted ties to be continued

[74] Ibid. 27–9.

[75] Nixon Presidential Materials Project, White House Central Files, Country Files. (CO), CO 34-2, Box 19, Box 33, July 1971, NA.

[76] Nixon Project, CO 34-2, Box 35, NA. Whiting comments that the Chinese had picked the date for Kissinger's second visit, and the White House had agreed without offering a counter-proposal that 'would have avoided this coincidence of events'. See his 'Sino-American *Detente*', 340.

with the Nationalists, and the public disapproved 7 to 1 of the idea of withdrawing recognition from the regime.[77]

From Rapprochement *to Normalization*

Rapprochement was, then, very much in line with a public that had been advocating involvement with the PRC since the mid-1960s. However, after that a good deal of the momentum went out of the burgeoning Sino-American relationship, once Watergate had been instrumental in removing Nixon from power and age and infirmity had caught up with Mao and Zhou. Moreover, once the North Vietnamese had successfully unified the country under their leadership, a certain hollowness to the *rapprochement* was revealed: Beijing after all had supposedly been enlisted to help control the pace of the final stages of the Vietnam war, allowing at least a 'decent interval' before the inevitable collapse of the south and unification under the Communists.

Within China itself, and despite Lin's downfall, the opening to the United States remained a matter of some controversy. Jiang Qing (Mao's wife) and the group of Shanghai radicals associated with her remained a political force in the country. Premier Zhou came under attack for his so-called opportunism and search for 'white friends', 'big friends', and 'wealthy friends'.[78] Even after Mao's death in September 1976 and the speedy overthrow of the 'Gang of Four', opposition to the policy remained. Deng Xiaoping, clearly committed to normalization of ties, remained politically vulnerable until 1978, and in consequence was unwilling to appear too flexible in his meeting with US Secretary of State, Cyrus Vance, in mid-1977. Allegedly, he reacted furiously when it was leaked in Washington that in fact he had been conciliatory over Taiwan, leading him to deny that the visit had been a success.[79]

Political instabilities in China, and the continuation of the US domestic position supporting American links with both Taiwan

---

[77] Kusnitz, *Public Opinion*, 139–41; Nixon Project, CO 34–2, Box 39, 10 Mar. 1972, NA.

[78] Robert S. Ross, 'International Bargaining and Domestic Politics: U.S.–China Relations Since 1972', *World Politics*, 38, no. 2 (Jan. 1986), 267–8.

[79] Michel Oksenberg, 'A Decade of Sino-American Relations', *Foreign Affairs*, 61 (Fall 1982), 182; Ross, 'International Bargaining and Domestic Politics', 269.

and the PRC, together with a generally warmer public attitude to the Nationalists than the Communists, led Ford to endorse the policy of *rapprochement* but to avoid any new initiatives.[80] The Chinese developments noted above, and domestic differences in Washington also affected the course of Sino-American negotiations during the early Carter years. Despite these constraints, however, Carter came to power convinced of the need to move forward in relations with China. He believed, as Policy Review Memorandum 24 of May 1977 put it, that cultural and economic relations would regress without diplomatic ties, that China would no longer trust US pledges if full normalization did not occur, and that it might decide instead to reduce the threat from the north by seeking a *rapprochement* with Moscow.[81]

Carter's advisers were divided between those, such as the National Security Adviser, Zbigniew Brzezinski, who saw the normalization of relations as a 'key strategic goal' which would work to the US advantage in its global competition with Moscow, and those, such as Cyrus Vance, who wanted to give priority to Salt II, to strengthening NATO, and to restoring momentum to the Middle Eastern and Panama negotiations.[82] Opinion leaders gave indirect support to Vance's position in that they opposed by a massive 93 per cent to 5 per cent the suggestion that Washington accept the PRC's three demands for normalization: an end to US diplomatic ties with Taiwan, withdrawal of US military forces from the island, and the termination of the mutual defence treaty. Additionally, in July 1978, the Senate voted 94 to 0 that it be consulted before that treaty be modified.[83]

With the decision to go forward with the normalization of

---

[80] Michael Yin-mao Kau and Associates, 'Public Opinion and U.S. China Policy,' in Hungdah Chiu, ed., *Normalizing Relations with the People's Republic of China: Problems, Analysis and Documents*, Occasional Papers/Reprint Series in Contemporary Asian Studies, no. 2, 1978 (14), School of Law, Univ. of Maryland; Robert G. Sutter, *The China Quandary: Domestic Determinants of U.S. China Policy 1972–1982* (Boulder, Colo.: Westview, 1983), 3.

[81] Oksenberg, 'A Decade of Sino-American Relations', 182.

[82] Zbigniew Brzezinski, *Power and Principle: Memoirs of the National Security Adviser, 1977–1981* (New York: Farrer, Strauss and Giroux, 1983), 196; Cyrus Vance, *Hard Choices: Critical Years in America's Foreign Policy* (New York: Simon & Schuster, 1983), 75. In an oral history interview, Brzezinski described himself as playing the 'catalytic role' in normalizing relations with China, a role and outcome that obviously gave him enormous satisfaction. Zbigniew Brzezinski, Exit Interview, 20 Feb. 1981, pp. 18–20, JCL.

[83] Kau, 'Public Opinion', 98; Kusnitz, *Public Opinion*, 143.

relations, clearly such an unpromising domestic environment required skilful handling. But there were few indications that the Carter administration intended to try to persuade the public and Congress of the correctness of its stance. Certainly ambassador Leonard Woodcock in the liaison office in Beijing did begin to lobby those visitors to the PRC from the Congress, media, and business groups for an agreement with Beijing based on Carter's terms: that the United States would continue to sell arms to Taiwan, that unofficial cultural and economic ties would continue, and that Washington could make a statement at the time of normalization—that Beijing would not contradict—to the effect that the Taiwan unification issue would be settled peacefully; but in all other respects Congress was perceived as a hurdle to be surmounted, not as an important body to be wooed.

The State Department argued that the best moment for normalization would occur after the November 1978 Congressional elections and before the anticipated fight over the approval of SALT II. Yet the normalization statement released on 15 December still angered many on Capitol Hill. The Republican right was particularly scathing about an administration set 'to sell Taiwan down the river'. Barry Goldwater filed a suit in the Federal Court in Washington D.C. which led the judge to rule that Carter had acted unconstitutionally in rescinding the defence treaty without Senate approval—a ruling that was overturned on appeal. More damaging to the smooth development of Sino-American relations was the passage of the Taiwan Relations Act (TRA) in February 1979, which was more explicit than Carter's negotiators had been on the matter of continued arms sales to Taiwan. It read: 'The United States will make available to Taiwan such defense articles and defense services in such quantity as may be necessary to enable Taiwan to maintain a sufficient self-defense capability.' Carter considered vetoing the TRA, but the numbers supporting it in Congress, 339 to 50 in the House and 85 to 4 in the Senate, suggested that such a veto would easily have been overridden.[84] At this final stage, therefore, the executive had

---

[84] Oksenberg, 'A Decade of Sino-American Relations', 189; Harry Harding, *A Fragile Relationship: The United States and China since 1972* (Washington, DC: The Brookings Institution, 1992), 84–7. During interviews in Beijing in Sept. 1993, a number of specialists on the United States claimed that Carter deliberately instigated the TRA.

become distanced from the views of Congress and the public, denting the authority of a policy that had been debated for so long and that had been so complicated to enact.

China's political culture combined with communist ideology has ensured that policy has been decided at the highest levels and that the population has been mobilized, as necessary, to support it. A series of anti-American campaigns instigated by the centre, reinforced by events such as the Korean fighting and the US role in the protection of Taiwan, ensured a close fit between the leadership's positions towards the United States and societal attitudes, at least as they were outwardly manifested. When the *rapprochement* came, relatively little was done to prepare the Chinese for such an abrupt change of direction. As Zi Zhongyun has written, the 'decision was first made under Mao's authority, only then was there a change in the public debate, everyone studied it and caught up with the idea'. Moreover, if anyone other than Mao had produced such a change, she states, they would have been criticized as a 'rightist'. But once Mao had been directly identified with the decision, 'everyone realized that it would be easy to transform rapidly'.[85]

So it turned out to be, although not without some loss of legitimacy for a Communist leadership that so abruptly changed direction. Although doubts among Chinese leaders have surfaced regularly, at the societal level contact with the United States has tapped into a reservoir of pro-American sentiment, especially among the young. This has shown itself in a great hunger for things American, whether that is the Voice of America, or the desire to study in the United States. Between 1979 and 1988 some 56,000 students and scholars visited America, many recording their fascination with this 'mysterious land'[86] previously denied to them.

Similarly, although not necessarily for the same reasons, there has frequently been a close fit between American governmental policies towards China and views held within the wider society.

[85] Zi, [Gradual Thawing], 32.

[86] For discussion of this and of generational differences see David L. Shambaugh, 'Anti-Americanism in China', Annals of the *American Academy of Political and Social Science*, 497 (May 1988); Yuan Ming, 'Chinese Intellectuals and the United States: The Dilemma of Individualism vs. Patriotism', *Asian Survey*, 29, no. 7 (July 1989).

In the 1950s, this served to strengthen and harden America's stance in negotiations with primary allies who desired a less rigid China policy, and to enhance the authority of that policy in the domestic environment.

During the Truman era, it was relatively simple for administration and domestic attitudes to keep in step, Chinese entry into the Korean conflict guaranteeing a hostile perception of the Beijing regime. During Eisenhower's period, when minority voices spoke in favour of a greater flexibility in policy, Eisenhower, over the UN question, and Dulles, more broadly, both made public statements designed to bolster their inflexible position. Given Eisenhower's domestic popularity, this generally proved effective, except over the crisis involving the Offshore Islands. Only in the Kennedy period did bureaucratic changes allow for a consolidation of expertise and new thinking at middle levels of the bureaucracy; but such experts could not yet bind together with those in Congress, the media, and interest groups who wanted change to come about.

During the Johnson era administration policies became more distant from Congressional, public, and media attitudes, and it was then in particular that China policy began to lose its domestic legitimacy. Domestic groups still feared China, still saw it overwhelmingly as a state that was disruptive of world order; nevertheless, they paid heed to the longevity of the regime in Beijing, its entry into the nuclear club, and its attraction as a trading partner for America's allies. Thus, it was a relatively uncontroversial matter for Johnson to call for reconciliation with former enemies, although the specific details of that reconciliation could not be taken far while US involvement in Vietnam remained at a high level, and the Chinese themselves began their Cultural Revolution and a period of isolation.

Nixon's inheritance was, then, a powerful one in the domestic realm. As James Thomson has described it, perhaps understating that inheritance, it comprised a 'talented and well-trained China bureaucracy dedicated to innovation; a decade-old "laundry list" of possible U.S. initiatives towards China and a great deal of internal paper to support them; at least one specific policy shift, on the matter of China travel; a gradually evolving rhetorical foundation for a new China policy; and clear indications, in response to Democratic incrementalism, that the American public was probably ready and willing to move towards accommodation with Peking.'[87] In many respects, therefore, Nixon's moves towards the PRC served to regain a significant domestic consensus, already severely weakened over Asian policy as a result of the Vietnam experience, but additionally damaged by the maintenance of a policy that had come to be seen as lacking legitimacy and as difficult to justify.

Even with these clear signs of a desire for change, Nixon moved forward cautiously, testing the level of Chinese interest, but also ensuring that conservatives at home would not turn on him. In a number of respects, the two Presidents that came after Nixon experienced the backlash that Nixon feared, the first because of the unrealistic expectations that had been raised about the Sino-American *rapprochement*, and the second because at a time when Congress still desired to play a more central role in the foreign policy-making process, when public opinion polls demonstrated that Taiwan was still considered to be deserving of support, Carter chose to ignore those who advised him to consult seriously the legislative branch. If in the Johnson era policy had lagged behind public sentiment, in the Carter era it had moved too far ahead of it, thus casting a shadow over this final, formal stage.

[87] Thomson, 'On the Making of U.S. China Policy', 243.

5

Balancing Against Threats: The Rise and Fall of the Sino-Soviet Alliance

The Sino-Soviet Treaty of Friendship, Alliance, and Mutual Assistance signed in February 1950 represented one of the most significant formal alliances of the post-war era. It promised *inter alia* that the two contracting parties would 'consult together on all important international questions involving the common interests of the Soviet Union and China', 'develop and strengthen the economic and cultural ties' between them, and 'render each other all possible economic assistance'. It also pledged in its most significant clause that 'should either of the Contracting Parties be attacked by Japan or by States allied with Japan and thus find itself in a state of war, the other Contracting Party shall immediately extend military and other assistance with all the means at its disposal'.[1] For the new government in Beijing, such a pledge represented a significant enhancement of its security at a time of high cold-war tension, and a means of counteracting what it saw as the major threat to its survival, the United States. Furthermore, the alliance portended the augmentation of its economic, political, and military capabilities after a century of decline and perceived national humiliation.

For the United States, the voluntary movement by the Chinese Communists into the Soviet-controlled bloc, at a time when its relationship with Moscow tended to be viewed in zero-sum terms, represented an adverse shift in the balance against the threat posed by the Communist bloc to the vulnerable, East Asian theatre. The mighty Sino-Soviet alliance seemed to stand in stark contrast to the uneasy and untidy relationships that the United

[1] This translation of the treaty is taken from Xue Mouhong and Pei Jianzhang, eds., *Diplomacy of Contemporary China* (Hong Kong: New Horizon Press, 1990), 491–3. As such, it differs slightly from the translation given elsewhere, e.g. Raymond L. Garthoff, ed., *Sino-Soviet Military Relations*, Appendix A (New York: Praeger, 1966).

States had with such putative allies as the Japanese, the South Koreans, and the Nationalists on Taiwan. Moreover, during the period when the alliance functioned relatively smoothly, many Americans' former perceptions of China as a weak and chaotic country were transformed. The country instead came to be viewed as a land of burgeoning power, with enormous potential that, with Soviet help, was on the verge of being realized.

Within ten years, however, the alliance between the PRC and Soviet Union no longer appeared operable, as interests diverged and Moscow as the dominant partner found it increasingly more difficult to constrain the behaviour of its ally.[2] Some twenty years after that, on 11 April 1980, the Sino-Soviet treaty formally expired, three months after the US Defense Secretary, Harold Brown, had been in Beijing, where he suggested that China and the United States planned to 'facilitate wide cooperation on security matters', in order to remind others that 'if they threaten the shared interests of the United States and China, we can respond with complementary actions in the field of defense as well as diplomacy'.[3] A quasi-alliance between Washington and Beijing seemed in 1980 to have come into being, representing a dramatic change in international strategic relationships over the course of the cold-war era. As later events were to show, the basis of that co-operation was not as firm as Brown's comments had implied; nevertheless, the reversal in alignments after 1972 represented a substantial gain to the United States at a time when many had been reflecting upon the apparent loss in America's relative power.

This chapter focuses on US perceptions of Chinese power during successive phases in the Sino-Soviet relationship: the per-

[2] Work on alliances has proven helpful to the understanding of the Sino-Soviet relationship. It argues *inter alia* that most alliances are formed to balance against threats, threats which are a function of 'power, geographical proximity, offensive capabilities, and perceived intentions'. Once formed, they provide one means by which an alliance partner, the dominant partner, can restrain the behaviour of other alliance members. The strength and longevity of alliances depend on the extent to which interests remain convergent and affinities remain present, thus reducing to an acceptable level the need for restraint. See e.g. Stephen M. Walt, *The Origins of Alliances* (Ithaca, NY: Cornell University Press, 1986), p. vi; Robert E. Osgood, *Alliances and American Foreign Policy* (Baltimore: Johns Hopkins University Press, 1968), 19–20.
[3] Quoted in A. Doak Barnett, *China's Economy in Global Perspective* (Washington, DC: Brookings Institution, 1981), 554.

ceived impact of the alliance on China's capabilities and levels of security; the effects of its demise on Beijing and on the socialist bloc more generally; and finally the consequences of its eventual replacement in the 1970s by a tacit alignment between China and the United States.

The Formation of the Alliance

Chinese leaders began to consider building a closer, more formalized relationship with the Soviet Union from September 1948 for reasons associated with ideology, national security, and regime security.[4] The decision to lean towards the Soviet Union and eventually to sign a treaty with it was the logical outcome of a perception that the Chinese revolution was an inseparable part of the Soviet-led revolutionary struggle on behalf of progressive forces. Chinese leaders at this time also believed the United States might well intervene in support of the Chinese Nationalists in the final stages of the civil war. Even as the Truman administration failed to act, and as that immediate fear of US intervention receded, Washington was still seen as a long-term threat to the revolution. In China's view it was, after all, an imperialist power that would not readily be reconciled to the establishment of a progressive regime but, instead, might seek to attack China from without or, more probably, to subvert its revolution from within. To that end, Washington might try to use those within China who still hankered after a more independent and neutral stance in international affairs—those whom Mao called the 'middle-of-the-roaders or right-wingers . . . They are the supporters of what Acheson calls "democratic individualism"', Mao claimed, affording the United States 'a flimsy social base in China'.[5]

---

[4] Chen Jian, 'The Sino-Soviet Alliance and China's Entry into the Korean War', Working Paper no. 1, *Cold War International History Project*, Woodrow Wilson International Center for Scholars, Washington, DC, pp. 8 ff. For a discussion which places greater weight on the elements of *realpolitik* and national interest in the relationship, see Sergei N. Goncharov, John W. Lewis, and Xue Litai, *Uncertain Partners: Stalin, Mao, and the Korean War* (Stanford, Calif.: Stanford University Press, 1993).

[5] Mao Zedong, 'Cast Away Illusions, Prepare for Struggle', *Selected Works*, iv (Beijing: Foreign Languages Press, 1969), 427.

The material benefits of the 'lean to one side' decision came quickly. Two days after Mao had made his speech on that theme, Liu Shaoqi travelled to Moscow. During the course of that visit Stalin offered help to the People's Liberation Army (PLA) in gaining control of the strategically sensitive province of Xinjiang, agreed to the supply of Yak fighters and heavy bombers, and assistance with training Chinese pilots and technicians in schools to be established in Manchuria. General Zhang Aiping quickly followed on from Liu and he discussed Soviet aid in the development of a Chinese navy.[6] Mao's visit to Moscow in December 1949 was to push these contacts on to a significantly higher plane. The Chinese now wanted to establish a formal alliance in order to give greater precision to the relationship, as well as to replace the 1945 treaty between the Chinese Nationalists and the Soviet Union.

Once in Moscow, Mao's task was to set out the broad outlines of a treaty, leaving Premier Zhou Enlai to work out the details.[7] China wanted, in Mao's words, and much to the amusement of Beria, the Minister of Internal Affairs, something that 'would look pleasant outside and taste nice inside'.[8] When Zhou Enlai arrived in the Soviet capital on 20 January 1950, greater content was given to this statement, especially with respect to the military relationship between the two allies. As the text of the Sino-Soviet treaty began to emerge, Zhou did not consider the paragraph dealing with military obligations to be firm enough. In its original form it read: 'In the event that one of the Contracting Parties was invaded by a third state, the other Contracting Party shall render assistance.' Zhou sought the addition of the phrase 'by all the means at its disposal', which hardened the commitment and implied a future willingness on the Soviet part to use its developing nuclear weapons capability in support of its new ally.[9] Stalin, on the other

[6] Chen, 'The Sino-Soviet Alliance', 15; Bo Yibo, 'The Making of the "Lean-to-one-side" Decision', tr. by Zhai Qiang, *Chinese Historians*, 5, no. 1 (Spring 1992).

[7] Goncharov *et al.*, *Uncertain Partners*, 82, and chs. 3 and 4.

[8] *International Affairs* (Moscow) (Nov. 1990), 115. Chen, in 'The Sino-Soviet Alliance', translates Mao's statement as follows: 'For this trip we hope to bring about something that not only looks nice but also tastes delicious' (p. 17).

[9] Excerpts from Wu Xiuquan's memoirs in *Beijing Review*, 26, no. 47 (21 Nov. 1983), 18. According to Wu, the phrase was 'discussed and disputed for quite some time'. Note that Wu's rendering of the military clause differs in other respects from that provided in the publication *Diplomacy of Contemporary China*.

hand, made Soviet assistance to China in the event of an attack conditional on the formal declaration of 'a state of war'.[10]

Although the negotiation of this treaty was clearly a sobering experience for the Chinese delegation (as Wu Xiuquan later put it, 'all the symptoms' of Soviet expansionism and hegemonism were there 'in the period of Stalin'[11]), a subsequent semi-official Chinese publication has come to describe the new treaty as being of 'great significance in preserving the security of both sides, maintaining peace in the Far East, and the world as a whole, strengthening the friendship between the two peoples and promoting the cause of socialist construction of the two countries'. Beijing also believes that it was one of the factors that prevented US extension of the Korean war into Chinese territory.[12] And although China had to pay for the *matériel* the Soviet Union provided to its forces during that war, at least Moscow did make available equipment for more than sixty army divisions and ten air-force divisions. It also provided 80 per cent of the ammunition for the Chinese 'Volunteer' forces and, though concerned about possible US retaliation, it reluctantly and fearfully allowed its airmen to take part in actual combat operations.[13]

Post-Korea, the Soviet Union additionally gave concrete assistance to China in the nuclear weapons field. Chinese and Soviet strategic thinking had come into line in 1955, with China echoing Soviet writings on pre-emptive and surprise attacks arising out of developments in tactical weapons and technological developments in delivery systems. In January 1955, and in light of its recent experience of US atomic threats, China took its decision to acquire its own nuclear arsenal with Soviet assistance. Moscow duly announced publicly its intention to give aid to China to help with research into the peaceful uses of atomic energy, and secretly the two allies agreed to undertake joint exploration for uranium in China. By 1957, this developing relationship in the nuclear area produced a secret agreement, the 'Sino-Soviet New Defense Technical Accord', in which Moscow 'agreed to supply China the

[10] Goncharov *et al.*, *Uncertain Partners*, ch. 3 and p. 211.

[11] *Beijing Review* (21 Nov. 1983), 21.

[12] Xue and Pei, eds., *Diplomacy*, 35–6.

[13] Details of the equipment transfer are contained in Zhai Zhihai and Hao Yufan, 'China's Decision to Enter the Korean War: History Revisited', *China Quarterly*, 121 (Mar. 1990), 111–12. For details on Russian air activity see n. 24 below.

prototype atomic bomb and missiles as well as related technical data'.[14]

Certainly, the specific testing of the Sino-Soviet alliance during the first crisis in the Taiwan Straits in 1954–5 revealed some of its deficiencies (the Soviet government gave no explicit commitment to aid the Chinese in the event of a direct US attack on the mainland); nevertheless, given the essentially political objectives that were behind China's decision to attack the Offshore Islands at this time, this failure to offer an explicit guarantee or to threaten Washington does not seem to have been a major source of tension in the relationship. As the Chinese leadership stated in February 1955, on the fifth anniversary of the signature of the Sino-Soviet treaty, the friendship and alliance between Moscow and Beijing was playing a vital role in guaranteeing peace, it was 'a great peace treaty', and by implication not a treaty that raised global tensions.[15]

US Assessments in the First Phase

There were several strands to the American understanding of Sino-Soviet relations in the late 1940s and early 1950s. As the Chinese civil war was nearing its close, the argument that had arisen from within the Policy Planning Staff (PPS) predominated. John Paton Davies, the China specialist, and George Kennan, the director of the PPS, described the impending Chinese Communist victory as 'regrettable' though not 'catastrophic' to US interests. They believed that China would be in a weak and chaotic condition for some time to come and thus that victory in the civil war, rather than representing a vast accretion of power to the communist bloc, could actually prove debilitating, especially to Moscow. Moreover, the PPS believed that Soviet leaders faced an

[14] John Wilson Lewis and Xue Litai, *China Builds the Bomb* (Stanford, Calif.: Stanford University Press, 1988), 40–1, 62. Lewis and Xue record the hesitancy and haggling that the Soviets from the start engaged in this area of the relationship. See esp. p. 62. The nuclear weapons debate is covered more extensively in my Ch. 7.

[15] Michael Y. M. Kau and John K. Leung, eds., *The Writings of Mao Zedong, 1949–1976*, i., *Sept. 1949–Dec. 1955*, 'tel. to USSR, Feb. 12 1955' (Armonk, NY: Sharpe, Inc., 1986), 519–21. Details of China's objectives during the first Offshore Islands crisis are contained in He Di, 'The Evolution of the People's Republic of China's Policy Toward the Offshore Islands', in Warren I. Cohen and Akira Iriye, eds., *The Great Powers in East Asia, 1953–1960* (New York: Columbia University Press, 1990).

enormous task in trying to bring the Chinese Communists under control. Mao had 'Titoist tendencies', which might soon cause problems between his regime and Moscow. As National Security Council (NSC) document 34 of 13 October 1948 put it, potentially Mao was even more of a heretic than Tito because he had been 'entrenched in power for nearly ten times the length of time'.[16]

Mao's 'lean to one side' speech in June 1949, and then the signature of the alliance in February 1950 did cause alarm, however, and brought into question this perception of Chinese power and of Sino-Soviet relations. Davies read the June speech as an indication that the more pragmatic Chinese leaders—such as Zhou Enlai—had lost out to the pro-Soviets—such as Liu Shaoqi.[17] For some US officials, the signature of the alliance ended even medium-term prospects for any improvement in US relations with China and undermined the arguments of those counselling the administration to wait for the dust to settle in the country and for the Sino-Soviet relationship to founder.[18] True, the negotiations had taken over two months to complete, did not contain the generous provisions of aid the Chinese might have expected, and contained territorial provisions that the Chinese were believed to have resented.[19] Yet, there was still the problem of the passivity of the current US policy: when would Sino-Soviet hostility manifest itself? Would it be, as the US Secretary of State, Dean Acheson, had suggested in December 1949, in six to twelve year's time?[20]—a time-scale which in itself made the current policy line vulnerable.

[16] Gordon H. Chang, *Friends and Enemies: The United States, China, and the Soviet Union, 1948–1972* (Stanford, Calif.: Stanford University Press, 1990), 14; Wilson D. Miscamble, *George Kennan and the Making of American Foreign Policy, 1947–1950* (Princeton, NJ: Princeton University Press, 1992), 224–6; Rosemary Foot, *The Wrong War: American Policy and the Dimensions of the Korean Conflict, 1950–1953* (Ithaca, NY: Cornell University Press, 1985), 46.

[17] Miscamble, *George Kennan*, 235.

[18] For a discussion of this latter argument see Nancy B. Tucker, *Patterns in the Dust: Chinese–American Relations and the Recognition Controversy 1949–1950* (New York: Columbia University Press, 1983); Warren I. Cohen, 'Acheson, His Advisers, and China, 1949–1950', in Dorothy Borg and Waldo Heinrichs, eds., *Uncertain Years: Chinese–American Relations, 1947–1950* (New York: Columbia University Press, 1980).

[19] Foot, *The Wrong War*, 47.

[20] *Foreign Relations of the United States, 1949* (Washington, DC: Government Printing Office, 1974), 9: 466, 29 Dec. 1949.

Despite these doubts about its timing, the expectations of a rift between China and the Soviet Union at some point in the future remained in place during both the Truman and Eisenhower administrations. This perspective always gave a conditional quality to the Sino-Soviet alliance as far as the United States was concerned. Dulles, at his least optimistic, was to speak of national rivalries manifesting themselves within 100 years; on another occasion he spoke of having to wait twenty-five years, and on yet another of the break-up possibly coming within a year, but then adding quickly 'it might be some years away'. Vice-President Richard M. Nixon had predicted that it would take twenty-five to fifty years.[21] The best hope for intensifying the rift, Dulles told the British and French in December 1953, was to 'keep the Chinese under maximum pressure rather than relieving such pressure'. This would cause them to increase their demands on the Soviets, 'which the latter would be unable to meet and the strain would consequently increase'.[22]

However, implicit in this view of the alliance and in the need to split it apart was, first, that it would remain in place when cold-war tensions were likely to remain high, and secondly that despite its conditionality this alignment did matter—it had indeed tipped the balance of power in Asia in favour of America's strategic enemy. In consequence, the United States closely observed the relationship in order to determine the extent to which it improved China's power resources; the degree of control the Soviets exercised in the relationship; and the frequency with which interests converged or diverged.

As noted above, during the course of the Korean conflict, the Soviet Union transferred a vast amount of military equipment to the Chinese. In the view of an NSC staff study compiled at the end of 1951, this demonstrated that the Soviet Union was 'exerting substantial effort to create a well-trained, well-armed and effec-

---

[21] *Foreign Relations, 1955–7* (Washington, DC: Government Printing Office, 1986), 3: 292, 31 Jan. 1956; John Lewis Gaddis, 'The American "Wedge" Strategy', in Harry Harding and Yuan Ming, eds., *Sino-American Relations, 1945–1955: a Joint Reassessment of a Critical Decade* (Wilmington, Del.: Scholarly Resources Inc., 1989), 173; Gaddis, 'The Unexpected John Foster Dulles: Nuclear Weapons, Communism, and the Russians', in Richard H. Immerman, ed., *John Foster Dulles and the Diplomacy of the Cold War* (Princeton, NJ: Princeton University Press, 1990), 63.
[22] *Foreign Relations, 1952–4* (Washington, DC: Government Printing Office, 1979), 5: 1808–18, 7 Dec. 1953.

tive Chinese fighting force to strengthen the military capabilities of the Sino-Soviet partnership'. US intelligence determined that over a thousand jet aircraft had been made available and that an estimated 90 per cent of the ground force equipment and munitions were Soviet-supplied. A year after the war's end, Chinese air-force strength was estimated at more than 1,500 planes.[23] Moreover, it was also established during the course of that war that Russian airmen were taking part in combat operations in support of their Chinese and North Korean allies, a fact that Washington denied at the time for fear that the American public, as Paul Nitze subsequently put it, 'would expect us to do something about it and the last thing we wanted was for the war to spread to more serious conflict with the Soviets'.[24]

The Soviet contribution went well beyond the provision of *matériel* and training of Chinese armed forces, however. US studies noted that in these early years it also took the form of technical rehabilitation of Chinese industry, transportation systems, mining, and power generation. In the political field, the Soviets supported Chinese membership of the UN and acknowledged 'their status as a great power'.[25] It seemed apparent to Washington that China's resources had increased substantially as a result of its decision to lean to one side.

However, while this enhancement of its power and of that of the socialist bloc more generally was plain, there were some elements that detracted from this overall increase in Chinese and bloc capabilities. For example, the bolstering of China's great-power status had a double-edged quality to it. While it improved the security of both Beijing and Moscow, it could also represent a potential source of friction between the two communist allies. The same US study that had noted the Soviet contribution to China's *matériel* and political status also remarked that the

[23] *Foreign Relations*, 1952–4 (Washington, DC: Government Printing Office, 1985), 14: 290, 6 Nov. 1953, 'NSC Staff Study of US Policy Towards Communist China'; *Foreign Relations*, 1952–4, 14: 453, 3 June 1954, Table 11, National Intelligence Estimate, 'Communist China's Power Potential Through 1957'.

[24] Nitze quoted in Jon Halliday, 'Air Operations in Korea: The Soviet Side of the Story', in William J. Williams, ed., *A Revolutionary War: Korea and the Transformation of the Postwar World* (Chicago: Imprint Publications, 1993), 160. Nitze, at the time director of the Policy Planning Staff, was asked to write a paper entitled 'Removing the Fig Leaf from the Hard Core of Soviet Responsibility'. He recommended a cover-up.

[25] *Foreign Relations*, 1952–4, 14: 296, 6 Nov. 1953.

Russians 'could hardly view with equanimity the development of an independent China on its frontiers which was powerful, well armed, industrially competent, and politically united'.[26] China's military successes in Korea, and the death of Stalin and consequent rise in Mao's prestige, all had to be accommodated. The Soviets own acknowledgement that the Chinese had a part to play in determining communist policy in Asia—as shown by Moscow's sponsorship of Beijing's attendance at the 1954 Geneva conference—required the Soviets to consult the Chinese but also led them to attempt constraint where attitudes and policies differed. John Foster Dulles thought he had picked up hints of both these elements in the relationship in conversations with Molotov, the Soviet Foreign Minister, during the Berlin conference in February that year.[27] In conversations between the US Under-Secretary of State, Walter Bedell Smith, and Molotov in Geneva, Smith had commented on the US sense of a Chinese lack of restraint. Molotov had replied that China 'was still a very young country, and you must also remember that China is always going to be China, she is never going to be European'. He also remarked that, one day, it would become known that 'in the Korean matter the Soviet Union had acted as a restraining influence'.[28] What made the relationship potentially even more difficult was that the ability to constrain was diminishing not increasing over the course of the 1950s, and lessened still further after the revolts in Poland and Hungary in 1956 had led Khrushchev to call on his Chinese ally for support and counsel.

Such a prominent role in bloc affairs dramatically illustrated that China's soft power had increased alongside its hard-power resources. In a US assessment, 'the tone of authority in the Chinese Communist statements and the need apparently felt by the Kremlin for Chinese support on Eastern European issues have made a deep impression on the Communist world, and have

---

[26] Ibid.

[27] *Foreign Relations*, 1952–4, 14: 366, 26 Feb. 1954. Dulles reported orally: 'They treat the Chinese Communist regime as a partner who has to be consulted and, in certain instances, even restrained by persuasion and by economic pressures. It seems quite possible that the Soviet Union is worried over the possibility of new aggression by the Chinese Communists. The Soviets are anxious to avoid a major war, and they realize that the Chinese Communists are in a position to initiate such a war if they choose to do so.'

[28] Dulles–Herter files, Box 2, 23 May 1954, DDEL.

further weakened the concept that Moscow is the only authoritative interpreter of Communist ideological guidance'.[29]

The rise in Chinese prestige and related lessening of its dependence on Moscow was significant in the Eisenhower administration's view because it would allow for the emergence of basic conflicts of interest between the two allies. More negatively, however, and perhaps of greater moment, it could lead eventually to the development of a disruptive period in the global system. Leaving aside Sino-Soviet tensions concerning rival territorial claims, or the 'niggardly' nature of Soviet economic assistance,[30] in terms of bloc policy towards the non-communist world, it was assumed that Soviet caution and desire to preserve gains 'already won' would soon conflict with Chinese 'headier revolutionary elan'. This condition, in combination with Beijing's intention to restore the country's traditional great-power status, implied that China represented an ambitious, anti-*status quo* power. Furthermore, whereas Soviet interests were world-wide, Chinese interests for the most part were confined to Asia. This would lead the former to weigh the impact of conflict in Asia on developments in the more significant European and Middle Eastern theatres, whereas the latter might grow impatient with such cautious deliberation.[31]

Washington's assessment of this difference in world outlooks inevitably affected its appraisal of the alliance itself. During the Korean conflict, its conditional nature had been noted: for example, the Truman and Eisenhower administrations determined that the Soviets would not risk global war, would not risk coming openly to China's support, unless the overthrow of the Chinese Communist government appeared imminent.[32] At the time of the first Offshore Islands crisis in 1954–5, the Eisenhower administration concluded that the Soviet Union's entire discussion of the crisis 'had been characterized by a withholding of

[29] *Foreign Relations*, 1955–7, 3: 502, 19 Mar. 1957. NIE, 'Communist China Through 1961'.

[30] A word used to describe the new Sino-Soviet economic aid agreements signed in October 1954. See *Foreign Relations*, 1952–4, 14: 776, 18 Oct. 1954.

[31] *Foreign Relations*, 1952–4, 14: 103, 10 Sept. 1952, and 14: 404, 6 Apr. 1954, 'Relations between the Chinese Communist Regime and the USSR', and 'The Sino-Soviet Relationship and its Potential Sources of Differences'.

[32] Intelligence estimates constantly reiterated this point throughout the Korean conflict. See Rosemary Foot, *The Wrong War, passim.*

commitment or of official support for the Chinese "liberation" program'. No Soviet source had cited the treaty of alliance. When a US correspondent attempted to cable a dispatch that quoted Khrushchev to the effect that there needed to be a common struggle with the Chinese against US aggression, the censor insisted that he amend it to 'reflect Khrushchev's "actual position": Mr. Khrushchev had said that the Chinese Communist "liberation" of Taiwan had the sympathy of the Soviet people, not the support of the Soviet government'.[33] Eisenhower himself believed that while the Soviets would 'pour supplies into China' they would not go to war over Taiwan.[34] Part of the explanation for Dulles's early recommendation that the crisis be taken to the United Nations was that such action would seriously strain Sino-Soviet relations: if the Soviets used the veto, this would 'gravely impair' their peaceful coexistence policy; if they did not, the Chinese would not react well.[35]

Nevertheless, it was not until the late 1950s that evidence started to accumulate that Sino-Soviet interests were diverging in more fundamental ways, reducing bloc unity and Chinese levels of security. Although during the 1958 crisis, President Eisenhower appeared to have reversed his 1955 view, arguing instead that the Soviet Union not only supported the Chinese position but also was behind their efforts to raise tension, and Dulles believed Beijing and Moscow were jointly probing Washington's resolve, US intelligence advisers were of a different opinion. As the crisis unfolded and a wider war became a possibility, the Director of the Central Intelligence Agency (CIA), Allen Dulles, and his staff came to conclude that Moscow was concerned about China's bellicosity and was desperate to avoid a devastating conflict (an assessment that is now given wide support in Soviet and Chinese sources).[36]

---

[33] RG 59, Policy Planning Staff Office Files, Lot 66D70, Box 66, 23 May 1955, NA.

[34] Chang, *Friends and Enemies*, 131.

[35] Gaddis, 'The Unexpected John Foster Dulles', 62.

[36] Chang, *Friends and Enemies*, 187–8 and 199–200. Qiang Zhai, *The Dragon, the Lion, and the Eagle: Chinese–British–American Relations, 1949–1958* (Kent, Ohio: Kent State University Press, 1994), 199. According to Chinese sources, in Aug. 1958, prior to the shelling of the Offshore Islands, China had informed the Soviet Union about its proposed bombardment of Jinmen and Mazu. Soviet leaders were reportedly 'apprehensive', seeing in China's actions the possible destruction of 'their plan of Soviet–U.S. cooperation for world domination and that it might even lead to a possible Soviet–U.S. conflict'. When Gromyko came secretly to Beijing in early

Even though the US Secretary of State believed Beijing and Moscow to have co-ordinated their activities, he did not think formal treaty commitments were likely to be invoked. In one of the few direct references that Washington seems to have made to the Sino-Soviet alliance during this period, John Foster Dulles, in the course of a confidential background press briefing, argued that in the event of US bombing of Chinese air bases, the Soviets 'might or might not think it was expedient to come to the help of China under those circumstances. I don't think they would do it merely because of a treaty obligation.'[37] Later, after action in the Straits had abated, assumptions about tensions in the relationship grew firmer. The US embassy in Moscow reported that American efforts to tie Moscow to this 'reckless' behaviour of the Chinese had led Khrushchev in October 1959 to reject his country's responsibility for the acts of a 'fully sovereign' People's Republic of China, even as he reaffirmed the Chinese Communists' right to Taiwan.[38]

In these tests of the Sino-Soviet alliance, therefore, and where China was effectively involved in direct conflict with the United States, Washington affirmed that Soviet support for the PRC was

Sept., Chinese leaders allegedly reassured him that China 'would undertake all the consequences by itself and would not get the Soviet Union involved' (a recollection that is seriously at odds with that suggested in Gromyko's memoirs). Only then did Khrushchev write to Eisenhower stating that US retaliation against China would invite a Soviet response. Subsequently in China to celebrate the tenth anniversary of the establishment of the PRC, the Soviet leader apparently called for the abandonment of the use of armed force in the recovery of Taiwan, and 'hinted broadly' that China should consider temporarily a two-Chinas solution. Gromyko's alternative formulation claims that Mao had stated that if the United States attacked China with nuclear weapons, the Chinese armies would 'retreat from the border regions into the depths of the country. They must draw the enemy in deep so as to grip U.S. forces in a pincer inside China.' Mao's advice to the Soviets, according to Gromyko, was that 'in the event of war, the Soviet Union should not take any military measures against the Americans in the first stage. Instead, you should let them penetrate deep inside the territory of the Chinese giant. Only when the Americans are right in the central provinces, should you give them everything you've got.' Gromyko speedily declined the suggestion. See Andrei Gromyko, *Memories* (London: Hutchinson, 1989), 322–3. For the Chinese side see Xue and Pei, eds., *Diplomacy of Contemporary China*, 143–4; Lewis and Xue, *China Builds the Bomb*, 72.

[37] John Foster Dulles Papers, White House Memo Series, Box 7, News Conference, 4 Sept. 1958, DDEL.

[38] Dwight D. Eisenhower, Papers as President of the United States, 1956–61, Ann Whitman File (hereafter Ann Whitman File), Dulles–Herter Series, Box 10, telegram from Moscow embassy to Sec. of State, 31 Oct. 1959, DDEL.

indeed qualified. Furthermore, even in areas where the stakes were lower, it was obvious to the American administration that Chinese and Soviet policies were divergent and that Soviet support was not likely to be forthcoming. With respect to India, for example, where Moscow's behaviour—according to Chinese sources—was such as to make its differences with Beijing 'public to the world',[39] Allen Dulles noted in September 1959 that the Soviets were anxious to see the conflict between New Delhi and Beijing settled. The US embassy in Moscow recorded Khrushchev's 'absolutely neutral position' on the border skirmishes which the Soviet leader 'deeply regretted'. At the Bucharest meeting in June 1960, it had become known that the Soviet News Agency, TASS, had refused to handle the business of its Chinese counterpart in New Delhi when the latter had been thrown out of the country. To add insult to injury, the CIA noted that Moscow had also 'offered helicopters to India which it knew would be used on the Chinese frontier'.[40]

Washington had additionally been informed by October 1960 of Chinese reluctance to consolidate ties in the military field: secret monitoring of Khrushchev's speech to satellite leaders meeting in New York that month revealed to the Eisenhower administration that the Chinese had refused to allow Soviet submarines access to bases in their harbours.[41]

In addition to these specific conflicts of interest between Moscow and Beijing, and lack of military co-ordination, Washington also focused on the more general divergence of view between the two allies, differences that had far-reaching implications for bloc policy. The points at issue charted in 1959 and 1960 by the US

[39] Xue and Pei, eds., *Diplomacy*, 144.

[40] Ann Whitman File, NSC Series, Box 11, 10 Sept. 1959; Dulles–Herter Series, Box 10, 31 Oct. 1959; NSC Series, Box 13, 18 Aug. 1960; all at DDEL.

[41] Ann Whitman File, NSC series, Box 13, 20 Oct. 1960, DDEL. In fact, disputes in the conventional military field apparently went well beyond this, with the Chinese rejecting a Soviet suggestion for joint construction of a long-wave radio transmission centre and a radio receiving centre for long-range communications designed for commanding Soviet submarines in the Pacific; and the suggestion for the building of a joint submarine fleet. See Xue and Pei, eds., *Diplomacy*, 141–2. Mao is reported to have stated in connection with this suggestion: 'The question of sovereignty may not be bargained or negotiated to the slightest degree.' Later, he stated that the Soviet offer was an attempt 'to block the China seacoast, to launch a joint fleet in China to dominate the coastal area, and to blockade us'. Quoted in Lowell Dittmer, *Sino-Soviet Normalization and its International Implications, 1945–1990* (Seattle: University of Washington Press, 1992), 178.

intelligence community concerned the inevitability of war, the prospects for peaceful coexistence, the peaceful intentions of the West, and the possibility of a peaceful transition to socialism. Khrushchev's speech on the tenth anniversary of the establishment of the PRC was interpreted as implying that a 'test of force between communism and capitalism would be wrong', a view that Washington noted had quickly been contradicted by China's Minister of Defence. The Bucharest meeting in June 1960, in the US intelligence community's view, provided the most serious evidence of friction to date. There the Soviet Party Secretary argued forcefully that 'only madmen and maniacs can speak of a new world war'. In defence of his revision of Lenin's position on the inevitability of war, Khrushchev 'charged those who abided by letter of Lenin's utterances [were] no further along mentally than were children learning the alphabet'.[42] In Khrushchev's review of the dispute for satellite leaders in October 1960, he accused the Chinese of refusing to understand that war with the capitalist world 'would now set humanity back centuries'. Beijing did not comprehend that Lenin had spoken of the inevitability of war before the existence of a socialist community. In Khrushchev's view, Lenin would also have revised his doctrines if he had been alive in 1960.[43]

The nuclear dimension of the Sino-Soviet dispute had been made clear to the Chinese in June 1959 when the Soviets reneged on the agreement to supply a prototype bomb because of the test-ban negotiations then taking place in Geneva. Moscow also made it clear that it was Western and not Chinese perceptions that were critical to its decision: 'If the Western countries learn that the Soviet Union is supplying China with sophisticated technical aid, it is possible that the socialist community's efforts for peace and relaxation will be seriously sabotaged.'[44]

It was about at this time that the US realized Moscow's apprehensiveness about China's possible acquisition of these weapons. This was brought home even more forcefully after the election of John F. Kennedy to the presidency when Mikhail A. Menshikov, the Soviet ambassador to Washington, reported to Averell

[42] White House Office, Office of the Staff Secretary, Subject Series, Alpha. Subseries, Intelligence Briefing Notes, Box 14, 24 June 1960, DDEL.

[43] Ann Whitman File, NSC Series, Box 13, 20 Oct. 1960, DDEL.

[44] Lewis and Xue, *China Builds the Bomb*, 64–5.

Harriman in November 1960 his hopes that Washington and Moscow could come to some agreement on the control of nuclear weapons, 'as without such control China and other countries would obtain [them] in a few years, with attendant increase in the danger of nuclear war'.[45] Indeed, the USA perceived in 1961 that Soviet interest in an agreement banning the testing of nuclear weapons was related directly to Moscow's fears that China would soon join the nuclear club: 'There is little doubt that Moscow's desire to inhibit Communist China's acquisition of nuclear weapons has been one important reason why the Soviets have seriously entertained the idea of a supervised nuclear test ban.'[46] As one author has recently argued, and as is suggested in the briefing book prepared for Harriman's trip to Moscow in 1963, if the United States decided to take 'radical steps' against China— possibly a pre-emptive strike—to prevent the further development of its nuclear capabilities, Soviet co-operation was at least seen as worth exploring in mid-1963.[47]

The US intelligence community thus recognized almost from the beginning of the Sino-Soviet alliance that, while it had certainly led to an accretion in Chinese power, these same shifts in relative power could, and by the end of the 1950s were indeed beginning to operate as a serious source of tension in the relationship, representing a major loss in the Soviet ability to control its ambitious partner. In these circumstances, their differences in world outlook were becoming a significant block to the coordination of policies. But this realization did not necessarily translate into an assessment that the alliance was completely inoperable. This in part could be explained by the contradictory nature of the signals emanating from Moscow and from Khrushchev in particular; and by the assumption that the shared ideology—even if it embodied a difference over means—was a bond that was difficult to destroy.

With respect to Soviet signals, for example, despite circumspection in the 1958 Straits crisis, the Soviet leader had in the end sent

[45] John Fitzgerald Kennedy, President's Office Files (hereafter POF), Countries—USSR, General, Box 125, letter to John F. Kennedy from Averell Harriman, 15 Nov. 1960, JFKL.

[46] POF, Background Docs, G3, Vienna Meeting, Briefing Material, Box 126, 25 May 1961, JFKL.

[47] Chang, *Friends and Enemies*, ch. 8. ACDA—Disarmament, NSF Depts and Agencies, Harriman Trip to Moscow, Box 265, 20 June 1963, JFKL.

a letter to Eisenhower warning that an attack against China, Moscow's 'great friend, ally, neighbour', would be deemed equivalent to an attack on the Soviet Union itself. Khrushchev and Eisenhower were to have sharp disagreements at Camp David over Taiwan, and, just before that visit, the Soviet leader had falsely boasted to Harriman that Moscow had given Beijing missiles capable of hitting Taiwan and the US Seventh Fleet. Moreover, he claimed on that occasion that, should China decide to take Taiwan, Moscow would support it 'even if this meant war'.[48] Despite Allen Dulles's constant reports throughout 1959 and 1960 of serious friction between Beijing and Moscow, he would not go so far as to predict a complete break between the two. And in his deputy's view, without explicit identification of the opponent in the polemics, 'no irrevocable step had been taken'. Even the US embassy in Moscow, which had detailed every facet of the rift— its territorial, ideological, and power dimensions—concluded in September 1960 that a full break was not likely because both believed in the communist system and its eventual triumph, and both must also realize that the bloc 'would be seriously and fatally wrecked' if they allowed their relationship to be completely breached.[49]

Eisenhower seems rarely to have commented on these intelligence reports and assessments, although he heard and read many of them. Nevertheless, it seems probable that he shared the scepticism of his leading advisers over the seriousness of the rift between the two, especially given his belief in 1958 that Moscow had played a significant role in the Taiwan Straits crisis that year. As he argued in March 1959, for example, in reaction to a debate on US planning in the event of general war with the Sino-Soviet bloc, America's 'real enemy in the world is International Communism. Communist China was certainly a willing partner in this International Communist grouping.' Moreover, in his view 'it was virtually certain that in general war between the U.S. and the U.S.S.R. Communist China would be an ally of the U.S.S.R. The same could not be said for other Bloc countries but it certainly

---

[48] POF, Vienna Meeting, Background Docs, (C), Reading Material, Box 126, 26 Sept. 1959, JFKL; Chang, *Friends and Enemies*, 192 and 212.
[49] Ann Whitman File, NSC Series, Box 12, 22 June 1960; Dulles–Herter Series, Box 11, 11 Sept. 1960, both at DDEL.

could be said about Communist China.'[50] In other words, the assumption Eisenhower made was that, in the dire circumstance of a US war with the Soviet Union, Beijing and Moscow could still be relied upon to act in concert.[51]

The Fundamental Break and its Consequences

It took a new administration before the balance in the argument began to shift. A CIA special task force on Sino-Soviet relations concluded in April 1961 that there was a deep rupture in relations and that there were 'notable lapses' in the co-ordination of Chinese and Soviet foreign policies. However, the Agency still remained cautious, arguing that 'by and large the dispute did not appreciably lessen the ability of Moscow and Peiping to deal with the non-Communist world'.[52] But from 1962, there were officials bold enough to claim that the break between the two states was fundamental and the alliance inoperable. At a Policy Planning meeting in January 1962, attended by the Secretary of State, Dean Rusk, serious attempts were made to categorize the nature of the rift, and, in a way that was more explicit than in the past, to assess what the breach meant for Western and in particular for US policies. In the view of the respected Soviet expert, Charles Bohlen, the split could not be compared with the diversity of attitude that was prevalent in NATO. Others at the meeting argued that Soviet and Chinese objectives were no longer the same, a favourable development for the United States in that the energies of the former probably would be focused more on their own internal struggle and less on their competition with the West.[53]

[50] Ann Whitman File, NSC Series, Box 11, 5 Mar. 1959, DDEL.

[51] Other factors probably also encouraged caution when the Eisenhower administration contemplated the implications of the Sino-Soviet quarrel, including the timing of the dispute which coincided with the end of the Eisenhower administration. The President also seemed somewhat exhausted at the conclusion of his time in office, and less certain of the quality of the advice given by the secretary of state that had replaced John Foster Dulles.

[52] National Security File, (NSF), Country File, China, Central Intelligence Agency, 'The Sino-Soviet Dispute and its Significance', Box 22, 1 Apr. 1961, JFKL.

[53] James C. Thomson papers, Far East 1961–6, Comm. China General, Box 15, 12 Jan. 1962, JFKL.

By April 1962, intelligence officers with the help of outside specialists had prepared a policy paper on the Sino-Soviet conflict that was even more certain about the seriousness of the rupture between the two communist states. It argued that the 'differences are of a nature and to a degree that monolithic unity and control no longer exist in the Communist camp'. There was no longer any 'single line of command, no prime source of authority, no common program of action, no ideological uniformity'. Although both states would continue to adhere to the communist doctrine and therefore both would continue as enemies of the United States, that point of agreement was no longer seen as determining. Instead, the view now was that the break 'would . . . profoundly affect the nature and course of the cold war, and would contribute significantly to United States efforts to insure that the cold war does not produce a world situation with which it could not afford to live in peace'.[54]

Although there was some discussion in intelligence circles of the positive impact that a change of leadership in both China and the Soviet Union might have on the split, by 1963 and with the full opening of the polemics it was realized that the national antagonism was so great that any meaningful relationship was unlikely to be restored, whoever led the government in either state.[55]

With steadily increasing confidence, the CIA in 1963 charted the implications of Moscow's and Beijing's move to a position where they were national antagonists, and outlined the implications for China's capabilities and objectives in the region. Should the Chinese contemplate action beyond their borders, then China, in the CIA view, realized that Soviet support was unlikely. (Certainly this was made clear at the time of the 1962 Sino-Indian border war, when Moscow adopted an outward position of political neutrality, but continued its supply of military hardware to India.) This 'in turn raises the chances that the US would react vigorously to any extreme Chinese initiatives'. Soviet pressure on China's frontiers was also seen as likely to compromise Beijing's

[54] James C. Thomson papers, Far East 1961–6, Comm. China, Box 14, 'Sino-Soviet Conflict and U.S. Policy', 30 Apr. 1962, JFKL.
[55] James C. Thomson papers, Research Memoranda, 16–29 July 1963, Box 5, 'Soviets Declare Political War on Chinese Communist Leadership', 25 July 1963, JFKL.

foreign-policy moves in its other border areas. Finally, and as noted earlier, it was also deemed possible in 1963 that the Soviets would at least contemplate joint US–Soviet action to destroy China's burgeoning nuclear capability,[56] a clear indication that America's strategy towards China and the Soviet Union had moved from one designed to split Beijing away from Moscow to one that emphasized the common great-power interests of Washington and Moscow against Beijing. Although there were still the occasional doubts expressed as to the depth of the schism between the two (as Harriman said in July 1963, if Chiang Kai-shek landed on the mainland, he thought the Soviets would 'support the Chinese Communists fully'[57]), the balance of the argument had shifted during the latter part of the Kennedy administration towards those who were sceptical of the argument that there was either an ideological or a security basis to the relationship.

When Lyndon Johnson came to power, therefore, there was a solid phalanx of officials apprised of the nature of the Sino-Soviet split and ready primarily to focus on its national interest rather than its ideological dimensions. Well before the Sino-Soviet border war in 1969 or the Soviet hint that same year that it might launch an attack against Chinese nuclear installations at Lop Nor, officials in the Johnson administration were noting in 1966 and 1967 that the Soviet Union was more likely to be portrayed in Beijing as a country that would 'sooner join the US in an attack on China than come to China's aid', and that some degree of military action on the Sino-Soviet frontier, and 'some sort of strike against the Chinese Communist nuclear factories in the Gobi desert' were likely eventualities.[58] Reports in 1966 indicated that the Soviets were transferring some of their best trained forces from Eastern Europe to the Sino-Soviet border and with their best equipment. Also that year Moscow signed a 20-year defence pact with the Mongolian People's Republic which resulted in the early station-

[56] Vice-Presidential Security File, Box 11, 'SNIE 13-4-63: Possibilities of Greater Militancy by the Chinese Communists', 31 July 1963, LBJL; ACDA—Disarmament, Nuclear Test Ban, Briefing Book vol. II, NSF Depts & Agencies, Box 265, Harriman Trip to Moscow, 20 June 1963, JFKL.

[57] NSC Meetings, memoranda, Box 314, folder 10, 31 July 1963, JFKL.

[58] NSF Country File—China Memos, vol. VIII, Box 240, 'Chinese Prognosis for Sino-Soviet Mutual Defense Gloomy', 9 Jan. 1967, and 'Red China: The Prospects', 28 Nov. 1966, both at LBJL.

ing in the country of some 100,000 Soviet troops supplemented by tank and missile units.[59] The split was clearly moving into its military-strategic phase.

As suggested earlier, however, the dispute was not seen as being entirely beneficial to Washington. Despite this reduction in Chinese power, and the perceived constraints on Chinese actions around its border areas as a result this time of Soviet willingness to apply military pressure, the foundering of the alliance also implied the total diminishing of Moscow's ability to control China's 'revolutionary elan' other than by the use or threatened use of force. China's arguments in the dispute were also designed to prod Russia into adopting a more aggressive stance against US imperialism. Beijing portrayed itself as the centre of support for wars of national liberation and claimed that its past success with armed struggle stood as the sole source of inspiration for the world's oppressed peoples. Such claims did of course deepen America's commitment to South Vietnam, where it sought to defeat what it at first depicted as a Chinese-inspired revolutionary struggle; but they also served to reinforce the belief that China could no longer be ignored or ostracized but had, to whatever degree was possible, to be civilized or tamed. With the Soviets no longer able to play that role except by threatening or using its military strength, in the interests of world order, the United States itself might have to take up the task.

The Tacit Alignment

The Johnson administration attempted first steps in this civilizing mission with its policy of reconciliation with former enemies, and its offer to permit the free flow of ideas, people, and goods. The Nixon administration, mired in a war it could not win in Vietnam, faced with a rise in Soviet global military capabilities, with the stark example of the Sino-Soviet border war, and Soviet hints that it contemplated an attack on China's nuclear installations, went further. It seized an opportunity provided by the plain example of China's weakness, not only to attempt to draw China into the international community, but also to enlist it in an anti-Soviet

---

[59] Dittmer, *Sino-Soviet Normalization*, 188.

alignment that would help to restore America's global and regional standing, undercutting the perception that the United States had become the weaker of the two superpowers.

There was much discussion during this era of the multipolar world order that had emerged and that within this pentagonal framework the bases of power were mixed in form. Yet the Nixon administration, in part through its new China policy, hoped not for equality within this framework, but to regain its pivotal place within it. Nixon in the 1960s had been much impressed by the arguments of those such as Charles de Gaulle who pointed to the extent to which America's China policy had undermined Washington's authority with its allies.[60] Similarly, as Chapter 4 has shown, the majority of the American public and Congress no longer believed the government had been promoting the most sensible China policy (although Nixon remained concerned about the attitudes of right-wing Republicans). An opening to China could contribute to the restoration of authority in both the international and domestic arenas, and improve Washington's room for diplomatic manœuvre, especially where the Soviet Union was concerned. As Kissinger explained in a memorandum to Nixon in October 1971, a statement that demonstrated the unequal nature of the strategic triangle, whereas Beijing had little alternative but to turn to Washington, US options appeared to be much wider: 'We want our China policy to show Moscow . . . that it is to their advantage to make agreements with us, that they must take account of possible US–PRC co-operation . . . The beneficial impact on the USSR is perhaps the single biggest plus that we get from the China initiative.'[61]

The Nixon administration began a series of statements in 1969 designed to reassure the Chinese that it did indeed offer protection and that interests between Beijing and Washington were congruent where Moscow was concerned. As the Under-Secretary of State, Elliott Richardson, put it in September 1969—a time when Soviet military threats were at their most overt—the United

---

[60] Michel Oksenberg, 'A Decade of Sino-American Relations', *Foreign Affairs*, 61 (Fall 1982), 175.

[61] Henry Kissinger, *White House Years* (Boston: Little, Brown), 1979, 765. Stephen Sestanovich has argued that, in fact, this policy created very little leverage for Washington. See 'U.S. Policy Toward the Soviet Union, 1970–1990: The Impact of China', in Robert S. Ross, ed., *China, the United States, and the Soviet Union: Tripolarity and Policy Making in the Cold War* (Armonk, NY: M. E. Sharpe, 1993).

States 'could not fail to be deeply concerned ... with an escalation of this quarrel into a massive breach of international peace and security'.[62] This statement came one month after a Soviet embassy official had approached an official in the State Department to enquire about US reaction to a possible Soviet attack on Chinese nuclear facilities, and after Mao and his colleagues had become aware of Soviet contingency plans to conduct a 'surgical strike' against the country as a prelude to the use of airborne operations and the occupation of parts of China north of the Yangtze.[63] During private negotiations in Warsaw with the Chinese ambassador in January 1970, his US counterpart read a statement which affirmed that the US did not seek to 'join in any condominium with the Soviet Union directed at China'.[64] Presidents Ceauşescu and Yahya Khan were also invited to convey private messages to Beijing to the effect that Washington would not endorse the Soviet proposal for the establishment of an Asian collective security system, announced in 1969, and widely interpreted as an attempt to promote an anti-Chinese alliance.[65] In February 1970, the administration—somewhat belatedly—announced a change from the two-and-a-half war strategy it had based its planning upon to a one-and-a-half war strategy, with the intention of acknowledging publicly and graphically that Sino-Soviet co-operation was no longer seen as likely and that a conflict with the Soviet Union would not automatically involve the PRC.[66] During the Indo-Pakistani war of 1971, the USA moved an aircraft carrier task force to the Bay of Bengal, showing that Washington like Beijing supported Islamabad in that conflict. In addition, Nixon determined privately that if the Soviets attacked China during the course of that war, the United States 'would not stand idly by'.[67]

[62] Kissinger, *White House Years*, 184. See my Ch. 7 for a discussion of Soviet nuclear threats against China.

[63] Dittmer, *Sino-Soviet Normalization*, 200; William T. Tow, *Encountering the Dominant Player: U.S. Extended Deterrence Strategy in the Asia-Pacific* (New York: Columbia University Press, 1991), 213.

[64] Kissinger, *White House Years*, 687.

[65] Xue and Pei, eds., *Diplomacy of Contemporary China*, 269.

[66] Banning N. Garrett and Bonnie S. Glaser, 'From Nixon to Reagan: China's Changing Role in American Strategy', in Kenneth Oye, Robert J. Lieber, and Donald S. Rothchild, eds., *Eagle Resurgent? The Reagan Era in American Foreign Policy* (Boston: Little, Brown, 1987), 257. A two-and-a-half war strategy envisioned the possibility of fighting a war against China in Asia simultaneously with one against the Soviet Union in Europe, together with a minor conflict elsewhere.

[67] Kissinger, *White House Years*, 910.

The Chinese were receptive: the Soviet intervention in Czechoslovakia in 1968, the enunciation of the Brezhnev doctrine, the attacks on China itself, Soviet military contingency planning, and Moscow's promotion of 'encirclement' policies—including the stationing of 30 Soviet divisions along the border in 1970—convinced the Beijing leadership that the 'social-imperialist' Soviet Union was China's primary enemy and the most aggressive and expansionist of the two superpowers. Their secondary enemy, the United States, might in the circumstances of its relative global and regional decline form a useful temporary ally in a united front against Moscow.[68]

The Kissinger–Nixon visits were designed to cement US signals of support to China's security, but also to explore America's new-found opportunities: enlisting Chinese help in the American withdrawal from Vietnam, gaining Chinese acceptance—even agreement—to US alliance relationships in Asia, and sending signals to Moscow designed to promote the process of *détente*. To persuade the Chinese of the benefits of a joint anti-Soviet posture, Kissinger offered the Chinese intelligence information on Soviet deployments in the Far East.[69] The Shanghai communiqué broadened the commitment, pledging that each side was 'opposed to efforts by any other country or group of countries to establish . . . hegemony' in the Asia-Pacific region. But the high point of the strategic understanding came during Kissinger's visit in February 1973, where Soviet intentions were the overwhelming concern for the Chinese, even more so than in the previous visits—perhaps a result of the presence of forty-five Soviet divisions along the border that year. (As Mao told Kissinger, 'we can work together to commonly deal with a bastard'.[70])

During that visit, most of the objectives of the Nixon administration's China opening seemed to be bearing fruit, at least where those objectives pertained to Beijing. As Kissinger stated in a report to Nixon, the Chinese position in 1971 had been basically hostile. They had emphasized US 'withdrawals from Asia; the Japan–US military ties were at a minimum unhelpful; we were

---

[68] J. D. Armstrong, *Revolutionary Diplomacy: Chinese Foreign Policy and the United Front Doctrine* (Berkeley: University of California Press, 1977), 92 ff.

[69] Harry Harding, *A Fragile Relationship: The United States and China since 1972* (Washington, DC: Brookings Institution, 1992), 42.

[70] Nixon Presidential Project, President's Personal Files, Box 6, 24 Feb. 1973, NA.

told to get out of Korea; there was considerable attention to Taiwan; there was almost no interest in Europe; and the US might be capable of colluding with the USSR, Japan and India to carve up China'.[71] Now, in February 1973, the areas of agreement were wide, including a common interest in seeing that Vietnam developed as an independent state and not as an agent of Moscow, in maintaining the US–Japanese alliance, fostering stability on the Korean peninsula, and promoting coalition forces in Cambodia.[72]

Not surprisingly, China shortly after this began to indicate an interest in purchasing arms from Washington, a topic that was to become a contentious issue in the Ford and Carter administrations. Part of the struggle over how best to promote *détente* with Moscow, the debate in Washington basically divided between those who wanted to maintain a delicate balance in the employment of threats and blandishments, and those who wanted to promote a harder line in order to induce restraint in Soviet behaviour. Beijing's arguments supported those of the Washington hardliners. The Chinese had been critical in the mid-1970s of US attempts, as they put it, to stand 'on China's shoulders' to reach Moscow—or as Kissinger explained it to Nixon, 'to have our mao tai and drink our vodka too'.[73] Arms limitation agreements, grain sales, technology transfer, and the Helsinki accords were seen in China as examples of appeasement of the worst sort, not at all representing what the Chinese had in mind when they had decided on the opening to Washington. Mao and Zhou had wanted a united front with the United States against the state that China depicted as the most aggressive and expansionist power in the global system, not an alignment that served to promote US–Soviet *détente*.

China's position drew strength from a number of quarters in Washington, in part because the argument had already been tilted in China's favour. With the continuance in office of officials keen to make it clear that neither a vulnerable nor weakened China was deemed to be in America's national interest, the attraction of building military ties with Beijing and augmenting its military

[71] Nixon Presidential Project, President's Personal Files, Box 6, 27 Feb. 1973, NA.
[72] Ibid. See also Kissinger, *Years of Upheaval* (London: Weidenfeld and Nicolson, 1982), esp. 56–9.
[73] Ibid. 70.

capabilities were plain. In addition, with support for *détente* eroding in Washington, because of Soviet actions in Angola and elsewhere, those hard-line arguments eventually won out. One consequence was the Ford administration's acquiescence in December 1975 in the sale of British Rolls Royce Spey jet engines to China, a deal that could have been blocked under COCOM provisions, and French and German sales of defensive weapons shortly thereafter.[74] The USA edged cautiously forward too: in October 1976, Kissinger recommended to the NSC approval of the sale of two advanced Control Data Cyber 72 computers with military applications.[75]

A further deterioration in Soviet–American relations in early 1978, and the predominance of the geopolitical vision of Zbigniew Brzezinski, reduced more of the constraints. The National Security Adviser, during his first visit to China in May 1978, reaffirmed that a 'secure and strong China' was in Washington's national interest. To give tangible content to this statement, the Carter administration authorized discussions on the possible sale of American dual-purpose technology. Brzezinski himself also organized a NATO briefing on global strategic problems, and began negotiation of an agreement to establish monitoring stations on the Sino-Soviet border. In January 1979, when relations had at last been normalized, President Carter indicated his acquiescence to Western European defensive weapons sales to China and, after the Chinese intervention in Vietnam in February of that year, intelligence information was made available on the disposition of Soviet forces on the Chinese border.[76] On 3 April 1979, the PRC notified the Soviet Union that it would not be extending the alliance treaty, a decision that came into effect one year later.[77] In the meantime, military ties with the USA deepened further.

[74] Garrett and Glaser, 'From Nixon to Reagan', 262–3; A. Doak Barnett, 'Military-Security Relations between China and the United States', *Foreign Affairs*, 55 (Apr. 1977). See also my Ch. 3 for a discussion of COCOM and CHINCOM.

[75] Garrett and Glaser, 'From Nixon to Reagan', 263.

[76] Staff Offices, Speechwriters File, Chronological File, Box 40, Carter interview with Non-Washington Editors and News Directors, 26 Jan. 1979, JCL; Zbigniew Brzezinski, *Power and Principle: Memoirs of the National Security Adviser, 1977–1981* (New York: Farrer, Strauss, Giroux, 1983), 203; Garrett and Glaser, 'From Nixon to Reagan', 266; discussion with Professor Brzezinski, 4 Feb. 1994, Oxford, UK.

[77] The abrogation of this treaty is discussed in Xue and Pei, eds., *Diplomacy of Contemporary China*, 301. Somewhat disingenuously they have described the treaty

With the US Defense Secretary's visit to China in January 1980, a few days after the Soviet intervention in Afghanistan, the Carter administration indicated its willingness to consider the sale of non-lethal military equipment on a case-by-case basis. After that visit, China moved from export category Y to P, which permitted enhanced access to military equipment. At the same time, Washington embargoed all sales of high technology to Moscow 'until further notice'. Brown noted while in Beijing that he had come to explore the two countries' shared interests: Afghanistan was a good example of a crisis in which 'the United States and China find it in the self-interest of each of us to concert parallel responses to the world situation'.[78] A quasi-alliance seemed at that stage to have come into being. As outgoing Carter administration officials were to indicate, discussions with the Chinese on military matters had become 'almost like talking to an ally'.[79]

In the US assessment, the Sino-Soviet alliance in its early years served to augment China's security and its capabilities. It also enhanced the security of the communist bloc as a whole, especially of its leading member. The Soviet Union had at that time an apparently untroublesome 4,000-mile border with China and the demonstrated willingness of its ally to protect it from any pressure to intervene overtly in a conflict that involved the United States.

Nevertheless, the increase in China's prestige that resulted from its participation in the Korean war, from the consequent growth in its military strength, and—with the death of Stalin—the advent of a leader in Moscow willing to accord the Chinese greater equality of status, reduced Beijing's dependence on Moscow and sharpened the repercussions from any potential or actual divergence of interest. By the late 1950s, it had become clear that Chinese greater concern over US–Taiwanese relations, differing perceptions of developments in nuclear weapons technology

as having been designed to prevent the re-emergence of Japanese imperialism; with China's normalization of relations with Japan in 1972 and the signature in August 1978 of the Treaty of Peace and Friendship, the alliance treaty was therefore 'outdated'.

[78] Barnett, *China's Economy in Global Perspective*, 554; Robert S. Ross, 'U.S. Policy Toward China: The Strategic Context and the Policy-making Process,' in Ross, ed., *China, the United States, and the Soviet Union*, 163.

[79] Garrett and Glaser, 'From Nixon to Reagan', 269.

(including their impact on the inevitability of war), growing US–Soviet *détente* apparently at the expense of Chinese interests, and heavy-handed Soviet attempts to place controls on its ally's behaviour, were reducing the value of the alliance and undermining socialist-bloc unity.

As such differences continued to deepen, American administrations came to conclude in the 1960s that the Sino-Soviet rift was far reaching, the alliance inoperable, and the Soviet ability to restrain its ally would only come through the use or threatened use of force. By the midpoint of the Johnson administration, as better-armed and more numerous Soviet forces were being stationed on the Sino-Soviet border, some officials were arguing that China regarded Russia and not the United States as the state most likely to attack its territory and developing nuclear capability. This represented a significant change in the US perception of China and of the Sino-Soviet alliance compared with the view that had prevailed in the 1950s. Then, it had seemed plain that Chinese capabilities in all fields were being augmented. Now, Chinese access to various resources had gone, to be replaced by a concern in Beijing that the Soviets might well attack the PRC or at least operate to constrain its foreign policy behaviour.

Nixon was ready to take advantage of that assessment in order to gain leverage over Moscow and Beijing and to restore America's pivotal position in the global strategic balance. To reassure the Chinese of the seriousness of his intent, the President authorized statements and actions that demonstrated a willingness to help preserve the PRC regime in the event of any Soviet threat to its existence, a pledge that officials in the Ford and Carter administrations were to repeat. Such pledges demonstrated that, despite China's contributory role in the strategic triangle, the United States was the dominant actor. They also demonstrated that US containment policy had shifted from the containment of communism to the containment of Soviet power. For tripolarity and the balancing of Moscow to be made more meaningful still, Chinese–American 'collusion' had to be made more tangible; hence the decision to offer intelligence information, to establish a monitoring station, to support sales of Western arms and of American dual-use technology.

Much as had been the case in 1950, China in the 1970s sought to increase its security and to build up its capabilities, this time to diminish the threat from its northern neighbour. But, as also had been true before, it remained wary of being used by the dominant partner or of being abandoned, even in a quasi-alliance. The United States for its part had wider objectives to satisfy that encompassed its relationship with Moscow and its position in East Asia. As a result of its opening to China it found itself in the 1970s in the preferred position of having better relations with Moscow and Beijing than either had with each other. Moreover, it managed to exit somewhat more gracefully from Vietnam than would otherwise have been the case, and, despite initial resentments in East Asia about the secretive and cavalier way it had enacted its new China policy, Washington also managed to preserve its key bilateral ties in the region. With full normalization of relations in 1979, this was the first occasion, as Carter remarked, that the country had enjoyed good relations with both Japan and China at the same time.[80] The tacit alignment with Beijing and the consequences that flowed from that helped to return the United States to a central place in the global system.

---

[80] *Public Papers of the Presidents*, Jimmy Carter, 1980–1, vol. i, 19 Feb. 1980 (Washington, DC: US Government Printing Office, 1981), 345.

6

The Iron Wall: China's Conventional Military Capabilities

A tragic and influential feature of America's relations with the PRC has been that the armed forces of both countries have clashed on the battlefield. The Korean war experience strongly coloured American perceptions of China as a military power, helping shape its military decisions in that later costly conflict in Vietnam. But Beijing's frequent use of its armed forces subsequent to the Korean conflict allowed US administrations to make additional if less direct assessments of its capabilities. After Korea, the two Taiwan Straits crises, the Sino-Indian and Sino-Soviet border conflicts, the Vietnam war, and then Sino-Vietnamese fighting in 1979 prompted Washington to undertake regular appraisals of the strengths and weaknesses of what quickly became not only the largest land army in the world, but also the third-largest navy and air force.[1]

The dominant US perception in the 1950s was that China had a considerable military power potential. If those tough and courageous Chinese fighters could become technicians too, able, with Soviet help, to utilize heavy military equipment and master the techniques of modern warfare; and if the Chinese could go on to develop an independent military capability and thus no longer be reliant on the overstretched Trans-Siberian railroad for resupply,

---

[1] China's leaders have also spent time assessing US military capabilities. Using Mao's terminology, the Chinese leadership despised the United States strategically but respected it tactically: China developed a healthy regard for America's technical superiority, even as it publicly argued that Washington, because it lacked popular support for its policies, was in essence a paper tiger. The classic exposition of the paper tiger thesis is given in 'U.S. Imperialism is a Paper Tiger', 14 July 1956, in Mao Zedong, *Selected Works*, v (Beijing: Foreign Languages Press, 1977). 'Now U.S. imperialism is quite powerful, but in reality it isn't. It is very weak politically because it is divorced from the masses of the people and is disliked by everybody and by the American people too. In appearance it is very powerful but in reality it is nothing to be afraid of, it is a paper tiger' (p. 310).

then the PRC would become a formidable, world-class military foe. In the absence of such developments, Chinese military power would be no more than regional in scope, and the regime would continue to give primacy to the defence of its own territory and disputed border areas. Its military credibility would rest on the sheer size of its armed forces, its demonstrated willingness to employ arms and to sustain major losses, on its earlier successes in guerrilla warfare, and ability to support national liberation struggles close to its borders. These were hardly insignificant attributes, but were less daunting than those associated with great-power status.

Truman and Eisenhower administration appraisals of China's conventional strength suggested that Beijing was a 'candidate great power'[2] in military terms. By the 1960s and throughout the 1970s, however, it was clear that China had not developed advanced conventional forces, and had been sufficiently weakened through its domestic and foreign policies eventually to require it to embark on a domestic modernization programme that led to the reduction and then ending of its support for the national liberation struggles it had previously championed. Moreover, it needed American military protection to help it deal with Soviet encirclement. Such an evolution in the understanding of China's needs and capacities helped ease the path to the *rapprochement* and then normalization of relations between these two former military opponents, much as America's own defeat in Vietnam made it easier for Mao to turn to Washington.

A Candidate Great Power?

Combat between US and Chinese troops in Korea inevitably and powerfully shaped the US assessment of China's military capabilities and of Beijing's potential. Prior to Chinese entry into the

---

[2] Jonathan Pollack in his writings first used the term 'candidate superpower' to describe China. See, for example, 'China and the Global Strategic Balance', in Harry Harding, ed., *China's Foreign Relations in the 1980s* (New Haven: Yale University Press, 1984), 174. I prefer in this context to use the phrase 'candidate great power' in order to preserve something of the unique status of the two states designated as superpowers post-World War II. For a discussion of some of these terms see e.g. Martin Wight, *Power Politics* (Harmondsworth: Penguin Books, 1979).

fighting, officials in Washington had concluded that the PRC lacked the military capacity to undertake a full-scale involvement in the hostilities. Although domestic priorities in themselves were deemed sufficient to prevent Chinese intervention, US intelligence services also noted that the PLA's past combat experience was inappropriate to the operations in Korea. Previous fighting had involved 'hit and run' guerrilla tactics. The PLA had never met a 'well-trained force with high morale equipped with modern weapons and possessing the will and the skill to use those weapons'.[3] In addition, the Chinese had virtually no navy and only a small air force, perhaps '200 combat aircraft in tactical units' not tested in combat up to that time, comprising 40 TU-2 light bombers, 40 IL-10 ground attack aircraft, and 120 LA-9 fighters. The Chinese air force might also include 30 to 40 Soviet-type swept-wing fighters that were previously stationed near Shanghai.[4]

With China's entry into the Korean war such assessments were quickly overhauled. The stunning success of the first three Chinese offensives demonstrated that techniques used during the anti-Japanese and civil wars could in fact prove their worth against a modern, US-led army. On 28 November 1950, Mao ordered the Chinese forces to 'attack and eliminate the U.S. First, Second, and Twenty-fifth Divisions'.[5] Over two days, 30 November and 1 December, UN casualties exceeded 11,000. By 5 December, Chinese and North Korean forces had retaken Pyongyang; after the Chinese New Year's Eve Offensive, UN forces were driven back to the 37th parallel and Seoul changed hands once again. US forces had been propelled into the longest retreat in their military history by an army that had used the tactics of surprise, night fighting, and speed to overcome a professionally-trained, well-equipped, and technologically superior enemy. The shock of such an outcome can hardly be exaggerated, as US officials for a time considered total withdrawal from the peninsula, air force retaliation against Chinese bases, and the declaration of a state of national emergency. One Chinese document

---

[3] RG 319, Records of the Army Staff, G3 091 Korea, TS, 11 July 1950, NA.

[4] *Foreign Relations of the United States, 1950* (Washington, DC: Government Printing Office, 1976), 7: 1103, 8 Nov. 1950, NIE-2, 'Chinese Communist Intervention in Korea'.

[5] Zhang Shu Guang, *Deterrence and Strategic Culture: Chinese–American Confrontations, 1949–1958* (Ithaca: Cornell University Press, 1992), 110.

later captured by US forces crowed over these successes: US 'infantrymen are weak, afraid to die and haven't the courage to attack or defend. They depend on their planes, tanks, and artillery. At the same time, they are afraid of our fire power.' It also noted the US army's dependence on good terrain and weather to transport its large amounts of equipment, and remarked on its unfamiliarity with night fighting and hand-to-hand combat.[6]

This Chinese assessment of their superiority was premature, of course. By the spring of 1951 and especially after the disastrous Chinese offensive in May, military operations turned against them and a stalemate began to develop. Chinese supply lines had been over-extended, new UN tactics under the Command of General Matthew Ridgway had frustrated efforts to create a fluid battlefield operation, and UN air superiority had begun to take its toll. As casualties mounted, and rations ran short, morale and discipline among the Chinese soldiers had started to break down.[7] Nearly all of the Chinese prisoners of war taken throughout the three years of fighting came during this period.

Nevertheless, over the course of the war, Washington developed a deep respect for the Chinese armed forces which would later influence US strategy in Vietnam. Certainly Washington remained well aware of PLA weaknesses at war's end. US officials noted China's inability to use its air power except in defensive operations, its total lack of an amphibious capability, and its insufficient logistical support which made it difficult to maintain the momentum of offensives. Washington also noted the 'major weakness' associated with the absence of a domestic supply facility, thus rendering Beijing totally dependent on the Soviet Union for heavy military equipment.[8] Yet, its strengths were considerable too. As one NSC staff study put it four

---

[6] Lt. Col. Roy E. Appleman (Ret.), *Disaster in Korea: The Chinese Confront MacArthur* (College Station: Texas A and M University Press, 1989), 102.

[7] A compelling account of Chinese offensives is contained in Chen Jian, 'China's Changing Aims during the Korean War, 1950–51', *Journal of American–East Asian Relations*, 1 (Spring 1992), esp. 25–38. See also Alexander L. George, *The Chinese Communist Army in Action: The Korean War and its Aftermath* (New York: Columbia University Press, 1967).

[8] These points were made in, for example, *Foreign Relations*, 1951 (Washington, DC: Government Printing Office, 1983), 7: 1265, NIE-55, 7 Dec. 1951; *Foreign Relations*, 1952–4 (Washington, DC: Government Printing Office, 1985), 14: 290–1, NSC Staff Study, 6 Nov. 1953; *Foreign Relations*, 1952–4, 14: 393, NIE-10-2-54, 15 Mar. 1954; *Foreign Relations*, 1952–4, 14: 453–4, NIE-13-54, 3 June 1954.

months after the end of hostilities (the study is worth quoting at length):

The achievement of the Chinese Communist regime in Korea has been a military feat of no mean proportions, and instructive as to the extent of Chinese Communist military capabilities. The Chinese Communists, with Russian assistance, were able to organize, train, equip, supply, and commit massive ground forces in the Korean peninsula. These forces fought with courage, aggressiveness, and with notably few desertions. They demonstrated skill and energy in camouflage and entrenchment. As the war progressed the Communists demonstrated increasing capabilities and proficiency in the artillery arm. They accumulated considerable capabilities and limited experience in air warfare, although the bulk of air combat appears to have been undertaken by the Russians. The Communists devised means, frequently primitive, for logistic support of their front line units in the face of uncontested air and naval superiority on the part of the UN Command. Towards the end of the war Communist ground-to-air anti-aircraft capabilities were extensive.[9]

Subsequent official military assessments elaborated further on the merits of the Chinese infantryman: he patrolled energetically and skilfully, he was a master of the art of infiltration, and could move at great speed on foot. His rations were simple, personal comforts few, yet his morale was high. He was imaginative in making up for equipment deficiencies: lacking a sophisticated communications system, for example, Chinese forces had used bugles, horns, whistles, and coloured flares. These had the additional effect of causing panic within enemy ranks.[10] Overall, despite the deficiencies and high casualties sustained, it had been an impressive performance.

It was clear from the NSC Staff Study that, even during the course of the war, China had begun what one analyst has described as a process of 'modernization under fire'.[11] As noted in Chapter 5, the Soviet Union had, at a cost, provided China with a sizeable air force and equipment for sixty army divisions. Post-

[9] *Foreign Relations*, 1952–4, 14: 289–90, NSC Staff Study, 6 Nov. 1953.

[10] *The Chinese Armed Forces Today: The U.S. Defense Intelligence Agency Handbook of China's Army, Navy and Air Force* (London: Arms and Armour Press, 1979) (reproduced from *Handbook on the Chinese Armed Forces*, DDI-2680-32-76, U.S. Defense Intelligence Agency, Washington, DC, 1976). See also Walter G. Hermes, *United States Army in the Korean War: Truce Tent and Fighting Front* (Washington, DC: Office of the Chief of Military History, United States Army, 1966), esp. 510–12.

[11] William Whitson, *The Chinese High Command: A History of Communist Military Politics, 1927–71* (New York: Praeger, 1973), 95.

Korea, this process was taken further, with the transfer of additional Soviet equipment in 1954 as a result of their relinquishing of the base at Port Arthur, and the establishing of several military industrial enterprises.[12] General Peng Dehuai, who commanded Chinese forces in Korea, and had seen at first hand the devastation that could be wrought by a technologically superior foe, also set about the task of professionalizing the army. At his prompting, the Chinese leadership appeared ready to carry forward the lessons learnt during the Korean war and to allocate generous funding for the modernization of its forces. In the view of the Eisenhower administration, preparations indicated that China would probably continue to devote one-third of its national budget to the military and would use a major share of its foreign-exchange earnings to import military equipment and petroleum products.[13]

A formidable military required, of course, a solid industrial base to maintain and support it. By 1956, Allen Dulles, the director of the Central Intelligence Agency, was reporting 'remarkable developments in the industrialization of Communist China, especially in the areas relating to war potential'. He predicted that at the end of the year the Chinese would be producing their own jet-fighter aircraft, although these would depend on components and equipment of Soviet manufacture. He also spoke of a major naval building effort, underway at shipyards in Shanghai. Under Soviet supervision, the Chinese had 'launched their first destroyers, modelled on the Soviet "Riga" class', and they had also begun producing a number of smaller craft.[14] A 'slight measure' of Chinese independence of Moscow seemed to be developing, therefore, and was important because it had earlier been argued that a major weakness facing China had been its lack of domestic supply facilities, its dependence on the Soviet Union, and reliance on the vulnerable Trans-Siberian railroad for the transport of equipment.[15]

[12] Jonathan D. Pollack, *Defense Modernization in the People's Republic of China*, N-1214-1-AF, Oct. 1979 (prepared for the US Air Force by the RAND Corporation, California).

[13] *Foreign Relations*, 1952–4, 14: 460, NIE-13-54, 3 June 1954.

[14] Ann Whitman File, NSC Series, Box 7, 18 June 1956, 'Discussion at the 288th meeting of the National Security Council', DDEL.

[15] *Foreign Relations*, 1952–4, 14: 454, NIE-13-54, 3 June 1954.

China's growing military power and the increase in its political prestige post-Korea alarmed US officials and the wider public. Images detailed in the study undertaken by Harold Isaacs conveyed a picture of the Chinese not only as warriors but also as technicians. As Dulles told a Congressional Committee in April 1954, Chinese generals were now acting as technical advisers to Vietminh forces, a point of information that evoked a frightening reversal of image compared with the Guomindang era.[16] A report produced for Congress in 1957 reminded the legislative branch that the Chinese had massive ground forces of 2.5 million organized into 150 divisions with support units. It stated that since 1952, the Chinese military had been undergoing an 'important reorganization and modernization . . . to include standardization of weapons, increased service and support units, and a vastly expanded military school system'.[17]

Other estimates had assumed that, by 1957, the country would have expanded its industrial output by some 20 to 25 per cent over 1952, and that much of this would be put towards military modernization. Training was expected to be intensified, and selection and utilization of personnel improved. The air arm was likely to be expanded and made into a more balanced force, with an overall strength of 2,500 'including 1,400 jet fighters and 480 jet light bombers'. While the navy itself was not expected to develop much further, the naval air force would probably grow and be trained in new techniques. Beijing was shaping up to be a formidable enemy, likely to pose a significant 'challenge to the influence of Western nations in Asia' and to overawe its lesser neighbours.[18] Already the size of its armed forces far outstripped the numbers in other Asian nations: 2.5 million and a nationwide conscription campaign begun in 1955, compared with 600,000 on Taiwan, 190,000 in Indonesia, and 90,000 in Thailand, for example. The danger was that, being in awe, such neighbours would accommodate themselves to Beijing without the latter even having to resort to threats. To contain such fear, the USA

[16] Harold R. Isaacs, *Scratches on our Mind: American Images of China and India* (Westport, Conn.: Greenwood Press, 1977), 236–7.

[17] *United States Defense Policies in 1957*, report produced by Legislative Service of Library of Congress for House Armed Services Committee (Washington, DC: US GPO, 1958), 10.

[18] *Foreign Relations*, 1952–4, 14: 460–1, NIE-13-54, 3 June 1954.

determined on the difficult and frequently locally unpopular policies of establishing bilateral military alliances and naval and air bases in the area, proffering defence support and military aid, and integrating atomic forces into the defence network.

Reappraising China's Capabilities

Military clashes in the next few years provided opportunities for the United States to assess the effectiveness of such Chinese attempts to modernize and equip its armed forces. In 1958, the second Taiwan Straits crisis provided a test of the Chinese air force and its naval capabilities. The border wars with India in 1962 and with the Soviet Union in 1969 caused the army to come under scrutiny once again. These instances of the use of force were to allow the US government to develop a far more nuanced portrayal of China's military strengths and weaknesses. Such assessments were to undermine the earlier depiction of China's military as a modernizing force. While it had maintained the skills of the early 1950s, it came to be realized that it had more or less stagnated since that time.

During the Taiwan Straits crisis of 1958, Beijing certainly demonstrated its ability to manipulate tensions for political ends. China's main military activity involved an intensification of the bombardment of the Offshore Islands, further actions being deemed unwise because of the deterrent steps the US had taken. Presumably in the expectation that the Chinese Communists would be able to achieve their goal of forcing the Nationalist troops to surrender, the United States 'assembled off the China coast the most powerful armada the world had ever seen: six carriers, with a complement of 96 planes capable of delivering nuclear weapons, three heavy cruisers, forty destroyers, a submarine division, and twenty other support craft'.[19] Such actions, coupled with implicit US nuclear threats, alarmed America's Western allies and the neutral nations, and demonstrated the drawbacks to Washington of its support for Chiang Kai-shek. The Japanese sought reassurances that the United States would not use its sea and air bases in Japan if hostilities with the PRC

[19] Gordon H. Chang, *Friends and Enemies: The United States, China, and the Soviet Union, 1948–1972* (Stanford, Calif.: Stanford University Press, 1990), 185.

ensued; the Australian Prime Minister confirmed that the treaty linking Australia, New Zealand and the United States (ANZUS) could not be invoked; and the Canadian Minister of External Affairs stated that his government was not involved in this 'unilateral action' by the United States. Although the British were far less critical publicly of US actions than they had been in 1955—predominantly because of the government's painstaking efforts to rebuild relations after the Suez débâcle—Downing Street issued a statement to the effect that the British government had made no commitment to the United States to act in concert over the matter.[20] The Chinese Communists, therefore, at relatively little direct cost to themselves, had made a political point of some significance.[21]

As skilful as the Chinese leaders were at using force as an adjunct to political objectives, in other respects, however, their actual military activity was seen to be deficient, especially in comparison with Chiang Kai-shek's forces. The Chinese Nationalist air force had proven to be surprisingly good. It had shown itself capable of efficiently integrating and utilizing such weaponry as side-winder missiles and had shown that its pilots were superior to the Communists in aerial combat.[22] There had, then, been some shift in the balance of advantage towards the Chinese Nationalists, and one that had certain implications for the future safety of the islands. Any future blockade of Jinmen and Mazu (Quemoy and Matsu) was presumed to require Beijing to authorize air strikes—artillery alone in 1958 had been unable to prevent a combined US–Chinese Nationalist resupply operation—which would probably lead to high attrition rates for Communist pilots and aircraft.[23]

[20] See *Japan Times*, 13 Sept. 1958; *The Times*, 6 and 12 Sept. 1958; *Christian Science Monitor*, 12 Sept. 1958; Coral Bell, 'Australia and China', in A. M. Halpern, ed., *Policies toward China: The View from Six Continents* (New York: McGraw Hill, 1965), 186.

[21] For further information on this crisis see e.g. He Di, 'The Evolution of the People's Republic of China's Policy Toward the Offshore Islands', in Warren I. Cohen and Akira Iriye, eds., *The Great Powers in East Asia* (New York: Columbia University Press, 1990); Gordon Chang, *Friends and Enemies*, esp. ch. 6; RG 218, CCS 319.1. Box 39, 11-18-58, 'Report of Lessons Learned in the Lebanon and Quemoy Operations,' NA.

[22] RG 218, 'Report of Lessons Learned,' NA.

[23] Roger Hilsman Papers, Box 1, China-OSI, Tab A 'Kinmen: The Cost of Capture', memorandum from Roger Hilsman to Dean Rusk, [1962], JFKL.

Against Indian troops in 1962, Chinese military successes were swift and impressive, quickly forcing a reluctant Nehru, in severe danger of compromising his policy of non-alignment, to seek assistance from the United States. In this conflict, Chinese infantry units dominated. They had planned and prepared well, paying particular attention to the movement in advance of essential supplies. It was a low-intensity operation, using small units over a short time period—the kind of operation where the PLA could excel.[24]

However, after tensions had diminished, and the Kennedy administration appraised the results of this military operation, it concluded that the future threat to a better-prepared India was essentially small, and that a Chinese attack could be held by 12 to 14 Indian divisions. Before the end of 1962, the British and the Americans had given military aid to India valued at $120 million, US engineers had helped with road-building, and had made the Leh airstrip operational for combat purposes.[25] Of course, much depended on the condition of Indo-Pakistani relations, and on India's level of determination in facing a future Chinese threat; nevertheless, Chinese capabilities in the area were perceived to be deficient in certain respects. According to the Secretary of Defense, Robert McNamara, China's maximum capability in the Tibet–Ladakh area amounted to 230,000 of whom about a half, some 120,000, would be combat troops; a sizeable force, perhaps, but it was estimated they would need 40,000 trucks and 40 per cent of the 1962 gasoline supply to support them.[26] The threat from the Chinese air force was also not seen to be great, because airfields then were distant from the disputed border areas and only six were over 6,000 feet with concrete, asphalt, or macadam runways.[27]

Some seven years later, China's conventional military capabilities seemed hardly to have altered. In the early engagements with

[24] Jonathan D. Pollack, 'China's Military Power and Policy', in Onkar Marwah and Jonathan D. Pollack, eds., *Military Power and Policy in Asian States: China, India, Japan* (Boulder, Colo.: Westview Press, 1980), 64.

[25] Gowher Rizvi, 'The Rivalry between India and Pakistan', in Barry Buzan and Gowher Rizvi, eds., *South Asian Insecurity and the Great Powers* (London: Macmillan, 1986), 104.

[26] NSF—NSC History, South Asia, 1962–6, Box 24, vol. I, 29 Apr. 1963, JFKL.

[27] Vice-Presidential Security File, Memo for NSC (no date), Box 5, 'Recommendations of NSC SubCommittee on South Asia for Nassau Talks', LBJL.

Soviet forces in 1969, PLA units, much as they had in Korea, relied on a superior concentration of strength, unhampered movement of personnel, and that vital element of surprise. The later encounters could rely on none of these factors and Chinese troops suffered from deficiencies in firepower—including anti-tank weapons and tactical aircraft—and from a lack of mobility.[28] Chinese troops were badly mauled and casualties increased, leading Mao in April 1969 to reiterate a conclusion already reached in Washington: that China could not fight convincingly beyond its borders, that it relied for defence on deterrence by denial of victory, and would even yield territory in order to be able to utilize 'people's war'. As Mao stated, presumably to remind Moscow of the task it would face if it tried to invade China: 'Others may come and attack us but we shall not fight outside our borders. We do not fight outside our borders. I say we will not be provoked. Even if you invite us to come out we will not come out, but if you should come and attack us we will deal with you . . . If it is on a small scale we will fight on the border. If it is on a larger scale then I am in favour of yielding some ground.'[29]

The failure to improve the conventional capabilities of the Chinese armed forces stemmed from at least four interrelated factors: the loss of Soviet military support after the rupture of relations in 1960; the slowing down of the pace of industrialization, particularly after the failure of Great Leap policies; the decision to revive the doctrine of people's war in 1958, with a central role being assigned to the people's militia rather than to a professional army; and the onset of the Cultural Revolution, which made it impossible to raise questions about the state of the armed forces. It also required such forces finally to be called upon to quell the 'Red Guard' violence and then to operate in a political role as the backbone of the so-called 'Revolutionary Committees' set up to replace the devastated party apparatus.

The US capture of authoritative Chinese military documents in 1961 had afforded Washington valuable early insight into the specific nature of these deficiencies, and where China's military leaders assumed their strengths lay. The documents asserted that China remained superior in 'close fighting, night fighting, or

[28] *New York Times*, 7 Aug. 1969; Pollack, 'China's Military Power', 65.
[29] Mao quoted in Gerald Segal, *Defending China* (Oxford: Oxford University Press, 1985), 184.

trench warfare'. Given the lack of advanced weaponry, training in the area where Chinese forces remained formidable, that is, in close combat, had to continue to be emphasized.[30] However, the secret military documents also revealed the PRC's vulnerabilities with respect to air defence, as one RAND analyst summarized it, arising from 'delays in the construction of airfields deeper in the interior, defects in night and all-weather flying, limitations on pilot training because of shortages of equipment and fuel, poor maintenance and repair of aircraft, numerous accidents, radar shortcomings, weaknesses in defence against low-altitude attack, and lack of intelligence about the enemy'.[31] The message to China's leaders was that in order to overcome some of these deficiencies they needed to intensify training, to acquire new technologies, to develop an independent capacity to produce spare parts, and to develop their own oil reserves. Communications units also required urgent attention: 'The point was made time and again that under existing conditions (1961) the communications system was unlikely to survive a surprise enemy attack and that, once communications were paralysed, commands would be paralysed.'[32] Such deficiencies could not speedily be overcome, and in the light of such vulnerability Mao in 1964 ordered that China should embark on a massive programme of investment in the remoter regions of the country to create a self-sufficient industrial base that would serve as a strategic reserve in the event of China being drawn into a major war.[33]

Loss of Soviet assistance had meant, among other things, an interruption in the supply of military equipment and of spare parts for those items previously transferred. A Kennedy administration study of China's military capabilities completed in June 1963 noted the dependence of the Chinese aircraft industry and air force on Russia until 1960, and in the circumstances of the breach in relations commented on the air force's current 'impaired effectiveness' and 'progressive obsolescence'. It noted, too,

[30] Alice L. Hsieh, 'China's Secret Military Papers: Military Doctrine and Strategy', *China Quarterly*, 20 (Apr.–June, 1964), 94. Twenty-nine issues of the secret *Bulletin of Activities* of the General Political Department of the People's Liberation Army covering the months January to August 1961 were captured and subsequently released by the US government.

[31] Ibid. 91.   [32] Ibid. 92.

[33] Barry Naughton, 'The Third Front: Defence Industrialization in the Chinese Interior', *China Quarterly*, 115 (Sept. 1988).

that in the past 'practically all aviation gas and jet fuel' had come from the USSR and that at combat consumption levels China probably had stocks for only about three weeks' supply.[34] Such shortages had cut flying time; indeed, one source argued that Communist pilots were only flying about ten hours a month, half the average of the Americans, Japanese, and Chinese Nationalists.[35] It was also recognized that Chinese aircraft were being cannibalized on a growing scale, Western intelligence estimates in 1964 claiming that some 500 planes had been grounded or dismantled since 1960, including 200 in 1963 alone.[36]

The Johnson administration had available to it in mid-1966 one of the most exhaustive studies of China's military capabilities. It examined all three branches of the armed forces, noting their strengths but emphasizing their deficiencies. Not surprisingly, it concluded that the Chinese army remained essentially 'a foot-borne infantry force', which in warfare against modern units in open terrain 'would be hampered also by shortages of armored equipment, heavy ordnance, mechanical transport and possibly POL [petroleum, oil, and lubricants]'. Although the *matériel* situation had improved somewhat with the provision of more infantry weapons, artillery, and tanks, the single most serious problem confronting the PLA was lack of logistical support.

Turning to the air force, the study concluded that it was not capable of 'conducting sustained aerial warfare against any considerable weight of U.S. or Soviet opposition'. The bulk of the fighter aircraft was made up of some '1800 obsolescent MiG-15 and MiG-17 jets'. There were also 350 MiG-19s and 35 MiG-21s, and in terms of offensive air power an estimated 270 K-28 jet light bombers, 12 Tu-4s, and 2 Tu-16 medium bombers. With respect to the navy, the study noted that it remained oriented towards coastal defence and its capabilities against a modern force were 'limited by obsolescent and numerically limited equipment and probably by limited seagoing experience under combat maneuver

[34] NSF Depts. and Agencies, ACDA: Disarmament, Nuclear Test Ban, Harriman Trip to Moscow, Briefing Book, vol. II, on Nuclear Diffusion, Box 265, 20 June 1963, JFKL.

[35] Samuel B. Griffith, II, *The Chinese People's Liberation Army* (New York: McGraw Hill, 1967; sixth in a series on United States in World Affairs sponsored by Council on Foreign Relations), 225.

[36] John Gittings, *The Role of the Chinese Army* (London: Oxford University Press, 1967), 141.

conditions'. In all three branches of the armed services, the difficulties caused by Soviet withdrawal of its technical and *matériel*
support were noted,[37] the implication being that China's independent capabilities had neither been developed to a significant
degree before 1960 nor subsequent to that.

This particular study was designated as confidential, but information of this kind about the Chinese military was widely disseminated. In 1964, Donald Zagoria published a long magazine
article in the *New York Times*, detailing China's weaknesses in the
military, agricultural, and scientific areas.[38] In testimony before
the Senate Foreign Relations Committee in 1966, General Samuel
B. Griffith described China, except in regional terms, as a 'paper
tiger' that would be unable to project conventional military power
beyond its borders for ten to twenty years. He also reminded the
Senators that, despite apparent successes against India in 1962,
the Chinese armed forces could not have supported a sustained
operation.[39]

A year later in 1967, General Griffith published his book on the
PLA under the auspices of the Council of Foreign Relations. In it,
he commented in detail on the captured military documents referred to earlier, and voiced his doubts that the deficiencies indicated in these papers had been rectified. The general also
cautioned against the 'fallacious conclusion' that progress with
regard to nuclear weapons was representative of developments in
other fields. In many important areas, such as aircraft, chemicals,
electronics, and computer technology, China was far behind the
West; and he quoted Foreign Minister Chen Yi, who 'observed in
September 1965 that it would take "30–50 years" to catch up'.[40]
Zhou Enlai had said much the same thing in 1964: 'We Chinese do
not want any war, and what is more, we cannot even start a war.
For this we lack a long-range airforce, which we do not possess at
all, and our navy is far too small.'[41]

[37] NSF Country File—China, Communist China Long Range Study, vol. III, Box
245, annex II, Chinese Communist Military Threat, June 1966, LBJL.

[38] *New York Times*, magazine section, 18 Oct. 1964.

[39] Testimony by General Samuel B. Griffith, in Akira Iriye, ed., *U.S. Policy
Toward China: Testimony Taken from the Senate Foreign Relations Committee Hearings
1966* (Boston: Little, Brown, 1968), 77.

[40] Griffith, *Chinese People's Liberation Army*, 202, 222–5.

[41] James C. Thomson papers, FE—Communist China, General, Box 16, 'Chinese
Communist Interview on War in Southeast Asia', [presumed to be Zhou Enlai], 5
Aug. 1964, JFKL.

A 1964 survey of US defence policies, produced by the Legislative Reference service of the Library of Congress and at the request of the House Committee on Armed Services, reported—much as Zhou had done in his interview—that the PRC had 'little in the way of air force or navy compared to even second-rate powers', and that the army lacked strategic mobility while railroads and all-weather highways remained undeveloped. A fuller statement to the legislative branch in 1965 noted shortages of spare parts, strategic airlift, motor transportation, jet fuel, and a more general absence of the industrial infrastructure necessary to support armed forces in sustained operations.[42] Whatever McNamara might have been saying in the context of Vietnam, he rightly stated in 1964 that he did not expect China to be a first-class military power for 'many many years'.[43]

Not a first-class power, or even a modern military force, perhaps, but the PLA still retained credibility as a deterrent force. China did, after all, have the world's largest standing army, coupled with a militia sometimes calculated at 12 million which helped give support to Beijing's claims that it was impregnable to conquest by military means. As one author later put it: 'if China were to deploy the same proportion of men in the 18–45 age group as does the United States, its standing army would rise to 8,470,000'.[44] It had also demonstrated a willingness to engage in fighting, even against the most powerful armed forces in the world. Moreover, although China could not sustain large-scale operations beyond its borders, it was still regarded as capable of overrunning all of it smaller neighbours in conflicts of limited duration. Although open terrain did not favour its forces, it was assumed that mountainous or jungle conditions did. The individual soldier was regarded as rugged and loyal, and defections were thought by the CIA to be 'extremely unlikely'.[45] Clearly, these kinds of conclusions rested on the Korean war experience and on the conflict against India in 1962, and they had relevance

[42] *United States Defense Policies in 1964; United States Defense Policies in 1965*, both published in Washington, DC by the US Government Printing Office, 1965 and 1966.
[43] *New York Herald Tribune*, 7 May 1964.
[44] Lowell Dittmer, *Sino-Soviet Normalization and its International Implications* (Seattle: University of Washington Press, 1992), 149.
[45] NSF Country file, Vietnam, CIA Report, Boxes 50–1, 'Probable Effects in China and Taiwan of a GRC Attack on the Mainland', 18 Aug. 1965, LBJL.

for the kind of fighting the United States was being drawn into in Vietnam.

The Johnson administration, in determining the scope of its Vietnam operations in 1965, most frequently resorted to the Korean analogy.[46] The failure to take Chinese threats to enter the Korean peninsula seriously in October 1950, and the subsequent overwhelming of UN Command armies in December 1950 ('the ghost of the Yalu debacle', as William Bundy later put it[47]) were powerful memories, readily stirred by engagement in another conflict involving a country on China's borders divided into its communist and non-communist halves. Korea 'shaped the administration's definition' of the challenge raised by Vietnam, and helped to convince the US administration of the need to intervene. But it also served to contain the area of fighting because leading figures in the Johnson administration, including the President and his Secretary of State, estimated that the PLA would become directly involved in ground operations if US forces crossed the 17th parallel or bombed the North in a way that suggested the US sought the total destruction of North Vietnam.[48] Indeed, in most respects Johnson was right to assume this: in March 1965, the Beijing leadership determined that, although it would try and avoid direct military confrontation with the United States, it would send combat forces to Vietnam, if Hanoi requested it; moreover, if the US retaliated against China, it would meet that attack. In April, the Beijing leadership decided to hit back at any American planes that invaded the country's air space. More specifically still, by June 1965, Vietnamese and Chinese leaders had agreed that, if the US did not put its combat troops into the North, the Vietnamese would fight on their own; but, if US troops crossed the 17th parallel, the PLA would both operate as a strategic reserve and carry out operational tasks as necessary.[49]

The fear in Washington was not necessarily that the United States would lose such a war—here, China's presumed inability to sustain a protracted conflict if its supply lines came under

---

[46] This is discussed in detail in Yuen Foong Khong, *Analogies at War* (Princeton, NJ: Princeton University Press, 1991), esp. ch. 5.

[47] Bundy quoted ibid. 143.   [48] Ibid. 140–3.

[49] Chen Jian, 'The Failure of an "Alliance Between Brotherly Comrades": China's Involvement with the Vietnam War, 1964–1969', paper given at Nobel Institute, Oslo, Apr. 1993, 11, 14, 23.

attack proved relevant—but that US casualties would become prohibitively greater, and that there would be serious domestic and international costs attached to such action. As William Bundy later described it, it was *'assumed* that any such war would be a national disaster'.[50] Thus, the Johnson administration chose to launch graduated bombing attacks against the North rather than immediate, heavy, and sustained barrages, and decided against a US ground intervention in North Vietnam.

The Vietnam war also bore a relationship to China and its military standing in other respects. With Vietnam depicted at first as a Chinese-inspired 'war of national liberation', Washington was concerned to defeat a Chinese model of warfare that might be viewed as instructive elsewhere in the Third World. The long-range study of China, already referred to, argued that it was in these areas where Beijing's leaders believed they could 'best contend for world power status and influence, because the doctrine Mao and his colleagues developed through their revolutionary struggle is peculiarly relevant to these areas, because strong anti-Western attitudes and dismal economic situations reinforce that relevance, and because the capitalist-imperialist states are ill-prepared by habit, bent, and stance to resist protracted "people's wars of national liberation"'.[51] The absence of a well-equipped, modern fighting force paradoxically could be an advantage to China, if Beijing sought to demonstrate the relevance of its experience to certain struggles in the Third World, and to claim that the centre of world revolution was no longer in Moscow but was now in Beijing.

In the early stages of the Vietnam conflict, administration rhetoric and that of the informed public tended to underscore these commonalities between Beijing and revolutionary struggles in less-developed nations. Mao's writings on guerrilla warfare had 'become classic references' McNamara noted in March 1964.[52] General Griffith's study concurred with this assessment, noting that both General Giap in Vietnam and Che Guevara in Cuba had based their thinking on Mao's ideas: 'The Chairman's unique

[50] William Bundy quoted in Khong, *Analogies at War*, 143.

[51] NSF Country File—China, Communist China Long Range Study, vol. III, Box 245, annex v, June 1966, LBJL.

[52] F. M. Kail, *What Washington Said: Administration Rhetoric and the Vietnam War 1949–1969* (New York: Harper and Row, 1973), 26.

contribution to military literature will continue to exercise a profound influence over the organization and conduct of revolutionary guerrilla operations',[53] he asserted. A long and well-publicized exposition of Mao's ideas came with the publication in September 1965 of Lin Biao's 'Long Live the Victory of People's War!' With Lin's call to surround the cities—i.e. the developed world—by the countryside—the Third World—McNamara and other administration spokespersons reacted in an alarmist way to this document. The Secretary of Defense described it in October 'as a program of aggression . . . that ranks with Hitler's *Mein Kampf*'; an analogy that resonated with those keen to portray Beijing not only as inherently aggressive but also as expansionist.[54]

But this perception of Beijing was difficult to sustain. China kept secret—and the US drew little attention to—the direct clashes that occurred over the course of the war between US fighter planes and Chinese anti-aircraft batteries in North Vietnam, only reporting the shooting down of American aircraft over Chinese air space.[55] Reinterpretations within the US scholarly community of Lin Biao's statement noting its emphasis on self-reliance in revolutionary struggle,[56] and—more significantly—tacit signalling between the American and Chinese governments through which the latter laid down the conditions under which Chinese forces would find it necessary to enter the Vietnam fighting,[57] contributed to a reduction in tension. With reduced fear of intervention, US references to China's role as a model or to its direct support of the North Vietnamese and Vietcong dwindled.[58] Indeed, instead, China began to be depicted as somewhat pragmatic and cautious, much as Allen Whiting among others had been arguing for some time. As William Bundy (Assistant Secretary of State for Far Eastern Affairs) put it in

[53] Griffith, *The Chinese People's Liberation Army*, 290.

[54] Kail, *What Washington Said*, 27.

[55] Chen, 'The Failure of an Alliance', 23; Allen S. Whiting, *The Chinese Calculus of Deterrence* (Ann Arbor: University of Michigan Press, 1975), 186–8.

[56] See e.g. Edmund Stillman, 'The Political Issues: Facts and Fantasies', in Frank E. Armbruster, Herman Kahn, *et al.*, *Can We Win in Vietnam?* (London: Pall Mall Press, 1968); David P. Mozingo and Thomas W. Robinson, *Lin Piao on 'People's War': China Takes a Second Look at Vietnam* (Santa Monica, Calif.: Rand Corporation, 1965); Donald Zagoria's testimony before Senate Foreign Relations Committee, Iriye, ed., *U.S. Policy Toward China*, 101.

[57] Franz Schurmann, *The Logic of World Power* (New York: Pantheon, 1974), 511–15; Chang, *Friends and Enemies*, 272.

[58] Kail, *What Washington Said*, 27–9.

February 1966, the Chinese leaders had not sought 'a confrontation of military power with us, and in any situation that would be
likely to lead to wider conflict they are tactically cautious'.[59] A few
months later, Johnson announced concrete conciliatory gestures
which indicated a growing belief that Chinese caution might lead
them to be receptive to US overtures, or, more negatively, if
Beijing chose not to respond, could show to world and domestic
opinion that it was China itself that was the rigid actor in the Sino-
American relationship. The policy of 'containment without isolation' began to take formal shape.

There were then important shifts in US perceptions taking
place, despite the inauspicious circumstances of the Cultural
Revolution and the continuance of the Vietnam war. China did, of
course, remain an enemy, and with its testing of a thermonuclear
device in 1967 potentially a formidable one. Rusk, for one, was
clearly uncertain about the development of a policy that was
designed to contain China but also to draw it into the community
of nations. In October 1967, he reminded his audience that 'within
the next decade or two, there will be a billion Chinese on the
mainland, armed with nuclear weapons, with no certainty about
what their attitude toward the rest of Asia will be'.[60] In his last
major statement on China in January 1968, he admitted that
Beijing was not the 'real' enemy in Vietnam, but it still mattered
that Beijing was an advocate of the violent overthrow of legally
constituted governments. China was a 'state antagonistic to what
we and virtually every other state in the world see as the rule of
law and order in international relations'.[61]

Rusk's 1967 speech did draw attention to some important issues: it emphasized that significant change had come about as a
result of China's acquisition of a nuclear capability, and it
dredged up fears of a country with a huge population apparently
willing to bear enormous burdens in the pursuit of objectives that
challenged world-order principles. Yet, in respect of conventional
military capabilities, it came to be accepted in the United States
that China's military potential had never been fully realized.
Moreover, Beijing now faced on its northern border an enemy that
knew much about the outdated equipment it utilized, and about

---

[59] Quoted in Chang, *Friends and Enemies*, 272.
[60] Quoted in Stillman, 'The Political Issues', 130. See also Warren I. Cohen, *Dean
Rusk* (Totowa, NJ: Cooper Square publishers, 1980), 280.
[61] Cohen, *Dean Rusk*, 288.

the organization of its military command. The 1969 border war demonstrated only too clearly that Chinese weaknesses in firepower, anti-tank weaponry, and aircraft, left northern China 'extremely vulnerable to a combined Soviet ground and air assault'.[62] The Nixon administration clearly feared that any escalation in the conflict could lead to China being '"smashed" in a Sino-Soviet war', an outcome which it had then decided would be against American strategic interests.[63]

Earlier chapters have suggested how this revolutionary conclusion came to be reached: the steady loss of domestic and international support for America's China policies; the recognition that the ending of the Sino-Soviet alliance had cost Beijing dearly in material terms in the US perception; and the development of the belief that the time had come to draw China into an alignment directed against a more powerful Soviet Union.

Given the eventual success of this strategy of alignment under Nixon, US administration officials continued to have an interest in discerning the quality of China's armed forces, perhaps now in helping to improve them. Following the *rapprochement* in relations after 1972, US officials and other specialists were able to observe Beijing's armed forces at first hand on China's own territory. In the winter of 1976, for example, the respected military correspondent of the *New York Times*, Drew Middleton, reached a series of telling conclusions about the PLA following a three-week visit at the invitation of the Chinese Ministry of Defence and Foreign Affairs. In his published assessment, he noted that the military had to work with an outdated defence doctrine and with weapons at least 10 to 15 years behind those of the major powers. It had but fifty MiG-21s, the only aircraft that would be able to compete with the MiG-23 or Su-17 and Su-19s of the contemporary Soviet air force. In 1976, he found that the army was still spending a great deal of its time on close combat and bayonet fighting. China was, he argued, in a highly exposed position with respect to enemy air attack, with inadequate radar and no practical military communications system.[64] The inevitable conclusion

---

[62] Pollack, 'China's Military Power', 70.

[63] Henry Kissinger, *White House Years* (Boston: Little, Brown, 1979), 182 ff. See my Ch. 5 for further discussion of this assessment.

[64] *New York Times*, 1–3 Dec. 1976.

was, therefore, that with respect to the Soviet Union China could do little more than tie down forces that might otherwise be available for employment elsewhere.

Before long, these conventional weaknesses were to be demonstrated in graphic form in the context of a fight against an Asian state on China's borders, when China attacked its erstwhile ally, Vietnam. Launched one week after Deng Xiaoping's visit to the United States, and one month after the formal establishment of diplomatic relations between the United States and China, the war to teach Vietnam a lesson appeared to be taking place in quite propitious international circumstances. Nevertheless, such circumstances could not make up for China's combat deficiencies. Some twenty Chinese divisions were thrown into the conflict, together with border support units. As in the past, China used light-infantry tactics and relied on deception and surprise. At a later stage of this brief but bloody conflict, it launched a set-piece battle designed to take the town of Langson using tank infantry and following this up with night and close-quarters fighting. For the movement of supplies it relied on trucks and human porters. Although the Chinese did try to combine large-scale artillery into their operations, one student of this war has nevertheless concluded that the PLA 'basically just integrated light tanks and heavy artillery into the same tactics used in India in 1962, during the early months in Korea in 1951, and during the later phases of the civil war'. There was still 'no reason to believe the PRC [could] project conventional military power any further beyond its borders today than it could in 1950'.[65]

The strategic alignment that developed between the United States and China and directed against Moscow encouraged the Ford and especially Carter administrations to make good some of these deficiencies. The previous chapter noted America's tacit acceptance of the British sale of the Spey jet engine, the effect of which would be to 'advance China's jet propulsion technology by at least a halfdozen years'.[66] In 1980, Washington itself issued 400 export licences to China, the majority of which were for the export of military technology, to include radar, electronics, transport

[65] Harlan W. Jencks, 'China's "Punitive" War on Vietnam: A Military Assessment', *Asian Survey*, 19, no. 8 (Aug. 1979).
[66] Pollack, 'China's Military Power', 80.

aircraft, and helicopters.[67] But both governments realized that any major transformation of China's military capabilities would be a prolonged process. In 1979, a Pentagon study concluded that it would cost between $41 and $63 billion for China to procure the military goods and services needed to defend itself with confidence against a Soviet conventional attack, that its ability to absorb advanced systems would be limited, and that to make an effective contribution in any joint US–Chinese operation against Russia, US combat troops would require prepositioned munitions, equipment, and a supporting base structure. China had 'virtually no capacity to project meaningful forces against the Soviet Union and if they [the Chinese] chose to attack, would have to content themselves with intermittent shallow raids'. Should the West choose to remain neutral in any Sino-Soviet conflict, although China would survive, it would be 'weakened substantially'.[68] Such conclusions exposed well the military limitations of the strategic triangle; and at the time they were published probably reinforced an impression in the United States that Beijing needed Washington more than the latter needed Beijing.

From the 1950s to the 1970s, US perceptions of China as a conventional military power underwent considerable refinement. During the 1950s, the US assessment of China's growing military potential, a potential spurred on by impressive industrial growth levels and the Soviet transfer of equipment and scientific knowledge, seriously alarmed the Eisenhower administration. With the shift in emphasis in Chinese military doctrine in 1954 and the continuing closeness in relations with the Soviets at that time, it appeared that the rugged and resourceful Chinese infantryman would soon undertake advanced training to include the use of more modern equipment.

However, observation of China's use of force in 1958, 1962, and 1969, Beijing's removal of General Peng Dehuai from his position as Minister of Defence in 1959, and renewed emphasis on

[67] *SIPRI* Yearbook (London: Taylor & Francis, 1981), 181. China in 1984 became the second socialist country after Yugoslavia to receive equipment under the US Foreign Military Sales Program. *SIPRI* Yearbook, 1985, 359.

[68] The Pentagon prepared this study as guidance for policy-makers, and not in order to forward policy proposals. Its conclusions were reported in the *New York Times*, 4 Jan. 1980.

'people's war' and on training a people's militia, led to a more restrained assessment of China's capabilities. The obvious strains in the Sino-Soviet relationship from 1958 and eventual loss of Soviet military assistance and technology transfer, together with the economic weaknesses arising out of the failure of Great Leap policies, and the nature of the activities that had to be undertaken by the PLA in order to bring the violent and chaotic Cultural Revolution to a speedier close, added to this perception that China would not after all soon develop modernized armed forces. Its apparent reluctance to intervene openly in the Vietnam fighting in 1965 reinforced a perception that it would only engage in combat when its own territory (or disputed territory that it claimed), was under direct threat of attack. Whereas in these circumstances China could probably intimidate many of its neighbours with the threat of a swift campaign, had already demonstrated its mastery at integrating political with military objectives, and could effectively deter a land war on Chinese soil, it could not project power beyond its borders in any kind of sustained way, and had shown no ability to fight a modern war using combined operations.

Moreover, in later years, the actions of a few of its neighbours began to cast doubt on its military predominance in the region: Vietnam in 1979 was able to hold regular Chinese divisions for some time solely with its border forces, and India, which may not have had the occasion (fortunately) to demonstrate its strength in a further border conflict with the PRC, nevertheless between 1964 and 1980 had spent some $30 billion on force modernization, acquiring in the course of this an airforce that was more advanced than China's.[69]

The single most important factor in prompting US administrations to downgrade their assessments of China's military capabilities may have been the loss of Soviet support from 1960. Until that date, Chinese and Soviet aircraft and missile forces had been quite similar in their technical standards, with the Soviets retaining a lead of only a few years. After 1960, the Chinese more or less marked time and the gap began to grow. It took until 1970 before

---

[69] Onkar Marwah, 'India's Military Power and Policy', in Marwah and Pollack, eds., *Military Power and Policy*; Rajan Menon, 'The Military and Security Dimensions of Soviet–Indian Relations', in Robert H. Donaldson, ed., *The Soviet Union in the Third World: Successes and Failures* (Boulder, Colo.: Westview Press, 1981).

the F-9, the country's first domestically designed and produced fighter aircraft appeared, but then only in limited numbers. Apparently, it was judged a failure by outside military observers.[70] By 1979, the US military reinforced these earlier perceptions and repeated that any major transformation of China's armed forces would be enormously costly, that China would find it virtually impossible to launch an attack on the territory of its primary enemy, and that this would continue to be the case for many years to come.

Over the whole period, therefore, China's strength has lain in defence rather than offence and it has wisely avoided the serious, protracted warfare it had engaged in on the Korean peninsula. This realization contributed in the United States to a more sober and less alarmist appreciation of China's capabilities, and helped to create an environment which promoted the *rapprochement* in relations. Such an ability to deter military attack is not to be denigrated as a source of power, however. As one author has noted, no outside military force has seen fit to engage China in areas over which it has unquestioned territorial control for fear of being sucked into a people's war.[71] The sheer size of China's armed forces and its potential to increase the numbers thrown into combat, together with the status accorded Mao's writings on and experience with guerrilla warfare, have made up for some of its deficiencies in the techniques of modern warfare, and in its inability to project power. Governments have also been in little doubt that China would fight to support its sovereign claims and territorial integrity. The United States and other states in the global system recognized that China had built this 'wall of iron' even as Washington recognized the corollary: that China on its own could not convincingly break through it.

---

[70] Pollack, *Defense Modernization*, 8.
[71] Pollack, 'China's Military Power', 63.

7

The Politics of Nuclear Weapons: China as a Nuclear Power

The PRC has the dubious distinction of having been threatened with nuclear attack more frequently than any other state in the global system. During the conflict in Korea, the tensions in 1954 over Indo-China, and during the two Taiwan Straits crises, the United States issued explicit and implicit threats of a compellent and deterrent nature. As China's relations with the Soviet Union deteriorated in the 1960s, culminating in the border war of 1969, nuclear threats formed part of the discourse of that crisis, too. Beijing's decision to develop its own nuclear arsenal owed much to Washington's resort to nuclear coercion; and the break with Moscow at the end of the 1950s forced China's decision to strike out on its own in this field. Yet China's determination to acquire these weapons was not only connected with national security but also with questions of national autonomy and self-esteem. It seems probable that, although these direct nuclear threats resurrected or reinforced painful memories of past humiliations by great powers, China would have taken the nuclear route anyway.

China's explosion of its atomic device in October 1964 added new complexities to the Sino-American relationship and to their respective broader foreign-policy agendas. For the Chinese, there was the concern that the United States might attack its facilities before it had developed a credible strike force. Having described the two superpowers as 'self-ordained nuclear overlords', they also feared that developing countries might perceive China also as having joined the ranks of the 'oppressor nations'. For the United States, there was the problem of what difference this made to China's power position in the global system, the security and psychological impact on China's neighbours, and whether in these circumstances Washington's policy of isolating China remained workable. In terms of its structural concerns, Washington also needed to assess the ramifications of this change in China's status on the developing non-proliferation norm. Predictably, the non-recognition policy came under increased domestic and international scrutiny as a result of China's nuclear test, a test that increased Beijing's prestige, especially in the Third World, where fear of this technological achievement was mixed with admiration that the industrialized world's monopoly had at last been overcome.

At a time, therefore, when the United States had begun to make a more sober and informed assessment of China's conventional military, economic, and political capabilities, the atomic development complicated the overall assessment that China so far had failed to fulfil its power potential. More broadly, the atomic test demonstrated that with sufficient determination and the necessary scientific and technological skills any nation could overcome objective weaknesses in other areas; any adversary could render inoperable what it perceived as America's nuclear blackmail.

Acquiring the Bomb

There were both proximate and longer-term causes that led to China's decision to acquire a nuclear capability. As noted above, these were connected with explicit and implicit American threats and with the assumption that such a capability conferred a great power status that could not be ignored. It was widely agreed that such weapons constituted 'a vivid demarcation of power in the international system'.[1]

During the Korean war, both the Truman and Eisenhower administrations had searched for the means of exploiting their nuclear arsenal in ways that would influence both the fighting and the negotiating process. The Truman administration believed that it had a clear, if qualified, nuclear superiority over the Soviet Union that ought to be usable, and its first moves in early July 1950 were designed to deter the Soviets from entering the fighting. At the end of the month, however, China was the major

---

[1] Jonathan D. Pollack, 'China and the Global Strategic Balance', in Harry Harding, ed., *China's Foreign Relations in the 1980s* (New Haven: Yale University Press, 1984), 172.

focus of the deterrent effort. To this end, the US administration decided to add ten nuclear-configured B29s to the Strategic Air Command (SAC) task force that was due to cross the Pacific. This deterrent action was unsuccessful, of course, but resorted to again in April 1951, this time in response to a Communist force buildup of personnel and aircraft which led to fears in Washington that UN forces would be attacked from the air and cut off at sea from Japanese bases. In these circumstances, Truman approved the transfer of B29s carrying complete atomic weapons to the Pacific theatre.[2] During the same period, C. B. Marshall of the State Department's Policy Planning Staff, in conversations with a Chinese national identified with non-Communist elements in the Beijing government, issued generalized threats. He outlined the difficulties of constraining American emotions during the Korean fighting when these feelings dictated laying waste to Chinese cities and destroying Chinese industries.[3]

During the Eisenhower era, his administration's use of nuclear coercion, closely followed by the resolution of the one remaining issue at the Korean armistice talks,[4] encouraged the President and his Secretary of State to believe that these threats had been effective in compelling China to end the fighting. (Chinese sources suggest that Beijing's leaders had in fact discounted a nuclear attack, and feared instead an amphibious landing, given American generals' experience and success with such operations.[5]) The belief in the efficacy of America's warnings to Beijing

[2] Roger Dingman, 'Atomic Diplomacy During the Korean War', *International Security*, 13, no. 3 (Winter 1988/9), 62, 72.

[3] Rosemary Foot, *A Substitute for Victory: the Politics of Peacemaking at the Korean Armistice Talks* (Ithaca, NY: Cornell University Press, 1990), 32, 35. There were other instances during the Truman era, including Truman's press conference on 30 Nov. 1950 at which he had implied that the use of atomic weapons was under active consideration. One message of the Senate Hearings into General MacArthur's dismissal from his UN and Far Eastern commands was that if the enemy widened the war the United States would retaliate in ways and by means of its own choosing. Similar expectations were raised in the so-called 'Greater Sanction' statement, negotiated during the Truman era and issued one week after the signature of the Korean Armistice agreement. It stated: 'if there was a renewal of the armed attack . . . we should again be united and prompt to resist. The consequences of such a breach of the armistice would be so grave that, in all probability, it would not be possible to confine hostilities within the frontiers of Korea.'

[4] Rosemary Foot, 'Nuclear Coercion and the ending of the Korean Conflict', *International Security*, 13, no. 3 (Winter 1988/9).

[5] See, in particular, Zhang Shu Guang, *Deterrence and Strategic Culture: Chinese–*

reinforced the US administration's decision to develop the 'New Look Strategy' based on the threat of massive retaliation against any attack on America's allies. As a result, atomic threats were issued during later crises involving the two countries. For example, on the assumption that after Korea China would step up its involvement in Indo-China, Dulles warned in September 1953 that a 'second aggression could not occur without grave consequences which might not be confined to Indo-China', a warning that he repeated at a press conference at the end of the year. At numerous press conferences during the first Taiwan Straits crisis in 1954–5, the US President, Vice-President, and Secretary of State all hinted at the possible use of atomic weapons.[6] Dulles's *Life Magazine* article of January 1956 foreshadowed the continuation of such threats, given the repetition of his belief in their efficacy: 'Nobody is able to prove mathematically that it was the policy of deterrence which brought the Korean War to an end and which kept the Chinese from sending their Red armies into IndoChina, or that it has finally stopped them in Formosa. I think it is a fair inference that it has.'[7] With the US decision in May 1957 to station Matador missiles on Taiwan, missiles that were capable of flying 650 miles per hour, that had a range of 600 miles, and that could carry atomic warheads, the nuclear threat against China became more tangible still.

These experiences alone were—not surprisingly—enough to lead Chinese officials to a firm determination to manufacture a bomb, at that stage preferably with Soviet assistance. But clearly there were always other reasons for acquiring nuclear weapons: their association with great-power status, with Beijing's desire to right the wrongs of a humiliating past, and with its goal of economic modernization.[8] For example, during the Korean conflict,

American Confrontations, 1949–1958 (Ithaca, NY: Cornell University Press, 1992), 133.

[6] Jan H. Kalicki, *The Pattern of Sino-American Crises* (London: Cambridge University Press, 1975), 82; Richard K. Betts, *Nuclear Blackmail and Nuclear Balance* (Washington, DC: The Brookings Institution, 1987), 59–62; He Di, 'The Evolution of the People's Republic of China's Policy Toward the Offshore Islands', in Warren I. Cohen and Akira Iriye, eds., *The Great Powers in East Asia* (New York: Columbia University Press, 1990), 144 ; Zhang, *Deterrence and Strategic Culture*, 213–15.

[7] James Shepley, 'How Dulles Averted War', *Life Magazine*, 16 Jan. 1956.

[8] These motives for acquiring nuclear weapons are not unknown outside of China, a point made by Brahma Chellaney in 'South Asia's Passage to Nuclear

although there is evidence to support the position that Chinese leaders believed that Washington had greatly exaggerated the power and effectiveness of nuclear weapons, and that properly designed underground shelters and tunnels could be used to shield troops from nuclear attack,[9] Beijing clearly recognized their political power. As one leader put it in 1951, 'only when we ourselves have the atomic weapon, and are fully prepared, is it possible for the frenzied warmongers to listen to our just and reasonable proposals'.[10] It was a perspective that was to resurface on numerous occasions after that: Mao in 1956 stated that 'if we are not to be bullied in the present day world, we cannot do without the Bomb'; he said again in 1958, as it was becoming clear that China could not rely on Soviet assistance, without the bomb 'others don't think what we say carries weight'. Although China derided the United States for dividing the world into those which possessed nuclear weapons and those which did not, China wanted to make sure that it counted by becoming a member of the nuclear club.[11]

Chinese leaders also made the argument that harnessing such technology was a reflection of a country's level of development and that it enhanced a state's overall ability to modernize. Chen Yi, China's Foreign Minister, explained in 1963 why China should make every effort to acquire a nuclear weapons capability: 'Atomic bombs, missiles, and supersonic aircraft are a reflection of the technical level of a nation's industry,' he said. Without a

---

Power', *International Security*, 16, no. 1 (Summer 1991). For example, when India successfully tested its first IRBM, the head of the missile programme said: 'Agni [the missile] is a technological strength. Strength respects strength. Weaklings are not honored. So we should be strong' (p. 60). During the discussions in Britain to decide whether to build a hydrogen bomb, Churchill argued that 'we could not expect to maintain our influence as a world power unless we possessed the most up-to-date nuclear weapons'. Quoted in Norman Dombey and Eric Grove, 'Britain's Thermonuclear Bluff', *London Review of Books*, 22 Oct. 1992, 8; see too Margaret M. Gowing, *Independence and Deterrence: Britain and Atomic Energy, 1945–1952* (London: Macmillan, 1974).

[9] Mark A. Ryan, *Chinese Attitudes toward Nuclear Weapons: China and the United States during the Korean War* (Armonk, NY: M. E. Sharpe, 1989), esp. ch. 7.

[10] William R. Harris, 'Chinese Nuclear Doctrine: The Decade Prior to Weapons Development, (1945–55)', *China Quarterly*, 21 (Jan.–Mar. 1965), 94.

[11] Mao Zedong, 'On the Ten Great Relationships', *Selected Works*, v (Beijing: Foreign Languages Press, 1977), 288; John Wilson Lewis and Xue Litai, *China Builds the Bomb* (Stanford, Calif.: Stanford University Press, 1988), 36; Morton H. Halperin, *China and the Bomb* (New York: Praeger, 1965), 52.

mastery of this technology, China would, he suggested, 'degenerate into a second-class or third-class nation'.[12]

The acquisition of nuclear weapons could also contribute to overcoming the psychological drain associated with the humiliations of China's past. Mao's reference to being bullied in the present-day world harked back to an era marked by the imposition of unequal treaties and to past encroachments on China's sovereignty. Premier Zhou Enlai made that historical link plainer still when, two months after China's detonation of its first atomic device, he triumphantly declared: 'Have we not exploded an atom bomb? Has not the label, "sick man of the east," fastened on us by Westerners, been flung off?'[13] These longer-term historical influences, the concern with international prestige, combined with the actual threats to the security of new China, were sufficient to push Beijing towards its decision to acquire the bomb.

The actual timing of that decision owed much to the threats and boasts after the conclusion of the Korean armistice which had sensitized the Chinese to the nuclear issue. From the Western news media they had obtained a fairly full picture of the US 'New Look' defence strategy, and had noted its emphasis on nuclear attack. Nehru also commented on the doctrine of massive retaliation and on the possibility of a US attack on the Chinese mainland, a comment to which the Chinese apparently paid special attention.[14] Partly in response to a widening of the strategic debate in post-Stalinist Russia, and partly because of the American development of the hydrogen bomb, Chinese leaders started to explore more openly the relationship between nuclear weapons and warfare. They began with a consideration of the possible role

[12] Alice Langley Hsieh, 'The Sino-Soviet Nuclear Dialogue: 1963', in Raymond L. Garthoff, ed., *Sino-Soviet Military Relations* (New York: Praeger, 1966), 164.

[13] Chong-pin Lin, *China's Nuclear Weapons Strategy: Tradition within Evolution* (Lexington, Mass.: Lexington Books, 1988), 106. Also worth noting in this regard is the PLA statement after China's first SLBM test in 1982. That statement recalled the sinking of China's warships by the Japanese navy in 1894–5: 'the billowing waves splashed up by the SLBM washed clean the historical shame imposed on this great nation' (ibid.). General Nie Rongzhen has also written in his memoirs: 'In order to terminate the bullying and humiliation of our country by the imperialists for more than a century, we [decided we should] develop sophisticated weapons, symbolized by missiles and A-bombs.' Quoted in William T. Tow, *Encountering the Dominant Player: U.S. Extended Deterrence Strategy in the Asia-Pacific* (New York: Columbia University Press, 1991), 210.

[14] Lewis and Xue, *China Builds the Bomb*, 256 n. 39.

of tactical nuclear weapons, and of the consequences of surprise attack, now thought more likely as a result of technological developments in delivery systems and the greater destructive power of thermonuclear weapons.[15] It was also in 1954 that the decision was taken to make the Chinese Academy of Sciences (CAS) an independent body under the State Council and to step up research into the basic sciences. These decisions had funding implications: by 1957, CAS's budget had been increased threefold over 1953, with a large proportion going towards the purchase of Western scientific literature.[16]

The most critical moment for the development of the nuclear programme came on 15 January 1955. All senior members of the Chinese politburo attended an enlarged meeting of the Central Secretariat called to explore the possibility of starting to build nuclear weapons. With a sample of uranium on the table, the scientists present conducted an introductory seminar in nuclear physics. Mao quickly reached the decision that China should 'devote major efforts to developing atomic energy research'. In typically optimistic vein, he made the move towards testing an atomic device seem capable of early realization: 'we possess the human and natural resources, and therefore every kind of miracle can be performed'.[17]

Those human resources needed to undergo further training, however, and the natural resources had to be discovered and adapted. Certain of the scientists who were to play a crucial role in the nuclear programme—for example, Qian Sanqiang, He Zehui, and Peng Huanwu—had received training in Europe during the war years, the first two studying nuclear physics at the Curie Institute in Paris, and the latter working with the Nobel Laureate, Max Born, in Edinburgh.[18] But in the 1950s, the link with the Soviet scientific community and access to its publications was to prove vital. In 1954, Moscow invited several Chinese military leaders, including Defence Minister Peng Dehuai, to the Soviet Union to observe a military manœuvre after a simulated atomic explosion.[19] In October that year, the two socialist allies signed an

[15] Harris, 'Chinese Nuclear Doctrine', 91–3.
[16] Ibid. 95; Lewis and Xue, *China Builds the Bomb*, 42.
[17] Ibid. 38–9.   [18] Ibid. 44.
[19] He Di, 'Paper or Real Tiger: America's Nuclear Deterrence and Mao Zedong's Response', unpublished paper in my possession, dated 26 Apr. 1992, p. 44 .

agreement on scientific and technical co-operation and decided to establish a Sino-Soviet Scientific Commission. On 17 January 1955, the Soviet government announced that it would give aid to China and several Eastern European countries to help their research into the 'peaceful uses of atomic energy'. This was the first of six accords signed between 1955 and 1958 and designed to develop China's nuclear science industry and weapons programme. Notably, this first agreement included a secret plan to undertake joint exploration for uranium in China.[20]

Later Sino-Soviet polemics, together with the nature of the accord, ensured that most international attention was subsequently given to the agreement signed in October 1957. Moscow agreed in this 'New Defence Technical Accord' to provide China with a prototype bomb and missiles, along with related technical data. This breakthrough in Sino-Soviet co-operation was negotiated not long after the unrest in Poland and the Soviet intervention in Hungary in 1956, which explained much about the timing of it in General Nie Rongzhen's view. Nie, who was formally in charge of national scientific and technological development between 1956 and 1966, later claimed that this agreement only came about as a result of the difficulties Khrushchev experienced over Eastern Europe, difficulties that improved China's value as a socialist ally and thus strengthened its bargaining position. Prior to that agreement, Moscow had been cautious in offering support in this area: aid had been slow in reaching the Chinese scientists and had 'excluded assistance on the advanced weapons themselves'. The Soviets had also asserted that they could only assist with the training of some fifty personnel in missile research.[21]

Despite the 1957 agreement, however, this cautious Soviet approach to nuclear co-operation soon resurfaced. Most analysts place Moscow's decision to renege on the 1957 accord as coming early in 1958, although the agreement was not officially rescinded until June 1959. It arose primarily from a clear difference between the two communist allies over strategic doctrine. The Maoist approach to nuclear war was to regard it as one stage of a protracted conflict that China would eventually win, given its large population and predominantly rural economy. The PRC's deterrent strategy rested, then, on the notion of the denial of victory to any

---

[20] Lewis and Xue, *China Builds the Bomb*, 41, and n.
[21] Ibid. 62; and *Beijing Review*, 17 (29 Apr. 1985), 15–16.

aggressor—what has been referred to as active defence—and not on the concept of retaliatory punishment. As in many other areas, Mao tended to extrapolate from Chinese demographic conditions to the global arena. Moreover, he believed it essential to overcome the fear and resulting paralysis that development of nuclear weapons had brought in its wake. He stressed, therefore, that the conditions that made it possible for China to survive a nuclear war were more widely applicable. As the Chinese have quoted Mao as stating: 'If the worst came to the worst and half of mankind died, the other half would remain while imperialism would be razed to the ground . . . in a number of years there would be 2,700 million people again.'[22]

Also in this period, Mao interpreted Soviet achievements in the satellite and missile fields in 1957 as underlining a trend where the East was beginning to prevail over the West. A static measurement of capabilities meant little to Mao, who tended to emphasize the psychological boost that could come as a result of this kind of technological breakthrough, a boost which he claimed would allow liberation movements to take to the offensive against imperialists who were now on the defensive.

Moscow, on the other hand, interpreted these scientific developments quite differently from Beijing and argued that nuclear weapons had changed the nature of the relationship between the two blocs. Soviet leaders were coming, then, to appreciate the connection between war prevention and the doctrine of mutual retaliation. They interpreted these technological developments as contributions to the policy of peaceful coexistence with the United States, based on a common great-power understanding of the destructive nature of nuclear war. The Chinese, in their view, did not seem to share this understanding. Their reaction to Khrushchev's speech in Beijing in September 1959, during which he warned them not to use armed force to test the West, demonstrated to the Soviets that they were 'keen on war like a bellicose cock'.[23] As Khrushchev was to put it in October 1960, Beijing refused to accept that war with the West 'would now set humanity back centuries'.[24]

It was in 1958 that Moscow began the negotiations that eventually led to the signing of the Partial Test Ban Treaty in 1963 with

---

[22] Lewis and Xue, *China Builds the Bomb*, 66.   [23] Ibid. 72.
[24] Ann Whitman file, NSC Series, Box 13, 20 Oct. 1960, DDEL.

Britain and the United States. In a note dispatched to Washington
and Beijing on 4 April 1958, Moscow noted that only three states
at that point had nuclear weapons and that as a consequence it
would be relatively easy to end nuclear weapons testing.[25] In the
summer of 1958, its scientists worked with their American counterparts to determine the feasibility of developing a monitoring
system designed to detect secret atomic tests. In August, Eisenhower invited the Soviets to a meeting with the objective of
banning all tests, and talks began in October. Much of this
conciliatory activity coincided with the tensions over the Offshore
Islands in the Taiwan Straits.

By the middle of 1959, Moscow was willing to tie its position in
these negotiations more directly to the question of China's acquisition of a nuclear capability, refusing because of these test-ban
talks to supply Beijing with the prototype bomb and related technical information. It may have been that the Soviets were trying to
trade West Germany's non-acquisition of nuclear weapons for a
guarantee that China would also be restrained from developing
this capacity. Whatever their calculations, Soviet leaders also confirmed that Western perceptions of its stance in this policy area
mattered far more than did Chinese views of this breach of an
agreement. As a letter from the Soviet Party Central Committee
put it, 'if the Western countries learn that the Soviet Union is
supplying China with sophisticated technical aid, it is possible
that the socialist community's efforts for peace and relaxation will
be seriously sabotaged'. An angry and defiant Chinese politburo
meeting a few days later 'vowed that China would produce its
first atomic bomb within eight years'.[26]

In fact, it was only five years later that the Chinese tested their
first atomic device, a period in which, as some of its leaders
realized, it was vulnerable to attack. While Mao continued
ostensibly to 'despise the enemy strategically', leaders in more
private venues voiced their unease. It was revealed in an official
1961 PLA publication, circulated only to regimental commanders
and above, that China's military leaders were realistic about the
country's overwhelming military and technological inferiority
when compared with the United States. They also took note of its

[25] Harold P. Ford, 'The Eruption of Sino-Soviet Politico-Military Problems,
1957–1960', in Garthoff, ed., *Sino-Soviet Military Relations*, 105.
[26] Lewis and Xue, *China Builds the Bomb*, 64–5.

vulnerability to nuclear attack, especially in the light of their inability to rely on Soviet backing for China's foreign-policy objectives.[27]

As China neared testing, its government may have attempted to undercut this vulnerability by repainting the picture that had been built up of a bellicose China willing to risk nuclear war. During the Sino-American ambassadorial talks in Warsaw in August 1963, Ambassador Wang Bingnan appeared to some in Washington to be distancing his government from the view attributed to it: that it favoured war between the United States and the communist bloc. He was even willing to acknowledge his government's feelings of insecurity. As Wang put it, the United States should remove its nuclear threat to China which came from all parts of the compass—from the fortifications in Guam, from the units in Korea and Taiwan, and from the US air force, attack aircraft carriers, and submarines that operated in the Pacific Ocean.[28]

With the advent of the Chinese test in October 1964, the Beijing government issued a statement that also underlined this sense of vulnerability. Beijing declared that it would never be the first to use these weapons in any future war, that China's development of nuclear weapons was solely for defensive purposes, that its broader aims were to break the nuclear monopoly of the superpowers, and eventually to eliminate nuclear weapons altogether. In support of the argument that these weapons were for defensive use only, Beijing referred specifically to the source of the external threat: 'China cannot remain idle and do nothing in the face of ever increasing nuclear threat posed by the United States. China is forced to conduct nuclear tests and develop nuclear weapons . . . The development of nuclear weapons by China is for defence and for protecting the Chinese people from the danger of the United States launching a nuclear war.' One analyst of this and subsequent Chinese statements, made as it tested and developed its nuclear arsenal between 1964 and 1969, has found that there was 'virtually no evidence to support the argument that decisionmakers in Peking began to view China's strategic pos-

[27] Hsieh, 'China's Secret Military Papers: Military Doctrine and Strategy', *China Quarterly*, 20 (Apr.–June 1964). See also my Ch. 6.
[28] National Security File (NSF), Countries, Poland, General, Ambassadorial Talks with Ambassador Wang, Box 153, 10 Aug. 1963, JFKL.

ition as qualitatively improved by the mere possession of a limited nuclear capability', and that, on the contrary, various editorials and PLA documents showed that 'Chinese perceptions of external hostility and inferior capability remained very high throughout this period'.[29] Indeed, Chinese leaders were apparently so fearful of attack during this era that in 1964 they decided for security reasons to spend a huge proportion of the national budget on the creation of an industrial base area in remote and inhospitable regions of the country (much of which apparently still lies idle at this time).[30] It was a massive, costly, and ultimately ineffective effort by a country that ostensibly did not fear nuclear war.

The US Response to a Nuclear China

That China was vulnerable, both in the period preceding its atomic test and for several years after it, is clear from the American record and from indiscretions and hints given by Moscow at the time of the 1969 Sino-Soviet border war. To focus on American thinking, it is apparent that the United States viewed with dismay the growing evidence that China was moving towards its test, President Kennedy in particular worrying enormously about Beijing's emergence as a nuclear power.[31] Moreover, his administration was generally more concerned about proliferation than Eisenhower's had been.[32] The Soviets seemed concerned too: there had already been hints from Soviet statements, information from secretly monitored discussions, and a direct approach from the Soviet ambassador to Washington, all indicating their dismay over China's nuclear potential.[33]

Thus, in the preparations for the 1961 Vienna summit between the President and Nikita Khrushchev, Kennedy's advisers recommended that the opportunity be taken to exploit Sino-Soviet

[29] Jonathan D. Pollack, 'Chinese Attitudes Towards Nuclear Weapons, 1964–9', *China Quarterly*, 50 (1972), 249, 260.

[30] Barry Naughton, 'The Third Front: Defence Industrialization in the Chinese Interior', *China Quarterly*, 115 (Sept. 1988); He Di, 'Paper or Real Tiger', 94.

[31] James Fetzer, 'Clinging to Containment: China Policy', in Thomas G. Paterson, ed., *Kennedy's Quest for Victory: American Foreign Policy, 1961–1963* (New York: Oxford University Press, 1989), 179.

[32] George Quester, *The Politics of Nuclear Proliferation* (Baltimore, Md.: Johns Hopkins University Press, 1973), 38.

[33] Ch. 5 covers these points in more detail.

differences, especially in this promising area concerning Soviet fears of a nuclear-armed China. Apart from the general and longer-term hope of furthering the breach between the two communist states, although now it was Moscow rather than Beijing that was to be enticed, the more immediate objective was to promote the signature of a test-ban treaty which Kennedy seemed to believe would help to constrain China's own efforts to develop a nuclear arsenal.[34] (Chinese leaders were apparently in agreement with him, seeing the treaty as a means of exerting pressure on China to stop its programme. It simply represented 'collusion' between Washington and Moscow in an 'attempt to manacle China'.[35])

US administrations had always tended to evaluate China's possible development of nuclear weapons in the context of its relationship with the Soviet Union. In 1956, it was considered likely that Soviet pledges of assistance could lead to a small-scale Chinese nuclear research programme by 1960.[36] By 1959, the sense that Beijing would soon acquire these weapons had hardened and it was now deemed likely that nuclear forces would be based in China sometime before 1963, but probably under Soviet control.[37] But as America's intelligence reports began to detail the various facets of the emerging Sino-Soviet breach, particularly the opposing views concerning the possibility and likely outcome of a nuclear conflagration, the perception grew in Washington that Moscow might be willing to take a firmer stand against the Chinese. As Khrushchev had reported to socialist bloc leaders at a meeting in New York in October 1960—a statement monitored by US intelligence—'the US was now deterred from war by the military strength of the USSR'. He went on, 'while the USSR could liberate the world from capitalism by war, to do so would now set humanity back by centuries. Therefore, the USSR could not urge war. The Communist Chinese,' he added, 'did not understand this situation.'[38]

[34] Gordon H. Chang, *Friends and Enemies: The United States, China, and the Soviet Union, 1948–1972* (Stanford, Calif.: Stanford University Press, 1990), 230–1.
[35] Chinese statement quoted in Lewis and Xue, *China Builds the Bomb*, 193.
[36] *Foreign Relations of the United States, 1955–7* (Washington, DC: Government Printing Office, 1986), 3: 244, National Intelligence Estimate (NIE 13–56) 'Chinese Communist Capabilities and Probable Courses of Action Through 1960', 5 Jan. 1956.
[37] NSC 5913/1, 'US Policy in the Far East', 25 Sept. 1959, NA.
[38] Ann Whitman File, NSC series, 464th meeting of the NSC, Box 13, 20 Oct. 1960, DDEL.

The approach at the 1961 Vienna summit was the first concrete attempt to exploit this growing Soviet–American coincidence of interest, but on this occasion the Soviets did not make the required response, probably mindful of giving further support to Chinese charges that Moscow had come to value its relationship with Washington more highly than that with its socialist ally. However, further serious deterioration in Sino-Soviet relations through 1962 and 1963 encouraged Washington to persist in its attempts to obtain Soviet co-operation in action designed to prevent the emergence of a nuclear China. President Kennedy instructed Averell Harriman that, while he was in Moscow to negotiate the final stages of the Test Ban Treaty, he should 'elicit [Khrushchev's] view of means of limiting or preventing Chinese nuclear development and his willingness to take Soviet action or to accept U.S. actions aimed in this direction'.[39] The briefing books prepared for this trip indicated that such co-operation might even include joint military action; but it seems unlikely that Harriman presented these thoughts in his initial probes. He preferred instead to tackle the topic indirectly, asking Khrushchev what the Soviet response would be if Chinese missiles were targeted at the USSR. Again, as in 1961, the Soviet leader was unresponsive, making known his view that, over the course of this phase of the test-ban negotiations, it would be better if pressure on China appeared to be coming from other—perhaps Third World—countries. Only if China was seen to be isolated on this matter of the Test Ban Treaty could change in its behaviour possibly be effected.[40]

---

[39] Glenn T. Seaborg with Benjamin S. Loeb, *Stemming the Tide: Arms Control in the Johnson Years* (Lexington, Mass.: Lexington Books, 1987), 111. Kennedy's alarm seemed, if anything, to grow over the course of his administration. As he put it during a press conference in August 1963, China, with 'weak countries around it, 700 million people, a Stalinist internal regime, and nuclear power, and a government determined on war as a means of bringing about its ultimate success, [was] potentially a more dangerous situation than any we faced since the end of the Second [World] War'. Quoted in Allen S. Whiting, *The Chinese Calculus of Deterrence* (Ann Arbor, Mich.: The University of Michigan Press, 1975), 168.

[40] McGeorge Bundy, *Danger and Survival: Choices about the Bomb in the First Fifty Years* (New York: Random House, 1988), 460–1; Chang, *Friends and Enemies*, 246–7. Pressure on China did in fact come from other Third World countries: during Zhou's trip to Africa in the winter of 1963–4 he apparently spent a good deal of time explaining and defending his country's failure to support the Partial Test Ban Treaty. See Morton H. Halperin and Dwight H. Perkins, *Communist China and Arms Control* (Cambridge, Mass.: East Asian Research Center, 1965), 120.

As evidence proceeded apace that Beijing was making ready missile test sites, the Johnson administration returned to the question of joint pre-emptive action against China's nuclear weapons facilities. A paper produced in April 1964 queried once again whether the United States should engage in such action against the Chinese facilities that had been identified. The conclusion reached was that it would be 'undesirable except as part of military action against the mainland in response to major ChiCom aggression'.[41] In September 1964, about a month before China's first test, unilateral action was contemplated but rejected as a course of action: 'We would prefer to have a Chinese test take place than to initiate such action now. If for other reasons we should find ourselves in military hostilities at any level with the Chinese Communists, we would expect to give very close attention to the possibility of an appropriate military action against Chinese nuclear facilities.' Once again, the possibility of joint action with the Soviets was raised—from a range that included a warning to the Chinese not to test to 'a possible agreement to cooperate in preventive military action'. The memorandum added: 'The Secretary of State now intends to consult promptly with the Soviet Ambassador.'[42] But at a time when Soviet leaders were presumably preparing for Khrushchev's ouster and possibly even envisaging some means of repairing the rift with the Chinese,[43] it seems unlikely that the Soviets would have given serious consideration to any such proposal at this time. Moreover, Rusk may not have made the approach to Ambassador Dobrynin at all; at least, he does not recall doing so.[44]

Assessments of China's Power and the Impact on Non-Proliferation

Yet alongside this obvious US and Soviet concern about China's emergence as a nuclear weapons state there existed a more sober

[41] NSF Country File, China Cables, vol. I, 'The Implications of a Chinese Communist Nuclear Capability', Box 237-8, 17 Apr. 1964, LBJL.

[42] Chang, *Friends and Enemies*, 250.

[43] Polemics did diminish for a few months after Khrushchev's downfall, and it has been argued that his overthrow partly resulted from his inept handling of the dispute with China.

[44] Seaborg, *Stemming the Tide*, 112.

debate—at least in the United States—on the military and political consequences of this change in China's capabilities, the conclusion being that it made little objective *military* difference to US security, or to that of its Asian allies. The April 1964 study already referred to noted the great asymmetry in Chinese and American nuclear capabilities and vulnerabilities which made it highly unlikely that the PRC would either threaten or resort to the first use of nuclear weapons. A Chinese nuclear capability was also not seen as likely to impose any new military restrictions on the United States in its response to perceived aggression in Asia. Moreover, the paper argued, Beijing, which had already 'sought to avoid action which might provoke major military confrontation' resulting in an attack on the mainland, was deemed likely to be even more cautious given its 'soft, vulnerable' delivery systems,[45] systems that were not protected by any sophisticated radar or early warning devices. As partial confirmation of these arguments, when the Chinese test came in October 1964 Beijing did indeed adopt an explicit 'no first use' pledge.

Nevertheless, although objectively China as a nuclear weapons state hardly exercised any constraint on US activity, it was recognized that this change of status had political and psychological ramifications. Before the October test, it had already been acknowledged in Washington that such a test would have a powerful psychological impact globally. For some time, China had been denouncing the Partial Test Ban Treaty of 1963 on the grounds that it was an attempt to consolidate the nuclear monopoly of the big powers and to undermine the defence capability of the 'peace-loving countries'.[46] Breach of this monopoly would add significantly to the prestige of China and—of consequence for America's non-proliferation policy—it would mean that to be truly effective any agreement on arms control would require consideration of China's position.[47] As the April study argued, in order for the US to continue to demonstrate 'its peaceful and protective intentions' it would also have to make a 'positive statement' of its 'interest in involving the ChiComs in disarmament

---

[45] NSF Country file, China Cables, vol. 1 Box 237-8, 17 Apr. 1964, LBJL.

[46] Hsieh, 'The Sino-Soviet Nuclear Dialogue', 159.

[47] For an early academic statement of this argument see A. Doak Barnett, 'The Inclusion of Communist China in an Arms-Control Program', in Donald G. Brennan, ed., *Arms Control and Disarmament: American Views and Studies* (London: Jonathan Cape, 1961), esp. 300–3.

negotiations'.[48] Furthermore, a Chinese test would demonstrate, as a congressional study of US defence policy put it, 'that even an underdeveloped nation with tremendous economic and social problems could, if it were determined to put the nuclear goal ahead of the welfare of its people, master the art of making nuclear weapons, provided that it had the necessary scientific and technological skills and the essential basic resources'.[49] More particularly, Washington believed that an atomic test would lead neutral nations to push harder for Chinese membership in the United Nations, to calls for Beijing's participation in disarmament negotiations, and to demands within India and Japan for these countries to take the nuclear route.[50] Indeed, the US Secretary of State, Dean Rusk, showed that he too could be sympathetic to this possible Indian and Japanese argument, suggesting for a time that the United States might want to be in a position where New Delhi and Tokyo could offer a nuclear response to a Chinese threat.[51]

The means the USA first adopted to help reduce the impact on other governments and peoples of a future Chinese test was to build up the expectation that such a test would shortly occur and that the US had made ready for it. Thus, a variety of commentators began to project that an explosion would take place in 1963 or 1964. With definite evidence that a weapon was about to be tested, Rusk issued a statement on 29 September 1964 designed to reassure his audience that 'the United States has fully anticipated the possibility of Peiping's entry into the nuclear weapons field and has taken it into full account in determining our military posture and our own nuclear weapons program'.[52] He also attempted to show that China was out of step with world opinion, deploring the atmospheric test 'in the face of serious efforts made by almost all other nations to protect the atmosphere'.

After the actual detonation had taken place, the US administration's approach remained much the same, with further attempts to downgrade the significance of the event and to reduce China's moral stature as a result of it. President Johnson's statement immediately after the explosion adopted the tone of being

[48] NSF Country File, China Cables, vol. I, Box 237-8, 17 Apr. 1964, LBJL.
[49] 'United States Defense Policies in 1964', 89th Congress, 1st Session, House Document no. 285, 4 June 1965 (Washington DC: US GPO, 1965), 14.
[50] NSF Country file, China Cables, Box 237-8, 17 Apr. 1964, LBJL.
[51] Seaborg, *Stemming the Tide*, 135.   [52] Halperin, *China and the Bomb*, 83–4.

more in sorrow than in anger. The test came, he said, as 'no surprise', and its 'military significance should not be overestimated' because—as in fact turned out to be the case—many years separated the testing of a device and the acquisition of a stockpile of nuclear weapons that could be delivered reliably to their designated targets.[53] He also described the test as a tragedy for the Chinese: where other governments had chosen to work for the well-being of their people through economic modernization and the development of the peaceful uses of atomic energy, the PRC leadership, he said, had rejected that path. Two days later, on 18 October, Johnson declared that the United States would support any nation subjected to Chinese nuclear blackmail.

The British were primed, presumably, to make a response that offered similar reassurance, a Foreign Office statement saying that there was 'a vast difference between the first test of a crude device, and the emergence of a country as a nuclear power'.[54] A few days later, the US Secretary of Defense, Robert McNamara, further emphasized the crude technology employed, describing the Chinese device as 'primitive' and 'unwieldy', and arguing that it would take many years for China to move to the delivery stage.[55]

Despite this carefully worked out response to the test, however, many of the political reactions the US had feared did in fact occur. These partly came because, on the basis of incomplete intelligence, the USA had denigrated the test technically. The Johnson administration assumed it was a plutonium device, a miscalculation that allegedly came from not being able to employ photographic reconnaissance over one area of China.[56] Within a few days, the administration and scientists world-wide came to recognize that the device was in fact a sophisticated one: the Chinese had gone straight to the testing of a fission device using uranium-235, rather than first testing a heavier, dirtier plutonium bomb as the Americans and British had done before them. As the former editor of the *Journal of the American Rocket Society* and Professor of Aerospace Propulsion at Princeton put it: 'our newspaper editors and our statesmen ought to revise their beliefs and stop underestimating China's potential'. He called on his country's leaders

[53] NSF Country file, Box 22, C050–2, 16 Oct. 1964, LBJL.
[54] *The Times*, 17 Oct. 1964.   [55] *New York Herald Tribune*, 23 Oct. 1964.
[56] Seaborg, *Stemming the Tide*, 113.

to start reconsidering their foreign policy options because 'in fewer years than they think' China's nuclear weapons would be able to target America's Asian allies.[57] A Royal Institute of International Affairs (London) report, picked up by the *Egyptian Gazette*, suggested that Beijing might well have the hydrogen bomb in two to five years and not the five to ten years that had earlier been estimated.[58]

These subsequent commentaries added to a sense, already apparent from other quarters, that the test had indeed added to China's prestige and probably to that of the developing world more generally. The *Straits Times'* (Singapore) reaction was fairly typical: small as the test might have been it was 'clearly an event of almost shattering importance'. Quoting Kenya's ambassador to Beijing, the newspaper also described it as a great achievement in the Afro-Asian world, dispelling the myth that only Western countries were capable of developing atomic weaponry.[59] The *Japan Times*, even as its government strongly protested the explosion, also noted that it was 'increasingly evident' that China had 'risen to a markedly higher status among the nations of the world and its sayings and doings cannot be ignored'.[60] The US State Department's Office of Intelligence and Research (INR) conducted a survey of Afro-Asian opinion. It showed that Beijing had won loudest praise from its close allies in Asia—North Korea, North Vietnam, the Pathet Lao, the South Vietnamese Liberation Front, and Cambodia—and friendly approval from such states as Pakistan and Indonesia. In Africa, sympathetic statements were made in Ghana, Guinea, Mali, the Congo, and by the Organization of African Unity. Overall, newspaper comment in Cambodia, Indonesia, Pakistan, and in several African countries 'expressed a sense of pride in this achievement of a fellow Afro-Asian nation'. It was also observed that the harsh reaction from India, Japan, and the United States (together, it could have been added, with that from other West and East European governments) could be discounted as 'no more than a reflection of old enmities'. Generally, therefore, there were 'no unpleasant surprises' for Beijing in these reactions to the atomic test;[61] instead,

---

[57] *The New York Times*, 8 Nov. 1964.   [58] *Egyptian Gazette*, 4 Dec. 1964.
[59] *Straits Times*, 19 and 22 Oct. 1964.   [60] *Japan Times*, 18 Oct. 1964.
[61] NSF Committee File, Committee on Nuclear Proliferation—China, Box 5, 28 Oct. 1964, LBJL.

there was much from which to derive political satisfaction, despite no immediate enhancement of China's security.

Roger Hilsman, formerly the US Assistant Secretary of State for Far Eastern Affairs, added his own thoughts on this addition to China's capabilities. No longer a part of the Johnson administration, but now Professor of Government at Columbia University, New York, his views on China policy were still heeded by Washington's policy élite and by opinion-formers more generally. From his perspective, acquisition of the bomb had not altered the balance of power either in Asia or outside of it. But what was important was that it showed China's *potential* (not a word Hilsman used) ability to organize its resources in pursuit of national power: 'What makes Communist China formidable,' he said, 'is not possessing an atomic bomb, but 700 million people, the technical skills of those people, a national base of continental size, and the demonstrated determination and organization to control those people and resources and direct them toward the goals of national power and prestige.'[62] China might have displayed its weaknesses in other areas, but when the direction of a policy was shielded from changes in the centre's political line, as the nuclear programme was to be at least until the Cultural Revolution, then remarkable progress could be had.

Johnson himself betrayed his fears about the impetus China's test would give to others. In a television broadcast on 18 October he stated with some candidness that China's 'demanding effort' might tempt 'other states to equal folly. Nuclear spread is dangerous to all mankind. What if there should come to be 10 nuclear powers, or maybe 20 nuclear powers? What if we must learn to look everywhere for the restraint which our own example now sets for a few? Will the human race be safe in such a day?'[63] Before long, his predictions concerning possible proliferation proved to be accurate. Shortly after the detonation, the Indian ambassador to Washington called on the Director of the US Arms Control and Disarmament Agency and warned him of the domestic pressures on the Indian government to develop its own nuclear capability. Within a year, he claimed, China would be capable of dropping a

[62] This speech is contained within James C. Thomson's papers, Far East, Communist China, General, Box 16, 18 Nov. 1964, JFKL.

[63] Johnson's comments quoted in Roderick MacFarquhar, *Sino-American Relations 1949–71* (New York: Praeger, 1972), 211.

bomb on New Delhi without fear of retaliation. Soon after, some 100 Indian parliamentarians signed a petition calling for the development of India's nuclear capabilities, and the head of India's nuclear establishment added to the clamour by declaring that the only defence against nuclear attack 'appears to be the capability and threat of retaliation'.[64] India was *en route* to its 'peaceful nuclear explosion' of 1974.

There were also demands for increased diplomatic contact with China: 'Throughout the world', the INR report confirmed, the explosion had brought 'renewed calls for admitting Peiping to the United Nations and having Communist China participate in arms control arrangements and conferences'. Many governments and individuals were calling on the United States to take the kinds of initiatives that would bring China into the international community,[65] including the UN Secretary-General, who proposed a nuclear disarmament conference that brought together the five nuclear weapon states[66] (all of whom happened to be members of the Security Council, even if the PRC did not hold the China seat). China in turn gave an added boost to these demands: whereas Washington claimed its willingness to invite China to the 18-nation disarmament conference held in Geneva, Beijing pointed out that these talks were conducted within a UN framework of which it was not yet a part.[67] The United States also focused on persuading China to adhere to an agreement already in place—the Test Ban Treaty; however, Beijing suggested other avenues that were of little interest to Washington—the 'complete prohibition and thorough destruction of nuclear weapons', or failing that a joint pledge of no first use.[68]

Such demands from other states for Chinese participation were difficult for Washington to resist, of course. Thus, while the change in China's status might be limited militarily, the huge political and psychological impact helped to promote a more flexible line within the Johnson administration, reinforcing the arguments of those who believed that China needed to be inte-

[64] Seaborg, *Stemming the Tide*, 117–18; Richard K. Betts, 'Incentives for Nuclear Weapons: India, Pakistan, Iran', *Asian Survey* (Nov. 1979), 1056.

[65] NSF Committee File, Committee on Nuclear Proliferation—China, Box 5, 28 Oct. 1964, LBJL.

[66] Halperin, *China and the Bomb*, 94.

[67] Halperin and Perkins, *Communist China and Arms Control*, 130.

[68] MacFarquhar, *Sino-American Relations*, 227–8.

grated, subjected to the constraints of an arms control regime, and to the pressures that were an inevitable result of wider international contact.

US Assessments of China's Weapons Programme

In many respects, China's own behaviour as a nuclear weapons state bolstered the perception that China could be tamed; could, when it needed to, be cautious. Although China's programme of testing continued after 1964 and it was able to conduct a hydrogen test only 32 months after its first atomic explosion (a speed of advancement that did cause alarm in Washington), the perception of China as a defensive nuclear state, able above all to complicate Moscow's strategic picture, gained ground in the United States. A constant Chinese refrain had been to castigate the superpowers for their use of nuclear blackmail, and Beijing tried hard to differentiate itself from the other four members of the nuclear club, especially from the two major states. Despite earlier US fears, its obvious unwillingness to engage in nuclear coercion of its neighbours, its constant reiteration of the no-first-use pledge, its reluctance (at least in the 1960s and 1970s) to help others acquire the means to produce their own weapons, and its plainly inferior status when compared with the two superpowers, made the 1964 event less momentous as a threat to China's neighbours and to the non-proliferation norm than was initially thought to be the case.

Moreover, China moved steadily but—after the initial stages—slowly from a programme of development and testing to a position of deployment, and it never opted for large numbers of weapons in any category. As Mao explained his thinking to André Malraux in 1965: 'Once I have six atomic bombs, no one can bomb my cities.'[69] Both the Americans and the Chinese tended to overestimate the speed at which Beijing would be able to develop a missile system. At the height of the Cultural Revolution and immediately after China's thermonuclear test the director of the US CIA estimated that the Chinese would have an ICBM capability before 1972.[70] Even with the subsequent understanding

---

[69] Quoted in Dittmer, *Sino-Soviet Normalization*, 185.
[70] Seaborg, *Stemming the Tide*, 420.

of the destructive nature of the Cultural Revolution, the US Secretary of Defense, James Schlesinger, predicted in 1974 that the PRC would obtain ICBM operating capacity in 1976,[71] an over estimation of four years.

Chinese leaders also had unrealistic expectations about the speed their nuclear programme would develop. On 19 September 1958, China's missile academy had been directed to develop a *dongfeng* (DF) series of land-based ballistic missiles. Four types of missiles with different ranges were to be built: DF-2 to target Japan, DF-3 to target the Philippines; DF-4 for Guam; and DF-5 the continental USA.[72]

Over the years, this programme had been hampered by the economic crisis after the Great Leap Forward, by the political turmoil generated during the Cultural Revolution, and by the need for Beijing to develop difficult new technologies on its own. Thus, the DF-5 was not tested over its full range until May 1980, and by this time the Soviet Union had long since emerged as China's primary enemy, willing to threaten China with nuclear attack. During the border war in 1969, Soviet news and spokespersons had issued oblique and more obvious threats that appeared to show a nuclear strike was being contemplated. Victor Louis, a Soviet journalist who was often used as a conduit for his government's views, noted in a newspaper article that a Soviet air strike against the Chinese test site at Lop Nor was being considered, and recalled that the Brezhnev doctrine gave the socialist bloc the right to intervene in other socialist countries where leadership actions endangered the achievements of the state.[73] The Chinese leadership took these threats seriously, embarking on a massive civil defence programme, and pushing forward with its development of a second strike capability. Ironically, this time it

[71] Secretary of Defense James R. Schlesinger to the Congress on the FY 1975 Defense Budget and FY 1975–9 Defense Program, 4 Mar. 1974 (Washington, DC: US GPO, 1974).

[72] Lewis and Xue, *China Builds the Bomb*, 211–12. As analysts of this targeting have stated, China's weapons designers were not supposed to be concerned about the strategic purpose of their programme, but implicit in target selection was a doctrine of strategic retaliation, a topic that could be fully explored only after Mao's death. See John Wilson Lewis and Hua Di, 'China's Ballistic Missile Programs: Technologies, Strategies, Goals', *International Security*, 17, no. 2 (Fall 1992), 20.

[73] See the London *Evening News*, 16 Sept. 1969, quoted in Henry Kissinger, *White House Years* (Boston: Little, Brown, 1979), 185.

was the Soviets who wanted to involve the United States—if only by tacit consent—in an attack on Chinese installations. On 18 August a Russian embassy official during the course of a lunch with a Soviet specialist from the State Department asked him what the US reaction would be to a Soviet attack on Chinese nuclear facilities. (It was also rumoured that Moscow was sounding out European communist reaction to a pre-emptive strike.[74]) But, at this stage, when Nixon and Kissinger were concerned that China should remain intact as a participant in the balance of power game they were intent on playing, the contemplated Soviet action did not appeal to the US administration. Other attempts by Moscow between 1970 and 1979 to enlist Washington in joint undertakings against the Chinese 'nuclear threat' evoked a similarly lukewarm response.[75]

In the final irony, therefore, Beijing's ICBM was to be tested successfully at a time when the Soviet Union had been designated its primary enemy. In June 1980, it was 'delivered to China's Second Artillery for "operational training", and in December, for "trial operational deployment" in an experimental silo'.[76] Moreover, the programme as a whole had shown that Chinese leaders had opted for minimal deterrence and not entry into an arms race with the superpowers. Instead, they had decided to construct aircraft and missiles in moderate numbers with capabilities over various ranges. By 1972, China had conducted twelve nuclear tests, including thermonuclear and underground, and it had also launched a satellite. Mostly, it made one test a year, a number that reduced international criticism, as did the fact that, unlike France,

---

[74] Kissinger, *White House Years*, 183–4. A US intelligence cable, July 1967, also reported a Soviet official as stating that 'if and when the time comes to do something about China, the Soviet Union would expect the United States to help'. Seaborg, *Stemming the Tide*, 112 n.

[75] Dittmer, *Sino-Soviet Normalization*, details these: 'In July 1970, when SALT negotiations had been under way for just nine months, the Soviet delegation floated a proposal for Soviet-American "joint retaliatory action" against any third nuclear power that undertook "provocative" action against one of them.' Later, Washington was presented with '(1) the draft of an anti-Chinese treaty on preventing nuclear war (first given to Nixon in May 1972); (2) an offer of an alliance against China, made to Kissinger in early 1973; (3) frank discussion of the Chinese nuclear threat at the 1973 summit at San Clemente; (4) an offer of an anti-Chinese alliance made to Nixon in 1974 . . . (5) the same offer repeated to Ford at Vladivostok; and (6) the same offer revived for Carter upon the signing of SALT II in Vienna' (p. 201).

[76] Lewis and Hua, 'China's Ballistic Missile Programs', 18.

it was not testing overseas. By the end of the decade, it was believed to be developing a three-stage liquid-fuelled rocket capable of launching a satellite into geostationary orbit. It had also test-fired a ballistic missile from a submerged submarine.[77]

China's minimal but credible nuclear deterrent force was in place. General Nie Rongzhen's memoirs reflect the satisfaction of being in that position: published in 1984 they stated that development of these weapons had enabled China 'to own the minimal means to stage a counterattack in case our country suffered a surprise nuclear attack by the imperialists'.[78] One author has also noted the political benefits of this programme: since 1969 China has not been subjected to nuclear blackmail, thus confirming for the Chinese that the basic objectives of their nuclear policy had been attained.[79]

From the mid-1950s, if not earlier than that, Chinese leaders believed that they had to acquire nuclear weapons in order to ensure that major states in the global system would take them seriously, and that strategic enemies would not continue to exploit their nuclear advantage over China. An increase in material power could, then, have important political benefits in their view. Both in terms of increased status and in deterring nuclear blackmail, Beijing could be said to have learned well the lessons of the nuclear age.

US administrations were clearly sensitive to the increase in China's prestige and political power—and for Kennedy in particular, the military uncertainties that would arise from its acquisition of an atomic capability—and from 1961 through to 1964 seriously contemplated preventing the programme from advancing any further. But factors restraining the United States were many and varied. Certain of these related to the fact that China was objectively a weak, developing nation and moreover Asian. Any attack on China's burgeoning nuclear facilities would have given unequivocal support to Beijing's argument that the United States wanted to keep China and other Third World states in a relationship of dependency, that it was attempting to hold back

[77] *SIPRI Yearbook of World Armaments and Disarmament*, 1972 (London: Paul Elek Ltd.); *SIPRI Yearbook*; 1983, (London: Taylor and Francis).
[78] Quoted in Lewis and Xue, *China Builds the Bomb*, 216.
[79] Bundy, *Danger and Survival*, 534.

the technical development of other countries, and that it had few qualms about expending Asian lives. If the United States had managed to convince Moscow to combine with it to deny China its nuclear capability, then to a degree those kinds of arguments would have been undermined. Both Moscow and Washington would have argued that their actions were directed against a state that was cavalier about nuclear war and was willing to contemplate death and destruction on a massive scale. In the absence of that joint agreement, the US alternative was to try to reduce the impact of this increase in China's power and find other, more benign ways of propping up the non-proliferation regime. Washington would de-emphasize the significance of China's acquisition of nuclear weaponry, and assure its Asian allies that Washington's nuclear umbrella extended to them, in the hope of allaying any plans they might have either to accommodate to Beijing or to take the nuclear route themselves. In addition, at a superpower summit at Glassboro, New Jersey, in June 1967, Johnson and Kosygin committed their two countries to signing a nuclear non-proliferation treaty. In many respects, the PRC's own behaviour as a nuclear weapons state, together with the offer of the US nuclear umbrella, helped contain overt proliferation, except in the case of India, which led in turn to Pakistan's more *sub rosa* development of such a capability.

The political difference that China's acquisition of nuclear status made, always greater than any strategic change that had resulted, further legitimized the arguments of those in America and outside of it who were calling for China to be drawn into the international community—more specifically, into the United Nations and into disarmament and arms control negotiations. Beijing's own restraint and emphasis on the defensive aspects of its nuclear programme may have given heart to those convinced that moving closer to China was both a duty and not an entirely unrealistic quest. China's behaviour seemed to indicate that it had *de facto* embraced the non-proliferation norm and its pledge of 'no first use' undercut generally the perceived military utility of nuclear weapons. Thus, the weapons programme increased the political rather than the military power of China at a time when US thinking was showing signs of moving away from the earlier rigidities in its China policy.

After an impressive start, China's deployment programme moved slowly, only becoming of global strategic significance at a time when Moscow and not Washington was the state it wanted to deter. The policy decision that had been taken in large measure at American prompting came to full fruition at a time when China was ready to play its part in an anti-Soviet containment policy.

8

China as the 'Wave of the Future': The Chinese Politico-Economic Model

When the Chinese Communists finally triumphed on the Chinese mainland in 1949, the leaders of the new socialist state faced a series of formidable challenges; not least, the need to restore order in a country that had been laid waste by international and civil war. Immediate priorities were to re-establish the conditions conducive to the resumption of industrial and agricultural production and to extend a land reform programme that had already been embarked upon in the northeast of the country. The longer-term goal was to transform China into a prosperous and powerful socialist state, thus demonstrating conclusively that the Communist Party had fully liberated the Chinese people, that one quarter of the human race had indeed stood up. Impressive growth rates in the 1950s, together with political, military, and diplomatic successes within a hostile international environment, seemed to suggest that Beijing did have within its grasp the achievement of a strong, united country, able to put behind it that so-called 'century of humiliation', and to hold up its head proudly.

In the early to mid-1950s, the Chinese drew on the developmental and institutional experience of their Soviet ally. Disillusioned with this by 1956, Mao intensified the collectivization drive in the countryside, and two years later launched the 'Great Leap Forward', which emphasized a self-reliant path to development using techniques reminiscent of the Yan'an period. From this time, serious defects in the Chinese economic strategy became increasingly manifest until, in 1978, China initiated an ambitious and unprecedented economic reform programme, one in which the United States and other industrialized states were set to play a crucial part. In the context of this reform, Beijing's leaders reflected on a Maoist era that had some positive features but also many negative ones. As far as Mao himself was concerned, his record was indeed one that had 'deteriorated over time'.[1] China's rate of economic advance, though quite impressive overall, had been erratic and was punctuated by a famine of major proportions as a result of policies that bore Mao's imprimatur. Mass-mobilization campaigns had left the working population enervated and apathetic. Levels of technological advancement lagged ten to twenty years behind world levels, and some thirty to forty years in specific areas. Moreover, as China's rate of growth declined or stagnated between 1965 and 1973, those of its neighbours—notably, Japan, South Korea, and the Chinese communities in Taiwan, Singapore, and Hong Kong—accelerated. By the time of Mao's death in 1976, the Party's political credibility was at stake, given that the goal of achieving a powerful and prosperous China appeared to have eluded it. Mao's eventual successor—Deng Xiaoping—thus pushed through radical economic reform. 'In effect, the Chinese themselves repudiated the "Chinese model".'[2]

This Chapter will focus on US perceptions of the political economy of China and its perceived consequences for China's capabilities both internally and as a political and economic model for other developing countries. Although the decline in Beijing's hard and soft power resources, alluded to above, did not follow a linear trajectory, the apparent overall weaknesses of its economy eased America's fears about the Third World impact of its politico-economic model. It also reduced concerns that any contact between Washington and Beijing would raise the PRC's prestige to the point where its path to development would be revived as a serious source of inspiration in large parts of the developing world.

Domestic Order and Advancement in the 1950s

As noted earlier, the years 1949 to 1952 essentially marked a period of rehabilitation in China and the re-establishment of

[1] Harry Harding, *China's Second Revolution: Reform After Mao* (Washington, DC: The Brookings Institution, 1987), 30.

[2] Gordon White, *Riding the Tiger: The Politics of Economic Reform in Post-Mao China* (London: Macmillan, 1993), 3 and esp. ch. 1; Harding, *China's Second Revolution*, 29–39, provides a useful balance sheet for the Maoist period.

political and economic order. The effects of war had been profound, disrupting industrial and agricultural production, transport systems, and the distribution of goods. In 1948, US officials, such as George Kennan, had depicted China in Malthusian terms: a country 'with a population over three times that of the United States had, in proven reserves, less than half as much iron, a tenth as much coal, and no petroleum'.[3] Official Chinese Communist estimates were that in 1949 heavy industry output was about a third of the pre-war level and agricultural output about 70 per cent. The resultant hyperinflation contributed to the fragmentation of the national market and the development of a barter economy.[4] Despite the magnitude of the task the Communists faced, and the drain that participation in the Korean war imposed on economic resources, Communist leaders proclaimed themselves ready to embark on their first five-year plan from 1953. It was a plan that relied on Moscow's developmental experience, Stalinist forms of political organization, and Soviet aid and technological inputs of generous proportions.

Determination, enthusiasm, and Soviet assistance resulted in industrial growth rates during the first plan that were impressively high. Agricultural growth rates—though less impressive—were still creditable. US estimates put the increase in GNP at about 7 to 8 per cent a year between 1952 and 1957. Washington also suggested that between 1952 and 1960 China would probably have 'tripled its electric power output, more than doubled its coal production, and increased the value of its machine industry some two and one-half times'. Although its industrial base would remain small for some time to come, it would face difficulties in feeding its large population, and in finding enough trained personnel to carry out its aims; nevertheless, the overall conclusion was that since 1949 the Communists had shown a combination of 'flexibility, skill, and ruthless determination' which had allowed them to make 'significant progress' towards the achievement of their central objectives.[5] When they outlined a target of 9 per cent

[3] Ronald McGlothlen, *Controlling the Waves: Dean Acheson and U.S. Foreign Policy in Asia* (New York: Norton, 1993), 136.

[4] For further details on this see e.g. Alexander Eckstein, *China's Economic Revolution* (Cambridge: Cambridge University Press, 1977), ch. 1.

[5] *Foreign Relations of the United States*, 1955–7 (Washington, DC: Government Printing Office, 1986), 3: 230–55, National Intelligence Estimate, (NIE) 'Chinese Communist Capabilities and Probable Courses of Action Through 1960', 5 Jan.

growth per year in their second five-year plan, few would have denied their ability to reach it.

That flexibility and ruthlessness were well demonstrated after 1956, when Mao in particular began to criticize certain features of the Soviet developmental model. Mirroring some of Mao's own criticisms of economic practice, the Director of the CIA, Allen Dulles, noted that the Chinese first five-year plan had followed the Soviet model 'too slavishly', to the detriment of agriculture, which 'could not support the desired expansion of industry'. The Chinese had, he noted, 'introduced a realistic program to correct these evils'.[6] In its early stages, therefore, the acceleration of the collectivization programme and then the Great Leap Forward could be depicted as reasonable responses to China's overpopulated–underemployed condition, given the proclaimed rejection of reliance on heavy industry and capital-intensive modes of development. However, as far as Eisenhower and Dulles were concerned, these policies also contained elements that were especially ominous, because they appeared to indicate that the Chinese people were willing to allow themselves to be regimented on a massive scale,[7] further reinforcing the image of China as a militarized society, of a government in near total control, and all powerful.

In fact, the most common image of China in the 1950s in the United States, among the well and less well informed, was that of a country whose energy had been released, or of a civilization that had been bottled up for so long now bursting forth. A series of photographs published in *Life* Magazine in January 1957 reinforced this in its depiction of Chinese men and women laying rails, pumping oil, and engaging in productive work that would, in the magazine's opinion, lead to China becoming one of the top ten industrial states by 1962.[8] As one China specialist writing in

1956; *Foreign Relations*, 1955–7, 3: 497–510, NIE, 'Communist China Through 1961', 19 Mar. 1957.

[6] Ann Whitman File, NSC Series, Box 8, 16 May 1957, DDEL. Apparently, Eastern Europeans were equally interested in these innovations: in 1959 some 127 delegations visited the PRC and 104 Chinese delegations visited Eastern Europe to promote the Great Leap Forward and Commune movement. L. Dittmer, *Sino-Soviet Normalization and Its International Implications* (Seattle: University of Washington Press, 1978), 30–1.

[7] Dulles Papers, White House Memorandum Series, Box 7, 4 Nov. 1958, DDEL.

[8] Harold R. Isaacs, *Scratches on Our Minds: American Images of China and India* (Westport, Conn.: Greenwood Press, repr. edn. 1977), 220–3.

1958 argued, the Chinese Communists not only had exercised power more effectively than had the Soviets in the early years of their regime, but probably also more effectively than any previous regime in Chinese history.[9]

Similar if not equal anxiety prevailed in the United States when the Eisenhower administration contemplated the considerable improvement in China's diplomatic position that occurred in the mid-1950s. John Foster Dulles described the Chinese as 'drunk with power' because of their successes in Korea, at Dien Bien Phu, and in forcing the Nationalist evacuation of the Dachen islands in the Taiwan Straits.[10] But China's diplomatic successes depended less on these military aspects and more on its ability to project itself as a country that had at last 'stood up' and was now bent on consolidating its position through economic advances. Despite US attempts to diminish the significance of China's participation at the Geneva Conference on Korea and Indo-China in 1954, Beijing stressed the nature of the breakthrough that nevertheless had occurred. As a *Renmin Ribao* editorial put it: 'For the first time as one of the Big Powers, the People's Republic of China joined the other major powers in negotiations on vital international problems and made a contribution of its own that won the acclaim of wide sections of world opinion. The international status of the People's Republic of China as one of the big powers has gained universal recognition.'[11] The five principles of peaceful coexistence that it had negotiated with India that same year also won acclaim among developing countries interested in the emphasis on non-interference and equality of treatment.

Worse was to come. As preparations got underway for the holding of the first conference of Afro-Asian countries in 1955, US officials contemplated tactics designed to delay or even prevent

---

[9] A. Doak Barnett, *Communist China and Asia* (New York: Harper, 1960), 11.

[10] Dulles–Herter, Legislative Meetings Series, Box 1, 1955, DDEL.

[11] Quoted in Michael B. Yahuda, *Towards the End of Isolationism: China's Foreign Policy After Mao* (London: Macmillan, 1983), 100. Note also the reference to the Conference by Wang Bingnan, who conducted the negotiations at ambassadorial level with the United States, first in Geneva and then in Warsaw: the United States 'could not stop New China from stepping into the international political arena, striding like a giant'. *Joint Publications Research Services*, (JPRS-CPS-85-069) 'Nine Years of Sino–U.S. Talks in Retrospect, Memoirs of Wang Bingnan', 7 Aug. 1985, p. 3.

its start on the grounds that Bandung 'would provide Chou En-lai with an excellent forum to broadcast Communist ideology to a naive audience in the guise of anti-colonialism'.[12] When it became clear that the conference would go ahead, 'friendly' delegations, such as those from Japan, the Philippines, Thailand, Pakistan, Turkey, and Iran, were to be approached to ensure that they would deal effectively with 'Communist misrepresentations'. The outcome was a communiqué that the US Secretary of State felt his government could live with, but the broader view of US officials was that Zhou Enlai, largely through his 'diplomatic virtuosity', had left a favourable impression, especially in his several private meetings with Asian leaders.[13]

Further evidence of China's great power behaviour came with its decision to embark on an overseas aid programme in the mid-1950s, at first concentrating on neighbouring countries in Asia, and later giving priority to Africa. Its assistance terms were generous, and projects—labour-intensive, light industrial and agricultural—reflected a belief in the wider applicability of China's experience.[14] Such a programme also demonstrated a confidence that few other countries in China's objective economic position would have felt able to display.

In the Eisenhower administration's view, China had available to it a variety of resources that enhanced its power in the global system. Beijing received sympathetic treatment in the Third World because it was perceived as a 'former victim of imperialist and capitalist oppression', on the side of those nations that had taken a strong anti-colonialist stance, and as having successfully thrown off the foreign yoke. At Bandung, Zhou had asked the various delegations to put aside differences in ideology and to band together on the 'common ground' of overturning the 'sufferings and calamities of colonialism'. When the Chinese leader visited Pakistan in January 1957 and encountered a warm public reception, Pakistanis were—US officials believed—

[12] *Foreign Relations*, 1955-7 (Washington, DC: Government Printing Office, 1990), East Asian Security; Cambodia; Laos, 21: 1-3, 7 Jan. 1955.

[13] RG 59, R and A Reports, Country File, IR 6909, 20 May 1955, NA.

[14] For details of the Chinese aid programme see e.g. Janos Horvath, *Chinese Technology Transfer to the Third World: A Grants Economy Analysis* (New York: Praeger, 1976); and John F. Copper, *China's Foreign Aid: An Instrument of Peking's Foreign Policy* (Lexington, Mass.: Lexington Books, 1976).

contributing to 'their own self-esteem' in paying tribute to the Chinese victory over Western dominance.[15]

Officials in Washington also believed that by the mid-1950s Beijing had managed to create the impression in Asia that it was a 'dynamic, permanent and not unfriendly world power'. (In consequence, perhaps, several states established diplomatic relations with China in those years, including Yugoslavia, Afghanistan, Nepal, Egypt, Syria, and Yemen in 1955 and 1956; Ceylon in 1957; and Cambodia, Iraq, Morocco, and the Sudan in 1958.) In the administration's view, such governments were impressed by the PRC's effective control over a vast geographical area and population. Beijing's neighbours were also seeking to make profound changes in their societies, and, it was argued, the 'Chinese Communist pattern appears in certain respects to offer a solution'.[16] Moreover, these countries paid 'more attention to the apparent material progress in Communist China than to the methods by which it was attained'. China's apparent progress served to give a boost to the considerable intellectual sympathy for Marxist economic concepts among Asian leaders; anyway, for these countries, there was little alternative to a prominent state role in the planning and finance of major economic development projects.[17]

Advances in Chinese influence in the Third World were seen to be matched in the socialist bloc, where Beijing's prestige was at an all-time high, spurred on by the military burdens it had borne during the Korean conflict, the death of Stalin, and the establishment of a leadership in Moscow less certain of its stature in the communist world. Furthermore, the new Soviet leadership was willing from 1954 to put its relationship with Beijing on a more equal basis and treat it as a partner. In 1956, it openly sought Chinese assistance and support after the upheavals in Eastern Europe.

Thus, in the 1950s, the enhancement of the diplomatic and economic position of China, combined with increases in its military capability, contributed to the Eisenhower administration's belief that communism in Asia was now thought to be the 'wave

---

[15] *Foreign Relations*, 1955–7, 3: 251, 5 Jan. 1956; RG 59, Office of Chinese Affairs, Lot 60D648, Box 4, 12 Mar. 1957, NA.

[16] *Foreign Relations*, 1955–7, 3: 251, and 3: 505–6, 5 Jan. 1956 and 19 Mar. 1957.

[17] *Foreign Relations*, 1955–7, 3: 649–50, 3 Dec. 1957.

of the future'; worse still, as Dulles put it, there was no 'feeling of resistance' to it in Asia comparable with the attitude that existed in Western Europe.[18] The administration's major means of dealing with this unwelcome perception was to try to promote alternative models of economic and political development, ones that might appear to be more compatible with some Western values, and to refrain from undertaking any actions of its own that could further contribute to the power and prestige of China.

The main alternative models for Asian developing nations were considered to be India, and to a lesser extent Japan. Taiwan was also to be boosted in the hope that it would begin to display the economic dynamism being exhibited on the mainland. But in this case it was recognized that, with Taiwan in the economic doldrums and with the Chinese attachment to 'home place' and status favouring the PRC, there was not much mileage to be had in the promotion of Chiang Kai-shek's China as the 'wave of the future'. Figures compiled in the Office of Chinese Affairs between 1952 and 1956 showed that six times as many overseas Chinese in Southeast Asia were in fact choosing to return to the mainland rather than to the island of Taiwan.[19]

There were also difficulties when it came to the promotion of Japan: the anti-Japanese sentiment that existed throughout the region, together with the belief that its recovery came within the confines of a subordinate relationship with the United States, did nothing to help matters here. Moreover, its level of industrialization far outstripped those of its Asian neighbours, rendering it difficult to project it as a member of the developing world. Thus, attention focused on India, especially as a result of Chester Bowles's efforts as ambassador in New Delhi in 1951 to draw economic and political comparisons between China and India, and argue that if India failed as either a democratic political or economic experiment, then this would affect the whole of Asia. Walt Rostow, the influential 'modernization' theorist, then Professor at the Massachusetts Institute of Technology, was to put it more darkly in 1954: in the absence of tangible gains to point to in India, and with little else of comfort in the rest of 'Free Asia', he

[18] *Foreign Relations*, 1955–7, 3: 482, 18 Feb. 1957 (said by Dulles to representatives of the press in private conversation).
[19] RG 59, Records of the office of Chinese Affairs, 1957, Lot 60D648, Box 9, Mar. 1957, NA.

argued, even 'an indifferent outcome on mainland China could still represent an important relative achievement both to the Chinese and to Asians generally'. This would allow Beijing to 'maintain its posture as Asia's wave of the future, both in terms of military strength and, especially, as possessor of the "correct" formula for the solution of Asia's problems'.[20]

This Chinese–Indian comparison was a theme that was taken up strongly in the US Congress in the 1950s, and rather less forcefully in the executive branch. India's non-alignment, its championing of anti-colonialism, its nationalism, and its criticisms of America's China policy, made it an awkward partner for the administration, especially in comparison with Pakistan.[21] Nevertheless, State Department officials with responsibility for the area often stressed that US aid to India should be portrayed as a demonstration of its belief that 'free Asian nations' could meet the needs of their peoples. In their view, it was in Asia that the 'protagonists of freedom or force meet in today's world, for here the methods of both are being tried out'. India and China represented alternatives, the success of which would 'influence the economic and ideological pattern for all Asia'.[22]

But it was within Congress that these arguments were taken up most boldly, sometimes for partisan reasons, on other occasions because of a genuine concern for the issues that were seen to be at stake. In connection with debates concerning the economic assistance that was on offer to India, Senator John F. Kennedy put the

[20] To quote Rostow in full, in order to show the generally dispirited attitude of one influential commentator in the 1950s: 'If Japan is left to wallow along from year to year in the trough of a chronic balance of payments crisis; if the Philippines fail to make good in concrete results the social and economic promise of Magsaysay's political success; if Indonesia remains indolent and distracted in the face of its growing population problem; if India fails to produce major results from its efforts at a democratically engineered rural revolution; if Formosa fails to develop both as a creative element in Free Asia and a political rallying point for a new China—if, in short, Free Asia does not substantially improve its performance, an indifferent outcome on mainland China could still represent an important relative achievement both to the Chinese and to Asians generally'. In Walt W. Rostow, *The Prospects for Communist China* (New York: Wiley & Sons, 1954), 310.

[21] For further details on US relations with India and Pakistan in the 1950s, see Robert McMahon, 'United States Cold War Strategy in South Asia: Making a Military Commitment to Pakistan, 1947–54', *Journal of American History*, 75 (Dec. 1988).

[22] See e.g. statements by George V. Allen, Assistant Secretary for Near Eastern, South Asian and African Affairs, 28 May 1956; and by Kenneth T. Young, Director of Office of Southeast Asian Affairs, 13 Aug. 1956; both in *Department of State Bulletin*, 35 (1956).

comparison between China and India starkly. Depicting the Great Leap Forward, shortly after its launch, as the 'primary event of 1958', and the year as a whole as a 'win' for the Communists, he noted that China's economic growth rate was at least three times that of India, that the first cars were being produced in the PRC, that the Chinese would probably soon launch their first earth satellite, and before long could well have developed nuclear weapons. Describing India as the 'hinge of fate in Asia' and the 'one great counter to the ideological and economic forces of Red China', he also claimed New Delhi as 'the testing ground for democracy' throughout the region.[23] Kennedy apparently had been influenced by those such as Rostow who argued that judiciously applied US economic aid to the developing world would move these countries to the take-off stage of development, into a period of self-sustaining growth, and political maturity. The results, it was believed, would not only encourage more converts to the capitalist mode of development, but also increase the numbers of those who would act as bulwarks against communism.[24]

Partly in response to these vivid comparisons between Beijing and New Delhi, but also as a reaction to Soviet economic and political courting of non-aligned India,[25] aid to Nehru's government began to advance steadily in the second Eisenhower administration until, by Kennedy's time, New Delhi ranked as the world's largest recipient of US economic assistance. From January 1957, NSC deliberations had reflected this greater attention to India's prosperity 'in competition with China', NSC 5701 representing the first of a number of official policy statements that recognized that the outcome of the competition between Beijing and New Delhi would have a 'profound effect throughout Asia and Africa'.[26]

[23] *Congressional Record*, vol. 105, part 2, 86th Congress, 1st Sess., 19 Feb. 1959, pp. 2737–8; but see also speeches by Senators Zablocki, 8 June 1956; Celler, 12 July 1956; Humphrey, 13 July 1956, 15 Aug. 1957, and 23 Jan. 1958; Cooper, 16 Jan. 1958 as further examples of these arguments.

[24] Walt W. Rostow, *Eisenhower, Kennedy and Foreign Aid* (Austin, Tex.: University of Texas Press, 1985); Thomas G. Paterson, ed., *Kennedy's Quest for Victory* (New York: Oxford University Press, 1989), 13. Rostow, of course, became a member of the Kennedy administration, and Kennedy apparently remained convinced of the soundness of his development ideas.

[25] Burton I. Kaufman, *Trade and Aid: Eisenhower's Foreign Economic Policy, 1953–1961* (Baltimore, Md.: Johns Hopkins University Press, 1982).

[26] Quoted in Dennis Merrill, *Bread and the Ballot: The United States and India's*

Despite these efforts, however, as Rostow also noted,[27] as of 1958, India's economic development did not stir the imagination in the manner that China's did; neither did it offer many signs that New Delhi had chosen the right path. 'All its imperfections' were open to view in a way that Maoist China's were not. Such failings were debated vociferously in the Indian press and in parliament, whereas the Chinese leadership appeared in as firm a control of its people and its economy as it was of its media.[28]

Thus, faced with what was perceived as the challenge of the Chinese model, the Eisenhower administration saw it as essential to provide aid to India, but also to refrain from any action that would further heighten the power or prestige of the Beijing government. The US administration saw itself as the main brake on China's growing prestige and believed that any modification in its policy would markedly enhance Beijing's prospects. Diminishing the PRC's growing stature was made both more necessary and more difficult as a result of Zhou's accomplished performance during the so-called 'Bandung phase' of China's diplomacy, which undermined the American effort to depict the Chinese as unreasonable. Having been forced into direct negotiations with the Chinese after the 1955 Bandung conference, primarily as a means of settling the Offshore Islands crisis, the administration feared that such contacts would indeed enhance Beijing's prestige and reinforce the belief that Washington was about to make its own accommodation with the PRC. Zhou himself fostered this belief in an imminent modification in US policy via discussions with diplomats in Beijing and in messages to the authorities on Taiwan.[29]

The United States devised two main strategies to undercut what were seen as Chinese Communist gains in the 1950s, and to undermine the belief that Washington had begun to operate a 'two-Chinas' policy. It emphasized that there was to be no change in US policy and reiterated that the Chinese Communists should continue to be shunned because the Beijing regime had not so

---

Economic Development, 1947–1963 (Chapel Hill: University of North Carolina Press, 1990), 140. See also discussion of NSC 5909 (22 July 1959), 5.

[27] Rostow, *Eisenhower, Kennedy and Foreign Aid*, 33.

[28] A notable exception was the criticism levelled mainly by intellectuals during the 'Hundred Flowers Movement'.

[29] See e.g. Zhou's statement to the 'heads of mission' in Beijing, 11 Nov. 1957, in FO 371/127290, PRO.

altered its nature as to become a 'peaceloving state'. US diplomats were to remind those willing to listen that the PRC had been branded an aggressor by the United Nations in 1951; was violating the Geneva accords in its provision of war *matériel* to the North Vietnamese; was still refusing to renounce force in the Taiwan Straits; and was breaking an agreement recently made with Washington to release Americans detained in China. The refusal of 14,000 Chinese prisoners of war taken during the Korean conflict to return to the PRC and the large numbers of refugees who were continuing to enter Hong Kong was offered as evidence of widespread internal dissatisfaction in the country.[30]

The US Secretary of State, together with Walter Robertson, the Assistant Secretary for the area, played central roles in attempting to undermine China's growing stature. At a press conference in February 1957, in response to a question concerning possible changes in America's China policy, Dulles stated that the United States should not forget too quickly the hurt that China had done it. The Chinese, he said, had caused America 150,000 casualties during the Korean war, had prevented a political settlement on the peninsula, had seized Tibet, had been fomenting war in Indo-China, had continued unlawfully to hold 10 Americans in its custody, and had been threatening force against Taiwan. In August 1956, the Assistant Secretary described 'Red China' and its dedicated Marxist leaders as being 'like a giant octopus with tentacles of infiltration and subversion stretching into every country of the area'.[31] In January and February 1957 Robertson gave, respectively, an interview to *US News and World Report* and a speech in Indiana. At the latter event, he reminded his audience that 'Red China' was still 'hostile, aggressive, and building up its military capabilities ... By every standard of national and international conduct [it was] an outlaw nation.' It was a regime 'im-

[30] RG 59, Office of Chinese Affairs, Lot 60D648, Box 4, Mar. 1957, NA; evidence concerning the Sino-American ambassadorial talks and the one agreement signed between US and Chinese negotiators can be found in *Foreign Relations*, 1955–7, vols. 2 and 3, China, together with the microfiche supplement to these volumes; and the prisoner of war issue during the Korean war is discussed in my *A Substitute for Victory: the Politics of Peacemaking at the Korean Armistice Talks* (Ithaca, NY: Cornell University Press, 1990).

[31] Walter S. Robertson, 'The Problem of Peace in the Far East', address 13 Aug. 1956, US *Department of State Bulletin*, 35 (1956), 268.

posed by force' and should not be regarded as representative of the Chinese people.[32]

The Secretary of State's landmark speech in San Francisco in June 1957 quite closely approximated Robertson's own statements and should be interpreted in light of the strategy of undermining Chinese prestige. That speech was a further public counter to the Chinese projection of themselves as peaceful members of the international community who had interests that were legitimate and deserving of recognition. Domestically, he stated, the Chinese Communists had come to power by violent means and had subjected the people to 'massive forcible repression'. Unlike the Soviet Union at the time that the United States had recognized it, the PRC's record was 'one of armed aggression'. He introduced the experience of the Sino-American negotiations and used it negatively to castigate Beijing's leaders for their disregard of international law. Dulles also made clear his belief that the US role in the international system bestowed upon it certain obligations that did not apply to other states. US diplomatic recognition, he argued, 'gives the recipient much added prestige and influence at home and abroad'. If his government compromised on this or on other issues such as trade or cultural relations, the 'spirit and resolution' which the US provided would 'weaken free Asia' in its resistance to Chinese Communism. Although Dulles began his speech by reminding his audience that US policies should not be set in concrete, he closed it by warning those who sought change in China policy that Americans would 'never serve as rallying points for free peoples if the impression is created that our policies are subject to change to meet Communist wishes for no reason other than that Communism does not want to change'.[33]

The Secretary of State's speech satisfied a number of constituencies, including, of course, those in Congress distrustful of the administration's policy of talking with the Chinese Communists in Geneva, and fearful that this presaged trading and recognition. But it also represented an important contribution to the strategy designed to undermine China and to prevent its further em-

[32] FO 371/127289, 19 Feb. 1957; FO 371/127239, 18 Jan. 1957 and 6 Feb. 1957, all at PRO.
[33] *Foreign Relations*, 1955–7, 3: 558–66, 28 June 1957.

powerment. In addition, it demonstrated the administration's belief that the United States represented the one state that had it within its capacity to enhance or diminish Beijing's global position. Dulles recognized that he lived in a world of change, but as far as the PRC was concerned he wanted to keep that world as unchanging as possible via a policy of containment through isolation.[34]

The Chinese Model Under Stress

Mao's initiative in attempting to shift China's development strategy in a direction that would better reflect the concrete conditions within China was at first interpreted in the United States as a sign of the leadership's flexibility. That adjustment, combined with the militarization of society that took place in the early stages of the Great Leap programme, made the Chinese appear even more powerful, purposeful, and resolute than before. As Dulles warned Congressional leaders, 'in a state characterized by despotism, secret police, and ruled labor, there are possibilities of economic growth which we do not possess in a free society'.[35]

However, by the summer and autumn of 1959, when information began to filter in that the new policies were not doing well, a review of China's position seemed in order. The CIA Director reported that the system of communes was being reorganized, that agricultural production was 'facing serious trouble', and that the country was experiencing severe flooding, especially in the south. It was also noted that the regime was undergoing severe internal political unrest, with evidence of anti-Communist sentiment in Xinjiang and Tibet, including armed uprisings. In the foreign policy field, strains were increasing with Moscow, the Chinese showing 'exasperation' at Soviet criticism of their

[34] Eisenhower raised 'one or two' questions about the draft of the San Francisco speech that Dulles had passed on to him, but overall he declared it 'excellent' as a major statement of America's China policy. See *Foreign Relations*, 3: 588, n. 2 (28 June 1957). As Eisenhower prepared to hand over to his Democratic successor, the NSC still reaffirmed its earlier decision to do all it could to reduce the 'growth and power and prestige of China'. 10 Nov. 1960, 'U.S. Policy in the Far East', reaffirming policy conclusions in NSC 5913/1, 25 Sept. 1959, NA.
[35] Dulles–Herter, Legislative Meetings series, Box 3, 5 Jan. 1959, DDEL.

economic policy, and difficulties had arisen with India over Tibet.[36]

However, it was not until the Kennedy administration that the extent of the problems China was facing were fully realized. Certainly, it should be noted that Kennedy himself appeared to retain his view of China as a serious threat, which suggests that what concerned him most about Beijing was the fact of Stalinist rule being wedded to a growing nuclear capacity. Or perhaps he assumed that China would not face such economic problems for long. Whatever the reason he maintained that perception, his intelligence officials gathered information which suggested that China was in fact entering a period of severe and possibly prolonged weakness. They portrayed a people that were experiencing exhaustion and hunger, and that were becoming indisciplined, as shown by widespread looting, arson, and the murder of Communist cadres. Medical symptoms of undernourishment included nutritional œdema, with 15 per cent of cadres and other supervisory personnel in a work camp in East China reportedly suffering from dropsical swelling. There were widespread indications of cadre disillusionment with the Party centre, and of a loosening of the supervisory reins which gave the general population the opportunity to express its grievances (there was a hunger riot in Harbin in January 1961, which may have resulted in the summary execution of 70 persons). Indiscipline had also spread to the army, with soldiers in one billet apparently refusing to leave their beds and participate in manœuvres, and with military guards on the Hong Kong border professing to be 'too tired and hungry to chase villagers trying to escape to the Crown Colony'.[37] Figures available to the US Office of Intelligence and Research (INR) showed that while some 200 Chinese a day routinely moved across the border into Hong Kong, by 5 May 1962 there were 1,000 a day, and by 19 May some 5,000.[38]

[36] Ann Whitman file, NSC Series, Box 11, 25 June 1959, DDEL; RG 59, 793.00, Box 3930, 5 Sept. 1959, NA; Box 3931, 22 Dec. 1959, NA; Ann Whitman File, NSC Series, Box 11, 10 Sept. 1959, DDEL.

[37] NSF Country File, Box 22, CIA, 'Morale of Party Cadres and Armed Forces in Communist China', 18 May 1961, JFKL. (This memorandum was made available to Walt W. Rostow, then Deputy Special Assistant to the President for National Security Affairs.)

[38] Hilsman, *To Move A Nation*, 315.

There was also evidence of widespread division at the highest levels of the Party. A Rand report of June 1961 made available to Walt Rostow, then Deputy Special Assistant to the President for National Security Affairs, focused on the bitter divisions that existed over the pace and form of collectivization, the perceived degree of reliability of non-Party scientists, and the extent of dependence on Moscow's assistance and guidance.[39]

But it was the agricultural dislocation that was most consequential. A CIA report in July estimated that between 1958 and 1960 agricultural production had dropped 31 per cent and industrial production in the one year of 1960–1 by 42 per cent. The rapid withdrawal of Soviet technicians in July 1960 had exacerbated industry's position, but food shortages had also caused worker production to decline.[40] The State Department's INR noted that grain shortages in 1961–2 were likely to be between 10 and 15 million tons in relation to the 1957–8 level, but some 50 to 55 million tons below the Food and Agricultural Organization figure based on a per capita intake of 2,300 calories per day.[41] In response to this crisis, from 1961 the large-scale communes were reorganized into smaller units with the production team (roughly equivalent to a small village) being made the basic accounting unit; private plots were once again permitted; and food grains were purchased in foreign markets, even as foreign exchange reserves rapidly depleted.[42] Whereas Chinese dealt with a severe food crisis, Japanese looked back on agricultural growth rates of 6.5 per cent between 1952 and 1960, Taiwanese on rates of 4.5 per cent, and South Koreans, 3.5 per cent.[43]

Despite readjustments in Chinese policy, however, which did lead to a period of economic recovery, reports of serious problems

[39] NSF Country File, China General, Box 22, Rand report on Chinese food problems by Allen S. Whiting, 2 June 1961, JFKL.

[40] Peter Van Ness and Satish Raichur, 'Dilemmas of Socialist Development: An Analysis of Strategic Lines in China, 1949–1981', in *China From Mao to Deng*, ed. by the *Bulletin of Concerned Asian Scholars* (Armonk, NY: M. E. Sharpe, 1983), 81; NSF Country File, China General Box 22, CIA, 'The Situation in Mainland China', 27 July 1961, JFKL.

[41] James C. Thomson papers, FE, Comm. China, Box 15, Research Memorandum, INR-9, Director of Intelligence and Research, 21 Sept. 1961, JFKL.

[42] Van Ness and Raichur, 'Dilemmas of Socialist Development', 81; NSF Country File, China General, Box 22, CIA, 'The Situation in Mainland China', 27 July 1961, JFKL.

[43] James C. Thomson Papers, Far East, Comm. China 1961–6, Box 14, CIA Report, SNIE 13-2-61, 'Communist China in 1971', 26 Sept. 1961, JFKL.

in the country were still the norm within the Kennedy and then the Johnson administrations. Between 1961 and 1965 the general assessment that emerged among administration intelligence officers and specialists on China was that the country should not be seen as a modern industrial colossus, but—reminiscent of Kennan's view in 1948—an overpopulated country struggling to feed its people on a land base that was restricted to less than 0.5 acres per person, compared with 2.5 acres per person in the United States and Soviet Union. Discussions of industry between 1961 and 1965 emphasized much idle capacity in factories and a transport system that was underutilized. With the retardation of China's industrial base, this was putting it even further behind in technological terms, and leaving the Chinese in a position where they were 'running hard to get back where they started' while much of the rest of the world 'forged ahead'.[44] A CIA report in December 1965 focused on the food–population problem as being most crucial to China's military, political, and economic prosperity. In the agency's estimation, this could only be solved by generating substantial annual increments to agricultural production and introducing an effective birth-control programme, neither of which it believed would be given the necessary priority.[45]

To compound the difficulties, the decision to give high priority to developing advanced weaponry—which in itself was restricted in range because of the 'limited supply of high quality industrial and manpower units'—was estimated to be having an adverse impact on the civilian industrial sector. The weapons and civilian areas were in competition for inputs such as chemicals and petroleum, and for the country's scarce technical and scientific talent, a point that was reiterated in a later CIA report on science and technology.[46]

---

[44] Vice-Presidential Security File, Colonel Burns, Box 5, Memo to the Vice-President, 'Industrial Difficulties in Communist China', 11 June and 25 June 1962, LBJL; Panzer, Box 154, 'Economic Potential of Communist China, October 1963', report from Stanford Research Institute, LBJL; NSF Country File, China Cables, vol. ii, Box 237-8, CIA, 'Little Chance of Communist China Regaining Economic Momentum', 1 Apr. 1964, LBJL.

[45] NSF Country File, China Cables, vol. v, Box 239, Report from Director of Intelligence, Dec. 1965, (based on conclusions reached 15 Nov. 1965), LBJL.

[46] NSF Country File, China Cables, vol. v, Box 239, Director of Intelligence, Report, 'Economic Prospects for Communist China', Dec. 1965, LBJL; NSF Country File, China Cables, vol. v, Box 239, CIA Special Report, 'Science and Technology in Communist China', 28 Jan. 1966, LBJL.

That January 1966 report pin-pointed another of China's key weaknesses: the shortage of 'well-trained scientists in the middle and upper brackets of competence'. And while it acknowledged that the government could probably assemble a research team competent enough to make progress towards almost any single objective, this would be 'at the expense of other projects'. Thus, the conclusion reached was that, although China had considerable success in developing advanced, especially nuclear, weapons, overall the level of technology in the country was 'very backward' and the devotion of resources to weapons programmes was 'retarding seriously the growth of a strong technical base for the broader needs of the economy'.[47]

The intelligence service also turned its attention to other groups within Chinese society, arguing generally that levels of dissatisfaction were high in the early to mid-1960s. A CIA report on 'Popular Attitudes and Morale in Communist China', December 1965, claimed that China's youth were probably the most dissatisfied grouping within the country because opportunities for schooling were extremely limited. In one Beijing high school, for example, it was said that only 20 per cent of those in the junior school could continue to the higher levels and only 30 per cent of senior high-school students who wanted to go on to college could do so. In the large-scale exodus of refugees to Hong Kong many were young people, and some 10,000 out of 11,000 high-school and college students who arrived in Hong Kong in the summer of 1962 opted not to return.

Most of the country's four million intellectuals were also believed to find the government's erratic policies frustrating and, more seriously, directly harmful to themselves on each occasion they were targeted. Similarly, the peasantry were thought to be disaffected, still subsisting on some 2,000 calories a day, which was less than the allocation for 1957. The failure of the commune movement and the return to a limited form of individual private enterprise demonstrated the fallibility of the leaders in Beijing, and contributed to the passivity adopted in the face of new campaigns designed to generate yet further political and economic effort.[48] As the American Consul General in Hong Kong put it, the

---

[47] Ibid.
[48] NSF Country file, China Cables, vol. v, Box 239, CIA Special Report, 'Popular Attitudes and Morale in Communist China', 17 Dec. 1965, LBJL.

success of the newly-sanctioned private sector reflected the growing gap between the leadership's preference for selfless struggle
and the people's desire for material incentives.[49]

If there had been a dramatic loss of the economic and political
momentum in China when compared with the 1950s, the foreign
policy successes of that earlier era were also destined not to be
repeated in the 1960s. This was not uniformly so, because the
testing of the atomic device in 1964 was seen to have enhanced
China's prestige, the Chinese had initiated increased economic
contact with the West and Japan, and in January 1964 had established diplomatic relations with the French. But on balance China's foreign policy position by 1965—especially in the developing
world—was viewed as distinctly unfavourable compared with
the position in 1960, and almost unrecognizable compared with
the Bandung phase in the mid-1950s.

The vitriolic nature of Sino-Soviet polemics did not help
China's cause. In addition, the Sino-Indian border war, despite
the Third World's fearful admiration for China's military prow-
ess, had generated far higher levels of support for India than for
China in other developing countries, and surprisingly so in
Africa. In a Kennedy administration assessment, only one country
was rated as being moderately in support of Beijing's position
(Cambodia), and just one other (Pakistan, India's enemy, involved in its own territorial dispute with New Delhi) strongly in
support.[50]

Unrest in China's most vulnerable border areas, coupled with
domestic failures and the dispute with Moscow, led the Chinese
Communists to fear a Nationalist invasion in 1962. According to
Wang Bingnan, as a result of such fear Zhou Enlai had argued
that the PRC 'had to strive' to make the United States 'restrain
Chiang'. Thus, at the Sino-American ambassadorial talks (now
held in Warsaw) Wang raised the question of the tensions in the
Taiwan Straits and accused the United States of supporting and
encouraging Chiang. The US ambassador offered the assurances
the Chinese government sought: Washington would never sup-

[49] James C. Thomson papers, Far East, Comm. China, General, Box 16,
AmConGen, Hong Kong, to Sec. State, 17 Dec. 1965, JFKL.

[50] Roger Hilsman papers, India, Sino-Indian Border Clash, Box 1, from Office of
Intelligence and Research to the Secretary, 'Non-Communist Countries' Reactions
to Sino-Indian fighting', 27 Nov. 1962, JFKL.

port a Chinese Nationalist attack on the mainland.[51] But this search for reassurance was a telling indication of China's sense of weakness, and, according to the US Consul General in Hong Kong, a contribution to the tarnishing of its 'aura of invincibility'.[52] (Indeed, between 1959 and 1962, China's most vulnerable period, some Chinese leaders apparently advocated a more realistic turn in Beijing's foreign policy. Termed the 'Three Reconciliations and the One Reduction'—that is, reconciliation with US imperialism, Soviet revisionism, and Indian reaction, and the reduction of aid to revolutionary movements—this turned out to be a policy line that was ahead of its time.[53])

Further setbacks in Beijing's relations with the developing world were to occur over 1965 and 1966, with the State Department's INR recording for Dean Rusk's consideration in February 1966 that Burundi, Dahomey, and the Central African Republic had suspended diplomatic relations with Beijing; that President Kenyatta had termed China an unfriendly country and had refused to allow Zhou Enlai to visit in June 1965; and that relations had worsened with Bourguiba's Tunisia (he had called China 'expansionist'). In the INR estimation, matters were not much better in the Communist bloc: relations with Cuba had deteriorated sharply as Castro accused China of resorting to economic blackmail for political reasons; Hungary and Poland began openly to criticize Beijing; and Hanoi moved closer to Moscow, probably in response to the large shipments of Soviet military aid. Elsewhere in Asia, China's ultimatum to India during its 1965 war with Pakistan became an embarrassment when Islamabad unexpectedly accepted the Soviet–American call for a ceasefire and then Moscow's hosting of a peace conference in Tashkent between the two South Asian states. In Indonesia, China lost one of its most staunch supporters when the Indonesian Communist Party coup attempt failed. Allegations of PRC involvement in the coup did nothing to allay growing distrust of China in the Afro-Asian world.[54]

[51] Wang, *Nine Years*, 48–9.

[52] James C. Thomson papers, FE, Comm. China, General, Box 15, AmConGen, Hong Kong, 'Implications for US Policy of Latest Developments in Communist China', 18 July 1962, JFKL.

[53] Michael B. Yahuda, *China's Role in World Affairs* (London: Croom Helm, 1978), 169–76.

[54] NSF Country File, China Cables, vol. v, Box 239, Director of Intelligence and

The Chinese attempt to promote a 'second Bandung' conference in 1965 in Algiers, a conference without Soviet participation
and one that took a strong anti-imperialist position, was also
unsuccessful, to a large degree because Beijing pushed too forcefully and insensitively to persuade leaders in Africa and Asia to
accept these conditions.[55] Many Afro-Asian states wanted Soviet
participation and agreed with the argument that it was an Asian
as well as a European power. The conference was postponed in
June 1965 because of the overthrow of Ben Bella. By November,
China finally had to admit that it would never be held, concluding
that the 'current situation' was not favourable.[56] In the CIA's
view, the Beijing leadership appeared 'totally unaware' that its
inflexible and confrontational policies with respect to other states
had 'worked to its disadvantage throughout the world, changing
in one decade from the sympathetic world opinion of 1955 into
the suspicion and hostility of 1965'.[57]

The Impact of the Early Cultural Revolution

Despite these reverses in external and internal policies between
1961 and 1965, especially the 'colossal failure' of the GLF, the
Democratic administrations in the United States never thought it
probable that there would be a serious popular uprising in China.
The Kennedy and Johnson governments noted how well the control apparatus had functioned under stress. *In extremis*, the Beijing
leadership had exhibited some flexibility to include the purchase
of grain from abroad and the reinstatement of small private plots.
As a result, US intelligence organizations tended to describe the
Chinese people, even in the desperate year of 1961, as despairing
and resigned, but not 'near the point of revolt or of widespread
defiance of the regime'.[58]

Research, 'Communist China's Reverses in Foreign Relations Since January 1965',
25 Feb. 1966, LBJL.

[55] For some examples of the pressure tactics Beijing adopted see Yahuda,
China's Role in World Affairs, 155.

[56] NSF Country File, China Cables, vol. v, Box 239, Director of Intelligence and
Research, 'Communist China's Reverses in Foreign Relations Since January 1965',
25 Feb. 1966, LBJL.

[57] NSF Country File, China Cables, vol. vi, Box 239, CIA, 'Peking's View of the
United States', 10 Feb. 1966, LBJL.

[58] NSF, China General, Box 22, CIA, 'The Situation in Mainland China', 27 July
1961, JFKL.

However, the outbreak of the Cultural Revolution in China, an event which President Johnson appears to have followed quite closely in 1966 and 1967, prompted those assumptions to come under review. At the same time, this new mass movement reinforced the belief that China's economic problems were not about to be given priority; nor was its foreign influence likely to increase.

Officials in the Johnson administration proffered various explanations for the causes of this new turmoil. The American Consul General in Hong Kong in November 1966 focused on three factors: the pathological fear of Soviet-style revisionism in China (Hong Kong interestingly described anti-Soviet feeling as now exceeding 'the regime's antipathy toward the United States'); domestic policy differences; and personality clashes, heightened by the succession question. Domestic economic divisions were seen to revolve around the determination of the correct path to socialist construction: GLF-type policies versus the expedient policies that had been adopted to deal with the Leap's failings. In the foreign policy field such divisions centred on the deterioration in relations with the Indonesians and the Japanese Communist Party, the latter of which had advocated a repair to the Sino-Soviet rift mainly in order to bolster communist-bloc support to the North Vietnamese.[59]

Other officials concentrated on the internal consequences of the turmoil in China, Walt Rostow in a memorandum to the President concluding that there had been a further weakening of support for the Beijing leadership as it shifted away from material incentives and towards political exhortation; increased instability within that central leadership; and a decreased ability to effect an orderly succession to Mao. In terms of the economic consequences, Rostow claimed that China had produced less in 1965 than it had in 1958; that much of its heavy industrial plants were lying idle; and that unemployment levels were high.[60]

The CIA also took note of a central Cultural Revolution directive in June 1966 to abolish all college entrance examinations, to postpone entrance for six months, to base the curriculum on the

---

[59] NSF Country file, China, vol. VII, Box 240, AmConGen, Hong Kong, 'Comments on Current Scene in Communist China', 4 Nov. 1966, LBJL. For details on the foreign policy debate see Yahuda, *China's Role in World Affairs*, pp. 182–7.

[60] NSF Country File, China Memos, vol. VI, Box 239, Walt Rostow, 'Memorandum for the President', 25 July 1966, LBJL; and Box 9, 13 July 1966, LBJL.

study of Mao's thought, and to choose new entrants on the basis of their class background. In the agency's view, this move bore 'within it the seeds of eventual disaster for Communist China', and at least would result in a 'major setback for China's scientific and technological development'.[61] With the Cultural Revolution showing no signs of abatement, a further detailed report in December 1966 noted that the government and party machines were being seriously damaged—which could, it was argued, lead eventually to a more prominent role for the armed forces in governance. It also commented that policies were being adopted that were inauspicious for an industrial sector that required relatively advanced technology.[62]

The external constraints under which China operated were also seen to have increased in 1966. As Rostow informed the President, the internal crisis made it less likely that the Chinese would intervene in the Vietnam war, and because of the attack on Soviet revisionism in the Cultural Revolution it was highly unlikely that Beijing would repair its relations with Moscow.[63] With Sino-Soviet relations at an all-time low, to include the severance of Party-to-Party relations in 1966, there was clear evidence that elsewhere in the communist world China could only count on the support of Albania, the Communist Party of New Zealand, and a few other tiny splinter groups. In the Asian Communist movement, as was noted earlier, the Communist Parties of North Korea and North Vietnam had edged away from Beijing, the Japanese Communist Party no longer supported it, and the Communist Party of Indonesia—the PKI—had been shattered in the wake of the 1965 coup. China's quarrel with Cuba had the effect of forcing splinter groups in Latin America to choose between Beijing and Havana, with the majority turning to Castro.[64] A reduction of support for the seating of the PRC in the United Nations (the numbers voting against PRC entry rose from 47 in 1965 to 57 in 1966, the figures not coming down until 1969), the Chinese deci-

[61] NSF Country File, China Cables, vol. VI, Box 239, CIA, 'Educational Reform in Communist China', 8 Aug. 1966, LBJL.

[62] NSF Country File, China, vol. VIII, Box 240, [Name of agency and author sanitized], 'Political Issues in the Cultural Revolution', 19 Dec. 1966, LBJL.

[63] NSF Country File, China Memos, vol. VI, Box 239, Walt Rostow, 'Memorandum for the President', 25 July 1966, LBJL.

[64] NSF Country File, China Memos, vol. VII, Box 239, CIA, 'China's Growing Isolation in the Communist Movement', 5 Aug. 1966, LBJL.

sion to recall all but one of its ambassadors from abroad, and the rising number of disputes with neighbouring countries as Red Guards temporarily gained control of the Foreign Ministry,[65] obviously contributed to this perception of declining political support for China not only in the socialist bloc but also in the developing world more generally.

In 1967, the Cultural Revolution entered its most violent phase, and Rostow contemplated the prospect of civil war in the country.[66] Assessing the economic condition of China during the course of this upheaval, the CIA reaffirmed the conclusions of many of the reports produced after 1961: calorific intake in 1967 was probably still 10 per cent below the 1957 level, despite annual imports of grain of between five and six million tons. Simply to keep pace with a population growing at 2 to 2.25 per cent a year, China needed an extra four million tons of grain. There had been some gains in industrial production since 1963, especially as a result of investment in priority areas such as chemicals, petroleum, and modern weapons. But concentration on the latter had inevitably entailed greater demands being made on the scarce talent in the scientific, technical, and managerial fields. This continued drain on resources from civilian areas would further delay the development of a broad industrial base.

Turning to the effects of the Cultural Revolution itself, this was seen to be leading to sporadic disruption of industry, and a decline in efficiency and thus in production levels. The Agency confided that given China's 'present record of political turmoil and past record of twists and turns in economic policy', it was hazardous to draw general conclusions about China's economic future. However, the predictions contained within this report were remarkably forthright and thus are worth quoting in full:

The ambitions which have produced China's advanced weapons programme will almost certainly remain, and output in the military industries will probably continue to grow at a fairly rapid pace. At the same time, a substantial part of industry will remain in the backwater of outdated equipment and technology. The food–population problem will

---

[65] For an assessment of the impact of the Cultural Revolution on the Foreign Ministry see Melvin Gurtov, 'The Foreign Ministry and Foreign Affairs in China's Cultural Revolution', *China Quarterly*, 40 (1969).

[66] NSF Country File, China Cables, Box 240, Walt Rostow, 'Memorandum for the President: China's Vaulting Chaos', 9 Jan. 1967, LBJL.

not be solved, at least over the next few years. Barring spectacularly good weather and spectacularly good luck, agricultural output will have to be supplemented by continued imports of grain if the population is to be fed at even its present low level. Foreign trade will continue to grow and will continue to be oriented toward Japan and Western Europe. To an even greater extent than the USSR, China will remain a nation of extreme economic contrasts—a hungry nation with a dispirited population, albeit one with a growing arsenal of advanced weapons.[67]

Restabilization and Re-emergence, 1969–1978

Towards the close of the Johnson administration, the worst excesses of China's Cultural Revolution were over and, as the US had predicted, the army had been sent in to re-establish control over a movement that Mao himself acknowledged had got out of hand. Although there was much in China's domestic economic condition and external relationships to promote a turn away from international isolation, the Soviet intervention in Czechoslovakia, the onset of fighting on the Sino-Soviet border, and the perceived enfeeblement of the United States as a result of its defeats in Vietnam, were precipitating events instrumental in pushing Beijing towards a more flexible and moderate era in its foreign relations.

The Ninth Party Congress in April 1969 took the decision to return diplomats to their posts abroad. From 1970, China resumed people-to-people diplomacy on a grand scale and expanded state-to-state relations. In 1971 alone some 290 delegations representing 80 countries were invited to visit China. Between October 1970 and October 1971 China established diplomatic relations with fourteen countries (including Canada), it resumed relations with Burundi and Tunisia, and entered the United Nations. Following the Kissinger and Nixon visits in 1971–2, China's room for diplomatic manœuvre increased even more sharply. Some twenty-one states established, re-established, or elevated relations with the PRC in 1972, including the UK, Japan, Australia, New Zealand, and the Federal Republic of Germany.[68] It was a remarkably speedy shift out of diplomatic

[67] NSF Country File, China Memos, Box 241, CIA, 'Economic Prospects for Communist China Through 1970', Aug. 1967, LBJL.

[68] See Samuel S. Kim, *China, the United Nations, and World Order* (Princeton, NJ: Princeton University Press, 1979), 101–5, and app. A, 511–12.

isolation, almost a return to the heady days of the Bandung phase of diplomacy.

Such easy forward movement in relations suggested that large numbers of states in the global system still saw it as essential to incorporate China into international discourse and were ready to leap at the opportunity to establish contact provided by the moderation and adjustments in China's and America's policies. A further consequence of Beijing's shift in approach was an initial revival in enthusiasm among some groups in the West and in the developing world for the Chinese 'model' 'as a possible "third way" to prosperity and modernity', separate from capitalism or Eastern European socialism.[69]

This period of enthusiasm was not to last long, however, for internal political and economic conditions soon demonstrated China's continuing weaknesses. The opening to the United States was controversial among the Chinese leadership. As Mao told Nixon in 1972, Lin Biao had opposed such contact and had fled abroad once his attempted coup had been discovered.[70] Internal differences over foreign policy did not abate after 1972, Zhou Enlai becoming the target of a campaign in 1974 (the so-called 'anti-Lin Biao–anti Confucius' campaign).[71] Economic problems of the kind already identified by the CIA in the late 1960s remained prevalent. Even higher rates of investment were required to sustain growth rates: whereas in the 1950s the rate of investment had been equivalent to about one-quarter of national output, by the 1970s it was about one-third, with agriculture still receiving only 10 per cent of state investment between 1971 and 1975. Hence the burdens on the peasantry remained heavy and the growth in agricultural production only just kept pace with a population that had virtually doubled in size between 1949 and 1976. Incomes generally were stagnating or rising only very slowly and the final *coup de grâce* was given to material incentives with the elimination of the bonuses that had once been available to reward deserving workers.[72]

[69] White, *Riding the Tiger*, 3; see also Harding, *A Fragile Relationship*, 60–2, for details of favourable portrayals of 'egalitarian' China in the United States.

[70] Henry Kissinger, *White House Years* (Boston: Little Brown, 1979), 1061.

[71] For further details on such debates see e.g. Kenneth Lieberthal, 'The Foreign Policy Debate in Peking as seen Through Allegorical Articles, 1973–6', *China Quarterly*, 71 (Sept. 1977).

[72] See White, *Riding the Tiger*, esp. 32; and Harding, *China's Second Revolution*, esp. 31–7.

Modest purchases of Western equipment in selected areas were not going to be enough to overcome the gap between Chinese and world technological levels. Even Mao admitted to Kissinger in 1973, 'not without melancholy', that the Chinese would have 'to go to school abroad'.[73] A 1977 CIA study of China's oil industry recommended not just going abroad, but letting the outside in and 'changing policy to allow foreign participation'. Then 'virtually overnight', it promised somewhat optimistically, Beijing could remove—in this area at least—the technological handicaps from which it suffered.[74]

As the Chinese reform leadership began to consolidate its hold from late 1978, it accepted that China's advancement would depend on close involvement with the industrialized world and with international economic institutions. Such reformers, even the more conservative among them, tended to depict the period from 1966 to Mao's death in 1976 as ten lost years when no clear economic strategies were either formulated or implemented. On the thirtieth anniversary of the founding of the PRC, the Chinese veteran cadre, Ye Jianying, described those ten years as 'an appalling catastrophe suffered by all our people'.[75] The mass demonstration that had occurred in Tiananmen Square in April 1976, partly to honour the memory of Zhou Enlai but also to attack the Gang of Four, suggested that there were others in China who agreed with Ye.

The US perception of China as an economic and political model underwent significant change between the 1950s and 1970s. In the early to late 1950s, China's material power was seen to be increasing, abetting its presumed attractiveness as a politico-economic model to other developing countries. It appeared as a developing country that had found the key to rapid economic development, and to the means of controlling a large population through the adoption of Marxist, centralized economic policies. The Chinese development model seemed attainable to most developing countries, whereas the Western model appeared to be permanently out

---

[73] Henry Kissinger, *Years of Upheaval* (London: Weidenfeld and Nicolson, 1982), 69.

[74] Staff Offices, Press, Powell, Box 54, CIA Report, 'China Oil Prospects', June 1977, JCL.

[75] Quoted in Van Ness and Raichur, 'Dilemmas of Socialist Development', 82.

of reach. Furthermore, Beijing could reinforce its political links with the Third World by stressing their common desire for economic advancement, their colonial experience, and anti-colonialist aspirations.

In the wake of such perceptions of Beijing, the United States adopted policies designed to retard or undercut the growth in power and prestige of the PRC, refusing to trade, recognize, or allow travel to the country, and preventing Beijing assuming the UN seat. Additionally, alternative politico-economic models in Asia had to be bolstered, whether that was India, Japan, or Taiwan; alternatives that could be depicted as part of 'free Asia', friendly to the West, or at least neutral between East and West.

The US fear of empowering the Chinese Communists through various forms of recognition began to diminish, however, not as a result of the rise of alternative attractions (the economic advance-ment of China's neighbours was to become apparent later), but as a consequence of internal Chinese political and economic deci-sions that resulted in the disastrous Great Leap Forward, the alienation and then outright hostility of Beijing's major partners in the socialist world, the insensitive treatment of a number of developing countries, and the extreme isolation of the early years of the Cultural Revolution. From 1961, the Chinese were rarely depicted as the 'wave of the future' or the model for other devel-oping nations. Various US intelligence agencies and Johnson's National Security Adviser primarily depicted China as a state capable of causing trouble in its border areas, and developing advanced weaponry, but not capable of solving the food–popu-lation problem or developing a broad industrial base, at least not under the kinds of policies on offer in the Maoist era. In mid-1966, a major US study concluded that, realistically, China's current strength and potential for future decades was 'simply inadequate for the international role' to which it aspired, that Japan and not China would be 'the great power of Asia' with a per capita GNP probably 'more than ten times that of China and the economic gap between the two nations . . . still widening'. It also forecast that such a gap between aspirations and capabilities would 'become increasingly apparent to all thoughtful Chinese', inducing a 'fun-damental reappraisal and change in Chinese policy'.[76]

[76] NSF Country File—China, Communist China Long Range Study, vol. 1, Box 245, June 1966, LBJL.

In a statement in July 1971, President Nixon essentially flattered China, claiming it as one of the five great economic powers of the medium-term future. It was a remark that eased his passage to Beijing, since it appealed to China's sense of itself as a great nation and at last gave China a central place in the global great-power system. However, it was a potential that Nixon had directed attention to and, five months earlier, in a statement that suggested that it was not just the intelligence agencies in Washington that perceived China as economically weak, he had pointedly noted that the 'free Japanese economy' had a GNP two and a half times the size of China's with a population one-eighth the size, and that Chinese in Taiwan, Singapore, and elsewhere in Asia were remarkably successful economically, rebutting eloquently Beijing's 'claim of unique insight and wisdom in organizing the talents of the Chinese people'.[77]

Such an assessment fitted well with America's assessments of China's economic capabilities over the previous decade, and its expectations about Beijing's future. In such circumstances, the enhancement in China's prestige that inevitably came with the Nixon–Kissinger *rapprochement*, as evidenced by entry into the United Nations and the swiftness with which states moved to establish diplomatic relations with Beijing during that period, could be viewed somewhat sanguinely. The likely consequences of the Nixon breakthrough were no longer seen as dire in terms of their possible enhancement of the Chinese politico-economic model. On the contrary, the United States not only obtained a tacit strategic ally, and an admission from China that its security depended in large part on a relationship with the United States, but also the recognition that the radical Maoist policies of isolation and autarchy had rendered it economically weak and technologically backward. The 'wave of the future' had broken on the shore, but carrying little before it after all.

[77] President Nixon's second annual State of the World Report, 25 Feb. 1971, and speech to media executives, 6 July, in Congressional Quarterly, Inc., *China: US Policy Since 1945* (Washington, DC: 1980), 321–2.

9

International Order and US Structural Power: The US Relationship with China since 1979

How to get the Peking leadership into the international order, instead of their trying to destroy it according to their revolutionary vision, is primarily a psychological problem . . . [and] must follow the usual lines of therapy: it must lead the rulers of China gradually into different channels of experience until by degrees they reshape their picture of the world and their place in it.

Professor John K. Fairbank, 10 Mar. 1966

It is a truism that an international order cannot be secure if one of the major powers remains largely outside it and hostile toward it. In this decade, therefore, there will be no more important challenge than that of drawing the People's Republic of China into a constructive relationship with the world community, and particularly with the rest of Asia.

President Richard M. Nixon, 25 Feb. 1971

Our strategy toward China since 1971 has been to draw it out of its isolation and to integrate it in the international community . . . By building strong links to China strategically, intellectually, commercially, and even militarily in this early stage in its rise, we would reduce the chances of China's becoming a disruptive, expansionist power as it grew stronger militarily. Our expectation was that a forthcoming posture toward China would prompt its leaders gradually to accept and abide by international standards of behavior.

Professor Michel Oksenberg, 19 July 1989

The concept of international order, associated with ideas of consensus, predictability, and reciprocity has been defined more precisely as denoting 'stability and regularity in the pattern of assumptions, rules, and practices that are accepted as legitimate among the members of a given society and that concern the mechanisms of and limits to the process of change within that society'.[1] It is a concept that has a strong connection with the idea of structural power and, therefore, in the post-1945 context, with the United States, the state that many would see as central in shaping the current international order—the norms and rules of behaviour in the security, political, and economic fields.[2]

China, as a revolutionary state, post-1949 (and as with all revolutionary states), has long been perceived as a government that has found it difficult to accommodate itself to that prevailing international post-war order. As a result, one of the most persistent factors in determining the condition of US relations with China from the Truman to the Clinton eras has been the degree to which China has been perceived to be disruptive or supportive of that order. Furthermore, much of the debate in successive US administrations, among domestic opinion formers, and with America's allies, has been about the best means of inducing China to accept international norms: either through punishing and isolating Beijing until it reformed, or through selectively drawing it into international arrangements in order to channel and modify its behaviour. This division in approach has at different times separated US administrations from their primary allies, most notably the UK, Canada, and Japan, and from domestic constituencies. It has been a policy debate that has mattered because of the subjective sense in the United States that post-1945 it has had primary responsibility for preserving and reinforcing those international norms of behaviour. Such a responsibility has also carried with it the presumption that the United States should demonstrably command a wide degree of consensus in the international community for its efforts.

First steps to draw China more fully into international society through positive inducements were taken during the Johnson era, but were seriously constrained by the continuance of the US role in Vietnam, and by China's Cultural Revolution. Nixon took the opportunity that change in both these areas afforded to adjust policy more substantially, attempting to establish ties with China

---

[1] David Armstrong, *Revolution and World Order: The Revolutionary State in International Society* (Oxford: Clarendon Press, 1993), 6. The concept of order can also profitably be traced in the work of Hedley Bull. See in particular his *The Anarchical Society: A Study of Order in World Politics* (London: Macmillan, 1977). See too J. D. B. Miller and R. J. Vincent, eds., *Order and Violence: Hedley Bull and International Relations* (Oxford: Clarendon Press, 1990), for further elucidation.

[2] See Ch. 1 for further discussion of the concept of structural power.

on the basis of common interests with respect to Moscow, and in the promotion of stability in East Asia. Carter's vision of common interest still rested to a large degree on strategic alignment against the Soviet Union, but additionally comprised a desire to embrace China more fully still through the promotion of cultural, scientific, and economic ties. In the two years after the establishment of relations in January 1979, some thirty-five treaties, agreements, and protocols were signed between the two governments.

This was not a policy that flowed only in one direction, of course. Chinese leaders themselves signalled a concrete desire to rejoin and even extend their role in the international community from 1969, engaging nimbly in the 'intricate minuet'[3] that led to the Nixon visit of 1972. In the 1970s, China established diplomatic relations with some 72 countries, bringing the total to 124,[4] and as noted earlier received increasing numbers of foreign delegations in Beijing.

Nevertheless, until 1978, the PRC was still recognizably Maoist China, still challenging in certain respects the international *status quo*, still committed to the 'five "nevers": never permit the use of foreign capital; never run undertakings in concert with foreigners; never accept foreign loans (and by implication) never join the international capitalist IGOs; and never incur domestic nor external debts'.[5] Chinese leaders continued to pay homage to the 'Three Worlds Theory' and thought in terms of building united fronts against primary enemies—in this era against the Soviet Union. Although a member of the UN Security Council, Beijing essentially remained passive in its approach to that body,[6] not deeming it a significant aspect of its foreign policy, or an important independent actor in its own right. China also was largely

[3] The phrase is Kissinger's. See *The White House Years* (Boston: Little, Brown, 1979), 187. For a clear exposition of the normalization process see, Harry Harding, *A Fragile Relationship: Sino-American Relations Since 1972* (Washington, DC: Brookings Institution, 1992). An elegant synthesis is contained in Warren I. Cohen, *America's Response to China*, 3rd edn. (New York: Columbia University Press, 1990), ch. 8; and much insight is to be had from Michel Oksenberg, 'A Decade of Sino-American Relations', *Foreign Affairs*, 61 (Fall 1982).

[4] Harry Harding, 'China's Cooperative Behaviour', in Thomas W. Robinson and David Shambaugh, eds., *Chinese Foreign Policy: Theory and Practice* (Oxford: Clarendon Press, 1994), 395.

[5] Samuel S. Kim, 'China's International Organizational Behaviour', in Robinson and Shambaugh, eds., *Chinese Foreign Policy*, 426–7.

[6] See Samuel S. Kim, *China, the United Nations and World Order* (Princeton, NJ: Princeton University Press, 1979).

unengaged with Non-Governmental Organizations (NGOs), preferring instead to put its energies into the bilateral 'friendship'
organizations.

Not until Deng Xiaoping had consolidated his position from
December 1978 did this begin to change. With international and
especially American assistance Deng set out to modernize China
in ways yet untried, an objective which required the United States
to play two major roles: facilitating China's access to needed
advanced technology and skills; and contributing to a framework
of security that first would help shield China from a predatory
Soviet Union, and then more broadly help build a peaceful international environment that would allow for Beijing's absorption in
domestic issues. As a result of these decisions, within a few years,
many aspects of the Maoist legacy had been cast aside. No longer
a 'system reformer' but a 'system maintainer',[7] China began to be
drawn into an international society which in many areas reflected
the interests of the Western states in terms of the norms, rules, and
institutions that had been established.

These shifts in policy took place against the background of
international systemic change and considerable domestic turbu-
lence in China. Not surprisingly, therefore, it proved difficult at
times for Washington to maintain the domestic consensus necessary for the stable prosecution of its China policy. Similarly, at élite
levels within the PRC, profound doubts were exhibited especially
at times when the regime felt vulnerable over the possible ramifications of the course it had chosen to chart diplomatically and
economically. Thus, it has often proven difficult to maintain a
level of participation sufficient to demonstrate commitment to
international order.

The period since 1989 has been especially problematic, because
of the Tiananmen bloodshed and its aftermath, together with its
coincidence with fundamental structural change in the global
system associated with the ending of the cold war. Since then,
Washington has trained the spotlight more directly on those areas
where China failed to support those international norms the US
deemed as central. As one analyst has interpreted it, this represented part of Washington's ideological agenda which has led it
to promote, as so often in the past, a more extensive range of

---

[7] These terms are borrowed from Kim and are to be found in a number of his
works cited below.

demands where Beijing is concerned than other members of the G7. He argues that the United States has an 'ideologically motivated' objective to 'transform China in America's image' compared with other states' more straightforward desire for engagement in economic, cultural, and political, areas 'as ends in themselves'.[8] However, this difference in approach has not generated the levels of intra-allied tension associated with an earlier period when such fundamental matters as recognition, trading, and the use of force were at stake. What it has brought about, however, is a sharpening of the debate in Beijing and Washington about the nature of the global system and China's putative role within it.

The emphasis in this Chapter, then, is on China's closer involvement with the international community and on the exercise of US structural power designed to facilitate or retard the pace of that involvement. It also examines the US attempt to consolidate bilateral ties with China after normalization in pursuit of the particular objectives of its foreign policy, but more especially to encourage China's contribution to international order.

Normalization and Adjustment in the First Phase: 1979–1984

Domestic opinion in the United States supported administration moves to draw closer to Beijing, partly because it had perceived that as necessary for some time, and in part because of a more positive view of the kind of state China now appeared to be. In late 1979, some 65 per cent of respondents to a poll recorded a favourable perception of Beijing, a figure that was to rise to 70 per cent in 1980.[9] But those high levels of general support masked an unease about the official break in relations with Taiwan and the failure of the normalization agreement to guarantee firmly enough the future security of a long-standing ally that many believed had the right to self-determination. President Carter's decision not to consult Congress during the negotiations leading to the establishment of diplomatic relations represented a

[8] David Shambaugh, 'Peking's Foreign Policy Conundrum since Tienanmen: Peaceful Coexistence vs. Peaceful Evolution', *Issues and Studies*, 28, no. 11 (Nov. 1992), 77–8.
[9] Harding, *A Fragile Relationship*, appendix A, table A-1.

misperception of the intensity of feeling—especially within Congress—on this question of Taiwan's future, as well as a misreading of the continuing Congressional determination to play a more assertive role in foreign affairs.

The outcome of this unease and exclusion from the policy process was the Taiwan Relations Act of February 1979 (passed 339 to 50 in the House and 85 to 4 in the Senate), itself reflecting a suspicion that China had not given up its option on the use of force to regain Taiwan. That act declared that the United States would deem any attempt to overrun Taiwan by non-peaceful means a threat to the peace of the Western Pacific, and a matter of grave concern to Washington. More significantly for the longer-term progress of Sino-American relations, the Act provided for continuing arms sales to Taiwan to enable the island 'to maintain a sufficient self-defense capability'. Chinese leaders were dismayed, Carter was embarrassed, and it became the main cause of dispute between the two countries between 1979–82, affecting progress in other areas of the relationship. The matter of Taiwan's arms purchases was supposedly resolved between Beijing and Washington by the August 1982 Sino-American communiqué which agreed that the United States would 'reduce gradually its sale of arms to Taiwan'. However, in order to undercut Congressional criticism of the executive branch for signing such a document, Reagan's officials provided clarifications of the agreement which showed that it did not preclude the transfer of defence-related technology. Furthermore, it was not viewed as legally binding but more as a statement of policy. This latter point meant that its terms could be revised if Beijing were to threaten to use force to take over the island,[10] the major concern in this matter. To this day, Taiwan remains an issue that undermines the ties, because of the persistence of the perception in the United States that China might still resort to force in effecting reunification, and because of the belief in Beijing that US policy suggests a willingness to transgress the norm of state sovereignty where Taiwan is concerned; a willingness to interfere in an internal Chinese affair.

President Carter's neglect of this pro-Taiwan sentiment in the United States stemmed from his belief that establishing diplo-

---

[10] Harding, *A Fragile Relationship*, 117–18.

matic relations with Beijing would in itself be sufficiently popular
to overcome residual concerns about the island, and his view that
drawing China more fully into the international community
would help to resolve the Taiwan question peacefully, together
with other major objectives of US policy.[11] There was also the
matter of the strategic understanding between the two countries
concerning Moscow's role in the global system, a factor which
also was expected to contribute to full domestic acceptance of ties
with Beijing at Taiwan's expense. In consequence of this strategic
understanding, the President agreed to give Beijing Most
Favoured Nation (MFN) status where such was denied to Moscow; to sell selected items of equipment with military support
applications; to provide the Chinese with intelligence data on
Soviet deployments; and to establish facilities to monitor Soviet
nuclear tests.

More broadly, however, Carter believed the issues at stake with
the PRC went well beyond this question of Soviet containment,
important though that objective remained. Support for China's
modernization efforts, for its change of attitude towards methods
of development and towards other countries, almost appeared as
a duty for the administration. The deepening of bilateral ties was
important in itself but working in tandem with a quarter of the
world's population, Carter and his officials argued, would
supposedly contribute to the resolution of global tensions
associated with inequalities of wealth, access to resources, and
information.[12]

This question of the benefits of close ties with Beijing proved
more contentious in the Reagan administration. At first, at least
while Alexander Haig remained Secretary of State, the previous
supposition of China's central global importance remained intact.
As Haig was subsequently to argue in his memoirs, he believed
that China's role between East and West, North and South made

[11] He might also have thought that Deng himself had already accepted that the
PRC should extend the 'hand of peace' to its compatriots on Taiwan. Deng used
this phrase in discussions with Congressman Thomas Ashley in Jan. 1979 and
Ashley gave a full report to Carter. See Staff Secretary, Office of Staff Secretary,
Handwriting File, Box 117, 18 Jan. 1979, JCL. See also Oksenberg, 'A Decade of
Sino-American Relations'.

[12] A. Doak Barnett, *China's Economy in Global Perspective* (Washington, DC:
Brookings Institution, 1981), 504–5; Staff Offices, Counsel, Lipshutz, China—Misc
Pending, 1/79, Box 7, 'China Talking Points', 16 Jan. 1979, JCL. See also *Public
Papers of the President*, Jimmy Carter, vol. 1, 1980–1, *passim*.

it probably 'the most important country in the world'[13] for Washington, a statement that would have been welcomed in Beijing as it would have helped legitimize the current policies. With Haig's departure in June 1982, such hyperbole about China's centrality declined, however. More significantly, the Reagan administration began to re-evaluate the relationship in ways which injected a greater degree of realism into it, based on China's actual capabilities, and the limitations imposed by working with a non-democratic state. The new Secretary of State, George P. Shultz, in reassessing the basis to the relationship concluded that Japan and not China was at the core of America's relations in Asia. In his first major speech on Asia in March 1983, Schultz pointed to the ideological closeness with Japan, noting Tokyo's overwhelming importance in the global economy and Japan's democratic institutions that were conducive to US–Japanese co-operation. Where China was concerned, however, he avoided using the term 'strategic' to describe its position, noted the differences between the US and Chinese social systems, and pointed to the 'frustrations and problems' that would mark Sino-American relations in the future, as they had in the past.[14] China came to be seen as 'less than vital . . . too technologically backward to do more than tie down Soviet forces that would otherwise be available for employment on other fronts',[15] with only a limited ability to address the air and naval aspects of the threat the Soviet Union now posed in Pacific-Asia, and in many instances as unlikely to evaluate problems of world order from a perspective that would prove compatible with America's own.

A year later, however, the Reagan administration appeared a little more optimistic about the basis to the relationship. During the President's visit to Beijing in April 1984 he pointed to the ideological divisions, much as Shultz had done a year earlier, but he also emphasized some of the contributions China was making in Asia, and drew attention to areas where China and the United States might work together in the future. As he put it in a speech in Beijing: 'We must always be realistic about our relationship,

---

[13] Harding, *A Fragile Relationship*, 119.

[14] *Far Eastern Economic Review*, 21 Apr. 1983.

[15] Jonathan D. Pollack, 'China and the Global Strategic Balance', in Harry Harding, ed. *China's Foreign Relations in the 1980s* (New Haven: Yale University Press, 1984), 162.

frankly acknowledging the fundamental differences in ideology and institutions between our two societies.' But he went on, 'Yes, let us acknowledge those differences. Let us never minimize them. But let us not be dominated by them.' Both Washington and Beijing had condemned military expansion, the 'brutal occupation of Afghanistan, the crushing of Kampuchea, and we share a stake in preserving peace on the Korean peninsula'. He also referred to opportunities for increased scientific and economic cooperation and in the peaceful uses of nuclear energy on the basis of the 'shared principle of non-proliferation'.[16] These high-level statements were suggestions that China was perceived to be contributing to the maintenance of regional order, could contribute to the global norm of non-proliferation, but as yet did not have the kind of political economy in place that would make it a crucial global partner for the United States.

During 1981 and 1982 China also began its own reassessment of the value of the tie with the United States, and of the global balance of power. In the Chinese leadership's view, the US defence buildup under Reagan had succeeded in raising that country to the point where it represented a potential hegemonic threat at least equal to, certainly no longer less than, the Soviet threat. With Moscow bogged down in an unpopular and costly war in Afghanistan, its relations with key Eastern European allies in some disarray, and its economic and military support for Vietnam and Cuba burdensome, the trend of events seemed decidedly to be moving in Washington's favour. Moreover, there were some signs that the Soviets in 1982 sought a more productive relationship with the Chinese. At Tashkent, Brezhnev proposed a resumption of negotiations and of political, economic, and cultural ties. Where China was concerned, the Soviet leader appeared to renounce the applicability of the doctrine that carried his name; while Reagan was announcing one that foreshadowed a more active anti-communist stance, especially in the developing world.[17]

As a result of such reflections on global developments, domestic political tensions arising from too close an identification with the West, and with the specific irritations in the bilateral relation-

[16] *Public Papers of the Presidents of the United States, Ronald Reagan*, vol. I, 1984 (Washington, DC: US GPO, 1986), 579–80.
[17] Harding, *A Fragile Relationship*, 121–2.

ship with Washington—notably, arms sales to Taiwan—China announced at the Twelfth Party Congress in 1982 its 'independent foreign policy'. Thenceforth, China would retreat from its policy of confrontation with the Soviet Union and would give greater stress to matters of sovereign independence in the context of a more complex and balanced set of international relationships.[18] In Hu Yaobang's report to the Party Congress he explained that the policy shift meant that China would never attach 'itself to any big power or group of powers', and would never yield 'to pressure from any big power'.[19]

Certainly, this more flexible approach to foreign relations allowed China to explore the possibility of a *rapprochement* with Moscow and to be more selective in its criticism or support for US foreign-policy actions. Yet, an independent foreign policy did not necessarily mean equal involvement with the two superpowers in all functional areas. Although the tacit strategic alignment might be less in evidence, clearly the United States was the more beneficial partner for China: not only could it aid China's military and economic modernization efforts and facilitate its entry into and involvement with the keystone economic institutions deemed vital for the transformation of China's economy, it too was the one country that could provide China with critical military data on the Soviet Union. This was important at least until Beijing was more certain that Moscow no longer represented such a pressing military threat, and that the PRC had been correct to place the military last in line in the 'Four Modernizations'.

The centrality of Washington to Beijing's economic reform efforts and to the international acceptance of China's objectives was to be demonstrated on many occasions. Not until 1980 did China apply for and gain membership of the IMF and World Bank, the timing resting on the belief that a successful application would require US consent or at least its acquiescence. Thus normalization of relations would have to precede those applications for entry, for without the withdrawal of US recognition from Taiwan, difficulties were expected to arise.[20]

[18] Carol Lee Hamrin, 'China Reassesses the Superpowers', *Pacific Affairs*, 56, no. 2 (Summer 1983).

[19] *Beijing Review*, 25, no. 37 (13 Sept. 1982), 29.

[20] Harold K. Jacobson and Michel Oksenberg, *China's Participation in the IMF, the World Bank, and GATT: Toward a Global Economic Order* (Ann Arbor, Mich.: University of Michigan Press, 1990), 107.

The ideological power of such bodies was made manifest once China became a member. The advice and funds that China's reformers now had access to was instrumental, it has been argued, in altering the 'perceptions of many Chinese leaders about both the world economy and their own economic performance'.[21] Each concessionary loan came with feasibility studies and advice on the selection of technologies and international suppliers.[22] After Japan, the World Bank quickly became China's most important source of external funding, approving between 1980 and 1989 some $7.4 billion in loans covering 69 projects primarily in the areas of education, energy, transportation, and agriculture.[23] By the mid-1980s, China was to become the Bank's largest borrower; it had also successfully negotiated its first standby credit from the IMF, and had started to raise funds on the Eurodollar bond market.[24]

The success of China's modernization drive also depended on access to the American market. Although bilateral trading levels had declined between 1981 and 1983—as a result of macroeconomic problems in each economy, together with specific bilateral disputes—in May 1983 the Reagan administration further liberalized its technology transfer policy, declaring China a 'friendly nonallied country' and one that could therefore be shifted to country group 'V' alongside America's West European allies.[25] Such liberalization contributed to trading advances: between 1979 and 1985, the US share of China's exports more than doubled, from 6 per cent to 14 per cent. Two-way trade rose from $2.3 billion in 1979 to $7.7 billion in 1985, representing 11 per cent of total PRC trade, but only 1.4 per cent for the United States. US investment levels also began to rise after 1983: only $18 million in

[21] Ibid. 17. Discussions in Beijing in Sept. 1993 at the Chinese Academy of Social Sciences confirmed that knowledge about the success of neighbouring economies only became more widely known from 1979.

[22] Barry Naughton, 'The Foreign Policy Implications of China's Economic Development Strategy', in Robinson and Shambaugh, eds., *Chinese Foreign Policy*, 55. Useful additional detail about the World Bank group's role in China is provided in William R. Feeney, 'China and the Multilateral Economic Institutions', in Samuel S. Kim, ed., *China and the World: Chinese Foreign Relations in the Post-Cold War Era* (Boulder, Colo.: Westview Press, 1994), 229–38.

[23] Jacobson and Oksenberg, *China's Participation*, 118.

[24] Nicholas R. Lardy, *China's Entry into the World Economy: Implications for Northeast Asia and the United States* (London: UPA for the Asia Society, 1987), 4–5.

[25] Ibid. 21.

1983, investment totalled $280 million in 1984 and nearly $1 billion by the end of 1986.[26] But, as will be explored later, such economic contact came with specific pressure on China to open its market, transform its trading practices, and move towards the GATT norms of transparency and reduction of tariffs.

The Deepening of Ties: 1985–1989

The remaining years of the Reagan period were the most productive era in Sino-American relations, perhaps the best that could be expected of two states with different value systems, but also a number of shared interests. Military establishments continued their collaboration, and educational exchange visits multiplied, with some 75,000 Chinese students and scholars receiving visas to enter the United States between 1979 and 1989.[27] The two countries additionally signed a wide range of agreements on trade, nuclear co-operation, technical, cultural, and scientific exchange. Both sides had a more pragmatic and realistic approach to the relationship, developing a greater appreciation of its limitations and benefits. The geostrategic element lost its pivotal role as both countries drew succour from the dramatic changes in Soviet policy that were occurring in the Gorbachev era. China now was engaged in various forms of exchange with the US and its Western allies, activities that were promoting a social transformation in certain parts of the country.

Interestingly, neither Beijing or Washington chose to take advantage of the opportunities the new Soviet policies offered: in fact the Chinese, as *rapprochement* with the Russians accelerated, went out of their way to reassure the Americans that any improvement in Sino-Soviet ties would not be at Washington's expense. In explaining what was now termed China's 'independent foreign policy of peace', the then Premier, Zhao Ziyang, declared that China would 'never attach itself to any superpower, or enter into alliance or strategic relations with either of them'.[28] China would maintain its opposition to hegemonism, he said, but in doing that its aims were to advance world peace and stability,

[26] Harding, *A Fragile Relationship*, appendix A-2, p. 364, and p. 147.
[27] Harding, 'China's Cooperative Behaviour', 379.
[28] *Beijing Review*, 29, no. 16 (21 Apr. 1986).

promote common economic prosperity, and develop friendly relations with all countries. With Gorbachev's reforms proceeding
apace, genuine progress being made in US–Soviet arms control,
and on the 'three obstacles' that China had identified as central to
the restoration of normal ties with Moscow, each bilateral advance seemed independent of any action that the remaining pole
in the strategic triangle might take. The leverage that had supposedly once accompanied tripolarity no longer seemed relevant in
an era where China sought political stability, economic progress,
and reductions in tension.

The deepening of US–China co-operation in the period between
1985 and 1989 also owed much to a further strengthening of
Beijing's economic reform programme. One impetus for that
strengthening was the Chinese leadership's perception that in
the changed international circumstances global war no longer
seemed likely. Future contests would not be over military
strength, it was believed, but would arise from differing levels of
scientific and technological advancement.[29] This did not mean, of
course, that the Chinese considered all conflict as being unlikely.
Their new assessment included a decision to change China's strategic doctrine to one that required preparation for local or regional war. Given advances in Japanese, Indian, and Taiwanese
weaponry, and the poor performance of its armed forces during
the war with Vietnam in 1979, Chinese leaders decided to reduce
drastically the size of the PLA and to modernize all branches of
their armed forces. Once again, the United States was viewed as a
critically important partner in this task.

Armed forces modernization took several forms: army weaknesses in mobility and logistics, identified from recent past experience of conflict, were to be tackled; the air force was to acquire
radar systems allowing for all-weather operations; and the navy
was to change its strategy from 'brown water' to 'green water'
and eventually to 'blue water' defence, requiring an expansion of
the fleet and of its strategic nuclear force. The improvement of the
navy was deemed to be of particular importance because of the
new interests that China had acquired in the reform era: including

---

[29] Arthur S. Ding, 'Peking's Foreign Policy in the Changing World', *Issues and Studies*, Aug. 1991, p. 18. See also the informative discussion in Xu Xin, 'Changing Chinese Security Perceptions', *North Pacific Cooperative Security Dialogue: Working Paper no. 27*, Apr. 1993.

the ability to maintain control over a large number of islands and a vast expanse of sea rich in mineral resources; the protection of China's seaborne freight and the sea lanes through which it had to travel; and the provision of greater security for the wealth-producing areas of China, namely the thirteen coastal provinces.[30]

The US role in this modernization effort between 1985 and 1989 was indeed crucial. By the end of 1985, four areas for sales of defensive weapons had been identified and the value of arms deals rose from $8 million in 1984 (when China was first made eligible for the US foreign military sales programme) to $106 million in 1989. Although other countries sold to China, from the US alone Beijing acquired 'avionics to upgrade the J-8 interceptor, large-caliber ammunition, artillery-locating radars, antiship torpedoes, and commercially available items such as helicopters, naval gas turbine engines, coast defense radars, and a range of communications equipment'.[31]

Such weapons sales were never uncontroversial in the United States, because of residual fears about China's attitude towards the use of force. But other policy developments in China in 1985 made such sales more palatable, developments that suggested Beijing's leaders had decided to integrate the country more fully into international political and economic society and to deepen ties with Washington still further. In the first half of the 1980s, the opening of China's economy had been a means of earning foreign exchange in order to help finance domestic reforms. But that objective began to alter in September 1984 when the State Council promulgated a major foreign trade reform document which indicated that trade was to be a major engine of growth.

In that document, China announced an end to the monopoly of power that had long been enjoyed by the national foreign trade companies. As a consequence, by 1986, the Ministry of Foreign Economic Relations and Trade (MOFERT), had approved the creation of more than 800 separate import and export companies, and by the late 1980s there were more than 8,000 of these. A decision to reduce the scope of the foreign trade plan ac-

[30] Harry G. Gelber, 'China's New Economic and Strategic Uncertainties and the Security Prospects', *Asian Survey*, 30, no. 7 (July 1990), 665–6; You Ji and You Xu, 'In Search of Blue Water Power: The PLA Navy's Maritime Strategy in the 1990s', *The Pacific Review*, 4, no. 2 (1991), 137–9.

[31] Gelber, 'China's New Economic and Strategic Uncertainties', 666; see also table A-11 in Harding, *A Fragile Relationship*, and pp. 167–8.

companied this reform, the number of planned export commodities falling from 3,000 in the pre-reform era to 112 by 1988. The introduction of price reform, such that the domestic sale price of imported goods began to reflect world prices, together with currency devaluation, formed the final parts of this reform package.[32] Using customs data as an indicator of China's trading levels, foreign trade rose from $38.1 billion in 1980, to $69.66 billion in 1985 and $111.6 billion in 1989. Whether one refers to customs data or Chinese ministry figures (which are lower), China's foreign trade 'grew significantly more than world trade' in these years. Furthermore, from 1979 to 1989 the PRC's 'ranking as a trading country increased more than any other country in the world'.[33]

As noted earlier, over the first half of the 1980s, the United States grew in importance as a trading partner for China and that continued into the second half of the decade. In 1979, bilateral trade represented 8 per cent of China's total trade, by 1985 it stood at 11 per cent, and by 1989 at 16 per cent. The value of that trade rose from $2.3 billion in 1979, to $7.7 billion in 1985 and to $17.8 billion in 1989, with China enjoying significant trade surpluses from 1986.[34]

The United States, because of its market power, was also important in facilitating China's initial approach to the GATT. Having applied for and received permanent observer status in the GATT in 1984, China made a formal application to join (or rejoin as it put it) two years later. To help ensure the success of this, Beijing asked Washington to comment on a working draft memorandum that China was to submit to the GATT prior to its application. In the US view, Beijing still had much to do with respect to the transparency of its economic system, and its tariff and pricing policies; nevertheless, the general impression then was that Beijing appeared committed to satisfying the requirements of a GATT trading regime.[35]

Further suggestions of a Chinese desire for integration into the global economy came in the foreign investment field. Levels ac-

[32] Nicholas Lardy, 'Chinese Foreign Trade', China Quarterly, 131 (Sept. 1992), 701–4.
[33] Ibid. 694–5. See also Lardy, China in the World Economy (Washington, DC: Institute for International Economics, 1994), esp. ch. 2.
[34] Harding, A Fragile Relationship, table A-2, p. 364.
[35] Jacobson and Oksenberg, China's Participation, 88 ff.

celerated in the second half of the 1980s, including the direct investment from the United States which put it second only to Hong Kong. Virtually nil in 1978, the cumulative total investment reached $20 billion by 1990. US levels of utilized investment were low at the end of 1983 at $18 million, but had reached $751 million in 1985 and $1.6 billion by the end of 1988, about 10 per cent of the cumulative total.[36] Such investment was important to China's economic progress, first because the foreign investment sector of the economy became the major foreign exchange earner, and secondly it was the major means for introducing foreign capital into import substitution investment.[37]

A further dimension of China's economic enmeshment and political change was the decision to accept rather than to give foreign aid. Between 1956 and 1975, and in addition to the help it gave to its communist allies China had given assistance on generous terms to fifty-one non-communist developing countries, half of which had incomes higher than China's own.[38] By 1982, aid disbursements had dwindled sharply, with China choosing instead to become a major recipient. In October 1978 Beijing had made its first moves and asked the United Nations Development Programme (UNDP) for technical assistance. By the mid-1980s, it had become the largest borrower from the World Bank.[39] In March 1986, Beijing joined the Asian Development Bank and also began to draw on its resources. Its earlier conditions of entry had been the expulsion of Taiwan, but the United States threatened to withhold its funds from the Bank should this happen. Under US and Japanese prompting—the two largest of the Bank's shareholders—both China and Taiwan accepted a name change for the latter (Taipei, China). For the first time the two coexisted in an international organization.[40] By 1989, China had overtaken India in becoming the world's largest recipient of official bilateral and multilateral aid, receiving almost $2.2 billion a year.[41]

---

[36] Harding, *A Fragile Relationship*, table A-7, p. 368, and p. 147.
[37] Y. Y. Kueh, 'Foreign Investment and Economic Change in China', *China Quarterly*, 131 (Sept. 1992), 679–80.
[38] Harding, 'China's Cooperative Behaviour', 388, 393.
[39] Lardy, *China's Entry*, 4–5.
[40] Gerald Chan, *China and International Organizations: Participation in Non-Governmental Organizations since 1971* (Oxford: Oxford University Press, 1989), 160–1; Feeney, 'China and the Multilateral Economic Institutions', 239–40.
[41] Samuel S. Kim, 'International Organizations in Chinese Foreign Policy', Annals of the *American Academy of Political and Social Science*, 519 (Jan. 1992), 152.

China's eagerness to participate in and draw upon the material and technical resources of the keystone international economic institutions and to involve itself more generally within the international economy was mirrored in a more active role within the United Nations and in international and non-governmental organizations. As noted earlier, China was outside virtually all the major intergovernmental organizations in the period 1949–70. Once it had joined the United Nations, this changed: a member of 21 IGOs in 1977, by 1989 it had entered 37. Beijing also began to take note of international conventions: a signatory of 15 during the period 1971–6, between 1977 and 1987 it had signed 103.[42]

Similarly, it was only after 1978 that China began actively to participate in international NGOs. Prior to that time, Beijing either remained isolated from the vast bulk of them or treated them dismissively, preferring to focus on its friendship organizations. (Between 1971 and 1978, for example, at international meetings of the Red Cross, it contributed little of substance but used the meetings to voice its condemnation of the two superpowers, especially the Soviet Union.[43]) A member of 71 such NGOs in 1977, by 1989 it had joined 677.[44]

Most dramatic of all was the apparent change in China's attitude towards the United Nations and towards one of its central activities, that of peacekeeping. At the nadir of its relations with that body, in 1965, an authoritative *Renmin Ribao* editorial had called for the establishment of an alternative, revolutionary UN and categorized the body then as a 'dirty international political stock exchange in the grip of a few big powers'.[45] That same year, it described the Special Committee for Peacekeeping Operations as a plot to convert the UN 'into a U.S.-controlled headquarters of international gendarmes to suppress and stamp out the revolutionary struggles of the world's people'.[46] However, by 1985, China's Premier was fulsome in his praise of that organization,

---

[42] Chan, *China and International Organizations*, 16, puts the figure far higher at 94, probably as a result of a revision of classification procedures in the *Yearbook of International Organizations*. Kim's figure is lower; see his 'Thinking Globally in Post-Mao China', *Journal of Peace Research*, 27, no. 2 (1990), 193; Kim, 'China's International Organizational Behaviour', in Robinson and Shambaugh, eds., *Chinese Foreign Policy*, 406, table 15.1.

[43] Chan, *China and International Organizations*, 74.

[44] Kim, 'International Organizational Behaviour', 406, table 15.1.

[45] Quoted in Kim, 'Thinking Globally', 193.

[46] *Beijing Review*, 10 (5 Mar. 1965).

and described it as 'irreplaceable in the historical mission it shoulders and the impact it exerts on the world'. According to Zhao Ziyang, it was 'rare for a political international organization to have such enduring vitality like that of the United Nations, whose universality and importance grow with the passage of time'.[47]

One consequence of this more positive depiction of the UN was a changed attitude towards peacekeeping. During China's first decade in the UN it had refused to become involved in the creation and dispatch of peacekeeping forces. However, 4 June 1981 marked the last time that Beijing failed to participate in the vote on the extension of the UN force in Cyprus; and on 14 December 1981 the PRC changed its vote in favour of the extension. At the same time it began to support the mandates of UNIFIL (the UN Interim Force in Lebanon) and UNDOF (the UN Disengagement Observer Force), and from January 1982 started to pay its share of the expenses of these two operations.[48] Participation in the United Nations had subjected China to direct pressure from developing countries on both these issues, helping to persuade it to give up its earlier negative stance.[49]

The autumn of 1984 marked a further development as the PRC's deputy permanent representative to the UN Special Committee on Peacekeeping claimed that there was a 'universal demand for strengthening the peacekeeping capability of the United Nations'.[50] Given this more positive attitude, Chinese leaders began to explore the possibility of sending their own personnel to join peacekeeping forces. Shortly thereafter, a PRC delegation including two senior PLA officers and the deputy director of the Department of International Organizations in the Chinese Foreign Ministry made an inspection tour of the UN Truce Supervision Organization (UNTSO). In 1988, twenty Chinese officers were sent to join the UNTSO observer group in Beirut. The same year, the PRC applied, after Soviet prompting, for membership of the UN Special Committee. In 1989, twenty Chinese civilians were sent to the UN Transition Assistance Group (UNTAG) in Namibia and Beijing also offered five military observers for service in UNTSO.[51]

[47] Yitzhak Shichor, 'China and the Role of the United Nations in the Middle East', *Asian Survey*, 31, no. 3 (Mar. 1991), 262.

[48] Ibid. 259–62.   [49] Kim, 'International Organizational Behaviour', 421.

[50] Shichor, 'China and the Role of the United Nations', 262.

[51] Ibid. 265–6.

Participation in the Conference on Disarmament in Geneva also appeared to have encouraged a shift in China's stance on arms control, China proposing a number of 'partial disarmament meas-ures', in the fields of nuclear, chemical, and biological weapons, and acceding to or ratifying seven of the eleven multilateral con-ventions between 1982 and 1987.[52]

From 1981, therefore, and particularly after 1985, China entered more whole-heartedly into the work of the global institutions and offered its support to many of the norms that it had once rejected on the grounds that they reflected only the self-serving interests of the great powers. If China's behaviour in the 1950s and 1960s could be seen as 'system transforming', if it could be depicted as 'system reforming' in the 1970s, then the 1980s behaviour could be described as 'system maintaining', even 'system exploiting'. As Samuel Kim has argued, 'post-Mao China is concerned less and less with the making of new rules, new norms, and new principles for a more just international order. Rather, it is more and more concerned with the stability of the existing capitalist world sys-tem as a *sine qua non* for fueling its modernization drive.'[53]

A consequence of this has been a diminution in what might be termed China's soft power, or of its ideological appeal. In the Maoist era, China was perceived in many quarters as attempt-ing—against huge odds and not without many setbacks—to build a self-reliant national economy. This quest for autonomous non-capitalist development was seen, by many radicals at least, as virtuous,[54] doubly so in the light of the punitive economic measures that the US and then the Soviets took against the PRC. Once China had put behind it the chaos and violence of the Cultural Revolution, and had begun to deal more reasonably with other states in the global system, it came to be seen in parts of the developing world as the 'antihegemonic third world champion of the establishment of the New International Economic Order', a stance that 'led many *dependencia* theorists to embrace Beijing as a model of self-reliant development . . . as the only third world country that gave but never received any bilateral and multilat-eral aid'.[55] Neither these theorists, developing countries, nor

[52] Kim, 'International Organizational Behaviour', 419.
[53] Kim, 'Thinking Globally', 193.
[54] A point noted in Jacobson and Oksenberg, *China's Participation*, pp. vii–viii.
[55] Kim, 'China as a Regional Power', *Current History*, 91, no. 566 (Sept. 1992), 251.

Beijing itself have subsequently been much interested in promoting—or indeed been able to promote—China in such terms.

The reversal of China's policy of self-reliance, on the other hand, has been of benefit to the major institutions that were the foundations of the Bretton Woods system. In the view of World Bank and IMF officials, China's membership has legitimized their claims to be truly global organizations, blunting the charge that they were instruments of capitalist exploitation. Moreover, China's strong desire to 'regain' GATT membership has undercut the Third World argument that the UN Conference on Trade and Development (UNCTAD) should be used as an alternative forum for handling international trade negotiations. From the perspective of GATT officials, China's participation (though it is not yet a full member) has facilitated their work because Beijing (up to a point) has been 'espousing and adhering to their norms'.[56] Where once China had identified with the socialist bloc or the developing world against capitalist powers, from the mid-1980s it spoke of the goals of common economic prosperity within a single global market. Beijing also referred to common interests in peace and stability and the consequent need for China to have an omnidirectional foreign policy: friendly relations with all countries, including the formerly despised, such as Israel and South Africa; and a positive attitude towards the United Nations. In the 1980s, China as an alternative model of economic and political development no longer existed, as China strove to catch up with and emulate the approach to development of its more advanced neighbours. US power was now to be acknowledged as a crucial route of access to advanced technology, as an export market, as the provider of educational opportunity, and as a key actor in global economic and political organizations, many of whose norms China now apparently supported.

Reassessments: 1989–1994

From 1984 to 1988, Sino-American relations had clearly developed apace and China had begun to operate as an important contributor to the maintenance of international order. Much as

[56] Jacobson and Oksenberg, *China's Participation*, 126, and see ch. 6.

Shultz had predicted, however, there were several tangible points of friction, many of which indicated that China's embrace of international norms—such as universal protection of human rights and non-proliferation—were at best partial. Human rights abuses in China, particularly in Tibet, continued to provoke concern in Washington. China's continuing if reduced support for the Khmer Rouge, its missile and arms sales to the Middle East—most lucratively, to both sides during the Iran–Iraq war—together with suspicions that it had not in fact abided by the nuclear non-proliferation norm, particularly where its long-standing ally Pakistan was concerned, also caused friction. A difficult investment climate in China and the maintenance of barriers in the Chinese market similarly caused irritation within the US government and among business people, helping to generate a more sombre mood about economic possibilities in China, and about the extent of the transformation that had taken place. Chinese leaders had their own concerns about the social and cultural consequences of their reform policies, as their periodic campaigns against 'bourgeois liberalization' graphically illustrated.

Nevertheless, the beliefs of the incoming Bush administration were that China was on the correct path, and that the United States would continue to point out the way stations as ties with China continued to strengthen. In George Bush, the Chinese had the first American President who believed he had some specialist knowledge of China. He had lived and worked there as head of the liaison office set up as a quasi-embassy in 1973. That was a time when China's perceived geopolitical importance had been at its height. Of considerable gratification to Chinese leaders, his first trip abroad as President had included a visit to Beijing, and he soon established a pattern of maintaining regular and direct contact with Chinese leaders.

These fruitful beginnings were seriously damaged, however, as a result of the killings and repression that followed the political protests in China in the spring and early summer of 1989. The killings on 4 June close to the vicinity of the famous Tiananmen Square and the aftermath of the bloodshed coincided with the peaceful and not so peaceful collapse of communism in Eastern Europe, generating a siege mentality in Beijing, and a sense outside of the country that China should not be regarded as reformist at all, at least in the political sphere. Moreover, its economic advancement, once seen as a welcome development, now appeared more ominous as it became less clear that such increased power would be used in benign ways, domestically, regionally, or globally. The hackneyed image of China as an awakening dragon about to breathe fire over neighbouring areas soon resurfaced, especially when in February 1992 Beijing promulgated new legislation designating the South China Sea as part of China's inland waters, and began to acquire weaponry that indicated a growing interest in force projection.

The Tiananmen massacre in particular, but also the conjunction of these events with the collapse of communism elsewhere, led to a severe crisis in Sino-American relations, evoking memories of past episodes in their difficult history. China and America also focused attention on those issues to do with the global commons that had divided them in the past, and that had rumbled like distant thunder.

Human rights issues came sharply to the fore as a result of Tiananmen, a tragedy of particular concern in the United States. More than three-quarters of the American people who were polled said they had followed the 4 June events 'closely' or 'very closely' on their TV screens.[57] Reflecting the wave of horror that passed through the American populace, the Bush administration immediately imposed a ban on military sales to Beijing and on all high-level military exchange visits. (Prior to 4 June the US Defense Department had been receiving requests for over 30 licences per week. Subsequently, these were denied for any item on the munitions control list, applying both to new agreements and to commitments waiting to be fulfilled, dating from the 1970s.[58])

As it became clear that key Chinese leaders, most notably Deng Xiaoping, were not about to express regret at the violent official reaction to the demonstrations,[59] and, as political protesters con-

---

[57] Harding, *A Fragile Relationship*, 240.

[58] Robert S. Ross, 'National Security, Human Rights, and Domestic Politics: The Bush Administration and China', in Kenneth A. Oye, Robert J. Lieber, and Donald Rothchild, eds., *Eagle in a New World: American Grand Strategy in the Post-Cold War Era* (New York: Harper Collins, 1992), 293.

[59] As Michael Yahuda has put it: Deng 'regarded the clamour about human rights abuses in his country as less a sign of the existence of international norms of behaviour than as evidence of a dark plot by Western forces to undermine socialism in China'. 'Deng Xiaoping: The Statesman', *China Quarterly*, 135 (Sept. 1993), 563.

tinued to be picked up and jailed, further sanctions were imposed. As a demonstration of America's central role within international lending organizations and within the Western alliance, Washington recommended that all further lending to China by international financial institutions be suspended, and it urged its Western allies to impose sanctions similar to America's own. The Bush administration also announced that it would suspend all official exchange with China at or above the level of assistant secretary. In late June, the European Community (EC) similarly banned high level contacts and economic aid, and at the G7 meeting in Paris in July comparable decisions were taken, thus bringing Japan into line with Western governments. The ADB and World Bank halted all new lending, negotiations over China's GATT application were suspended, and the IMF deferred work on its technical assistance projects.[60]

However, the Bush administration's policy had another and perhaps predictable strand to it. Reflecting Bush's view that, despite the Tiananmen crackdown, the total isolation of China would be counter-productive, and that China remained an important strategic actor that needed to be engaged in diplomatic discourse, the President sent two secret missions to Beijing in July and December 1989. Despite the desire for continued engagement that these missions symbolized, the actual message conveyed was an uncomfortable and familiar one in the history of PRC relations with the United States: only with a change in China's behaviour could relations with America be fully restored.

To much of the US public and Congress, however, these two missions appeared overly conciliatory.[61] In Congress, pressure mounted to tighten economic sanctions, to question the continuation of MFN, and to allow Chinese students to remain in the country beyond the expiry date of their visas. Some in the legislative branch were genuinely appalled at Chinese behaviour; others were intent on using Bush's China policy for partisan ends, and as a means of denting his credentials as a foreign-policy President and putative China expert.

[60] Harding, *A Fragile Relationship*, 225–7; Jacobson and Oksenberg, *China's Participation*, 164.
[61] Much of what follows in this paragraph is drawn from Ross, 'National Security, Human Rights and Domestic Politics'.

With the executive branch searching for a way to maintain contact with the PRC and at the same time conciliate Congress, pressure was put on Beijing to offer some gesture. However, not all the steps Beijing had agreed to take during the December mission were fulfilled: the overthrow by the Romanian military of the Ceauşescus had shaken the confidence of Chinese élites, leading them to put police and army units on alert. Conservatives in Beijing temporarily reined in the moderates who were set to try to repair relations with the West. A lessening of tension came with the lifting of martial law on 10 January, and on 18 January 573 demonstrators were released. Many in the United States did not regard these moves as being of great moment, however; significantly, they did not include the resolution of the problem concerning the noted scientist and democracy activist, Fang Lizhi, then holed up in the American embassy, or the withdrawal of the military from the streets of Beijing.

Nevertheless, though Chinese moves to date had caused disappointment in Washington, the Bush administration still responded by easing its objections to World Bank loans. China for its part continued to test the political temperature in Washington, reacting in ways which it hoped would ease its relations with the United States. When the debate over the US granting of MFN status for another year reached a high pitch in early May 1990, Beijing released a further 211 prisoners. According to one Chinese analyst, advice from officials within particular government departments and from research institutes in Beijing and Shanghai was instrumental in convincing Chinese leaders—including Deng Xiaoping—of the 'economic cost if the United States should terminate China's MFN status'.[62] After Bush announced his support for the retention of MFN and the World Bank offered new loans to China, Beijing tried its own version of 'carrot and stick' and reminded Washington that there could be some cost to America if economic ties with the PRC were cut off: it signed an agreement worth $4 billion to purchase up to seventy-two aircraft from Boeing,[63] and the next day made the first of two

[62] Ding Xinghao, 'Managing Sino-American Relations in a Changing World', *Asian Survey*, 31, no. 12 (Dec. 1991), 1160. See also Carol Lee Hamrin 'Elite Politics and the Development of China's Foreign Relations', in Robinson and Shambaugh, eds., *Chinese Foreign Policy*, 92–3.

[63] A tactic that was resorted to again in May 1994 when MFN came up for renewal.

purchases of US wheat. At the end of June, China moved again, allowing Fang Lizhi to leave the US embassy and travel to Britain.[64]

Undoubtedly the Gulf war prosecuted through the United Nations speeded up the process of reconciliation between China and the West. Successful prosecution of a war that was authorized by the UN was of especial importance in the context of President Bush's statements about a new world order: 'a world where the rule of law supplants the rule of the jungle, a world in which nations recognize the shared responsibility for freedom and justice, a world where the strong respect the rights of the weak'.[65] Having raised the stakes in this manner, it was particularly important that China not obstruct the workings of the Security Council. Thus, American diplomats stationed in Beijing and Shanghai apparently hinted that this conflict represented an opportunity for China to improve relations with the United States, and Beijing responded.[66] It may well have been of some comfort to China to react under these circumstances since Beijing, as one of the Permanent 5 and thus with veto power, could be seen to exercise its own form of leverage. Beijing voted for all ten UN resolutions that imposed political, military, and economic sanctions against Iraq, and abstained on resolution 678 that permitted the use of armed force to compel an Iraqi withdrawal from Kuwait.

Such co-operative or at least non-obstructive behaviour appeared to reap its rewards. At the Luxembourg foreign ministerial meeting at the end of October, the EC decided to resume political, economic, and cultural relations with the PRC. In early November, Japan formally announced the resumption of its development aid programme to China, releasing $240 million under the Third Yen loans programme, and the World Bank announced a further loan of $275 million. The day after Beijing's abstention on Resolution 678, Foreign Minister Qian Qichen met President Bush, effectively and prominently putting an end to the ban on high-level diplomatic intercourse; and on 4 December the World

---

[64] Ross, 'National Security, Human Rights and Domestic Politics', 306.

[65] Quoted in Adam Roberts, 'A New Era in International Relations', paper for conference on 'Facing the Challenges of the Twenty-First Century', June 1991, Beijing, p. 21.

[66] Ding, 'Managing Sino-American Relations', 1159.

Bank voted to extend the first 'non basic needs' loan to Beijing since the Tiananmen killings.[67]

Thus, the Gulf war was important in reminding the United States and its allies that China, as a member of the Security Council, retained global significance and would continue to do so with regard to issues in which the United Nations could be expected to play a prominent role. Furthermore, given the dramatic changes that had taken place in East–West relations and the end to superpower rivalry, the UN was presumed likely to be more active in the future. However, the Gulf war also demonstrated the unique role that the United States still played in the global system: its ability to muster a coalition of states; to assemble and lead armed forces; and to put on an impressive and deadly military display, even if it called upon its richer allies to pay for the cost of those operations. As one Chinese officer was quoted as saying: 'the American troops are very strong and powerful and we are no match for them',[68] a sentiment that was echoed elsewhere in the world. A broader lesson some in the Chinese military learned was that 'whoever possesses high-tech weapons will have a bigger say in world military affairs, which in turn will promote those countries' political and economic development. Defence is the backing force behind politics and the economy.'[69]

The results of the Gulf war and US 'guidance' of UN activities led some within the Chinese leadership to fear that the United States might arrogantly bestride a unipolar world, making China the special target of its displeasure. One Chinese analyst in arguing that the UN role had been strengthened as a result of its action in the Gulf also noted the drawbacks that were evident: 'one outstanding manifestation was that the United States and some other Western countries have taken advantage of the drastic changes in the international situation and given enormous publicity to their values and priorities within the UN. They have attempted to force their views and policies upon others in order to achieve their own interests.'[70] The association with UN actions raised starkly for China, then, the dangers of becoming too closely integrated into international society.

---

[67] J. Mohan Malik, 'Peking's Response to the Gulf Crisis', *Issues and Studies*, Sept. 1991, pp. 115–17.

[68] Harding, *A Fragile Relationship*, 296.

[69] Xu Xin, 'Changing Chinese Security Perceptions', 9.

[70] *Beijing Review*, 34, no. 3 (21–7 Jan. 1991).

Such fears of US dominance of global institutions, of international discourse, even of the fate of weaker states, ran through Chinese commentaries in the early post-cold-war, post-Gulf-war era. During the period when China felt most vulnerable, the main argument focused on the PRC itself, noting that it was, as it had ever been, the target of a US strategy of peaceful evolution designed to undermine Communist Party rule and substitute a capitalist system in China.[71] But although the concern about US dominance was never removed entirely, a cause for especial anxiety because China benefitted from the economic relationship, it did begin to be subordinated to an argument that stressed the variety of constraints the US faced.

Such constraints arose from the fact that many developing countries were believed to share Chinese concerns about the emerging 'New World Order'. As the UN became seriously overstretched and its operations remained underfunded, Chinese leaders pointed to the virtues of a more restrained, less interventionist, international body, its actions based on respect for state independence and sovereignty.[72] In the context of UN actions in Somalia, and elsewhere, which had caused much international disquiet, China's Foreign Minister at the General Assembly in October 1993 bluntly stated that his country disapproved of the 'malpractice of indiscriminate use of sanctions or force in the name of the United Nations. We also believe that humanitarian missions must not be transformed into military operations and that a war could not be stopped by expanding it.'[73]

Beijing additionally attempted to demonstrate that its conception of human rights accorded closely or directly with such other major states as India. When Li Peng visited New Delhi in December 1991, the joint communiqué signed at the end of the visit stressed that 'for the vast number of developing countries the right to subsistence and development is a basic human right'.[74] In an article on the Bali meeting of the Nonaligned Movement (NAM) in June 1992, Chinese comments laid great emphasis on NAM agreement that the promotion of human rights could not take place through 'confrontation or imposing one's values upon

[71] See the report of Premier Li Peng's speech in *New York Times*, 19 Sept. 1991.
[72] See e.g. *Foreign Broadcast Information Service* (*FBIS*), China, Daily Report, 92/200 15 Oct. 1992.
[73] *Beijing Review*, 36, no. 41 (11–17 Oct. 1993).
[74] *Beijing Review*, 34, no. 51 (23–9 Dec. 1992), and no. 52 (30 Dec.–5 Jan. 1992).

others'.[75] Even Japan—a state that like India was once held up in the United States as the democratic alternative to the PRC—could be persuaded by Beijing to add its voice in mild support of China's position on human rights. In Tokyo's view, there were arguments against imposing the Western conception on other cultural areas.[76] As one analyst would later assert in *Beijing Review*, in a manner reminiscent of the Maoist approach, this meant that the US concept of human rights was endorsed 'by only 1 billion of the world's people, while the remaining 4 billion people disagree'.[77]

In the economic field, Chinese commentators made great play of China's growing status as a trading nation, noted that large numbers of jobs in the United States—some 100,000 according to a 1992 publication—had already come to depend on Chinese purchases from the American market, and over 500 American companies were investing in the country.[78]

This regaining of composure associated with a lessening of a sense of isolation and siege helped reinforce the arguments of those in Beijing committed to re-establishing the links that had been built with the industrialized world. Deng Xiaoping additionally argued that America's long-term strategy of peaceful evolution could be undermined provided China continued to improve the living standards of its people.[79] A significant boost to economic reform in China had come with Deng's visit to the South at Chinese New Year in 1992, where he described the region as a model for the rest of the country. This signal that the

[75] *Beijing Review*, 35, no. 23 (8–14 June 1992).

[76] A list of areas where Asian countries have supposedly disagreed with US policy and refused to follow it is contained in *Far Eastern Economic Review*, 19 May 1994.

[77] *Beijing Review*, 37, no. 22 (30 May–5 June 1994).

[78] See e.g. Guo Changlin, 'Sino–U.S. Relations in Perspective', *Contemporary International Relations*, 2, no. 7 (July 1992). On the eve of the 1994 decision regarding MFN, a Chinese analyst claimed that if the USA cancelled China's MFN status, this would mean that the US had abandoned the vast Chinese market, whereas for the PRC cancellation would not 'cause the sky to fall, and the earth to turn the other way round, and that the People's Republic of China would cease to exist and the Chinese economy would no longer develop'. *Beijing Review*, 37, no. 22 (30 May–5 June 1994).

[79] For discussion of the evolution in Chinese thinking see Bonnie S. Glaser, 'China's Security Perceptions: Interests and Ambitions', *Asian Survey*, 33, no. 3 (Mar. 1993), esp. 259–60; and Jianwei Wang and Zhimin Lin, 'Chinese Perspectives of the Post-Cold War Era: Three Images of the United States', *Asian Survey*, 32, no. 10 (Oct. 1992).

reformers were in the ascendant reassured outsiders and those inside China who were committed to reform. Trade, investment, and growth levels took off once again, growth rates reaching 12.8 per cent in 1992 and 13 per cent in 1993.[80] Contracted foreign investment for 1992 reached $14.6 billion, and $18 billion in 1993. Incentives were adopted to encourage foreign capital into new geographical regions and into new areas of high technology and the tertiary sector. China's export trade figures approached a value of $90 billion in 1992, making it the tenth largest exporting nation in the world. Expectations voiced in the West included the view that by 1994 China's economy would be four times larger than it was in 1978 and, if a steady course were to be maintained, eight times larger by 2002.[81]

China, then, might have failed badly in its support of the human rights regime, but there was still a chance that its economic reforms would continue to give a boost to a global economy normatively based on openness in trading and investment. Unlike in the cold-war era, however, when the United States for political reasons would allow non-communist allies a long period of adjustment, China would not be so fortunate in its timing. Bush and then Clinton thus were determined to reduce China's economic barriers still further, especially to America's export industries, using the steadily growing trade deficit with the PRC as a point of pressure. Standing at $6.2 billion in 1989 (US figures), that deficit rose to $12.7 billion in 1991, $18 billion in 1992, and $23 billion in 1993.[82]

In mid-1991 the United States began discussions on market access and on the protection of intellectual property. If these were to prove unsuccessful Bush warned that he intended to initiate trade sanctions against Chinese exports. In October that year,

---

[80] *Beijing Review*, 36, no. 24 (14–20 June 1993), 9; BBC *Summary of World Broadcasts*, Weekly Economic Report, FEW0320, 16 Feb. 1994.

[81] 'When China Wakes', *The Economist*, 28 Nov. 1992; Qimao Chen, 'New Approaches in China's Foreign Policy: The Post Cold War Era', *Asian Survey*, 33, no. 3 (Mar. 1993), 250; Lardy, 'China as a NIC', *International Economic Insights*, May–June 1993; Overseas Development Institute, London, *Briefing Paper*, 'China's Economic Reforms', Feb. 1993.

[82] Lardy, 'Chinese Foreign Trade', 718; Winston Lord, 'A New Pacific Community: Ten Goals for American Policy', opening statement at Confirmation Hearings for Ambassador Winston Lord, Washington DC, 31 Mar. 1993; *Far Eastern Economic Review*, 17 Mar. 1994, p. 43. The predicted deficit for 1994 is $28 billion: *Far Eastern Economic Review*, 25 Aug. 1994.

Washington launched an investigation of Beijing's trade practices under Section 301 of the 1974 Trade Act. Beijing had until October 1992 to satisfy specific American complaints or face export constraints. China agreed to increase its imports of American products, to phase out over 60 per cent of its import licences and other controls within two years, and to publicize its trading regulations.[83] On the eve of the expiry of a deadline for the imposition of punitive tariffs China also agreed to give better protection to patents and copyrights, to include computer software and sound recordings, and pharmaceutical products.[84] According to a Chinese analyst, in exchange for these trading and copyright agreements, the United States 'promised to support China's application to join GATT',[85] but in 1994 China was additionally required to reassure US and European Union officials that it would accept special safeguards against a surge in its exports to these economies after entry,[86] and GATT entry remains pending.

China's stance on these matters of openness and protection of property rights has been recognized to be important to the future of the GATT trading regime, particularly as Beijing's status as a trading nation advances. But other global norms were also recognized as requiring China's support or at least acquiescence in order to be fully effective. As US administrations have emphasized, China is a country that can advance or help to prevent the spread of conventional and nuclear weapons, can exacerbate or help resolve conflicts in Northeast and Southeast Asia, and can help protect or destroy the global environment. Such issues had already come to the fore during the Reagan and early Bush administrations, but in the post-Tiananmen era and in the light of China's growing economic power they became additionally important to tackle.

Timed to coincide with the Congressional debate over MFN in 1991, Beijing began to make some effort to bring arms sales under stricter control.[87] In early June, Premier Li Peng announced China

---

[83] Chen, 'New Approaches', 249.   [84] Lardy, 'Chinese Foreign Trade', 719.
[85] Chen, 'New Approaches', 249.
[86] *Far Eastern Economic Review*, 17 Mar. 1994. Lardy outlines the political and economic obstacles to GATT entry in *China in the World Economy*, 94–7.
[87] Some of the difficulties of bringing weapons sales under control are addressed in John W. Lewis, Hua Di, and Xue Litai, 'Beijing's Defense Establishment: Solving the Arms-Export Enigma', *International Security*, 15, no. 4 (Spring 1991).

would support Bush's moves to prevent the spread of nuclear, chemical, and biological weapons to the Middle East and would ban its missile sales to the area. Beijing also agreed to participate in a conference in early July 1991 designed to discuss guidelines for restraining the transfer of weapons to the Middle East. Subsequently in 1992, it made a commitment to abide by the Missile Technology Control Regime. In August 1991, during the Japanese Prime Minister's visit to Beijing, China agreed in principle to join the nuclear Non-Proliferation Treaty (NPT), which it did in 1992, and later announced its support for the extension of the NPT when that treaty comes up for renewal in 1995. It also agreed that the nuclear reactor it was helping to build in Algeria would be placed under International Atomic Energy Authority (IAEA) safeguards. That at least a part of this came as a result of US pressure using the lever of MFN was seemingly confirmed when Li Peng stated in late June 1991 that China 'would make no more concessions to the United States', alleging that Beijing 'had made "a great deal of efforts" to preserve most favored nation status'.[88]

With respect to the Cambodian peace process, China continued to give support to the UN effort, sending an engineering battalion to work under UN auspices. It also announced in 1993 that it would no longer be providing military aid to the Khmer Rouge; nor would it provide support to any of the Cambodian factions should civil war erupt.[89]

On the Korean peninsula, China has clearly put selective pressure on the North to continue its dialogue with the United States, to accept inspection of its nuclear facilities, and to retain its membership of the NPT. It has also indicated its firm support for Seoul in many areas, establishing diplomatic relations in 1992 and facilitating membership for both North and South Korea in the United Nations. But, prior to the agreement that was worked out between Washington and Pyongyang in October 1994, China's objection to the imposition of UN sanctions against the North, its

See also Eric Hyer, 'China's Arms Merchants: Profits in Command', *China Quarterly*, 132 (Dec. 1992).

[88] Chen, 'New Approaches', 244; Ding, 'Managing Sino-American Relations', 1164; Harding, *A Fragile Relationship*, 279.

[89] *International Herald Tribune*, 23 Apr. 1993.

constant reiteration that its influence on Pyongyang was limited, at the same time that it was calling for a solution to be worked out at the regional level, afforded an impression that China was only a reluctant participant in this proliferation crisis.

It is this perception of reluctance, on this and other issues, that has generated the belief that China's co-operation requires constant vigilance because it has not fully accepted certain norms. To many US officials, its behaviour seems to be wholly reactive, a response to pressure and a means of bargaining. The US record indicates that such vigilance is likely to be maintained, as shown by its reactions to Chinese sales of the M-ll missile to Pakistan in 1992 (which resulted in the imposition of sanctions on the sale of some high-technology items to China), and to the alleged shipment of chemical weapons to Iran in August 1993.[90]

The Clinton administration, despite expectations raised by its harsh campaign rhetoric, and the initial tying of MFN renewal to specific progress on human rights,[91] has shown by its overall behaviour that it retains a belief in the importance of maintaining contact with leaders in Beijing. Apart from the domestic economic consequences of imposing sanctions on China, it also accepts that the PRC is significant to the maintenance and reinforcement of global economic and political norms, and to the resolution of regional issues. Summits in Seattle and Bogor, and regular contact between other high-level officials indicate as much. As Winston Lord had reminded his audience during his Confirmation Hearings in March 1993 for the post of Assistant Secretary of State for East Asian and Pacific Affairs, one in five of the world's population lives in China, the country 'possesses nuclear weapons and

---

[90] See, for details on these two issues, *Far Eastern Economic Review*, 9 Sept. 1993. Interviews in Washington in Apr. 1994 nevertheless suggested that neither issue was believed to have been handled deftly by US officials. The sanctions which went into effect in Aug. 1993 were cancelled in Oct. 1994 on the signature of two Sino-US declarations where both promised to work for a ban on the production of fission materials, and China agreed not to export surface-to-surface guided missiles restricted under the MTCR. For details see BBC, *Summary of World Broadcasts*, FE/2119 G/1, 6 Oct. 1994.

[91] Clinton renewed MFN with China in May 1994 and removed the conditions attached to its yearly renewal. For a valuable discussion of this 1994 decision see David M. Lampton, 'America's China Policy in the Age of the Finance Minister: Clinton Ends Linkage', *China Quarterly*, 139, Sept. 1994; also see Lampton, 'China Policy in Clinton's First Year', in James R. Lilley and Wendell L. Willkie, II, eds., *Beyond MFN: Trade with China and American Interests* (Washington, DC: AEI Press, 1994).

exports nuclear technology. It launches satellites and sells missiles. It represents a huge market and one of the world's richest
civilizations. It holds a permanent seat on the United Nations
Security Council. It is central to key regional issues like
Indochina, Korea and disputed islands. It abuts the unsettled
Central Asian region. It is salient in new challenges that require
global action.' The United States, he stated, needed a 'nuanced
policy', one that 'condemned repression' yet preserved 'links
with progressive forces'. The serious issues affecting US relations
with China he listed as 'widespread human rights violation, including in Tibet. Chinese exports of dangerous weapons
and technology to volatile areas. Our fastest growing trade
deficit . . . second only to Japan. Collaboration at the United
Nations and on regional conflicts. Emerging challenges like the
environment and drugs'.[92] In an era of a more active United
Nations, of concern about the effects of weapons proliferation on
regional tensions, and of a President who had promised to focus
on the revitalization of America's economy, China has necessarily
been accorded a centrality that makes any use of American leverage an undertaking of great complexity. Lord's statement suggested that the complexity associated with the weighing of
different interests—from domestic, bilateral to global—was realized from the beginning of the new administration.

These matters will serve to keep the United States and China
warily engaged. From the Chinese perspective, in certain areas,
their position in these various sets of discussions and negotiations
remains inferior to that of the United States. As noted earlier, in
Deng's clarion call to accelerate reform in early 1992 he had made
the telling argument to his domestic critics, to those who feared
China would go the route of the former Soviet Union and Eastern
Europe, that stability would only come about in China if economic progress met the expectations of the population. With an
export-led strategy at the root of these advances and the desire for
rapid scientific and technological advancement, this suggested
the necessity for maintaining links with the United States and its
market, which in 1991 took some 26 per cent of China's exports
and in 1993 about a third. For most of the Maoist era, it was

[92] Lord, 'A New Pacific Community'. See also article by President Clinton
published in the *International Herald Tribune*, 1 June 1994, shortly after MFN
renewal.

evident that US policies helped to obstruct China's economic development, to deny it access to international organizations, and to prevent its reunification with Taiwan. The United States remains less dominant but still significant in each of these respects even now, a fact that the Chinese leadership recognizes. According to one Chinese scholar writing in 1992, who apparently has been close to Deng Xiaoping and other leaders, Deng has argued that the United States remains 'indispensable' to China's reform efforts and to its dealings with other Western countries. Other Chinese researchers have stated that the 'goal of creating a "socialist market economy" adopted by the Fourteenth Party Congress could not be realized in the event of a serious deterioration of Sino-American relations'.[93]

It is also the case that the Chinese search for domestic stability and comprehensive national strength, and its ability to contribute to international order in certain areas, may well be beyond a Communist Party leadership that in many respects has lost its legitimacy, may be losing control over large parts of the country, and is unable to command sections of the bureaucracy.[94] Other challenges facing Beijing include the difficulties of keeping up with the global technological revolution while at the same time providing for the needs of a population that increases by 15 million a year. Sustaining the growth rates to support this population is acknowledged to be problematic unless China can move to a higher stage of development.[95]

Although China recognizes, as the United States itself does, that America faces a welter of domestic problems, including the erosion of educational standards, and the relative decline of its economic strength, it also acknowledges that for the short and

[93] Wang and Lin, 'Chinese Perspectives', 917; Glaser, 'China's Security Perceptions', 259.

[94] For a recent statement of this argument see Gerald Segal, 'China Changes Shape: Regionalism and Foreign Policy', *Adelphi Paper*, 287 (Mar. 1994). David Shambaugh has also suggested that the Foreign Ministry has been unable to command the PLA in the important area of Sino-Japanese relations: the bilateral security dialogue that was agreed between the two states has been delayed because of a PLA refusal to discuss openly its planning and doctrine. 'Growing Strong: China's Challenge to Asian Security', *Survival*, 36, no. 2 (Summer 1994), 57. See also Lewis, Hua, and Xue, 'Beijing's Defense Establishment'.

[95] Chen, 'New Approaches', 245. Lardy, in raising the question 'Will China Become a Global Economic Superpower?' also points to a number of constraining factors. See *China in the World Economy*, 106–9.

medium term, the United States remains central to its efforts and to the inter-state system of which it is a part. America has a diverse and open market—especially in comparison with China's more developed neighbours such as Japan and South Korea; it retains a prominent role in global international institutions; largely shapes how major challenges to the international *status quo* are dealt with; and has offered and will probably continue to offer large numbers of Chinese citizens access to knowledge and training in new skills. In the light of this, Beijing's strategy remains one of treading a fine line between actions that the US would acknowledge as demonstrating its qualities as a responsible member of the international community, without compromising its position to a degree that would appear threatening to Communist Party rule.

These joint realizations on the part of Washington and Beijing suggest an uncertain and uncomfortable period where the two will neither be friends or enemies. Such a relationship does, however, indicate continuing if wary engagement, not a return to the estrangement and levels of hostility of earlier years.

10

Summary and Conclusion

Explaining change in international relationships has long been recognized as a challenge of great complexity but, in consequence, one of the most absorbing that is to be had.[1] Understanding the reversal in US relations with China, from hostility to *rapprochement*, is no exception to that, in part because of the distinctive elements in the relationship between 1950 and the early 1970s. As A. Doak Barnett once commented, during that period 'There were no formal diplomatic ties, no trade, no legal travel back and forth, and virtually no mutual contact between ordinary citizens of the two countries.' We would be hard put, he noted, to find two societies as isolated as this and for this length of time in the modern period.[2]

The establishment of Communist rule in Beijing in October 1949 was of great moment to Chinese everywhere and to the United States. Although, prior to the Korean conflict, Washington might have contemplated the eventual forging of a formal relationship with this new revolutionary state, nevertheless the US viewed China as an additional threat to be faced and accommodated in the global system. Once the war in Korea had thrown the two states and their respective armed forces together in the most desperate of circumstances, China provided the context for the establishment of a sizeable American presence in East Asia to include a system of alliances, and requisite basing arrangements. Major military crises involving Taiwan and Indo-China served to ensure that the US and China continued to confront each other in

---

[1] Barry Buzan and Roy J. B. Jones, eds., *Change and the Study of International Relations: The Evaded Dimension* (London: Pinter, 1981); Ole R. Holsti, Randolph M. Siverson, and Alexander L. George, *Change in the International System* (Boulder, Colo.: Westview Press, 1980). For a study that focuses on social transformation in international relations see Jan Aart Scholte, *International Relations of Social Change* (Buckingham: Open University Press, 1993).

[2] Barnett quoted in Harry Harding, *A Fragile Relationship: The United States and China since 1972* (Washington, DC: Brookings Institution, 1992), 33.

subsequent years, and that the US presence in Asia continued to deepen. For the Chinese too the United States represented a threat of major proportions: undermining regime security, constraining its relationships in Asia and beyond, and encircling it with military bases and some of its most advanced weaponry. Thus, emergence into an era where they were no longer implacable adversaries was of fundamental importance to the two states, as well as to regional and international actors.

That shift to *rapprochement* and then the normalization of the bilateral relationship can be better understood via a focus on the medium-term events that influenced the global and domestic contextual environments and proved conducive to bringing about change. Between the early 1950s and the mid-1960s, the United States experienced an erosion of support for its China policy in both environments, a matter of greater consequence for a state that sought to continue to play a leading role in establishing and reinforcing the norms and rules of behaviour associated with the post-war order. Furthermore, successive US administrations came to develop a more subtle and sober appreciation of China's capabilities, the overall conclusion being that Beijing was neither as menacing or powerful as had once been thought the case, and thus would not be dangerously empowered as a result of a change in America's policy. *Rapprochement* followed by normalization also meant that the PRC would have its entry into international society facilitated by a state largely responsible for establishing the patterns of international behaviour associated with the post-war order.

In the period after 1949, there were certain defining moments in the relationship, the most significant being China's entry into the Korean war, the onset and then failure of the Great Leap Forward, the Sino-Soviet rift, entry into the nuclear club, the Sino-American strategic alignment, and then China's economic modernization programme. Each of these events altered US and other countries' perceptions of China itself, and thus the environment in which China policy came to be debated and decided upon.

In the 1950s, the Truman and Eisenhower administrations, together with the majority of the American public, viewed China as a country that was *en route* to attaining great power status, and that already had shown its skills in organizing an enormous country with a huge population. Its hard power, material resources were growing, as a result of its own policies which seemed to be energetically and ruthlessly applied. Its links with the Soviet Union provided it with some strategic depth and access to goods and skills, including conventional military and nuclear technology. Its soft power resources were also not insignificant given its apparent early success with a politico-economic model that represented an outright rejection of liberal-capitalism, its transnational ideology, and the sympathetic treatment it received from countries that sought similarly to shed the humiliations associated with past status as a colony. The PRC's advancement occurred, therefore, within the context of policies the USA deemed as hostile to its national security and to its broader interests in the international system.

In these circumstances, Washington sought to ostracize Beijing and to undermine its growing power and prestige through the denial of recognition, constriction of China's trading relationships, and the bolstering of an alternative Chinese regime on the island of Taiwan. Moreover, even if administrations in the 1950s had sought a less harsh means of dealing with China, domestic, especially Congressional, pressure mainly engineered by right-wing Republicans, ensured that alternative means were not to be long contemplated. America's primary Western allies, although they often favoured a different approach towards China, were generally unwilling to cross the United States on matters connected with recognition for fear that Washington would withdraw its support from objectives that they considered more vital. It could not be described as willing consent, however, where America's China policy was concerned. Thus, the policy was not fully legitimized and was always difficult to carry through in the international arena.

In consequence of these difficulties and changes in various objective conditions, perceptions and policies began to alter in the late 1950s and early 1960s. Within the United Nations, new states espousing non-alignment joined the organization and the numbers in support of China's entry grew. America's primary allies became bolder in advocating change in US policy towards China on this and other questions: in part because of the perception that the UN without China would never be entirely credible as an international organization; because their own experience of trading with the PRC had demonstrated that, as with other members of the socialist bloc, it was possible to have contact on a stable, legal basis; and because their confidence in the security and political relationship with the United States had reached a point where disagreement with Washington did not appear as costly an undertaking. The two crises in the Taiwan Straits added to the pressure for change in that they served to suggest the dire consequences that could arise out of high levels of mutual Chinese–American misunderstanding and hostility.

Within US administrations themselves, to some degree the generation that had experienced the Korean war began to give way to one that focused on the Sino-Soviet rift, on China's objective condition, and the implications of the failure of the Great Leap Forward. The rift and the economic collapse, to be followed later by the Cultural Revolution, though tempered by Beijing's entry into the nuclear club, all suggested an overall reduction in China's hard and soft power resources, and that Washington now faced a less urgent situation than had appeared to be the case a few years earlier. The China bloc in Congress also began to lose its restraining hold on policy change, although the psychological damage it had wrought was more difficult to eradicate. Aware of the Sino-Soviet breach, of the loss of international support for America's China policy, and that China despite its lack of formal ties with Washington still had expended much US energy—whether that was in Korea, in Indo-China, or in the Taiwan Straits—Congressional leaders set out to explore the implications of these understandings, and whether limited contact would not be a wiser course to follow. By the mid-1960s, the majority of opinion formers and the mass public had concluded that such contact did have much to recommend it.

One area where China did advance in the 1960s was in the nuclear field. Although China remained vulnerable strategically for several years, attainment of such a capability was still an extremely rare event and carried with it a status that was difficult to ignore. However, such a development also contributed to this sense that a change in US policy had to be effected. The United States was closely involved with every other state that had such weapons, and Washington, along with Moscow, was the prime mover in the development of the norm of non-proliferation and in an arms control regime of which China needed to be a part. Some in Washington viewed China's violent unpredictability as a reason to incorporate Beijing into such arrangements; but China's circumspection once it had acquired these weapons reinforced an alternative perception that it was in fact an unofficial participant in the building of such regimes, to which it could contribute more profoundly if it were to become an official part of the process.

The perception of China had changed, then, from one where it was viewed as a 'candidate great power' in the 1950s to a portrait of a country which, although it had nuclear weapons, no longer had the backing of the Soviet Union or most of its socialist allies, was suffering serious economic setbacks, had an industrial capability that was plainly uneven, and had conventional armed forces that had failed to modernize at the pace once predicted for them. Certainly, the nuclear weapons capability had a psychological and political impact, but this went alongside an industrial base that was experiencing severe shortages of skilled personnel and in most other areas was undergoing technological decline.

From this perspective, the *rapprochement* with China can be seen as the culmination of several processes: changes in international attitudes as new states entered international forums and as old ones became more confident about the basis of their relationship with the United States, and thus more willing to challenge a policy that did not command their support and was not viewed as legitimate. And changes, too, in domestic opinion, as groups noted this loss of international support, the dangers of leaving a nuclear-armed China outside formal negotiating networks, and the longevity of a regime administrations had tried to undermine for more than a decade. In addition, there was a more nuanced understanding of the overall limitations in China's capabilities, especially as a result of the split with the Soviet Union, and the outcome of the ill-fated Great Leap economic reform programme.

These were Nixon's inheritance: the underpinnings of a broad understanding that China needed to be brought into the international community and, moreover, some believed, might be willing to be drawn in. If the Vietnam war had not so absorbed the Johnson administration, constraining its ability to embark on bold and innovative policies elsewhere in Asia;[3] if the Chinese leadership itself had not rejected the path that some in Beijing had advocated of easing tensions with its three major adversaries— America, India, and the Soviet Union—instead to become embroiled in its Cultural Revolution, which took it into a period of intense isolation; then positive moves beyond the small steps that Johnson did in fact authorize might have been made before 1971. As it was, change had to await the advent of a US administration more secure domestically, committed to the restoration of America's pivotal role in the global system, and that saw, arising out of Beijing's depiction of Moscow as its primary enemy, the opportunity to draw China not only into the international community but also into an alignment against the Soviets. Such an alignment would help, it was hoped, with the containment of growing Soviet power, and make the Moscow leadership, as well as Beijing, more supportive of international order.

The *rapprochement* and then normalization of relations with China at the beginning and end of the 1970s, respectively, did indeed contribute much to America's power, for three main reasons. First, in the domestic setting it helped to restore a consensus over Asian policy that had been severely damaged by the prosecution and loss of the war in Vietnam, and by the recognition that the United States had become internationally isolated with respect to its China policy. Secondly, in the international arena, the development of formal ties with China brought the United States into line with the approach of its major allies, removed the specific irritation surrounding its UN recognition policy, reduced the areas for disagreement over trading questions, and widened the opportunities for removing misunderstandings between Beijing and Washington that had served in the past to raise tensions to frightening proportions. More profoundly still, *rapprochement* reduced the sense that Washington's policies had been undermining and not buttressing many of the norms of the post-war order: a viable UN as the best approximation available to a collective security organization; a relatively open, world trading economy; and a nuclear non-proliferation

---

[3] A point made strongly in Nancy Bernkopf Tucker, 'Threats, Opportunities and Frustrations in East Asia', in Warren I. Cohen and Nancy Bernkopf Tucker, eds., *Lyndon Johnson Confronts the World* (New York: Cambridge University Press, 1994).

regime. Although its containment doctrine with respect to Moscow still rested primarily on deterrence, there had developed certain rules of behaviour and implicit understandings important to the management of that relationship. Where China was concerned, however, the possibility of effecting that transformation had seemed remote, given such levels of estrangement.

Finally, the repair of relations with China after 1971 exposed China more fully to the ideas and values that were dominant in the global system. In the 1970s, the change effected was relatively slight, though the level of China's challenge to the prevailing order had clearly diminished. But with the new reform leadership firmly in place from the end of the decade, and committed to economic modernization via close ties with Western countries and within the framework of established global economic and political institutions, the alteration in behaviour and rhetoric was more extensive. From the late 1970s and early 1980s, for example, China gave its support to institutions that espoused the values of liberal capitalism; began to participate in UN peacekeeping activities which in themselves implied that the organization could operate independently and neutrally of the states which made up that body; and offered to align its policies on arms sales and transfer of nuclear technology with those of the Western states. Even if not properly implemented, such activity gave credibility to the norms themselves, and provided a point of leverage for those with the ability to monitor adherence.

Examined from this perspective, therefore, the United States has clearly gained in terms of its structural power as a result of the normalization of ties and the introduction of reform policies in China. Those policies, and the actions that have flowed from them, have served to reinforce the belief that the 'rules' that have been largely shaped and promoted by the United States in fact have a universal quality to them: they can indeed embrace a state that at one time was perceived as having mounted a significant challenge to international order.

Nevertheless, China's embrace of such international patterns of behaviour remains incomplete, and it is still plainly desirous of determining its own international agenda. Moreover, the Tiananmen killings were one graphic suggestion that the security of the regime might matter more to the Beijing leadership than constructive participation in the management of international order as the leading Western states have defined it. From this perspective, it seems that China's search for comprehensive national strength has primarily been undertaken in order that the agenda eventually can be set not in Washington, or New York, or Geneva, but in Beijing. It seems an unlikely outcome, in part because of the political decay that has set in in the country, and because in the process of attempting to reach that objective it cannot avoid being socially transformed in ways that are difficult to control or reverse.

BIBLIOGRAPHY

Manuscript Collections

ACHESON, DEAN. Papers. Harry S. Truman Library. Independence, Mo. (HSTL)

BRITISH PUBLIC RECORDS OFFICE. Cabinet Files. Foreign Office Files. Prime Minister's Office Files. London. (PRO)

CARTER, JIMMY. Papers. Jimmy Carter Library. Atlanta, Ga. (JCL)

DULLES, JOHN FOSTER. Papers. Dwight D. Eisenhower Library. Abilene, Kan. (DDEL)

——. Papers. Seeley G. Mudd Library, Princeton University, Princeton. (SGML)

EISENHOWER, DWIGHT D. Papers. Dwight D. Eisenhower Library. Abilene, Kan. (DDEL)

HILSMAN, ROGER. Papers. John F. Kennedy Library. Boston. (JFKL)

JOHNSON, LYNDON B. Papers. Lyndon Baines Johnson Library. Austin, Tex. (LBJL)

JUDD, WALTER H. Papers. Hoover Institution on War, Revolution and Peace. Palo Alto, Stanford University, Calif.

KENNEDY, JOHN F. Papers. John F. Kennedy Library. Boston. (JFKL)

MURPHY, ROBERT D. Papers. Hoover Institution on War, Revolution and Peace. Palo Alto, Stanford University, Calif.

NIXON, RICHARD M. Papers. Nixon Presidential Project, National Archives, Alexandria, Va. (NA)

SCHLESINGER, ARTHUR. Papers. John F. Kennedy Library. Boston. (JFKL)

THOMSON, JAMES C. Papers. John F. Kennedy Library. Boston. (JFKL)

TRUMAN, HARRY S. Papers. Harry S. Truman Library. Independence, Mo. (HSTL)

United Nations Archives. Departmental Archive Group, New York.

US Council on Foreign Economic Policy. Papers. Dwight D. Eisenhower Library. Abilene, Kan. (DDEL)

US National Archives. Diplomatic Branch. Legislative Branch. Modern Military Records Branch. Washington, DC (NA)

Public Records: Published

The Chinese Armed Forces Today: The U.S. Defense Intelligence Agency Handbook of China's Army, Navy and Air Force. London: Arms and Armour

Press, 1979. (Reproduced from *Handbook on the Chinese Armed Forces*, *DDI-2680-32-76*, US Defense Intelligence Agency, Washington, DC 1976.)

Congressional Record, Washington, DC: Government Printing Office.

SCHLESINGER, JAMES R., to the US Congress on FY 1975 Defense Budget and FY 1975–9 Defense Program, 4 Mar. 1974. Washington, DC: Government Printing Office, 1974.

United Kingdom. *Parliamentary Debates*. Hansard.

UN General Assembly, proceedings.

US Congress. House. Subcommittee on the Far East and the Pacific of the Committee on Foreign Affairs. *Report on the Sino-Soviet Conflict and Its Implications*, and *Hearings on the Sino-Soviet Conflict*. 89th Cong., 1st. Sess., 1965. Washington, DC: Government Printing Office.

US Congress. Senate. Committee on Foreign Relations. *U.S. Policy with Respect to Mainland China. Hearings*. 89th Cong., 2nd Sess., 1966. Washington, DC: Government Printing Office.

US Department of State. *American Foreign Policy: Basic Documents*. Washington, DC: Government Printing Office.

—— . *Bulletin*. Washington, DC: Government Printing Office.

—— . *Foreign Relations of the United States*. 1948–57. Washington, DC: Government Printing Office.

US Library of Congress Legislative Reference Service. *United States Defense Policies*. Washington, DC: Government Printing Office.

US *Public Papers of the Presidents*. Washington, DC: Government Printing Office.

Newspapers, Monitoring Reports, Magazines

BBC Monitoring Reports, Summary of World Broadcasts, Far East. London: British Broadcasting Corporation.

Beijing Review. Beijing.

British Library Reference Division—Newspaper Library, Chatham House Press Files. London.

The Economist. London.

Far Eastern Economic Review. Hong Kong.

Foreign Broadcast Information Service, Daily Report, China.

International Herald Tribune.

New York Times.

Interviews/Discussions

BRZEZINSKI, ZBIGNIEW. 4 Feb. 1994, Oxford.

BUSH, RICHARD C. 14 Apr. 1994, Washington, DC.

Chinese Academy of Social Sciences. Sept.–Oct. 1993.
PAAL, DOUGLAS. 11 Apr. 1994, Washington, DC.
ROSTOW, WALT. W. 25 Apr. 1991, Austin, Tex.
US Department of State. Apr. 1994, Washington, DC.

Rand Reports and Books (Rand Corporation, Santa Monica, Calif.)

GOLDHAMER, HERBERT. 'Communist Reaction in Korea to American Possession of the A-Bomb and its Significance for U.S. Political and Psychological Warfare'. Aug. 1952.

GOTTLIEB, THOMAS M. 'Chinese Foreign Policy Factionalism and the Origins of the Strategic Triangle'. Nov. 1977.

HSIEH, ALICE LANGLEY. *Communist China's Strategy in the Nuclear Era.* 1962.

MOZINGO, DAVID P. and ROBINSON, THOMAS W. *Lin Piao on 'People's War': China Takes a Second Look at Vietnam.* 1965.

POLLACK, JONATHAN D. *The Lessons of Coalition Politics: Sino-American Security Relations.* 1984.

——. 'China in the Evolving International System'. Dec. 1983.

——. 'Defense Modernization in the People's Republic of China'. *N-1214-1-AF*, Oct. 1979. (Prepared for the US Air Force.)

SOLOMON, RICHARD H. 'Chinese Political Negotiating Behavior: A Briefing Analysis'. 1985. Unclassified (in part) as 'Chinese Political Negotiating Behavior, 1967–1984: An Interpretive Assessment(u)', Dec. 1985.

Unpublished Materials

BUSH, RICHARD C. 'The Evolution of U.S. Policy Toward China under the Clinton Administration'. Dec. 1993.

CHEN, JIAN. 'The Failure of an "Alliance Between Brotherly Comrades": China's Involvement with the Vietnam War, 1964–1969'. Nobel Institute, Oslo, Apr. 1993.

HE, DI. 'Paper or Real Tiger: America's Nuclear Deterrence and Mao Zedong's Response'. Apr. 1992.

KRUZE, ULDIS, 'Domestic Constituencies in Nixon's China Policy: A New Look from the National Archives'. Asian Studies on the Pacific Coast Conference, Honolulu, Hawaii, 29 June–2 July 1989.

PARK, JONG-CHUL. 'The China Factor in United States Decision Making Toward Vietnam, 1945–65'. Ph.D. dissertation, University of Connecticut, 1990.

Su, Lumin. 'Peaceful Coexistence and Anglo-Chinese Relations: The British Government's Policy towards China, July 1953–July 1954'. M. Litt. thesis, Oxford University, 1991.

Wilhelm, Alfred Donovan, Jun. 'Sino-American Negotiations: The Chinese Approach'. Ph.D. dissertation, University of Kansas, 1986.

Wu, Fumei Chiu. 'The China Policy of Richard M. Nixon: From Confrontation to Negotiation'. Ph.D. dissertation, University of Utah, 1976.

Yahuda, Michael B. 'China's Future: Peaceful Evolution?' BISA Conference, Swansea, Wales, Dec. 1992.

Books

Albrow, Martin. *Max Weber's Construction of Social Theory*. London: Macmillan, 1990.

Almond, Gabriel A. *The American People and Foreign Policy*. New York: Praeger, 1960.

Ambrose, Stephen E. *Nixon: The Triumph of a Politician, 1962–1972*, ii. New York: Simon and Schuster, 1987.

——. *Eisenhower: The President*. New York: Simon and Schuster, 1984.

Appleman, Lt. Col. Roy E. (Ret.) *Disaster in Korea: The Chinese Confront MacArthur*. College Station: Texas A. and M. University Press, 1989.

Arkush, R. David and Lee, Leo O. (eds.) *Land Without Ghosts: Chinese Impressions of America from the Mid-Nineteenth Century to the Present*. Berkeley: University of California Press, 1989.

Armbruster, Frank E., Kahn, Herman, et al. *Can We Win in Vietnam?* London: Pall Mall Press, 1968.

Armstrong, J. David. *Revolution and World Order: The Revolutionary State in International Society*. Oxford: Clarendon Press, 1993.

——. *Revolutionary Diplomacy: Chinese Foreign Policy and the United Front Doctrine*. Berkeley: University of California Press, 1977.

Bachrack, Stanley D. *The Committee of One Million: 'China Lobby' Politics, 1953–1971*. New York: Columbia University Press, 1976.

Ball, George, W. *The Past Has Another Pattern: Memoirs*. New York: Norton, 1982.

Barnett, A. Doak. *China's Economy in Global Perspective*. Washington, DC: Brookings Institution, 1981.

——. *China Policy: Old Problems and New Challenges*. Washington, DC: Brookings Institution, 1977.

——. *Communist China and Asia: Challenges to American Policy*. New York: Harper & Bros., 1960.

Beetham, David. *The Legitimation of Power*. London: Macmillan, 1991.

Bell, Roderick, Edwards, David V., and Wagner, R. Harrison (eds.)

Political Power: A Reader in Theory and Research. New York: The Free Press, 1969.

BETTS, RICHARD K. *Nuclear Blackmail and Nuclear Balance*. Washington, DC: Brookings Institution, 1987.

BOARDMAN, ROBERT. *Britain and the People's Republic of China, 1949–1974*. London: Macmillan, 1976.

BORG, DOROTHY and HEINRICHS, WALDO (eds.) *Uncertain Years: Chinese–American Relations, 1947–1950*. New York: Columbia University Press, 1980.

BOULDING, KENNETH E. *Three Faces of Power*. London: Sage, 1990.

BOWLES, CHESTER. *Promises to Keep: My Years in Public Life, 1941–1969*. New York: Harper and Row, 1971.

BRANDS, HENRY W. *The Specter of Neutralism: The United States and the Emergence of the Third World, 1947–1960*. New York: Columbia University Press, 1989.

BRENNAN, DONALD G. (ed.) *Arms Control and Disarmament: American Views and Studies*. London: Jonathan Cape, 1961.

BRUGGER, BILL. (ed.) *China: The Impact of the Cultural Revolution*. London: Croom Helm, 1978.

BRZEZINSKI, ZBIGNIEW. *Power and Principle: Memoirs of the National Security Adviser, 1977–1981*. New York: Farrer, Strauss and Giroux, 1983.

BULL, HEDLEY. *The Anarchical Society: A Study of Order in World Politics*. London: Macmillan, 1977.

Bulletin of Concerned Asian Scholars. (ed.) *China From Mao to Deng*. Armonk, NY: M. E. Sharpe, 1983.

BUNDY, MCGEORGE. *Danger and Survival: Choices about the Bomb in the First Fifty Years*. New York: Random House, 1988.

BUZAN, BARRY and JONES, ROY J. B. (eds.) *Change and the Study of International Relations: The Evaded Dimension*. London: Pinter, 1981.

—— and RIZVI, GOWHER (eds.) *South Asian Insecurity and the Great Powers*. London: Macmillan, 1986.

CARTER, JIMMY. *Keeping Faith*. New York: Bantam, 1982.

CHAN, GERALD. *China and International Organizations: Participation in Non-Governmental Organizations since 1971*. Oxford: Oxford University Press, 1989.

CHANG, GORDON H. *Friends and Enemies: The United States, China, and the Soviet Union, 1948–1972*. Stanford, Calif.: Stanford University Press, 1990.

CHANG, JAW-LING JOANNE. *United States–China Normalization: An Evaluation of Foreign Policy Decision Making*. Baltimore: Maryland Studies in East Asian Law and Politics, 1986.

CHIU, HUNGDAH. (ed.) *Normalizing Relations with the People's Republic of China: Problems, Analysis and Documents*. Occasional Papers/Reprint

Series in Contemporary Asian Studies, no. 2, 1978 (14), School of Law, Univ. of Maryland.

CLAUDE, INIS L., JUN. *Swords into Plowshares*. New York: Random House, 1971.

CLIFFORD, CLARK. M. *Counsel to the President: A Memoir*. New York: Random House, 1991.

COHEN, BERNARD. *The Public's Impact on Foreign Policy*. Boston: Little Brown, 1973.

COHEN, WARREN I. *America's Response to China*, 3rd edn. New York: Columbia University Press, 1990.

——. *Dean Rusk*, Totowa, NJ: Cooper Square, 1980.

—— and IRIYE, AKIRA (eds.) *The Great Powers and East Asia, 1953–1960*. New York: Columbia University Press, 1990.

CONGRESSIONAL QUARTERLY, Inc. *China: U.S. Policy since 1945*. Washington, DC, 1980.

COPPER, JOHN F. *China's Foreign Aid: An Instrument of Peking's Foreign Policy*. Lexington, Mass.: Lexington Books, 1976.

COX, ROBERT. *Production, Power and World Order*. New York, Columbia University Press, 1987.

DITTMER, LOWELL. *Sino-Soviet Normalization and Its International Implications, 1945–1990*. Seattle: University of Washington Press, 1992.

DONALDSON, ROBERT H. (ed.) *The Soviet Union in the Third World: Successes and Failures*. Boulder, Colo.: Westview Press, 1981.

DOWER, JOHN. *Empire and Aftermath: Yoshida Shigeru and the Japanese Experience, 1878–1954*. Cambridge, Mass.: Harvard University Press, 1979.

ECKSTEIN, ALEXANDER. *China's Economic Revolution*. Cambridge: Cambridge University Press, 1977.

——. *Communist China's Economic Growth and Foreign Trade*. New York: McGraw Hill, 1966.

EISENHOWER, DWIGHT D. *The White House Years*, i, ii. Garden City, NY: Doubleday, 1963 and 1965.

EVANS, PAUL M. *John Fairbank and the American Understanding of Modern China*. New York: Blackwell, 1988.

—— and FROLIC, MICHAEL B. (eds.) *Reluctant Adversaries: Canada and the People's Republic of China, 1949–1970*. Toronto: University of Toronto Press, 1991.

FINGAR, THOMAS (ed.) *China's Quest for Independence: Policy Evolution in the 1970s*. Boulder, Colo.: Westview Press, 1980.

FOOT, ROSEMARY. *A Substitute for Victory: The Politics of Peacemaking at the Korean Armistice Talks*. Ithaca, NY: Cornell University Press, 1990.

——. *The Wrong War: American Policy and the Dimensions of the Korean Conflict, 1950–1953*. Ithaca, NY: Cornell University Press, 1985.

FRANCK, THOMAS M. *The Power of Legitimacy Among Nations*. Oxford: Oxford University Press, 1990.

FUKUI, HARUHIRO. *Party in Power: The Japanese Liberal-Democrats and Policy-Making*. Canberra: Australian National University Press, 1970.

FUNG, EDMUND S. K. and MACKERRAS, COLIN. *From Fear to Friendship: Australia's Policies Towards the People's Republic of China, 1966–1982*. St Lucia, Queensland: University of Queensland Press, 1985.

GADDIS, JOHN L. *The United States and the End of the Cold War*. New York: Oxford University Press, 1992.

—— . *The Long Peace: Inquiries into the History of the Cold War*. New York: Oxford University Press, 1987.

—— . *Strategies of Containment*. New York: Oxford University Press, 1982.

GALBRAITH, JOHN KENNETH. *Ambassador's Journal: A Personal Account of the Kennedy Years*. London: Hamish Hamilton, 1969.

GARTHOFF, RAYMOND L. (ed.) *Sino-Soviet Military Relations*. New York: Praeger, 1966.

GARVER, JOHN W. *Foreign Relations of the People's Republic of China*. Englewood Cliffs, NJ: Prentice Hall, 1993.

—— . *China's Decision for Rapprochement with the United States, 1968–1971*. Boulder, Colo.: Westview Press, 1982.

GEORGE, ALEXANDER L. *The Chinese Communist Army in Action: The Korean War and its Aftermath*. New York, Columbia University Press, 1967.

GILL, STEPHEN (ed.) *Gramsci, Historical Materialism and International Relations*. Cambridge: Cambridge University Press, 1993.

GITTINGS, JOHN. *The Role of the Chinese Army*. London: Oxford University Press, 1967.

GONCHAROV, SERGEI N., LEWIS, JOHN W., and XUE, LITAI. *Uncertain Partners: Stalin, Mao, and the Korean War*. Stanford, Calif.: Stanford University Press, 1993.

GORST, ANTHONY, JOHNMAN, LEWIS, and LUCAS, SCOTT W. (eds.) *Contemporary British History, 1931–1961: Politics and the Limits of Policy*. London: Pinter, 1991.

GOWING, MARGARET M. *Independence and Deterrence: Britain and Atomic Energy, 1945–1952*. London: Macmillan, 1974.

GRASSO, JUNE M. *Truman's Two-China Policy*. Armonk, NY: M. E. Sharpe, 1987.

GRIFFITH, SAMUEL B. *The Chinese People's Liberation Army*. New York: McGraw Hill, 1967.

GROMYKO, ANDREI, *Memories*. London: Hutchinson, 1989.

HAAS, ERNST B. *When Knowledge is Power*. Berkeley: University of California Press, 1990.

HABERMAS, JÜRGEN. *Legitimation Crisis*. London: Heinemann, 1973.

HAIG, ALEXANDER M. JUN. *Caveat: Realism, Reagan, and Foreign Policy*. New York: Macmillan, 1984.

HALPERIN, MORTON H. *China and the Bomb*. New York: Praeger, 1965.

—— and PERKINS, DWIGHT H. *Communist China and Arms Control.* Cambridge, Mass.: East Asian Research Center, Center for International Affairs, Harvard University, 1965.

HALPERN, A. M. (ed.) *Policies Toward China: Views from Six Continents.* New York: McGraw Hill, 1965.

HAO, YUFAN and HUAN, GUOCANG (eds.) *The Chinese View of the World.* New York: Pantheon Books, 1989.

HARDING, HARRY. *A Fragile Relationship: The United States and China Since 1972.* Washington, DC: Brookings Institution, 1992.

——. *China's Second Revolution: Reform After Mao.* Washington, DC: Brookings Institution, 1987.

—— (ed.) *China's Foreign Relations in the 1980s.* New Haven: Yale University Press, 1984.

—— and YUAN, MING (eds.) *Sino-American Relations, 1945–1955: A Joint Reassessment of a Critical Decade.* Wilmington, Del.: Scholarly Resources Inc., 1989.

HARTSOCK, NANCY C. M. *Money, Sex and Power: Toward a Feminist Historical Materialism.* New York: Longman, 1983.

HELLMANN, DONALD C. *Japan and East Asia: The New International Order.* London: Pall Mall Press, 1972.

—— (ed.) *China and Japan: A New Balance of Power.* Lexington, Mass.: Lexington Books, 1976.

HERMES, WALTER G. *United States Army in the Korean War: Truce Tent and Fighting Front.* Washington, DC: Office of the Chief of Military History, United States Army, 1966.

HILSMAN, ROGER. *To Move a Nation: The Politics of Foreign Policy in the Administration of John F. Kennedy.* Garden City, NY: Doubleday, 1967.

HOLSTI, OLE R., SIVERSON, RANDOLPH M., and GEORGE, ALEXANDER L. *Change in the International System.* Boulder, Colo.: Westview Press, 1980.

HORNE, ALISTAIR. *Harold Macmillan, ii., 1957–1986.* New York: Viking, 1989.

HORVATH, JANOS. *Chinese Technology Transfer to the Third World: A Grants Economy Analysis.* New York: Praeger, 1976.

HSIAO, GENE T. (ed.) *Sino-American Detente and its Policy Implications.* New York: Praeger, 1974.

HSIUNG, JAMES CHIEH. *Law and Policy in China's Foreign Relations: A Study of Attitudes and Practice.* New York: Columbia University Press, 1972.

—— (ed.) *Beyond China's Independent Foreign Policy: Challenge for the U.S. and its Asian Allies.* New York: Praeger, 1985.

HUNT, MICHAEL H. *The Making of a Special Relationship: The United States and China to 1914.* New York, Columbia University Press, 1983.

IMMERMAN, RICHARD H. (ed.) *John Foster Dulles and the Diplomacy of the Cold War.* Princeton, NJ: Princeton University Press, 1990.

IRIYE, AKIRA (ed.) *U.S. Policy Toward China: Testimony Taken from the Senate Foreign Relations Committee Hearings 1966*. Boston: Little, Brown & Co, 1968.

—— and COHEN, WARREN I. (eds.) *The United States and Japan in the Post War World*. Lexington, Ky.: The University Press of Kentucky, 1989.

ISAAC, JEFFREY C. *Power and Marxist Theory: A Realist View*. Ithaca, NY: Cornell University Press, 1987.

ISAACS, HAROLD R. *Scratches on Our Mind: American Images of China and India*. Westport, Conn.: Greenwood Press, 1977.

JACOBSON, HAROLD K. and OKSENBERG, MICHEL. *China's Participation in the IMF, the World Bank, and GATT: Toward a Global Economic Order*. Ann Arbor: University of Michigan Press, 1990.

JOHNSON, LYNDON BAINES. *The Vantage Point: Perspectives of the Presidency, 1963–1969*. New York: Holt, Rinehart and Winston, 1971.

JOHNSON, U. ALEXIS (with MCALLISTER, JEF OLIVARIUS). *The Right Hand of Power*. Englewood Cliffs, NJ: Prentice Hall, 1984.

Joint Economic Committee of the United States Congress. *China under the Four Modernizations*. Washington, DC: Government Printing Office, 1982.

——. *Chinese Economy Post Mao*. Washington, DC: Government Printing Office, 1978.

——. *An Economic Profile of Mainland China*. New York: Praeger, 1968.

KAIL, F. M. *What Washington Said: Administration Rhetoric and the Vietnam War, 1949–1969*. New York: Harper and Row, 1973.

KALICKI, JAN H. *The Pattern of Sino-American Crises*. London: Cambridge University Press, 1975.

KAU, MICHAEL Y. M. and LEUNG, JOHN K. (eds.) *The Writings of Mao Zedong, 1949–1976*, i. *Sept. 1949 to Dec. 1955*. Armonk, NY: M. E. Sharpe, 1986.

KAUFMAN, BURTON I. *Trade and Aid: Eisenhower's Foreign Economic Policy, 1953–1961*. Baltimore, Md.: Johns Hopkins University Press, 1982.

KEGLEY, CHARLES W. JUN. and WITTKOPF, EUGENE R. *American Foreign Policy: Pattern and Process*, 4th edn. New York: St Martin's Press, 1991.

KEITH, RONALD C. *The Diplomacy of Zhou Enlai*. London: Macmillan, 1989.

KEOHANE, ROBERT. *International Institutions and State Power*. Boulder, Colo.: Westview Press, 1989.

KHONG, YUEN FOONG. *Analogies at War*. Princeton, NJ: Princeton University Press, 1991.

KIM, SAMUEL S. *China, the United Nations, and World Order*. Princeton, NJ: Princeton University Press, 1979.

—— (ed.) *China and the World: Chinese Foreign Relations in the Post-Cold War Era* 3rd edn. Boulder, Colo.: Westview Press, 1994.

KISSINGER, HENRY. *Years of Upheaval*. London: Weidenfeld and Nicolson, 1982.

——. *The White House Years*. Boston: Little, Brown & Co., 1979.

KUSNITZ, LEONARD A. *Public Opinion and Foreign Policy: America's China Policy, 1949–1979*. Westport, Conn.: Greenwood Press, 1984.

LANGDON, F. C. *Japan's Foreign Policy*. Vancouver: University of British Columbia Press, 1973.

LARDY, NICHOLAS R. *China in the World Economy*. Washington, DC: Institute for International Economics, 1994.

——. *China's Entry into the World Economy: Implications for Northeast Asia and the United States*. London: UPA for the Asia Society, 1987.

LARSON, DEBORAH. *Origins of Containment*. Princeton, NJ: Princeton University Press, 1985.

LEIGH, MICHAEL. *Mobilizing Consent: Public Opinion and American Foreign Policy*. Westport, Conn.: Greenwood Press, 1976.

LEVERING, RALPH B. *The Public and American Foreign Policy, 1918–1978*. New York: William Morrow, 1978.

LEWIS, JOHN W. and XUE, LITAI. *China Builds the Bomb*. Stanford, Calif. Stanford University Press, 1988.

LILLEY, JAMES R. and WILLKIE, WENDELL L. (eds.) *Beyond MFN: Trade with China and American Interests*. Washington, DC: AEI Press, 1994.

LIN, CHONG-PIN. *China's Nuclear Weapons Strategy: Tradition within Evolution*. Lexington, Mass.: Lexington Books, 1988.

LUKES, STEVEN. *Power: A Radical View*. London: Macmillan, 1974.

—— (ed.) *Power*. Oxford: Blackwell, 1986.

LUNDESTAD, GEIR. *The American 'Empire'*. Oxford: Oxford University Press, 1990.

MACFARQUHAR, RODERICK. *Sino-American Relations, 1949–71*. New York: Praeger, 1972.

——, WU, EUGENE, and CHEEK, TIMOTHY. *The Secret Speeches of Chairman Mao*. Cambridge, Mass.: Harvard University Press, 1989.

MCGLOTHLEN, RONALD. *Controlling the Waves: Dean Acheson and U.S. Foreign Policy in Asia*. New York: Norton, 1993.

MACKERRAS, COLIN. *Western Images of China*. Oxford: Oxford University Press, 1989.

MACMILLAN, HAROLD. *Riding the Storm*. London: Macmillan, 1971.

MAGA, TIMOTHY P. *John F. Kennedy and the New Pacific Community, 1961–63*. London: Macmillan 1990.

MAO ZEDONG. *Selected Works*, iv, v. Beijing: Foreign Languages Press, 1969 and 1977.

MARTIN, EDWIN. *Divided Counsel: The Anglo-American Response to Communist Victory in China*. Lexington, Ky.: University Press of Kentucky, 1986.

MARWAH, ONKAR and POLLACK, JONATHAN D. (eds.) *Military Power and Policy in Asian States: China, India, Japan*. Boulder, Colo.: Westview Press, 1980.

MAYERS, DAVID A. *Cracking the Monolith: U.S. Policy Against the Sino-Soviet Alliance, 1949–1955*. Baton Rouge: Louisiana State University Press, 1986.

MENDL, WOLF. *Issues in Japan's China Policy*. London: Macmillan, 1978.

MERRILL, DENNIS. *Bread and the Ballot: The United States and India's Economic Development, 1947–1963*. Chapel Hill: University of North California Press, 1990.

MILLER, J. D. B. and VINCENT, R. J. (eds.) *Order and Violence: Hedley Bull and International Relations*. Oxford: Clarendon Press, 1990.

MISCAMBLE, WILSON D. *George Kennan and the Making of American Foreign Policy, 1947–1950*. Princeton, NJ: Princeton University Press, 1992.

NIXON, RICHARD M. *The Memoirs of Richard Nixon*. London: Sidgwick and Jackson, 1978.

NYE, JOSEPH S. JUN. *Bound to Lead: The Changing Nature of American Power*. New York: Basic Books, 1990.

OGATA, SADAKO. *Normalization with China: A Comparative Study of U.S. and Japanese Processes*. Berkeley: Institute of East Asian Studies, University of California, 1988.

OKSENBERG, MICHEL and OXNAM, ROBERT B. (eds.) *Dragon and Eagle: United States–China Relations: Past and Future*. New York: Basic Books, 1978.

OSGOOD, ROBERT E. *Alliances and American Foreign Policy*. Baltimore, Md.: Johns Hopkins University Press, 1968.

OYE, KENNETH A., LIEBER, ROBERT J., and ROTHCHILD, DONALD (eds.) *Eagle in a New World: American Grand Strategy in the Post-Cold War Era*. New York: Harper Collins, 1992.

——. *Eagle Resurgent? The Reagan Era in American Foreign Policy*. Boston: Little, Brown, 1987.

——. *Eagle Entangled*. New York: Longman, 1979.

PATERSON, THOMAS G. (ed.) *Kennedy's Quest for Victory: American Foreign Policy, 1961–1963*. New York: Oxford University Press, 1989.

QUESTER, GEORGE. *The Politics of Nuclear Proliferation*. Baltimore, Md.: Johns Hopkins University Press, 1990.

RADTKE, KURT WERNER. *China's Relations with Japan, 1945–1983: The Role of Liao Chengzhi*. Manchester: Manchester University Press, 1990.

RAPKIN, DAVID P. *World Leadership and Hegemony*. Boulder, Colo.: Lynne Rienner, 1990.

RISKIN, CARL. *China's Political Economy: The Quest for Development since 1949*. Oxford: Oxford University Press, 1987.

ROBERTS, ADAM and KINGSBURY, BENEDICT (eds.) *United Nations, Divided World*, 2nd edn. Oxford: Clarendon Paperbacks, 1993.

ROBINSON, THOMAS W. and SHAMBAUGH, DAVID (eds.) *Chinese Foreign Policy: Theory and Practice*. Oxford: Oxford University Press, 1994.

ROSS, ROBERT S. (ed.) *China, the United States, and the Soviet Union:*

Tripolarity and Policymaking in the Cold War. Armonk, NY: M. E. Sharpe, 1993.

ROSTOW, WALT. W. *Eisenhower, Kennedy and Foreign Aid*. Austin, Tex.: University of Texas Press, 1985.

——. *The Prospects for Communist China*. New York: Wiley & Sons, 1954.

RUSK, DEAN. *As I Saw It*, as told to Richard Rusk and edited by Daniel S. Papp. New York: Norton, 1990.

RYAN, MARK A. *Chinese Attitudes Toward Nuclear Weapons: China and the United States during the Korean War*. Armonk, NY: M. E. Sharpe, 1989.

SCALAPINO ROBERT (ed.) *The Foreign Policy of Modern Japan*. Berkeley: University of California Press, 1977.

SCHLESINGER, ARTHUR M., JUN. *A Thousand Days*. Boston: Little, Brown, 1965.

SCHOLTE, JAN AART. *International Relations of Social Change*. Buckingham: Open University Press, 1993.

SCHULZINGER, ROBERT D. *Henry Kissinger: Doctor of Diplomacy*. New York: Columbia University Press, 1989.

SCHURMANN, FRANZ. *The Logic of World Power*. New York: Pantheon, 1974.

SEABORG, GLENN T. with LOEB, BENJAMIN S. *Stemming the Tide: Arms Control in the Johnson Years*. Lexington, Mass.: Lexington Books, 1987.

SEGAL, GERALD. *Defending China*. Oxford: Oxford University Press, 1985.

—— and TOW, WILLIAM T. (eds.) *Chinese Defence Policy*. Urbana: University of Illinois Press, 1984.

SHAMBAUGH, DAVID. *Beautiful Imperialist: China Perceives America 1972–1990*. Princeton, NJ: Princeton University Press, 1991.

SHAO, WENGUANG. *China, Britain and Businessmen: Political and Commercial Relations, 1949–1957*. London: Macmillan, 1991.

SHIH, CHIH-YU. *The Spirit of Chinese Foreign Policy: A Psychocultural View*. London: Macmillan, 1990.

SHULTZ, GEORGE. *Turmoil and Triumph*. New York: Scribner's, 1993.

SIPRI Yearbook of World Armaments and Disarmament. Oxford: Oxford University Press.

SNOW, EDGAR. *The Long Revolution*. London: Hutchinson, 1973.

SOLOMON, RICHARD H. (ed.) *The China Factor: Sino-American Relations and the Global Scene*. Englewood Cliffs, NJ: Prentice Hall, 1981.

SORENSEN, THEODORE C. *Decision-Making in the White House*. New York: Columbia University Press, 1963.

STEELE, A. T. *The American People and China*. New York: McGraw Hill, 1966.

SUTTER, ROBERT G. *The China Quandary: Domestic Determinants of U.S. China Policy, 1972–1982*. Boulder, Colo.: Westview, 1983.

——. *Chinese Foreign Policy After the Cultural Revolution, 1966–1977*. Boulder, Colo.: Westview Press, 1978.

SUTTER, ROBERT G. *China-Watch: Sino-American Reconciliation*. Baltimore, Md.: Johns Hopkins University Press, 1978.

SZULC, TAD. *The Illusion of Peace: Foreign Policy in the Nixon Years*. New York: Viking Press, 1978.

TAN, QINGSHAN. *The Making of U.S. China Policy: From Normalization to the Post-Cold War Era*. Boulder, Colo.: Lynne Rienner, 1992.

TOW, WILLIAM T. *Encountering the Dominant Player: U.S. Extended Deterrence Strategy in the Asia-Pacific*. New York: Columbia University Press, 1991.

TOW, WILLIAM T. (ed.) *Building Sino-American Relations: An Analysis for the 1990s*. New York: Paragon House, 1991.

TSAO, JAMES T. H. *China's Development Strategies and Foreign Trade*. Lexington: Lexington Books, D. C. Heath, 1987.

TUCKER, NANCY B. *Patterns in the Dust: Chinese–American Relations and the Recognition Controversy, 1949–1950*. New York: Columbia University Press, 1983.

TWITCHETT, D. and FAIRBANK, JOHN K. *The Cambridge History of China*, xv, *The People's Republic*. Cambridge: Cambridge University Press, 1991.

VANCE, CYRUS. *Hard Choices: Critical Years in America's Foreign Policy*. New York: Simon & Schuster, 1983.

WALT, STEPHEN M. *The Origins of Alliances*. Ithaca, NY: Cornell University Press, 1986.

WANG, BINGNAN. *Nine Years of Sino-US Talks in Retrospect: Memoirs of Wang Bingnan*. Joint Publications Research Services, JPRS-CPS-85-069, 7 Aug. 1985.

WELFIELD, JOHN. *An Empire in Eclipse: Japan in the PostWar American Alliance System: A Study in the Interaction of Domestic Politics and Foreign Policy*. London: Athlone Press, 1988.

WHITE, GORDON. *Riding the Tiger: The Politics of Economic Reform in Post-Mao China*. London: Macmillan, 1993.

WHITING, ALLEN S. *The Chinese Calculus of Deterrence*. Ann Arbor: The University of Michigan Press, 1975.

——. *China Crosses the Yalu: The Decision to Enter the Korean War*. Stanford, Calif.: Stanford University Press, 1960.

WHITSON, WILLIAM W. *The Chinese High Command: A History of Communist Military Politics, 1927–71*. New York: Praeger, 1973.

—— (ed.) *The Military and Political Power in China in the 1970s*. New York: Praeger, 1972.

WIGHT, MARTIN. *Power Politics*. Harmondsworth: Penguin Books, 1979.

WILLIAMS, MARC. *International Economic Organisations and the Third World*. London: Harvester Wheatsheaf, 1994.

WILLIAMS, WILLIAM J. (ed.) *A Revolutionary War: Korea and the Transformation of the Postwar World*. Chicago: Imprint Publications, 1993.

XUE, MOUHONG and PEI, JIANZHANG (eds.) *Diplomacy of Contemporary*

China. Hong Kong: New Horizon Press, 1990.

YAHUDA, MICHAEL B. *Towards the End of Isolationism: China's Foreign Policy After Mao*. London: Macmillan, 1983.

——. *China's Role in World Affairs*. London: Croom Helm, 1978.

YOUNG, KENNETH T. *Negotiating with the Chinese Communists: The United States Experience, 1953–1967*. New York: McGraw Hill, 1968.

ZHAI, QIANG. *The Dragon, the Lion, and the Eagle: Chinese–British–American Relations, 1949–1958*. Kent, Ohio: Kent State University Press, 1994.

ZHANG, SHU GUANG. *Deterrence and Strategic Culture: Chinese–American Confrontations, 1949–1958*. Ithaca, NY: Cornell University Press, 1992.

ZHAO, QUANSHENG. *Japanese Policy-Making, The Politics Behind Politics: Informal Mechanisms and the Making of China Policy*. Westport, Conn.: Praeger, 1993.

Articles

BALDWIN, DAVID A. 'Interdependence and Power: A Conceptual Analysis'. *International Organization*, 34, no. 4, Autumn 1980.

BARNETT, A. DOAK. 'Military-Security Relations between China and the United States'. *Foreign Affairs*, 55, Apr. 1977.

BETTS, RICHARD K. 'Incentives for Nuclear Weapons: India, Pakistan, Iran'. *Asian Survey*, 19, no. 11, Nov. 1979.

BLOOMFIELD, LINCOLN P. 'China, the United States, and the United Nations'. *International Organization*, 20, no. 4, 1966.

BO, YIBO. 'The Making of the "Lean-to-one-side" Decision'. Tr. by Zhai Qiang, *Chinese Historians*, 5, no. 1, Spring 1992.

BRANDS, HENRY W., JUN. 'Testing Massive Retaliation: Credibility and Crisis Management in the Taiwan Strait'. *International Security*, 12, no. 4, Spring 1988.

——. 'The Dwight D. Eisenhower Administration, Syngman Rhee and the "Other" Geneva Conference of 1954'. *Pacific Historical Review*, Feb. 1987.

BRIDGHAM, PHILIP. 'The Fall of Lin Piao'. *China Quarterly*, 55, July–Sept. 1973.

CHAI, TRONG R. 'Chinese Policy Toward the Third World and the Superpowers in the UN General Assembly, 1971–1977'. *International Organization*, 33, Summer 1979.

CHANCELLOR, JOHN. 'Who Produced the China Show?'. *Foreign Policy*, 7, Summer 1972.

CHANG, GORDON H. and HE, DI. 'The Absence of War in the U.S.–Chinese Confrontation over Quemoy and Matsu in 1954–55: Contingency, Luck, Deterrence'. *American Historical Review*, 98, no. 5, Dec. 1993.

CHELLANEY, BRAHMA. 'South Asia's Passage to Nuclear Power'. *International Security*, 16, no. 1, Summer 1991.

CHEN, JIAN. 'The Sino-Soviet Alliance and China's Entry into the Korean War'. *Cold War International History Project*, Working Paper no. 1, Washington, DC: Woodrow Wilson Center, 1992.

—— . 'China's Changing Aims during the Korean War, 1950–51'. *Journal of American–East Asian Relations*, 1, Spring 1992.

CHEN, QIMAO. 'New Approaches in China's Foreign Policy: The Post Cold War Era'. *Asian Survey*, 33, no. 3, Mar. 1993.

COX, ROBERT. 'Social Forces, States and World Orders: Beyond International Relations Theory'. *Millennium: Journal of International Studies*, 10, Summer 1981.

DAHL, ROBERT. 'The Concept of Power'. *Behavioral Science*, 2, 1957.

DEAN, ARTHUR. 'United States Foreign Policy and Formosa'. *Foreign Affairs*, 33, Apr. 1955.

DING, ARTHUR S. 'Peking's Foreign Policy in the Changing World'. *Issues and Studies*, 27, no. 8, Aug. 1991.

DING, XINGHAO. 'Managing Sino-American Relations in a Changing World'. *Asian Survey*, 31, no. 12, Dec. 1991.

DINGMAN, ROGER. 'Atomic Diplomacy during the Korean War'. *International Security*, 13, no. 3, Winter 1988/9.

DOMBEY, NORMAN and GROVE, ERIC. 'Britain's Thermonuclear Bluff'. *London Review of Books*, 22 Oct. 1992.

ELIADES, GEORGE C. 'Once More Unto the Breach: Eisenhower, Dulles and Public Opinion during the Offshore Islands Crisis of 1958'. *Journal of American East–Asian Relations*, 2, no. 4, Winter 1993.

FINGAR, THOMAS. 'Global Trends Affecting U.S.–PRC–Taiwan Relations'. In Gong, Gerrit W. and Lin, Bih-jaw, *Sino-American Relations at a Time of Change*, Washington DC: Asian Studies Program, the Center for Strategic and International Studies, Jan. 1994.

FOOT, ROSEMARY, 'Nuclear Coercion and the Ending of the Korean Conflict'. *International Security*, 13, no. 3, Winter 1988/9.

—— . 'Anglo-American Relations in the Korean Crisis: The British Effort to Avert an Expanded War, December 1950–January 1951'. *Diplomatic History*, 10, no. 1, Winter 1986.

FORLAND, TOR EGIL. ' "Selling Firearms to the Indians": Eisenhower's Export Control Policy, 1953–54'. *Diplomatic History*, 15, no. 2, Spring 1991.

GARST, DANIEL. 'Thucydides and Neorealism'. *International Studies Quarterly*, 33, no. 1, Mar. 1989.

GELBER, HARRY G. 'China's New Economic and Strategic Uncertainties and the Security Prospects'. *Asian Survey*, 30, no. 7, July 1990.

—— . 'Nuclear Weapons and Chinese Policy'. *Adelphi Paper*, 99, 1973.

GILL, STEPHEN. 'American Hegemony: Its Limits and Prospects in the Reagan Era'. *Millennium*, 15, Winter 1986.

GLASER, BONNIE S. 'China's Security Perceptions: Interests and Ambitions'. *Asian Survey*, 33, no. 3, Mar. 1993.

GOLDSTEIN, STEVEN M. and HE, DI. 'New Chinese Sources on the History of the Cold War'. *Cold War International History Project Bulletin*, Spring 1992.

GU, NING. [Kennedy Administration Policy Towards China] (in Chinese). *Journal of World History*, 6, 1991.

GUO CHANGLIN. 'Sino-U.S. Relations in Perspective'. *Contemporary International Relations*, 2, no. 7, July 1992.

GURTOV, MELVIN. 'The Foreign Ministry and Foreign Affairs in China's Cultural Revolution'. *China Quarterly*, 40, 1969.

HALPERIN, MORTON H. 'Chinese Nuclear Strategy'. *China Quarterly*, 21, Jan.–Mar. 1965.

HAMRIN, CAROL LEE. 'Competing "Policy Packages" in Post-Mao China'. *Asian Survey*, 24, no. 5, May 1984.

—— 'China Reassesses the Superpowers'. *Pacific Affairs*, 56, no. 2, Summer 1983.

—— and POLLACK, JONATHAN D. 'The Origins and Evolution of the Sino-American Alignment'. Forthcoming in Harding, Harry (ed.) *China's Cooperative Relations: Partnerships and Alignments in Modern Chinese Foreign Policy*.

HARDING, HARRY. 'China's American Dilemma'. Annals of the *American Academy of Political and Social Science*, 519, Jan. 1992.

—— 'From China with Disdain: New Trends in the Study of China'. *Asian Survey*, 22, no. 10, Oct. 1982.

HARRIS, WILLIAM R. 'Chinese Nuclear Doctrine: The Decade Prior to Weapons Development, (1945–1955)'. *China Quarterly*, 21, Jan.–Mar. 1965.

HE, DI. 'The Most Respected Enemy: Mao Zedong's Perception of the United States'. *China Quarterly*, 137, Mar. 1994.

HSIEH, ALICE L. 'China's Secret Military Papers: Military Doctrine and Strategy'. *China Quarterly*, 20, Apr.–June 1964.

HUO, HWEI-LING. 'Patterns of Behavior in China's Foreign Policy: The Gulf Crisis and Beyond'. *Asian Survey*, 32, no. 3, Mar. 1992.

HYER, ERIC. 'China's Arms Merchants: Profits in Command'. *China Quarterly*, 132, Dec. 1992.

IKENBERRY, JOHN G. and KUPCHAN, CHARLES A. 'Socialization and Hegemonic Power'. *International Organization*, 44, no. 3, Summer 1990.

IRIYE, AKIRA. 'Chinese–Japanese Relations, 1945–1990'. *China Quarterly*, Dec. 1990.

JENCKS, HARLAN W. 'China's "Punitive" War on Vietnam: A Military Assessment'. *Asian Survey*, 19, no. 8, Aug. 1979.

JOHNSON, CHALMERS. 'The Pattern of Japanese Relations with China, 1952–1982'. *Pacific Affairs*, 59, 1986.

KELLEHER, CATHERINE MCCARDLE. 'The Changing Currency of Power'. *Adelphi Paper*, 256, Winter 1990/1.

KEOHANE, ROBERT O. 'Reciprocity in International Relations'. *International Organization*, 40, no. 1, Winter 1986.

KIM, SAMUEL S. 'China as a Regional Power'. *Current History*, 91, no. 566, Sept. 1992.

——. 'International Organizations in Chinese Foreign Policy'. Annals of the *American Academy of Political and Social Science*, 519, Jan. 1992.

——. 'Mainland China and a New World Order'. *Issues and Studies*, 27, no. 11, Nov. 1991.

——. 'Peking's Foreign Policy in the Shadows of Tienanmen: The Challenge of Legitimation'. *Issues and Studies*, 27, no. 1, Jan. 1991.

——. 'China In and Out of the Changing World Order'. Princeton: Center of International Studies, World Order Studies Program, Occasional Paper, no. 21, 1991.

——. 'Thinking Globally in Post-Mao China'. *Journal of Peace Research*, 27, no. 2, 1990.

——. 'Whither Post-Mao Chinese Global Policy?'. *International Organization*, 35, no. 3, Summer 1981.

——. 'Behavioural Dimensions of Chinese Multilateral Diplomacy'. *China Quarterly*, 72, Dec. 1977.

KRAUSE, KEITH. 'Military Statecraft: Power and Influence in Soviet and American Arms Transfer Relationships'. *International Studies Quarterly*, 35, 1991.

KUEH, Y. Y. 'Foreign Investment and Economic Change in China'. *China Quarterly*, 131, Sept. 1992.

Lampton, David. 'America's China Policy in the Age of the Finance Minister: Clinton Ends Linkage'. *China Quarterly*, 139, Sept. 1994.

LARDY, NICHOLAS R. 'China as a NIC'. *International Economic Insights*, May/June 1993.

——. 'Chinese Foreign Trade'. *China Quarterly*, 131, Sept. 1992.

LEE, DENG-KER. 'An Analysis of Peking's Assessment of the Changing World Environment'. *Issues and Studies*, 27, no. 11, Nov. 1991.

LEVINE, STEVEN I. 'China and America: The Resilient Relationship'. *Current History*, 91, Sept. 1992.

LEWIS, JOHN W. and HUA, DI. 'China's Ballistic Missile Programs: Technologies, Strategies, Goals'. *International Security*, 17, no. 2, Fall 1992.

——, —— and XUE, LITAI. 'Beijing's Defense Establishment: Solving the Arms-Export Enigma'. *International Security*, 15, no. 4, Spring 1991.

LIEBERTHAL, KENNETH. 'The Collapse of the Communist World and Mainland China's Foreign Affairs'. *Issues and Studies*, 28, no. 9, Sept. 1992.

——. 'The Foreign Policy Debate in Peking as seen Through Allegorical Articles, 1973–76'. *China Quarterly*, 71, Sept. 1977.

LORD, WINSTON. 'China and America: Beyond the Big Chill'. *Foreign Affairs*, Fall 1989.

McMAHON, ROBERT J. 'United States Cold War Strategy in South Asia: Making a Military Commitment to Pakistan, 1947–54'. *Journal of American History*, 75, Dec. 1988.

——. 'Eisenhower and Third World Nationalism: A Critique of the Revisionists'. *Political Science Quarterly*, 101, Fall 1986.

MALIK, J. MOHAN. 'Peking's Response to the Gulf Crisis'. *Issues and Studies*, 27, no. 9, Sept. 1991.

MASTANDUNO, MICHAEL. 'Trade As a Strategic Weapon: American and Alliance Export Control Policy in the Early Postwar Period'. *International Organization*, 42, no. 1, Winter 1988.

MELISSEN, JAN, 'The Restoration of the Nuclear Alliance: Great Britain and Atomic Negotiations with the United States, 1957–58'. *Contemporary Record*, 6, no. 1, Summer 1992.

NAUGHTON, BARRY, 'The Third Front: Defence Industrialization in the Chinese Interior'. *China Quarterly*, 115, Sept. 1988.

NELSON, ANNA K. 'John Foster Dulles and the Bipartisan Congress'. *Political Science Quarterly*, 102, no. 1, Spring 1987.

NIXON, RICHARD M. 'Asia After Vietnam'. *Foreign Affairs*, 46, no. 1, Oct. 1967.

NYE, JOSEPH S. 'The Changing Nature of World Power'. *Political Science Quarterly*, 105, no. 2, 1990.

OGATA, SADAKO. 'Japanese Attitude Toward China'. *Asian Survey*, 5, Aug. 1965.

OKSENBERG, MICHEL. 'The China Problem'. *Foreign Affairs*, 70, no. 3, Summer 1991.

——. 'A Decade of Sino-American Relations'. *Foreign Affairs*, 61, Fall 1982.

Overseas Development Institute. 'China's Economic Reforms'. Briefing Paper, Feb. 1993.

POLLACK, JONATHAN D. 'Chinese Attitudes Towards Nuclear Weapons, 1964–9'. *China Quarterly*, 50, 1972.

PUTNAM, ROBERT D. 'Diplomacy and Domestic Politics: The Logic of Two-Level Games'. *International Organization*, 42, 1988.

ROSS, ROBERT S. 'From Lin Biao to Deng Xiaoping: Elite Instability and China's U.S. Policy'. *China Quarterly*, 118, 1989.

——. 'International Bargaining and Domestic Politics: U.S.–China Relations Since 1972'. *World Politics*, 38, no. 2, Jan. 1986.

RUSSETT, BRUCE. 'The Mysterious Case of Vanishing Hegemony; Or is Mark Twain Really Dead?'. *International Organization*, 39, no. 2, Spring 1985.

SCHRAM, STUART. 'Mao Zedong a Hundred Years On: The Legacy of a Ruler'. *China Quarterly*, 137, Mar. 1994.

SEGAL, GERALD. 'China Changes Shape: Regionalism and Foreign Policy'. *Adelphi Paper*, 287, Mar. 1994.

SHAMBAUGH, DAVID. 'Growing Strong: China's Challenge to Asian Security'. *Survival*, 36, no. 2, Summer 1994.

—— . 'Peking's Foreign Policy Conundrum since Tienanmen: Peaceful Coexistence vs. Peaceful Evolution'. *Issues and Studies*, 28, no. 11, Nov. 1992.

—— . 'China's Security Policy in the Post Cold War Era'. *Survival*, 34, no. 2, Summer 1992.

—— . 'Anti-Americanism in China'. Annals of the *American Academy of Political and Social Science*, 497, May 1988.

SHEPLEY, JAMES. 'How Dulles Averted War'. *Life Magazine*, 16 Jan. 1956.

SHICHOR, YITZHAK. 'China and the Gulf Crisis'. *Problems of Communism*, Nov.–Dec. 1991.

—— . 'China and the Role of the United Nations in the Middle East'. *Asian Survey*, 31, no. 3, Mar. 1991.

SNYDER, WILLIAM P. 'Dean Rusk to John Foster Dulles, May–June 1953: The Office, the First 100 Days, and Red China'. *Diplomatic History*, 7, no. 1, Winter 1983.

SPAULDING, ROBERT MARK JUN. 'Eisenhower and Export Control Policy, 1953–1955'. *Diplomatic History*, 17, no. 2, Spring 1993.

STEVENSON, ADLAI E. 'Putting First Things First: A Democratic View'. *Foreign Affairs*, 38, no. 1, Jan. 1960.

STRANGE, SUSAN. 'The Persistent Myth of Lost Hegemony'. *International Organization*, 41, no. 4, 1987.

SULLIVAN, ROGER W. 'Discarding the China Card'. *Foreign Policy*, 86, Spring 1992.

THOMSON, JAMES C. JUN. 'On the Making of U.S. China Policy, 1961–9: A Study in Bureaucratic Politics'. *China Quarterly*, 50, Apr./June 1972.

TUCKER, NANCY BERNKOPF. 'Threats, Opportunities and Frustrations in East Asia'. In Cohen, Warren I. and Tucker, Nancy B. (eds.) *Lyndon Johnson Confronts the World*, New York: Cambridge University Press, 1994.

—— . 'China and America: 1941–1991'. *Foreign Affairs*, 70, Winter 1991/2.

—— . 'American Policy Toward Sino-Japanese Trade in the Postwar Years: Politics and Prosperity'. *Diplomatic History*, 8, no. 3, Summer 1984.

WANG, JIANWEI and LIN, ZHIMIN. 'Chinese Perspectives of the Post-Cold War Era: Three Images of the United States'. *Asian Survey*, 32, no. 10, Oct. 1992.

WENG, BYRON S. 'Communist China's Changing Attitudes Toward the United Nations'. *International Organization*, 20, no. 4, Autumn 1966.

WHITING, ALLEN S. 'Sino-American *Detente*'. *China Quarterly*, 82, June 1980.

XU, XIN. 'Changing Chinese Security Perceptions'. *North Pacific Cooperative Security Dialogue: Working Paper no. 27*, Apr. 1993.

YAHUDA, MICHAEL B. 'Deng Xiaoping: The Statesman'. *China Quarterly*, 135, Sept. 1993.

YASUHARA, YOKO. 'Japan, Communist China, and Export Controls in Asia, 1948–52'. *Diplomatic History*, 10, no. 1, Winter 1986.

YOU, LI and YOU, XU. 'In Search of Blue Water Power: The PLA Navy's Maritime Strategy in the 1990s'. *Pacific Review*, 4, no. 2, 1991.

YUAN, MING. 'Chinese Intellectuals and the United States: The Dilemma of Individualism vs. Patriotism'. *Asian Survey*, 29, no. 7, July 1989.

ZHAI, QIANG. 'Britain, the United States, and the Jinmen-Mazu Crises 1954–55 and 1958'. *Chinese Historians*, 5, Fall 1992.

ZHAI, ZHIHAI and HAO, YUFAN. 'China's Decision to Enter the Korean War: History Revisited'. *China Quarterly*, 121, March 1990.

ZI, ZHONGYUN. ['Gradual Thawing: The Process of Change in American Public Opinion During the Decade prior to the Opening-Up of Sino-U.S. Relations'] (in Chinese). *American Studies*, 1, no. 2, Summer 1987.

INDEX